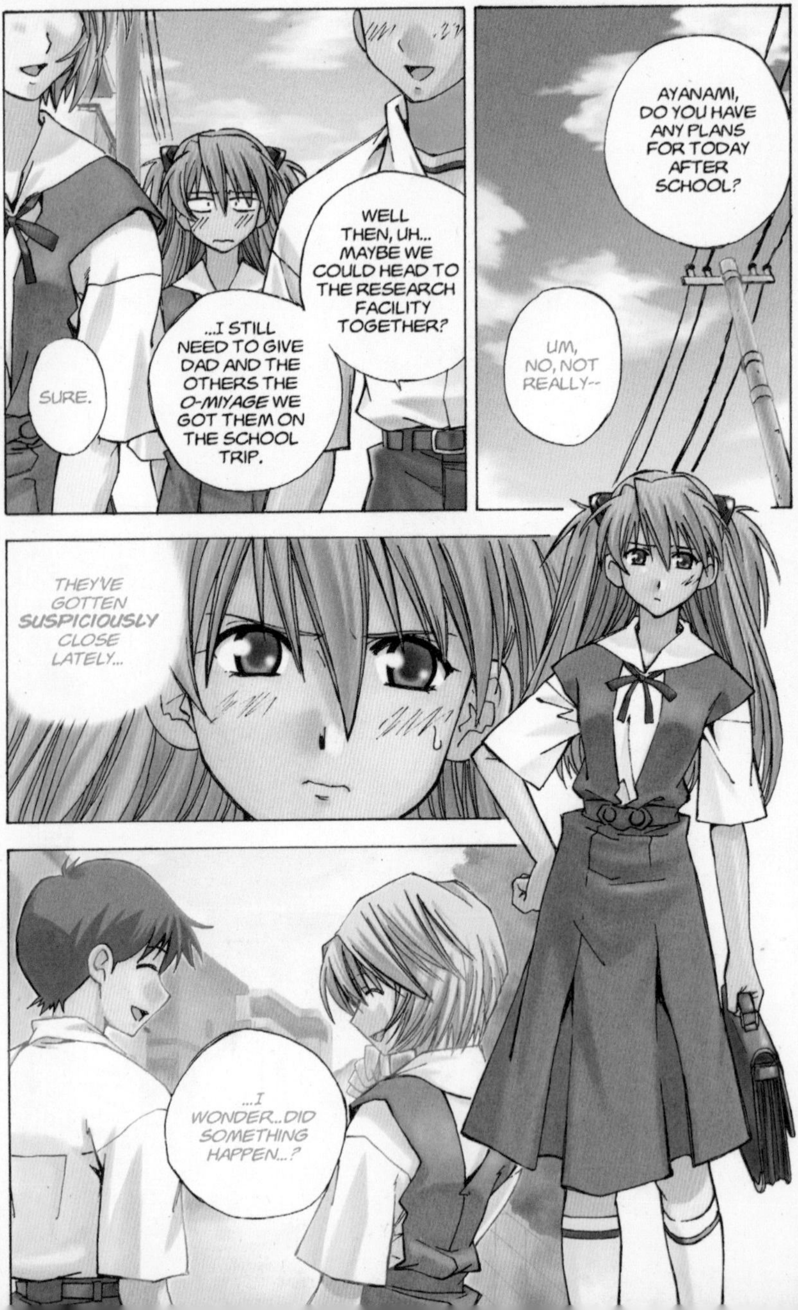
AYANAMI, DO YOU HAVE ANY PLANS FOR TODAY AFTER SCHOOL?
UM, NO, NOT REALLY--
WELL THEN, UH... MAYBE WE COULD HEAD TO THE RESEARCH FACILITY TOGETHER?
...I STILL NEED TO GIVE DAD AND THE OTHERS THE *O-MIYAGE* WE GOT THEM ON THE SCHOOL TRIP.
SURE.
THEY'VE GOTTEN **SUSPICIOUSLY** CLOSE LATELY...
...I WONDER...DID SOMETHING HAPPEN...?

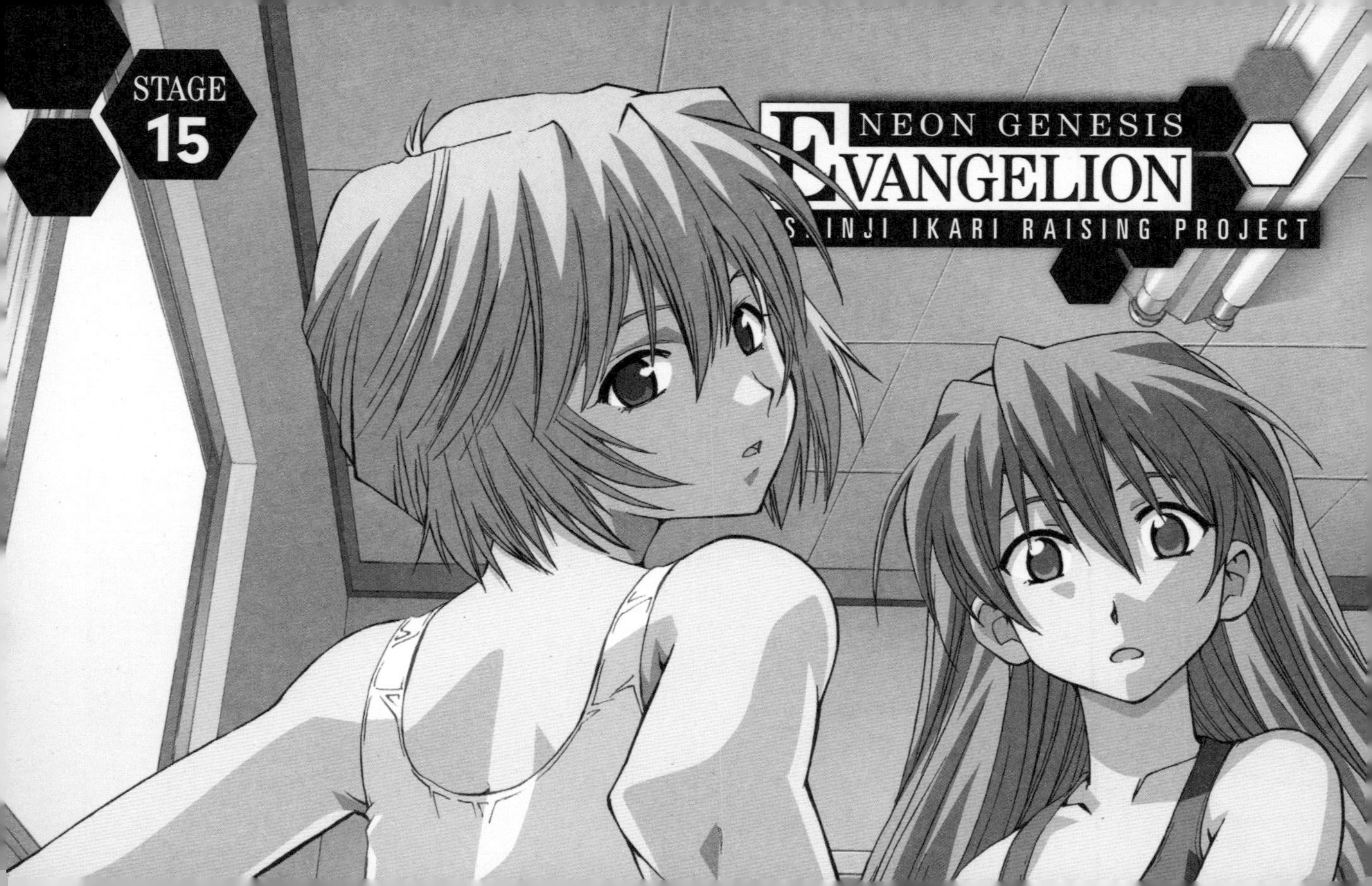
STAGE 15
NEON GENESIS EVANGELION
SHINJI IKARI RAISING PROJECT

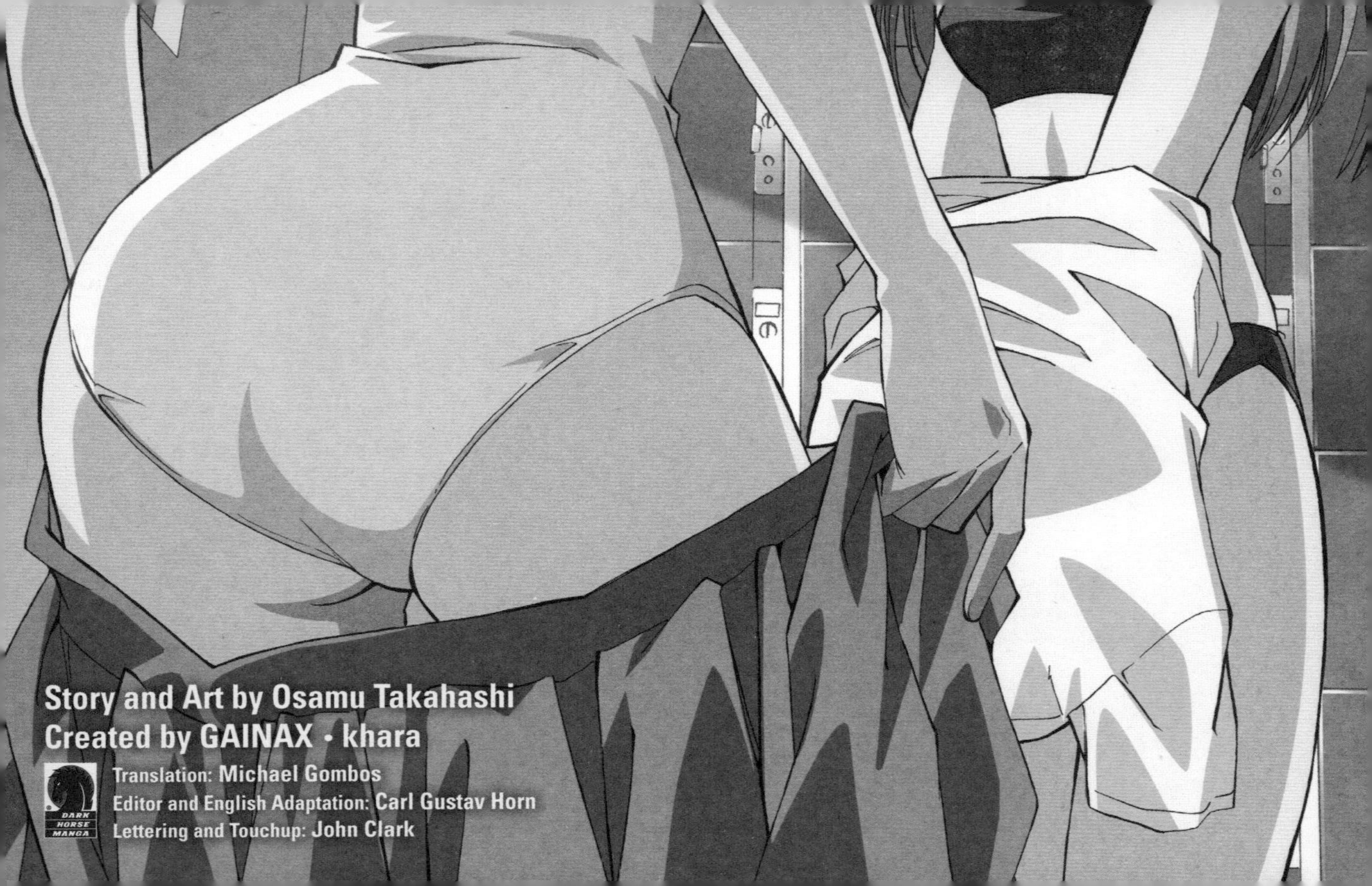
Story and Art by Osamu Takahashi
Created by GAINAX • khara
Translation: Michael Gombos
Editor and English Adaptation: Carl Gustav Horn
Lettering and Touchup: John Clark

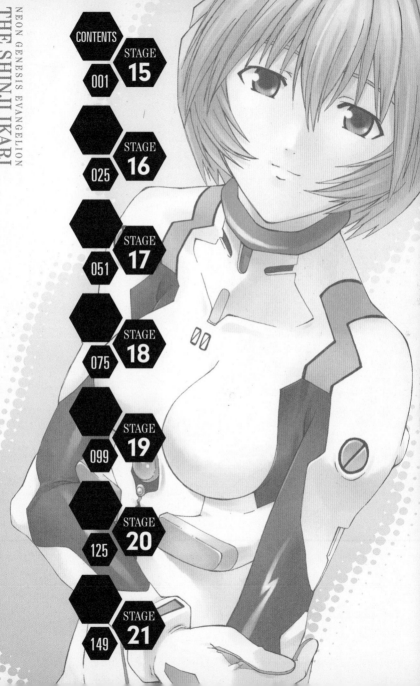

NEON GENESIS EVANGELION
THE SHINJI IKARI RAISING PROJECT

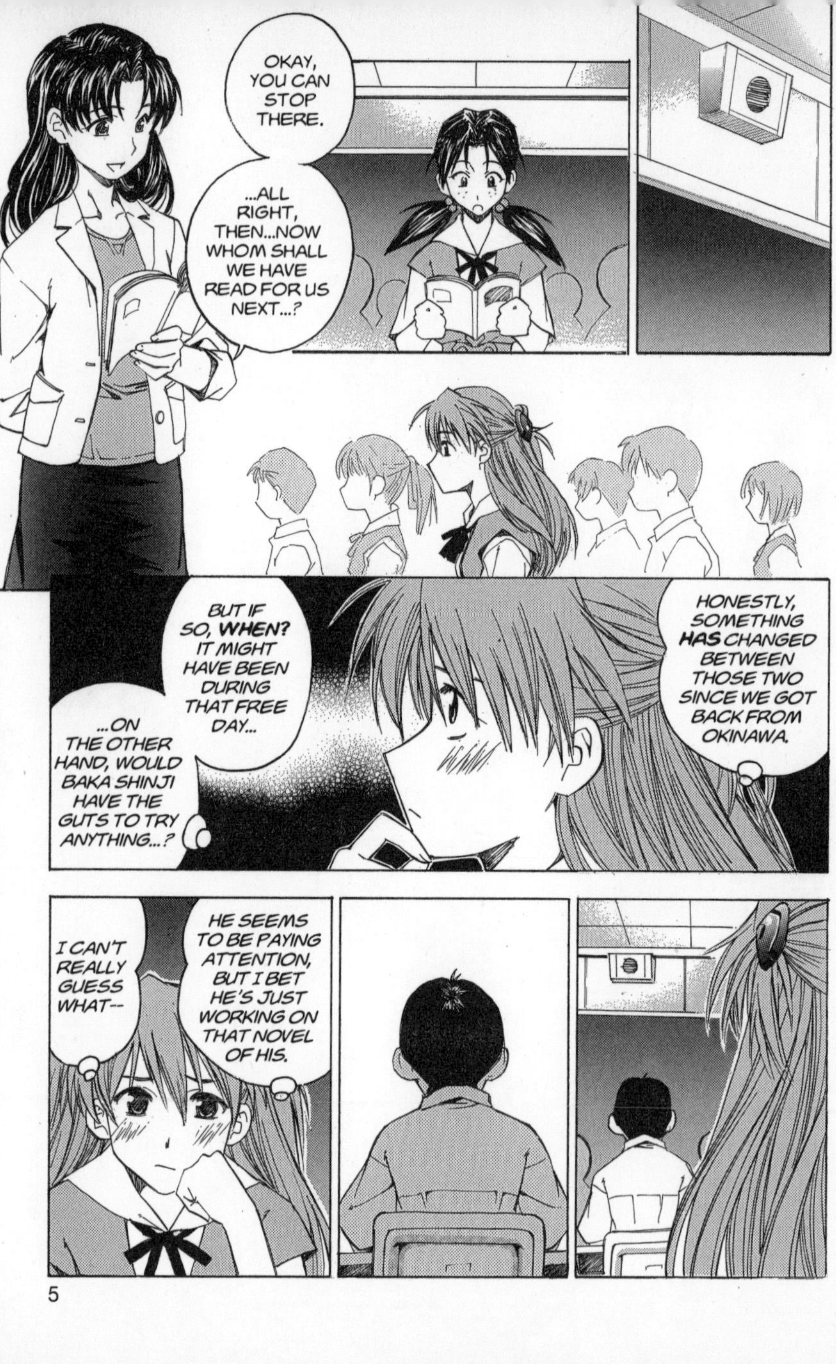
OKAY, YOU CAN STOP THERE.
...ALL RIGHT, THEN...NOW WHOM SHALL WE HAVE READ FOR US NEXT...?
HONESTLY, SOMETHING HAS CHANGED BETWEEN THOSE TWO SINCE WE GOT BACK FROM OKINAWA.
BUT IF SO, WHEN? IT MIGHT HAVE BEEN DURING THAT FREE DAY...
...ON THE OTHER HAND, WOULD BAKA SHINJI HAVE THE GUTS TO TRY ANYTHING...?
HE SEEMS TO BE PAYING ATTENTION, BUT I BET HE'S JUST WORKING ON THAT NOVEL OF HIS.
I CAN'T REALLY GUESS WHAT--

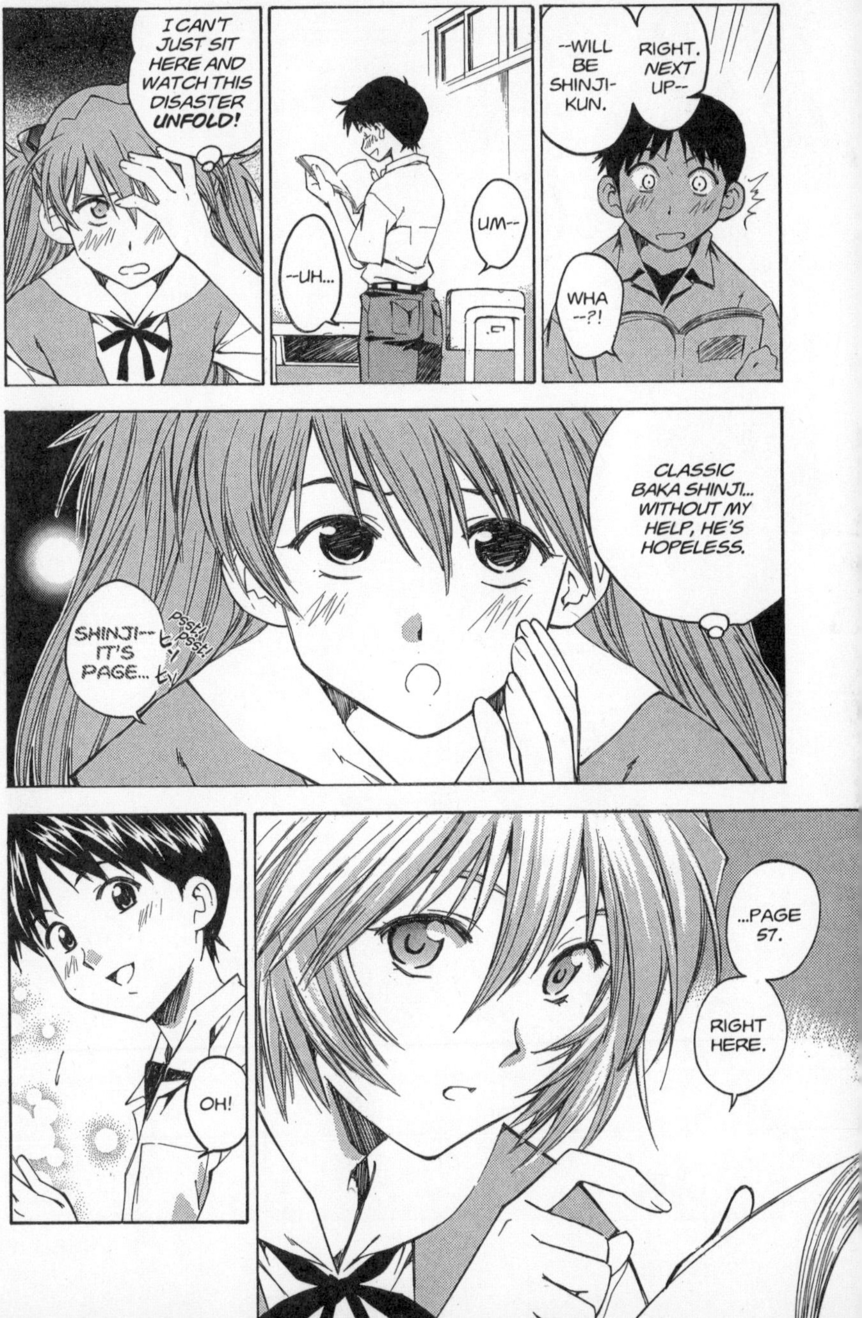
RIGHT. NEXT UP--
--WILL BE SHINJI-KUN.
WHA--?!
UM--
--UH...
I CAN'T JUST SIT HERE AND WATCH THIS DISASTER **UNFOLD!**
CLASSIC BAKA SHINJI... WITHOUT MY HELP, HE'S HOPELESS.
psst! psst!
SHINJI-- IT'S PAGE...
...PAGE 57.
RIGHT HERE.
OH!

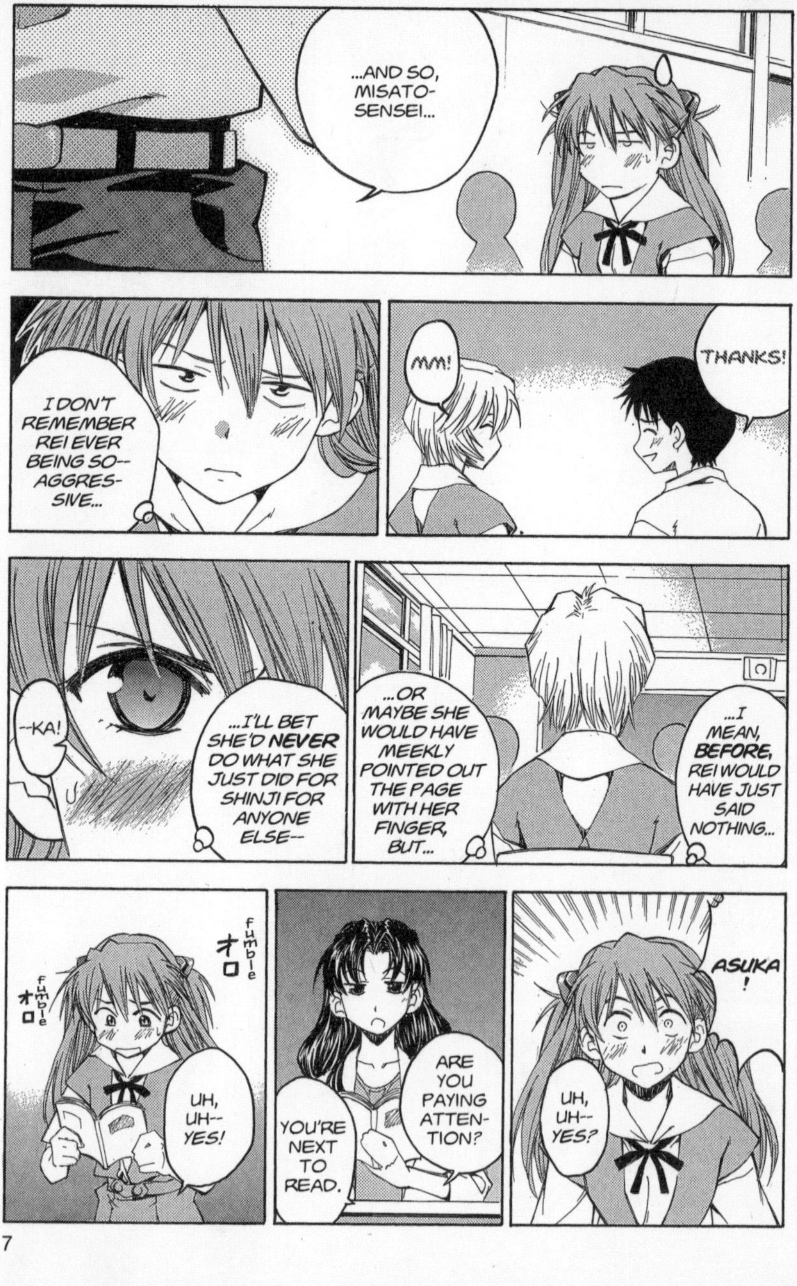
...AND SO, MISATO-SENSEI...
THANKS!
MM!
I DON'T REMEMBER REI EVER BEING SO-- AGGRES-SIVE...
...I MEAN, **BEFORE,** REI WOULD HAVE JUST SAID NOTHING...
...OR MAYBE SHE WOULD HAVE MEEKLY POINTED OUT THE PAGE WITH HER FINGER, BUT...
...I'LL BET SHE'D **NEVER** DO WHAT SHE JUST DID FOR SHINJI FOR ANYONE ELSE--
--KA!
ASUKA!
UH, UH-- YES?
ARE YOU PAYING ATTEN-TION?
YOU'RE NEXT TO READ.
オロ fumble
オロ fumble
UH, UH-- YES!

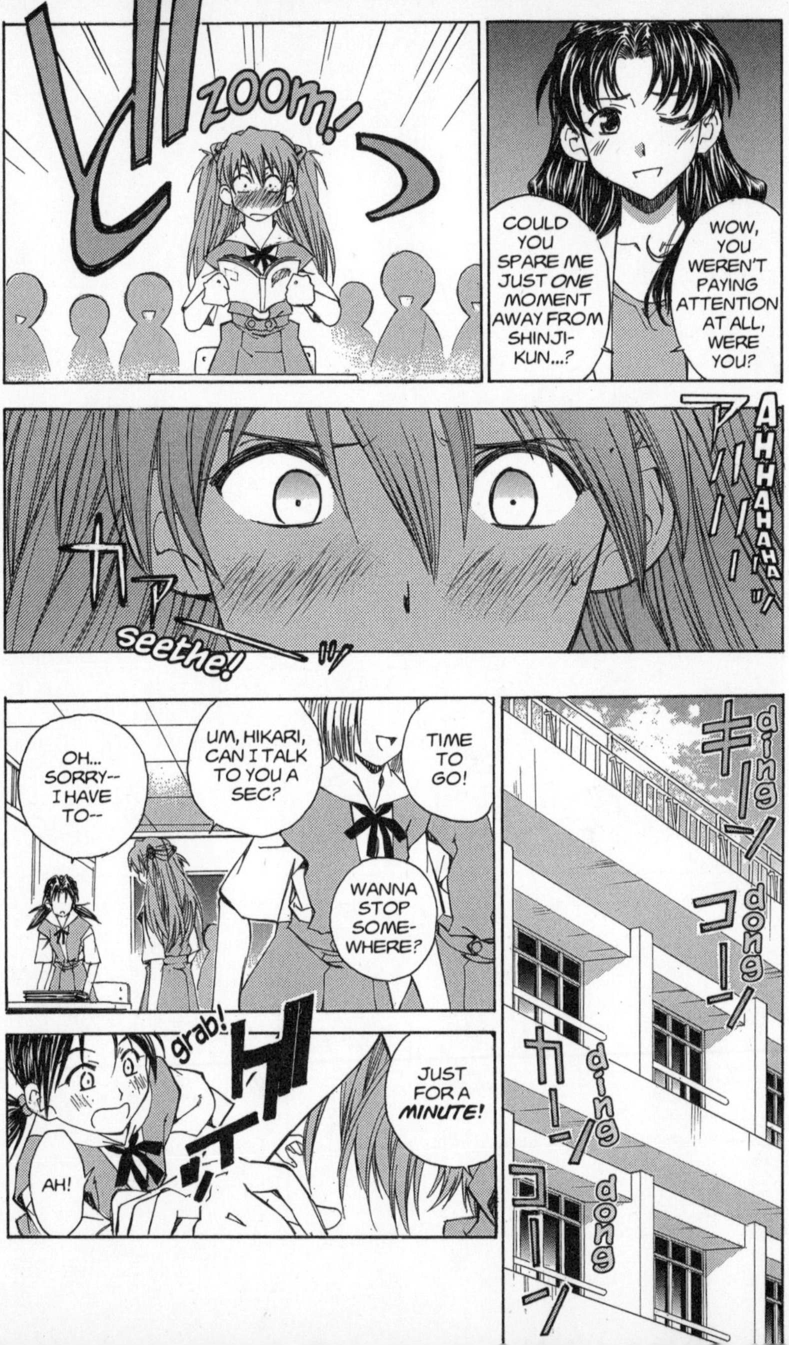
WOW, YOU WEREN'T PAYING ATTENTION AT ALL, WERE YOU?
COULD YOU SPARE ME JUST *ONE* MOMENT AWAY FROM SHINJI-KUN...?
zoom!
AHHAHAHAHA
seethe!
ding dong
ding dong
TIME TO GO!
WANNA STOP SOME-WHERE?
UM, HIKARI, CAN I TALK TO YOU A SEC?
OH... SORRY-- I HAVE TO--
JUST FOR A *MINUTE!*
grab!
AH!

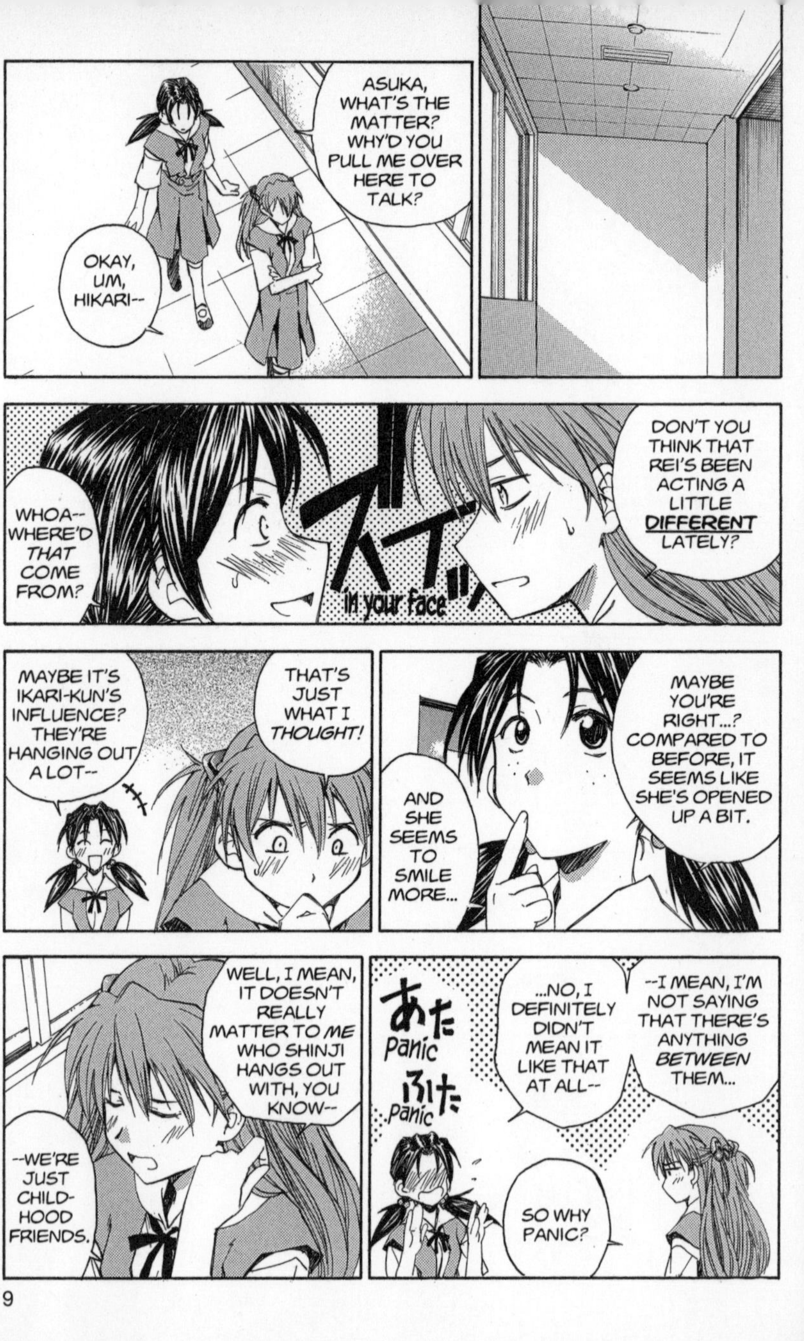
ASUKA, WHAT'S THE MATTER? WHY'D YOU PULL ME OVER HERE TO TALK?
OKAY, UM, HIKARI--
DON'T YOU THINK THAT REI'S BEEN ACTING A LITTLE DIFFERENT LATELY?
in your face
WHOA-- WHERE'D THAT COME FROM?
MAYBE YOU'RE RIGHT...? COMPARED TO BEFORE, IT SEEMS LIKE SHE'S OPENED UP A BIT.
AND SHE SEEMS TO SMILE MORE...
THAT'S JUST WHAT I THOUGHT!
MAYBE IT'S IKARI-KUN'S INFLUENCE? THEY'RE HANGING OUT A LOT--
--I MEAN, I'M NOT SAYING THAT THERE'S ANYTHING BETWEEN THEM...
...NO, I DEFINITELY DIDN'T MEAN IT LIKE THAT AT ALL--
あた panic
ふた panic
SO WHY PANIC?
WELL, I MEAN, IT DOESN'T REALLY MATTER TO ME WHO SHINJI HANGS OUT WITH, YOU KNOW--
--WE'RE JUST CHILDHOOD FRIENDS.

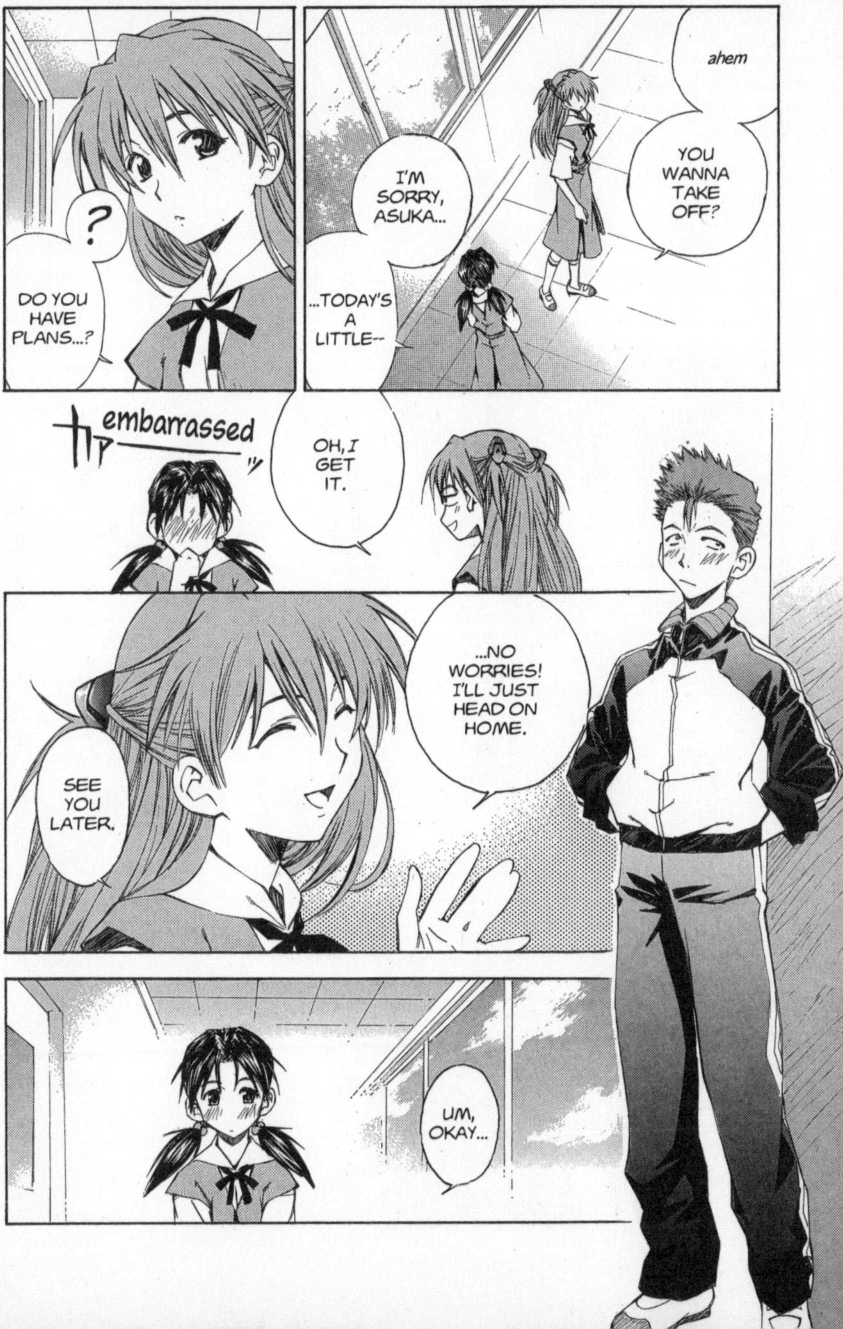
ahem
YOU WANNA TAKE OFF?
I'M SORRY, ASUKA...
...TODAY'S A LITTLE--
?
DO YOU HAVE PLANS...?
embarrassed
OH, I GET IT.
...NO WORRIES! I'LL JUST HEAD ON HOME.
SEE YOU LATER.
UM, OKAY...

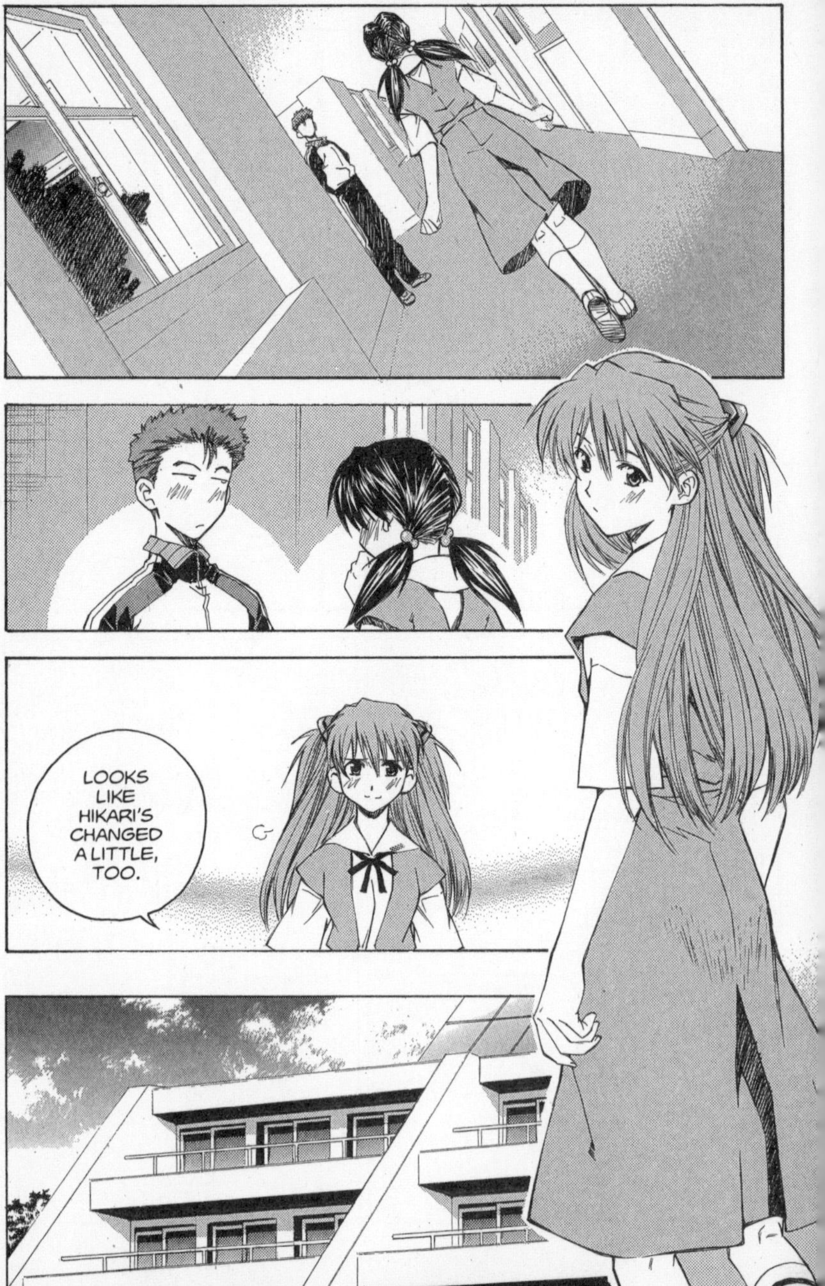
LOOKS LIKE HIKARI'S CHANGED A LITTLE, TOO.

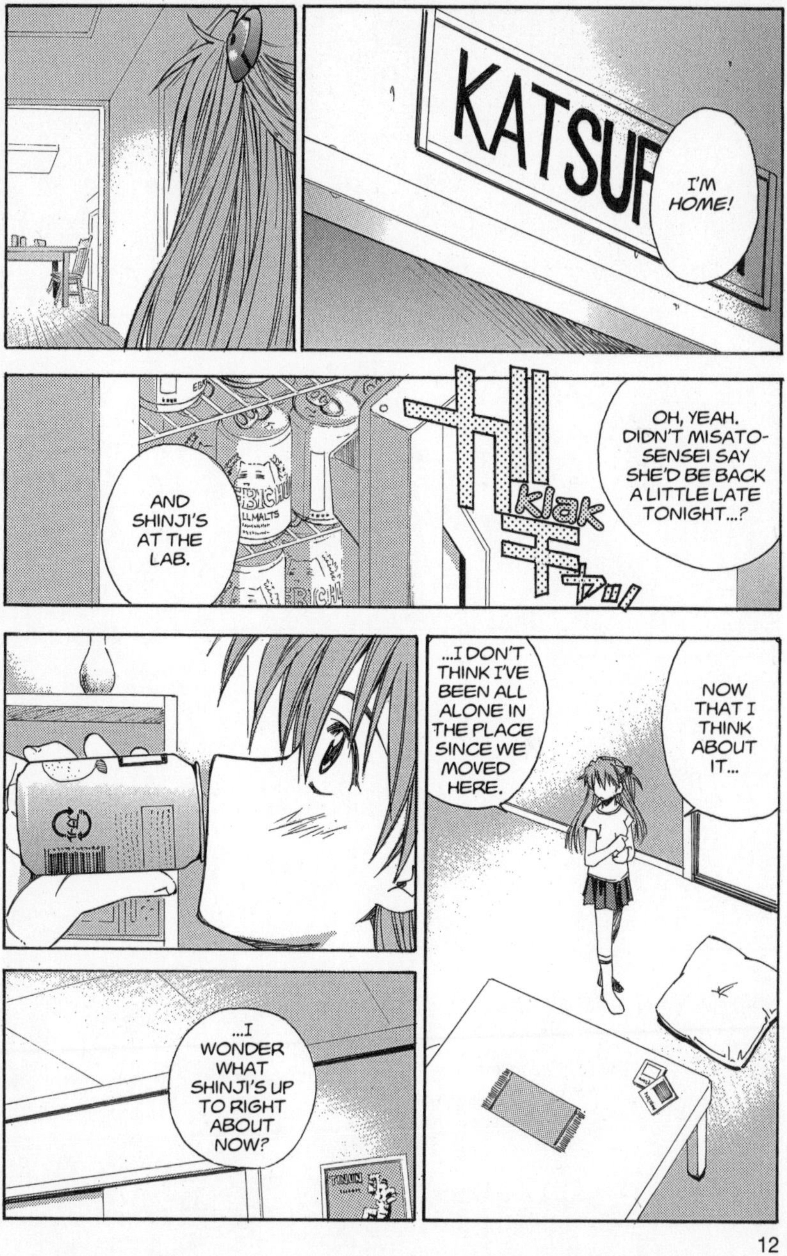
KATSUF
I'M HOME!
OH, YEAH. DIDN'T MISATO-SENSEI SAY SHE'D BE BACK A LITTLE LATE TONIGHT...?
klak
AND SHINJI'S AT THE LAB.
NOW THAT I THINK ABOUT IT...
...I DON'T THINK I'VE BEEN ALL ALONE IN THE PLACE SINCE WE MOVED HERE.
...I WONDER WHAT SHINJI'S UP TO RIGHT ABOUT NOW?

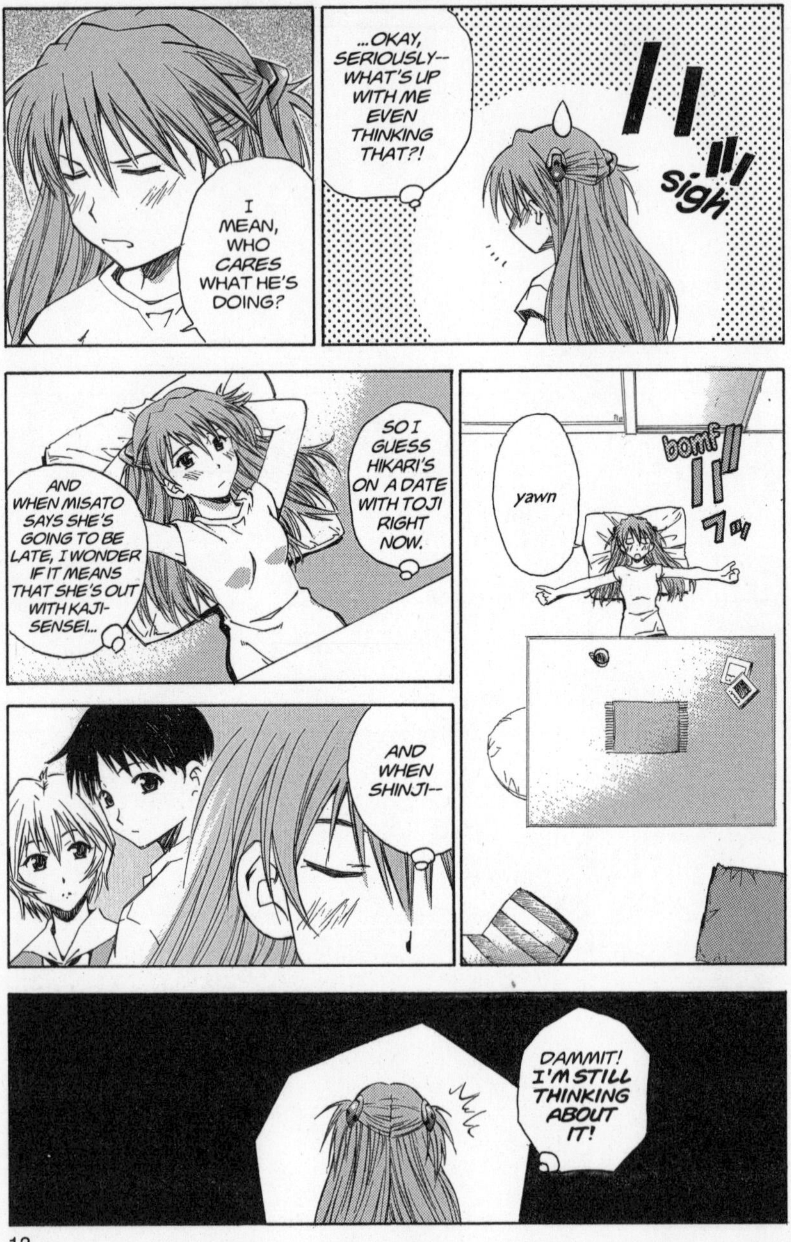
...OKAY, SERIOUSLY-- WHAT'S UP WITH ME EVEN THINKING THAT?!
sigh
I MEAN, WHO CARES WHAT HE'S DOING?
bomf
yawn
SO I GUESS HIKARI'S ON A DATE WITH TOJI RIGHT NOW.
AND WHEN MISATO SAYS SHE'S GOING TO BE LATE, I WONDER IF IT MEANS THAT SHE'S OUT WITH KAJI-SENSEI...
AND WHEN SHINJI--
DAMMIT! I'M STILL THINKING ABOUT IT!

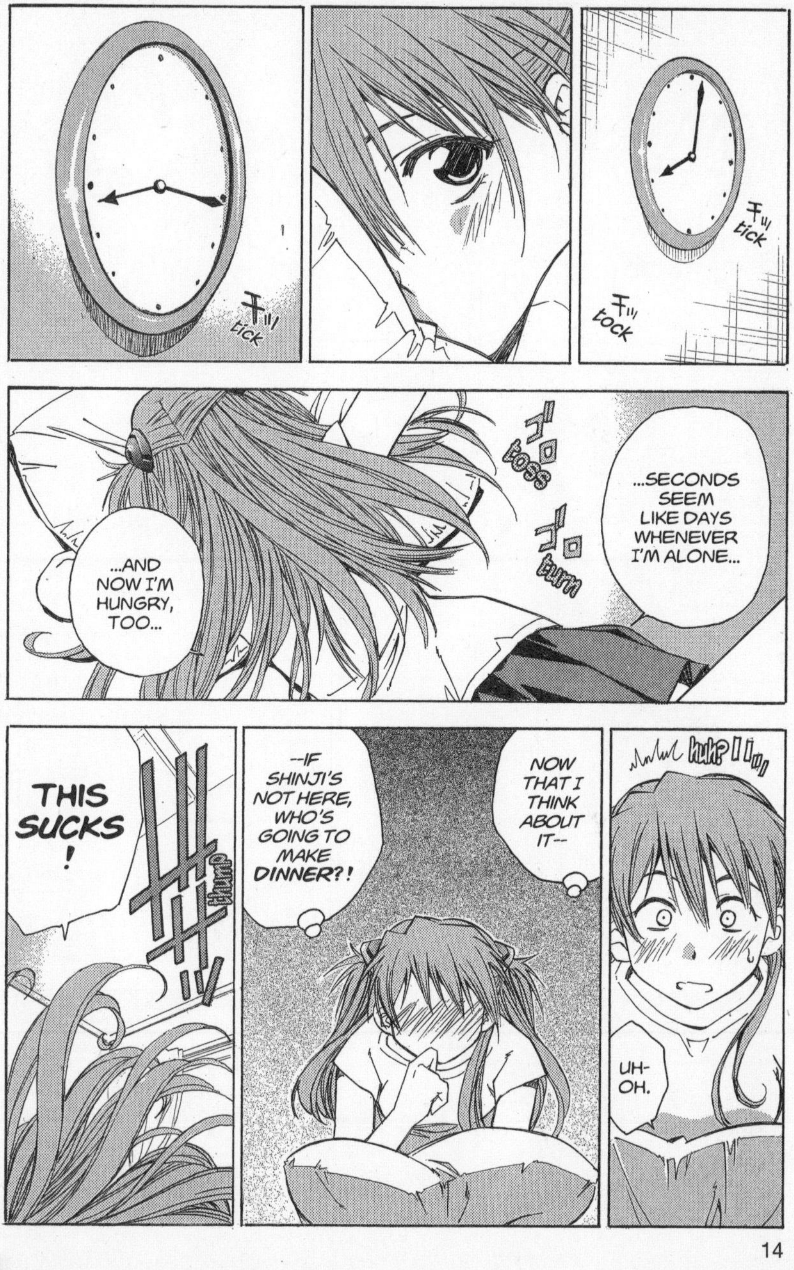
チッ tick
チッ tock
チッ tick
...SECONDS SEEM LIKE DAYS WHENEVER I'M ALONE...
ゴロ toss
ゴロ turn
...AND NOW I'M HUNGRY, TOO...
huh?
UH-OH.
NOW THAT I THINK ABOUT IT--
--IF SHINJI'S NOT HERE, WHO'S GOING TO MAKE DINNER?!
THIS SUCKS!
thump

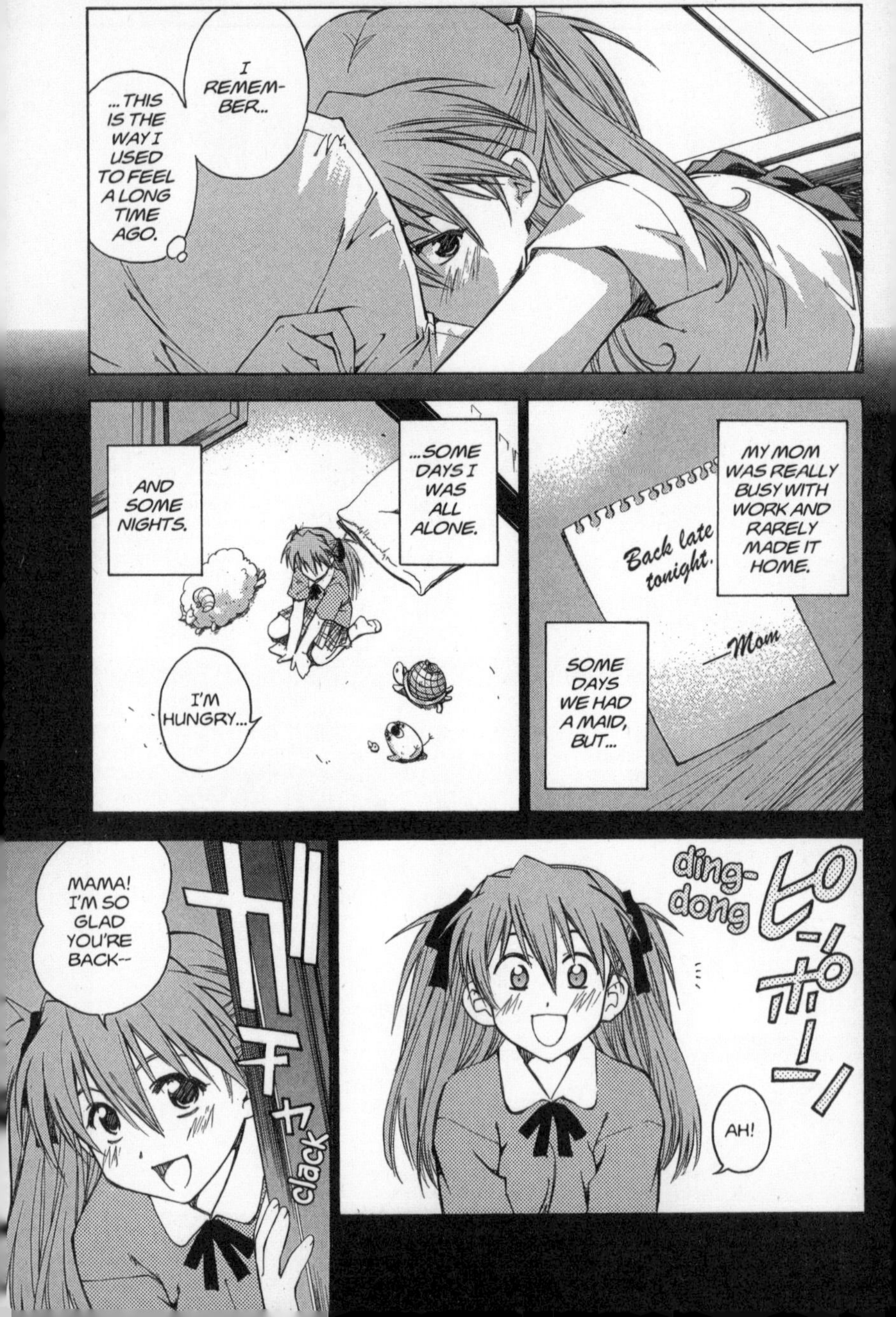
I REMEMBER...
...THIS IS THE WAY I USED TO FEEL A LONG TIME AGO.
MY MOM WAS REALLY BUSY WITH WORK AND RARELY MADE IT HOME.
Back late tonight.
—Mom
SOME DAYS WE HAD A MAID, BUT...
...SOME DAYS I WAS ALL ALONE.
AND SOME NIGHTS.
I'M HUNGRY...
ding-dong
AH!
MAMA! I'M SO GLAD YOU'RE BACK--
clack

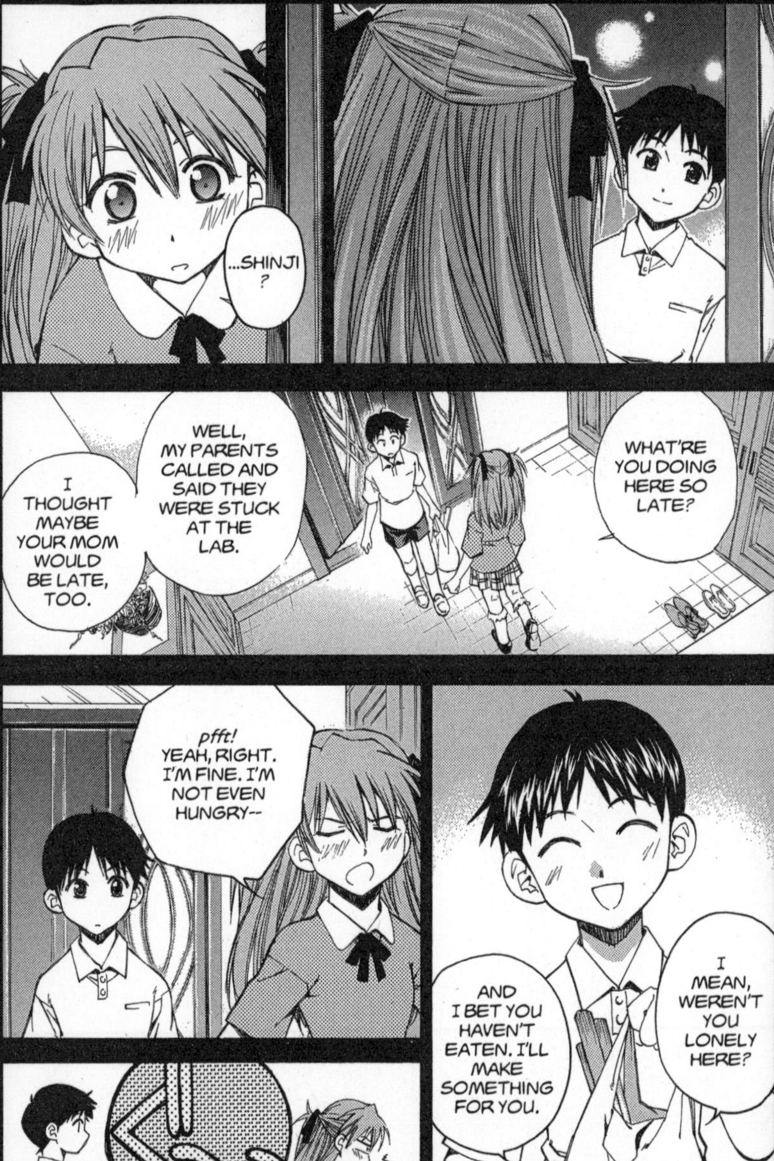
...SHINJI?
WHAT'RE YOU DOING HERE SO LATE?
WELL, MY PARENTS CALLED AND SAID THEY WERE STUCK AT THE LAB.
I THOUGHT MAYBE YOUR MOM WOULD BE LATE, TOO.
I MEAN, WEREN'T YOU LONELY HERE?
AND I BET YOU HAVEN'T EATEN. I'LL MAKE SOMETHING FOR YOU.
pfft! YEAH, RIGHT. I'M FINE. I'M NOT EVEN HUNGRY--
rumble

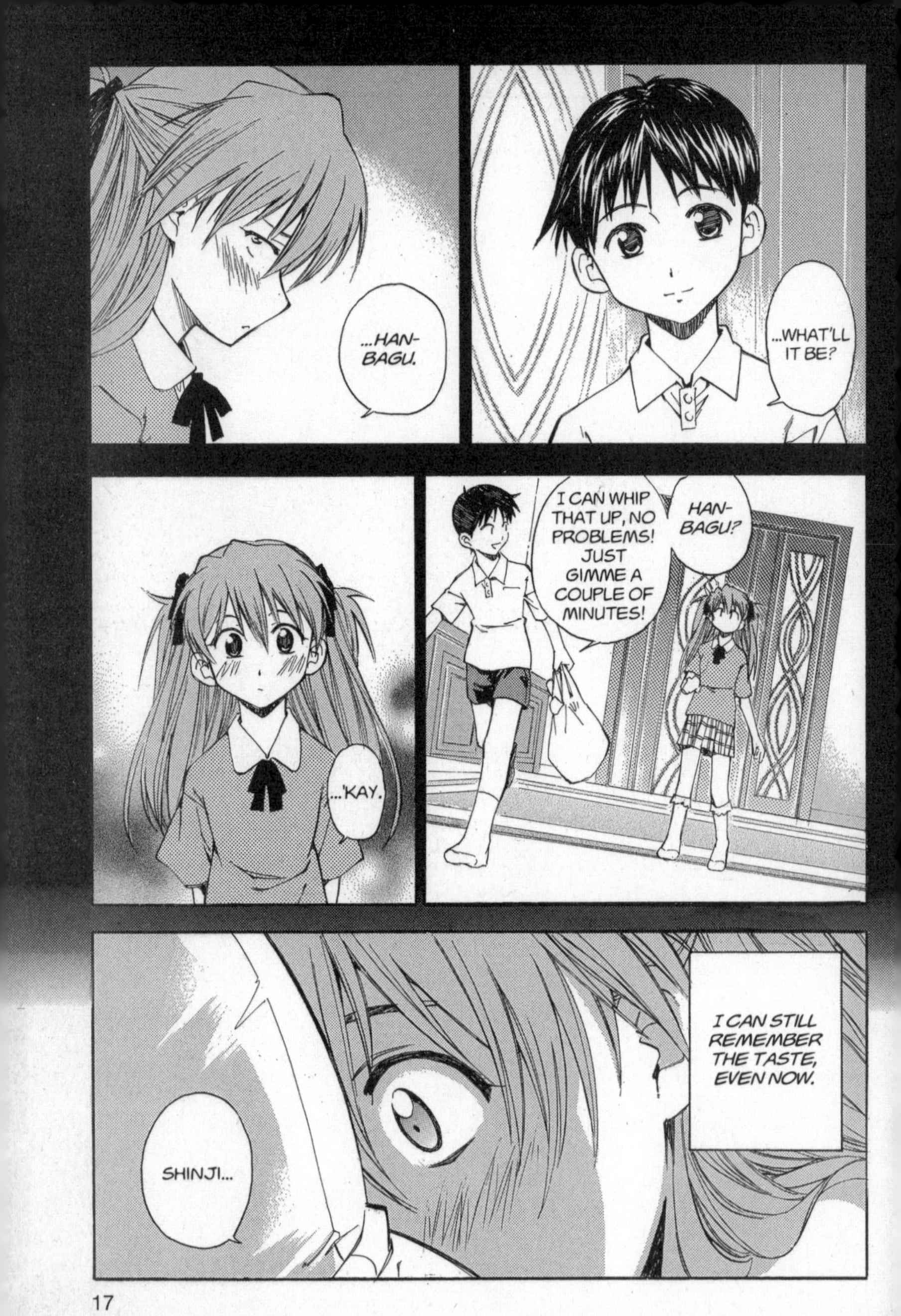
...WHAT'LL IT BE?
...HAN-BAGU.
HAN-BAGU?
I CAN WHIP THAT UP, NO PROBLEMS! JUST GIMME A COUPLE OF MINUTES!
...'KAY.
I CAN STILL REMEMBER THE TASTE, EVEN NOW.
SHINJI...

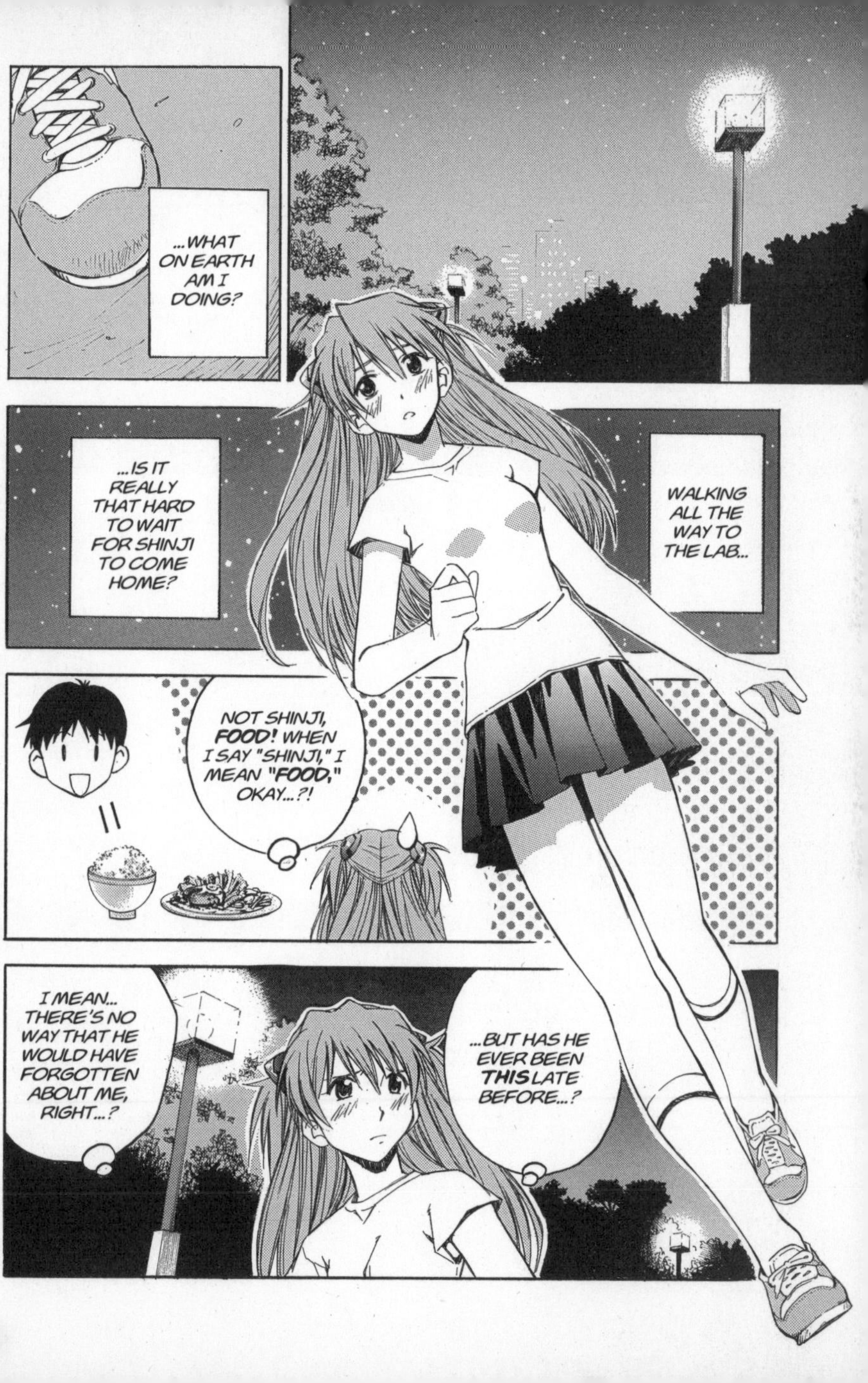
...WHAT ON EARTH AM I DOING?
WALKING ALL THE WAY TO THE LAB...
...IS IT REALLY THAT HARD TO WAIT FOR SHINJI TO COME HOME?
NOT SHINJI, FOOD! WHEN I SAY "SHINJI," I MEAN "FOOD," OKAY...?!
...BUT HAS HE EVER BEEN THIS LATE BEFORE...?
I MEAN... THERE'S NO WAY THAT HE WOULD HAVE FORGOTTEN ABOUT ME, RIGHT...?

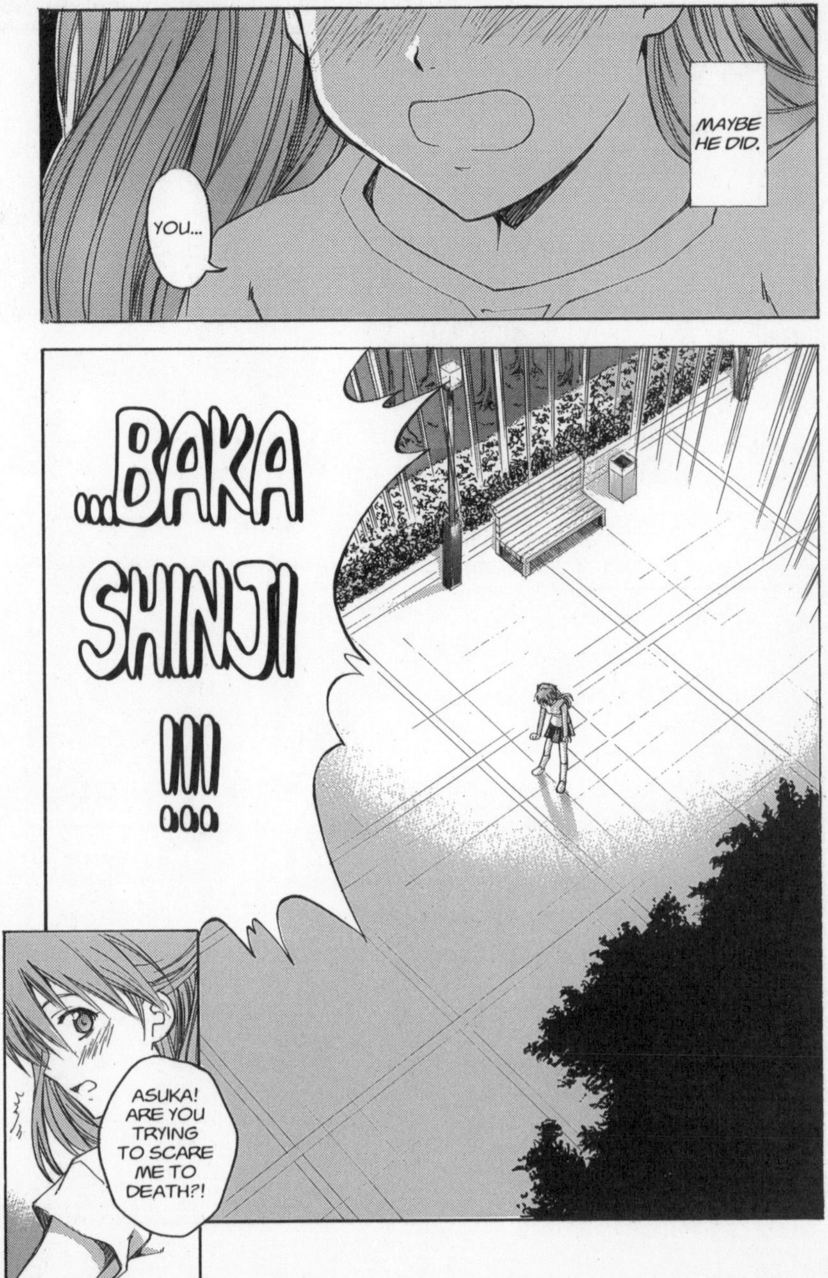
MAYBE HE DID.
YOU...
...BAKA SHINJI !!!!...
ASUKA! ARE YOU TRYING TO SCARE ME TO DEATH?!

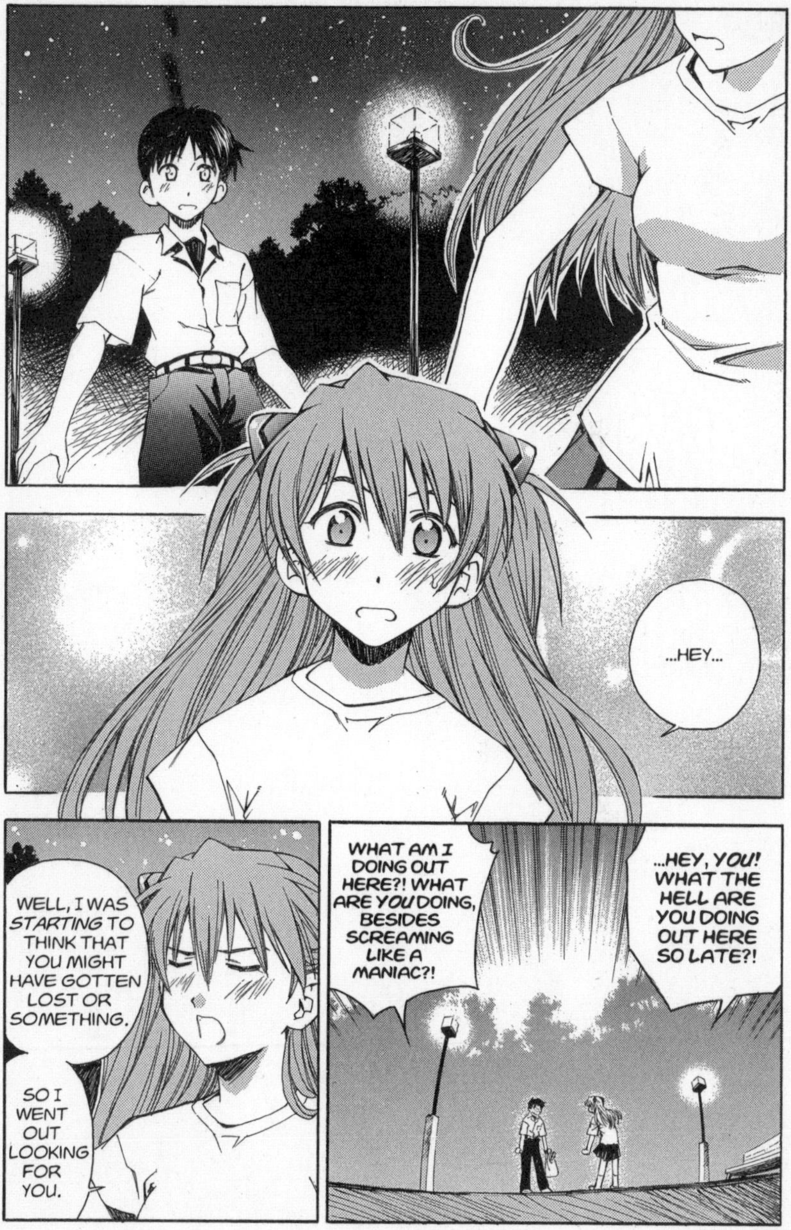
...HEY...
...HEY, *YOU!* WHAT THE HELL ARE YOU DOING OUT HERE SO LATE?!
WHAT AM I DOING OUT HERE?! WHAT ARE *YOU* DOING, BESIDES SCREAMING LIKE A MANIAC?!
WELL, I WAS *STARTING* TO THINK THAT YOU MIGHT HAVE GOTTEN LOST OR SOMETHING.
SO I WENT OUT LOOKING FOR YOU.

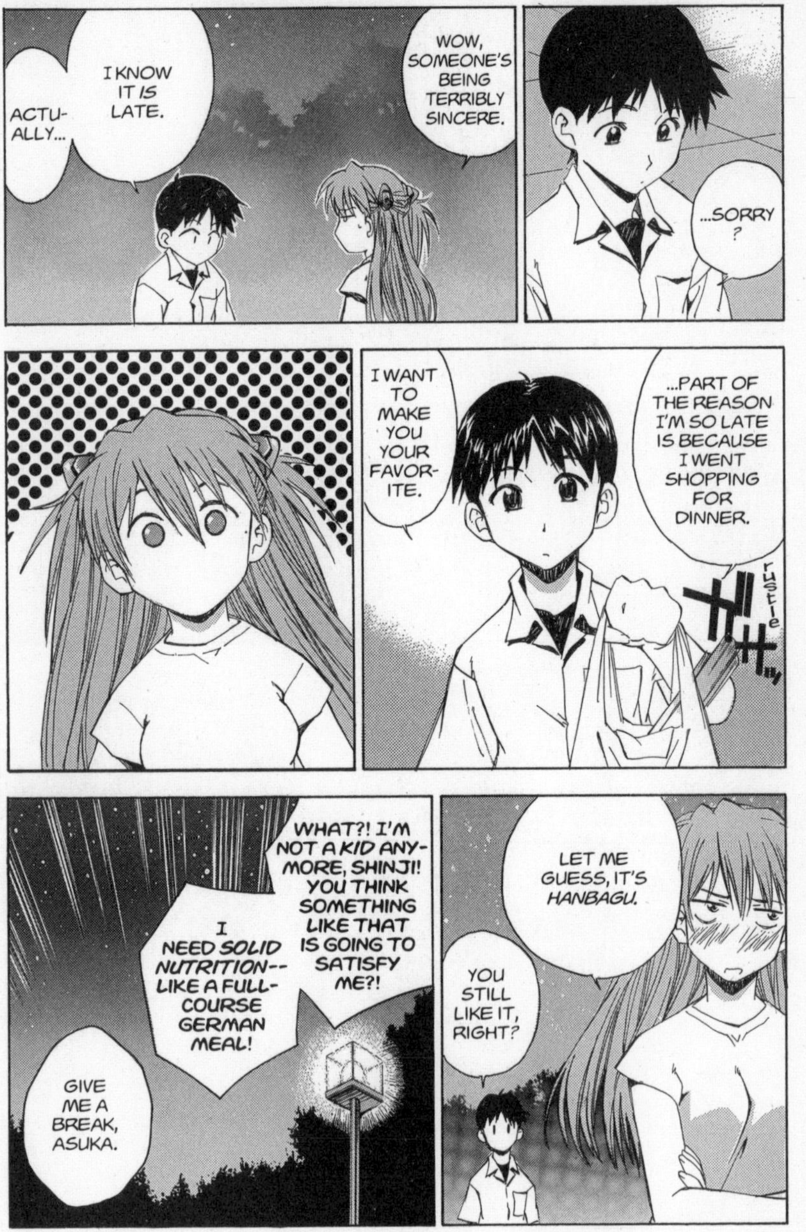
...SORRY?
WOW, SOMEONE'S BEING TERRIBLY SINCERE.
I KNOW IT *IS* LATE.
ACTU-ALLY...
...PART OF THE REASON I'M SO LATE IS BECAUSE I WENT SHOPPING FOR DINNER.
rustle
I WANT TO MAKE YOU YOUR FAVOR-ITE.
LET ME GUESS, IT'S *HANBAGU*.
YOU STILL LIKE IT, RIGHT?
WHAT?! I'M NOT A *KID* ANY-MORE, SHINJI! YOU THINK SOMETHING LIKE THAT IS GOING TO SATISFY ME?!
I NEED *SOLID* NUTRITION--LIKE A FULL-COURSE GERMAN MEAL!
GIVE ME A BREAK, ASUKA.

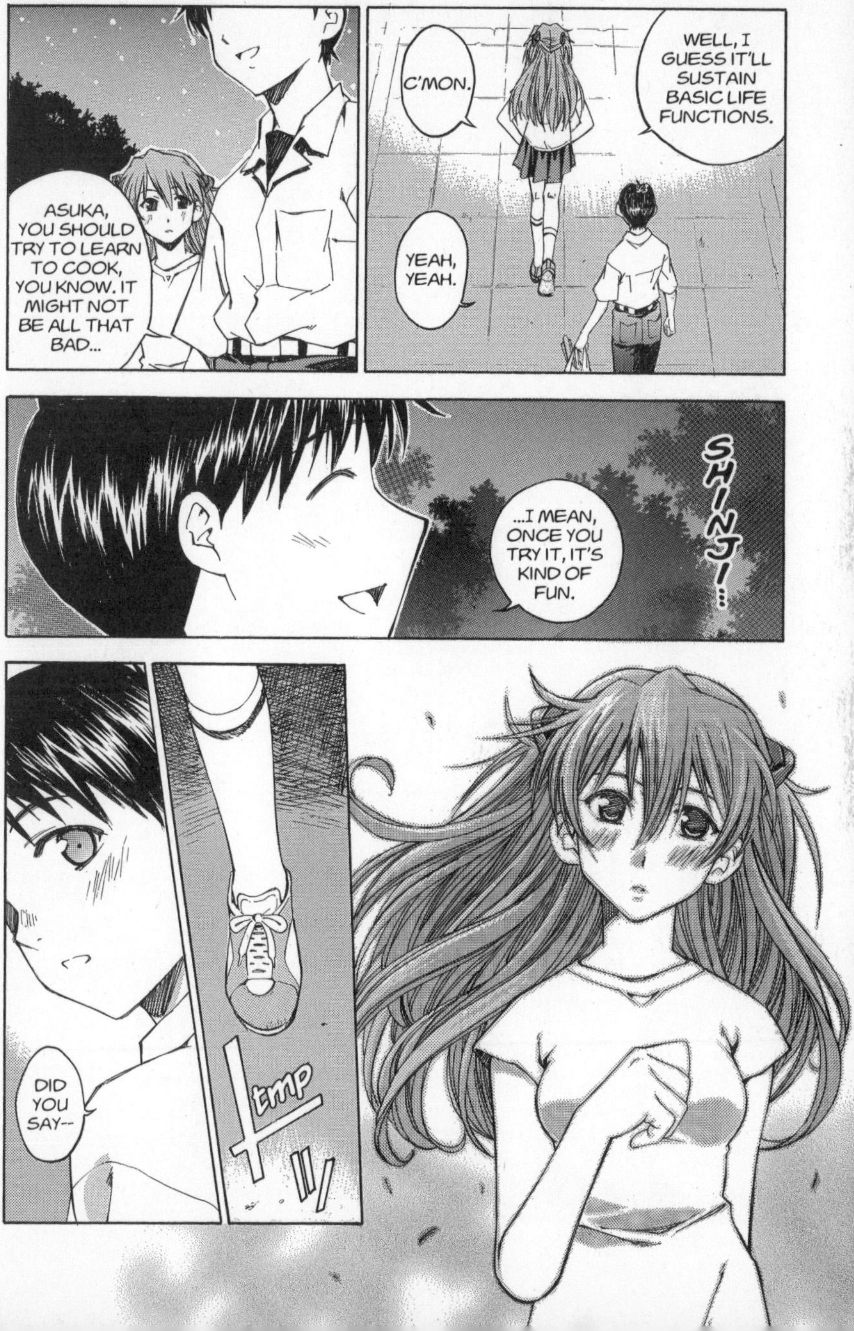
WELL, I GUESS IT'LL SUSTAIN BASIC LIFE FUNCTIONS.
C'MON.
YEAH, YEAH.
ASUKA, YOU SHOULD TRY TO LEARN TO COOK, YOU KNOW. IT MIGHT NOT BE ALL THAT BAD...
SHINJI...!
...I MEAN, ONCE YOU TRY IT, IT'S KIND OF FUN.
tmp
DID YOU SAY--

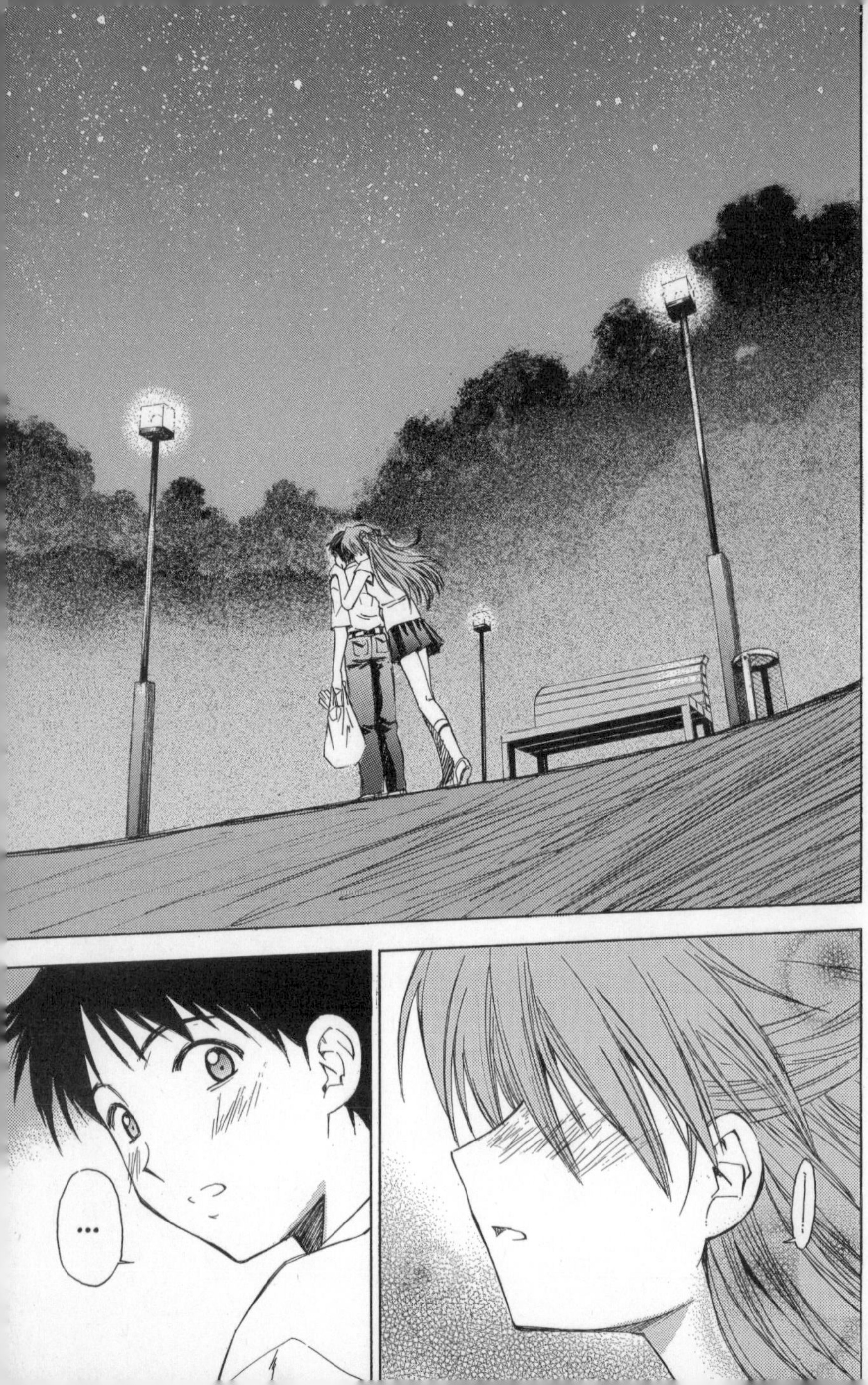
...

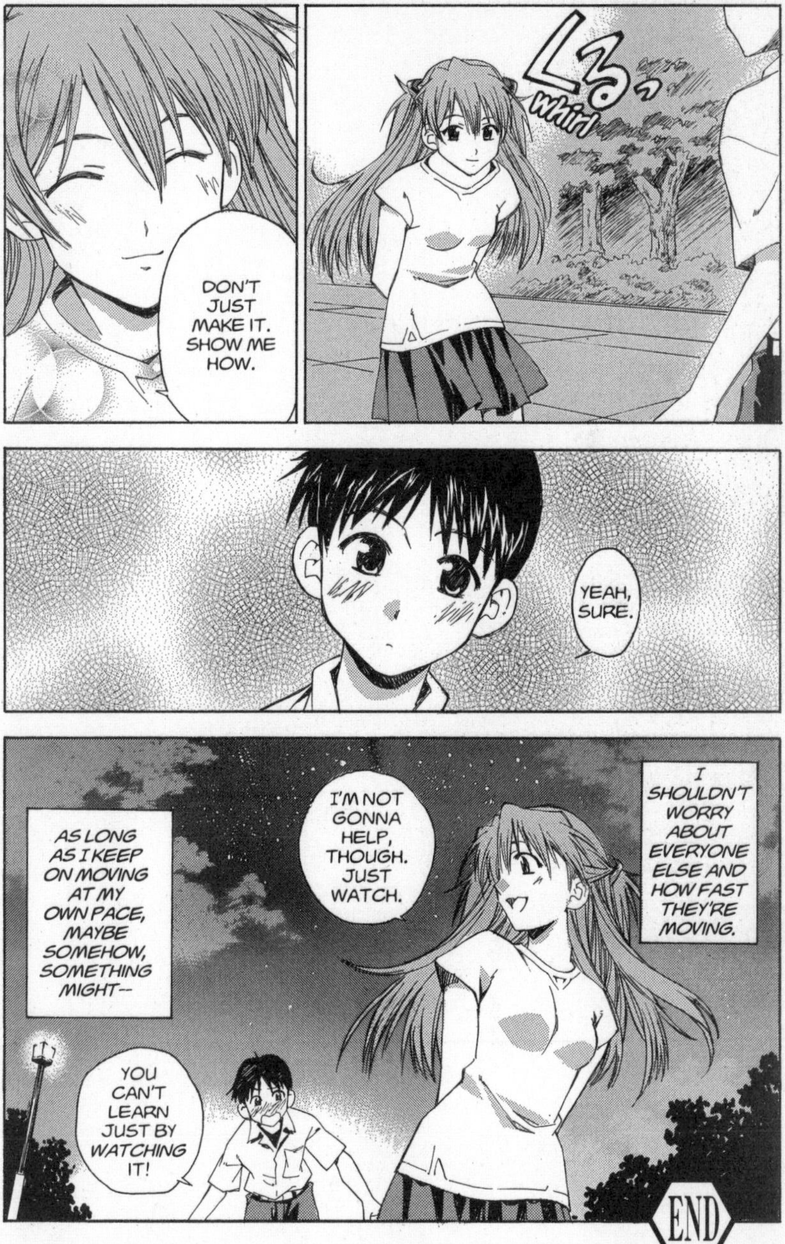
くるっ
whirl
DON'T JUST MAKE IT. SHOW ME HOW.
YEAH, SURE.
I SHOULDN'T WORRY ABOUT EVERYONE ELSE AND HOW FAST THEY'RE MOVING.
I'M NOT GONNA HELP, THOUGH. JUST WATCH.
AS LONG AS I KEEP ON MOVING AT MY OWN PACE, MAYBE SOMEHOW, SOMETHING MIGHT--
YOU CAN'T LEARN JUST BY WATCHING IT!
END

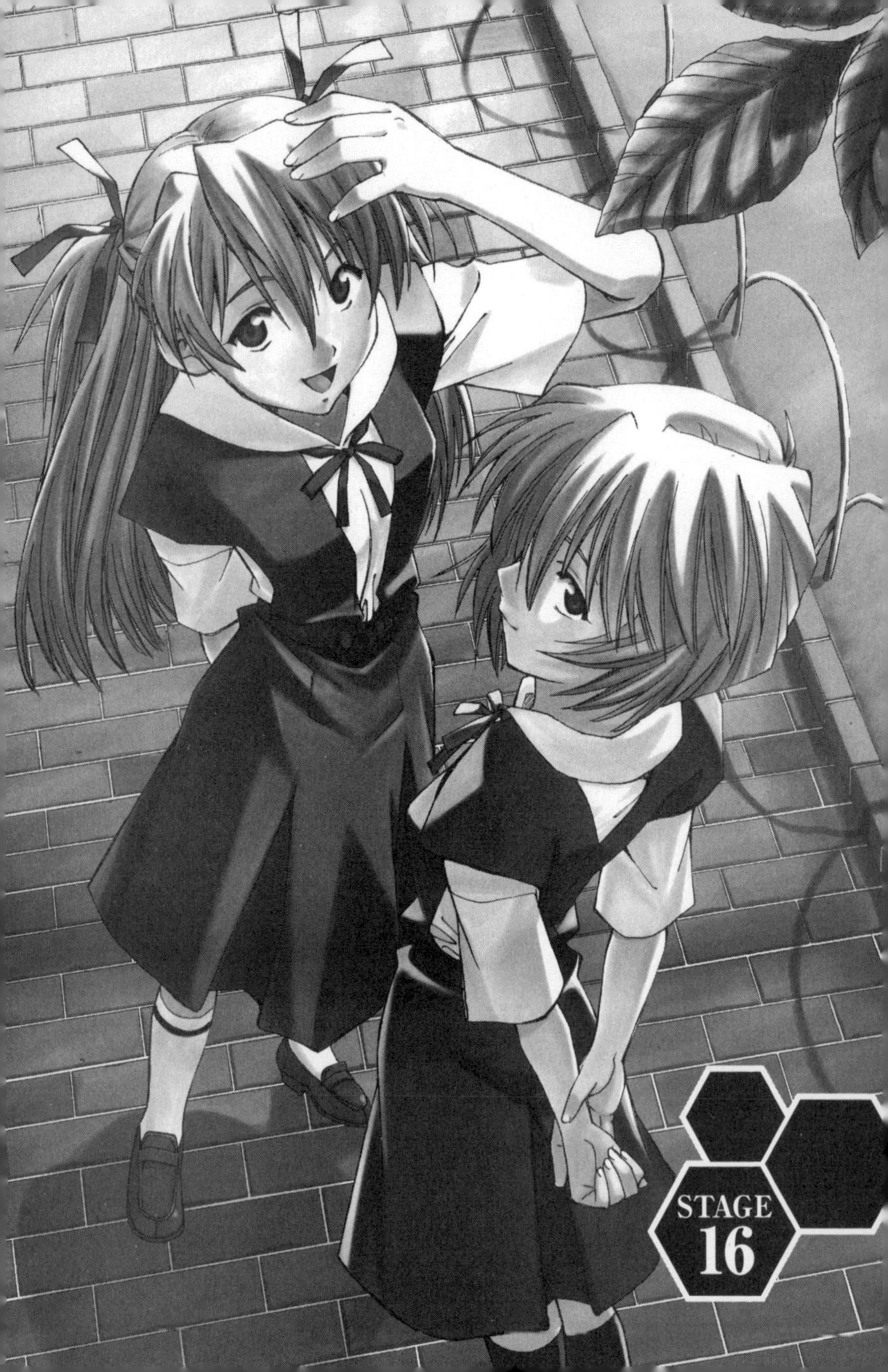
STAGE
16

NEON GENESIS
EVANGELION
THE SHINJI IKARI RAISING PROJECT

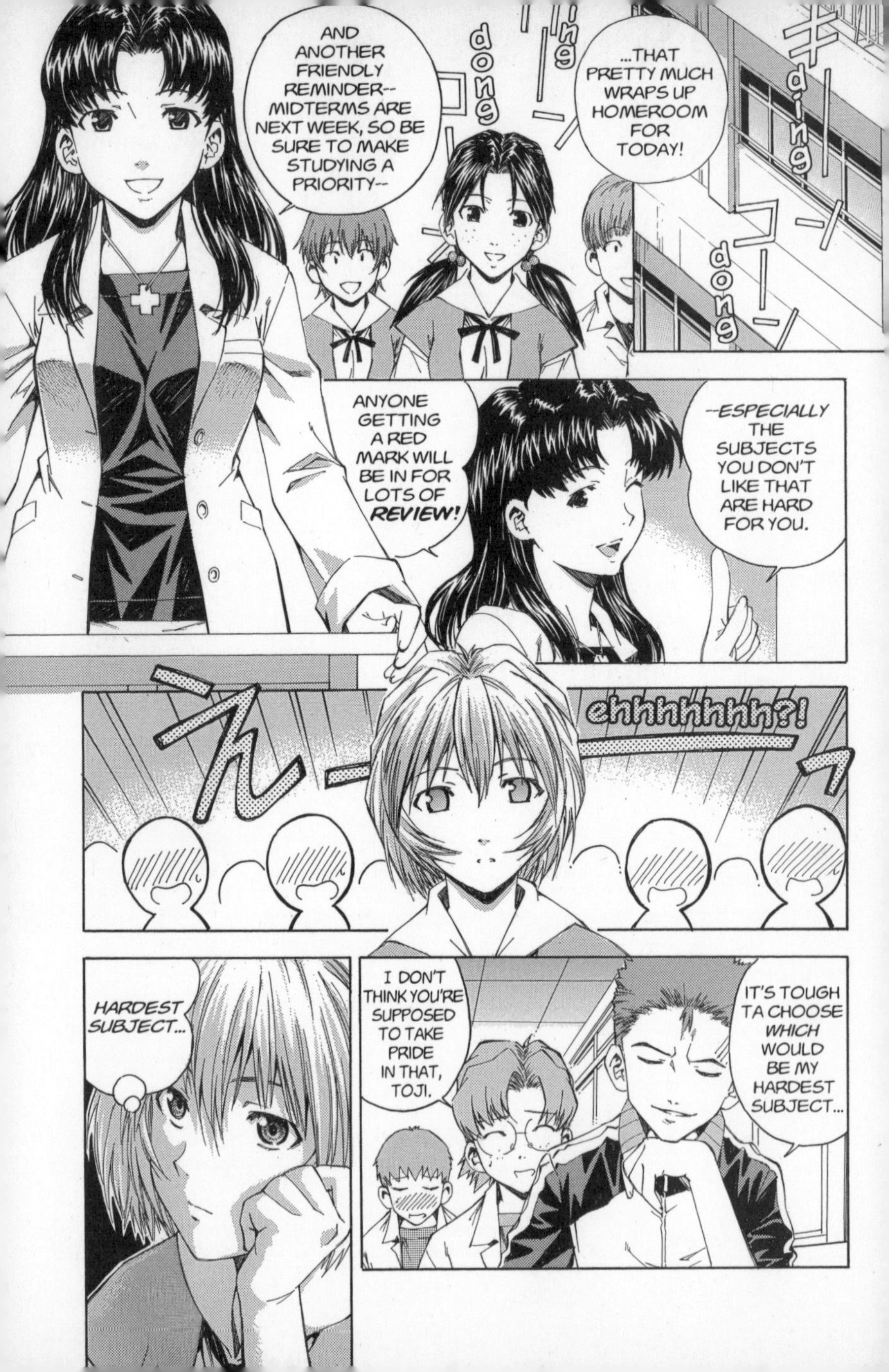

ding
dong
...THAT PRETTY MUCH WRAPS UP HOMEROOM FOR TODAY!
ding
dong
AND ANOTHER FRIENDLY REMINDER-- MIDTERMS ARE NEXT WEEK, SO BE SURE TO MAKE STUDYING A PRIORITY--
--ESPECIALLY THE SUBJECTS YOU DON'T LIKE THAT ARE HARD FOR YOU.
ANYONE GETTING A RED MARK WILL BE IN FOR LOTS OF *REVIEW!*
ehhhhhhhh?!
IT'S TOUGH TA CHOOSE *WHICH* WOULD BE MY HARDEST SUBJECT...
I DON'T THINK YOU'RE SUPPOSED TO TAKE PRIDE IN THAT, TOJI.
HARDEST SUBJECT...

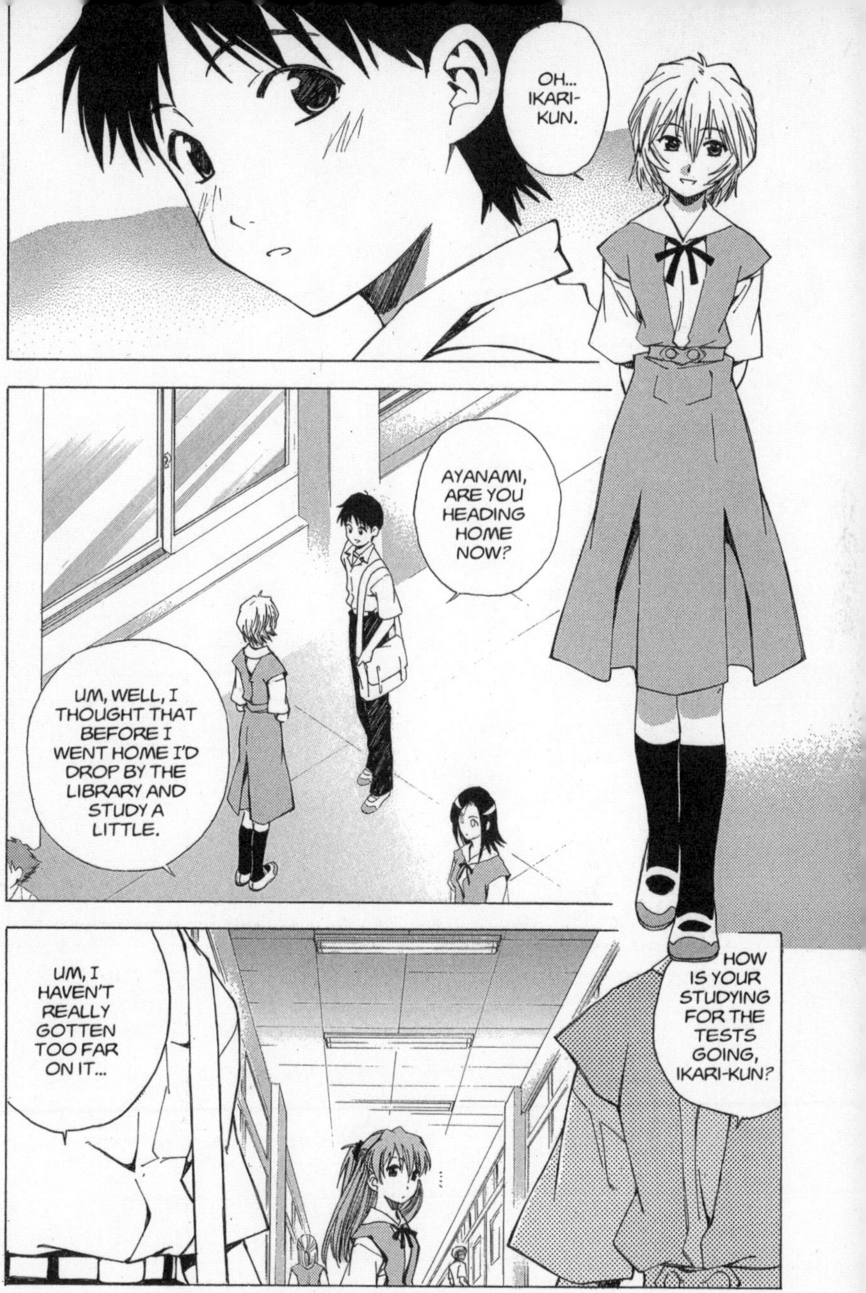
OH... IKARI-KUN.
AYANAMI, ARE YOU HEADING HOME NOW?
UM, WELL, I THOUGHT THAT BEFORE I WENT HOME I'D DROP BY THE LIBRARY AND STUDY A LITTLE.
HOW IS YOUR STUDYING FOR THE TESTS GOING, IKARI-KUN?
UM, I HAVEN'T REALLY GOTTEN TOO FAR ON IT...
...

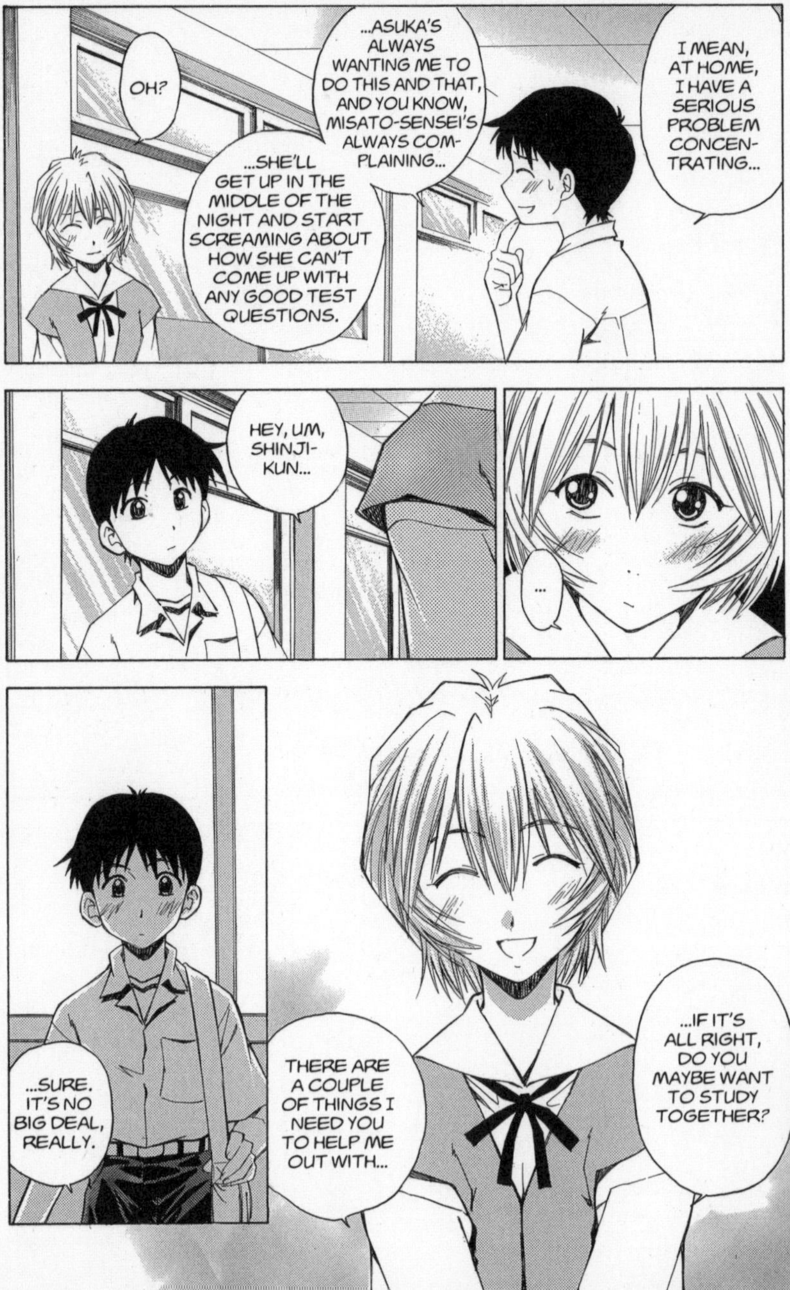
I MEAN, AT HOME, I HAVE A SERIOUS PROBLEM CONCEN-TRATING...
...ASUKA'S ALWAYS WANTING ME TO DO THIS AND THAT, AND YOU KNOW, MISATO-SENSEI'S ALWAYS COM-PLAINING...
...SHE'LL GET UP IN THE MIDDLE OF THE NIGHT AND START SCREAMING ABOUT HOW SHE CAN'T COME UP WITH ANY GOOD TEST QUESTIONS.
OH?
...
HEY, UM, SHINJI-KUN...
...IF IT'S ALL RIGHT, DO YOU MAYBE WANT TO STUDY TOGETHER?
THERE ARE A COUPLE OF THINGS I NEED YOU TO HELP ME OUT WITH...
...SURE. IT'S NO BIG DEAL, REALLY.

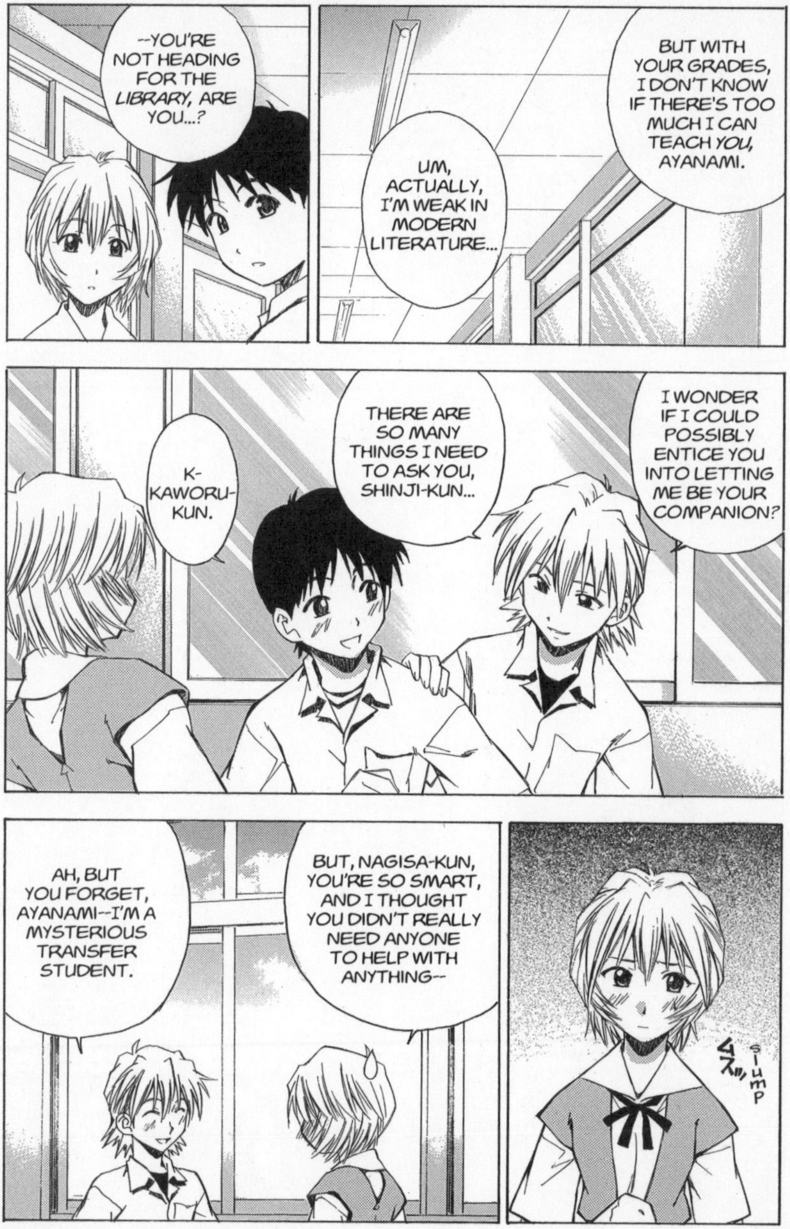
BUT WITH YOUR GRADES, I DON'T KNOW IF THERE'S TOO MUCH I CAN TEACH *YOU*, AYANAMI.
UM, ACTUALLY, I'M WEAK IN MODERN LITERATURE...
--YOU'RE NOT HEADING FOR THE *LIBRARY*, ARE YOU...?
I WONDER IF I COULD POSSIBLY ENTICE YOU INTO LETTING ME BE YOUR COMPANION?
THERE ARE SO MANY THINGS I NEED TO ASK YOU, SHINJI-KUN...
K-KAWORU-KUN.
ムスッ
SLUMP
BUT, NAGISA-KUN, YOU'RE SO SMART, AND I THOUGHT YOU DIDN'T REALLY NEED ANYONE TO HELP WITH ANYTHING--
AH, BUT YOU FORGET, AYANAMI--I'M A MYSTERIOUS TRANSFER STUDENT.

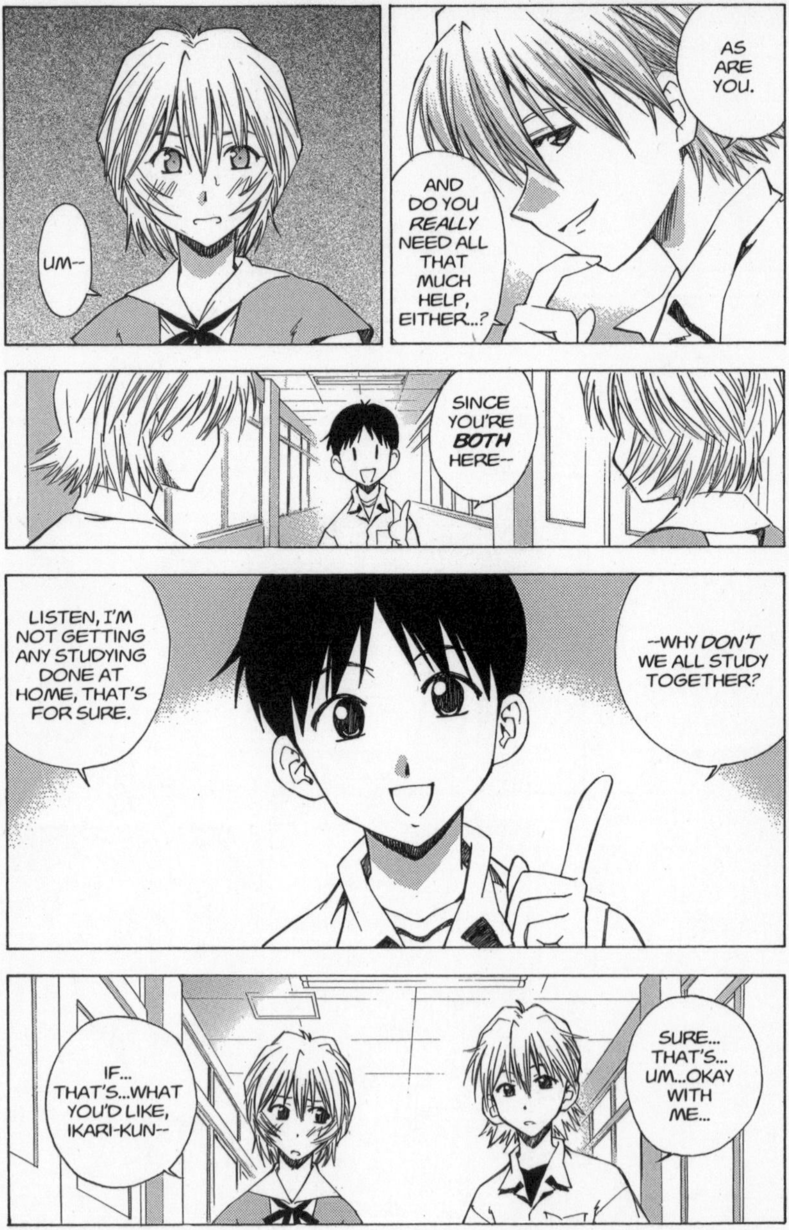
AS ARE YOU.
AND DO YOU *REALLY* NEED ALL THAT MUCH HELP, EITHER...?
UM--
SINCE YOU'RE ***BOTH*** HERE--
--WHY *DON'T* WE ALL STUDY TOGETHER?
LISTEN, I'M NOT GETTING ANY STUDYING DONE AT HOME, THAT'S FOR SURE.
SURE... THAT'S... UM...OKAY WITH ME...
IF... THAT'S...WHAT YOU'D LIKE, IKARI-KUN--

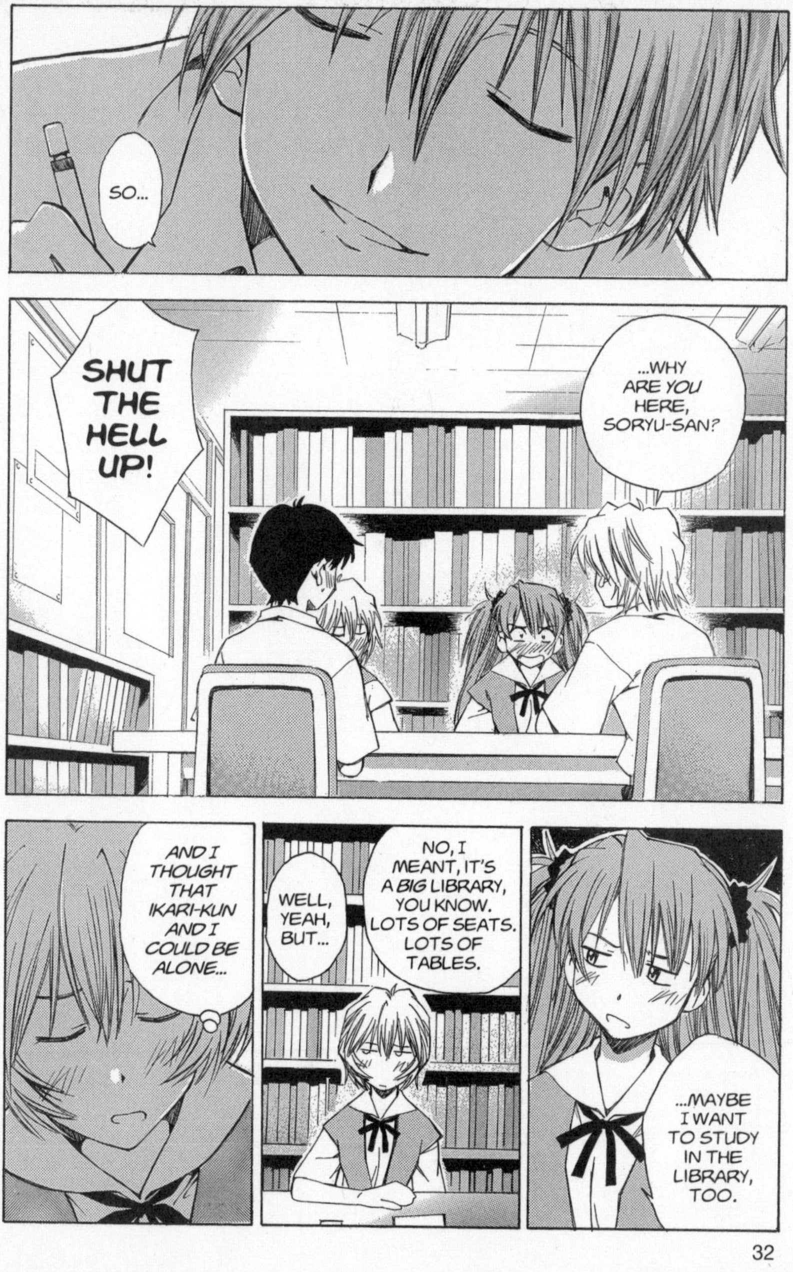
SO...
...WHY ARE *YOU* HERE, SORYU-SAN?
SHUT THE HELL UP!
...MAYBE I WANT TO STUDY IN THE LIBRARY, TOO.
NO, I MEANT, IT'S A *BIG* LIBRARY, YOU KNOW. LOTS OF SEATS. LOTS OF TABLES.
WELL, YEAH, BUT...
AND I THOUGHT THAT IKARI-KUN AND I COULD BE ALONE...

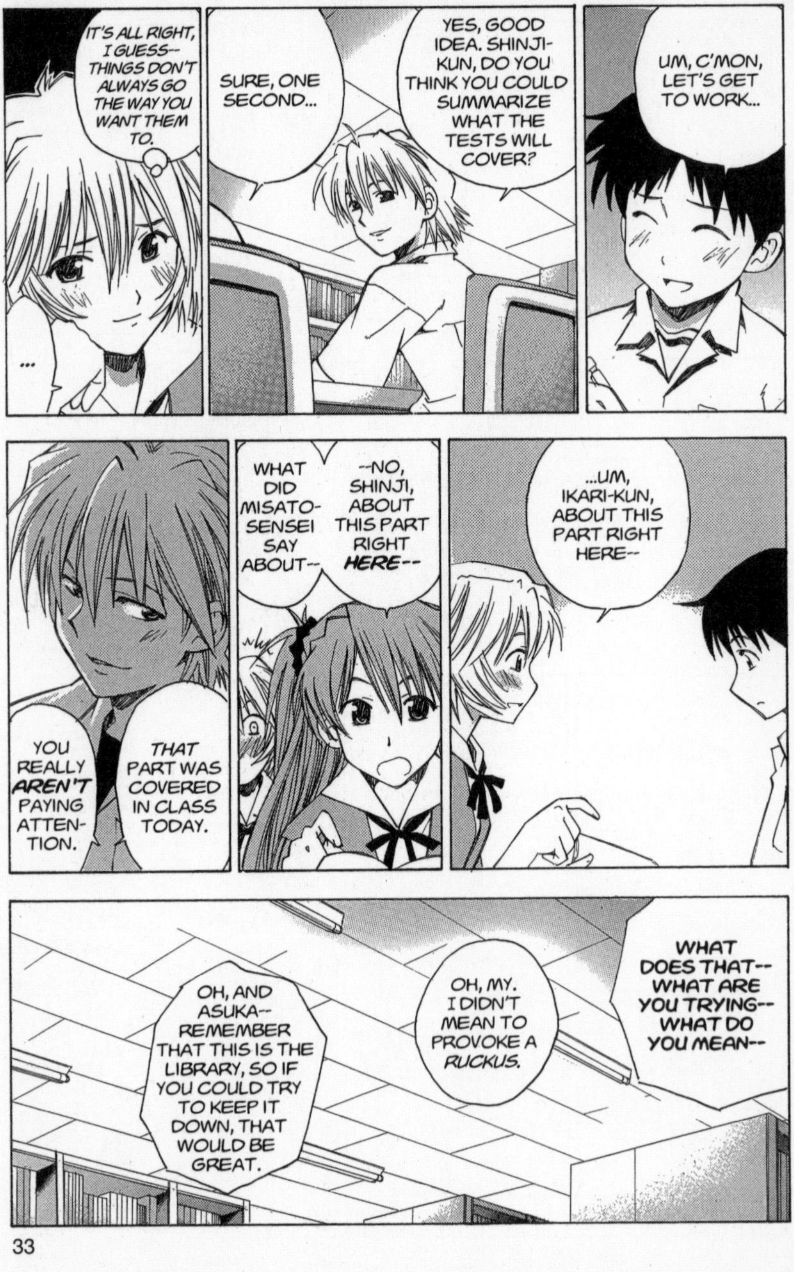
UM, C'MON, LET'S GET TO WORK...
YES, GOOD IDEA. SHINJI-KUN, DO YOU THINK YOU COULD SUMMARIZE WHAT THE TESTS WILL COVER?
SURE, ONE SECOND...
IT'S ALL RIGHT, I GUESS-- THINGS DON'T ALWAYS GO THE WAY YOU WANT THEM TO.
...
...UM, IKARI-KUN, ABOUT THIS PART RIGHT HERE--
--NO, SHINJI, ABOUT THIS PART RIGHT *HERE*--
WHAT DID MISATO-SENSEI SAY ABOUT--
THAT PART WAS COVERED IN CLASS TODAY.
YOU REALLY *AREN'T* PAYING ATTENTION.
WHAT DOES THAT-- WHAT ARE YOU TRYING-- WHAT DO YOU MEAN--
OH, MY. I DIDN'T MEAN TO PROVOKE A *RUCKUS*.
OH, AND ASUKA-- REMEMBER THAT THIS IS THE LIBRARY, SO IF YOU COULD TRY TO KEEP IT DOWN, THAT WOULD BE GREAT.

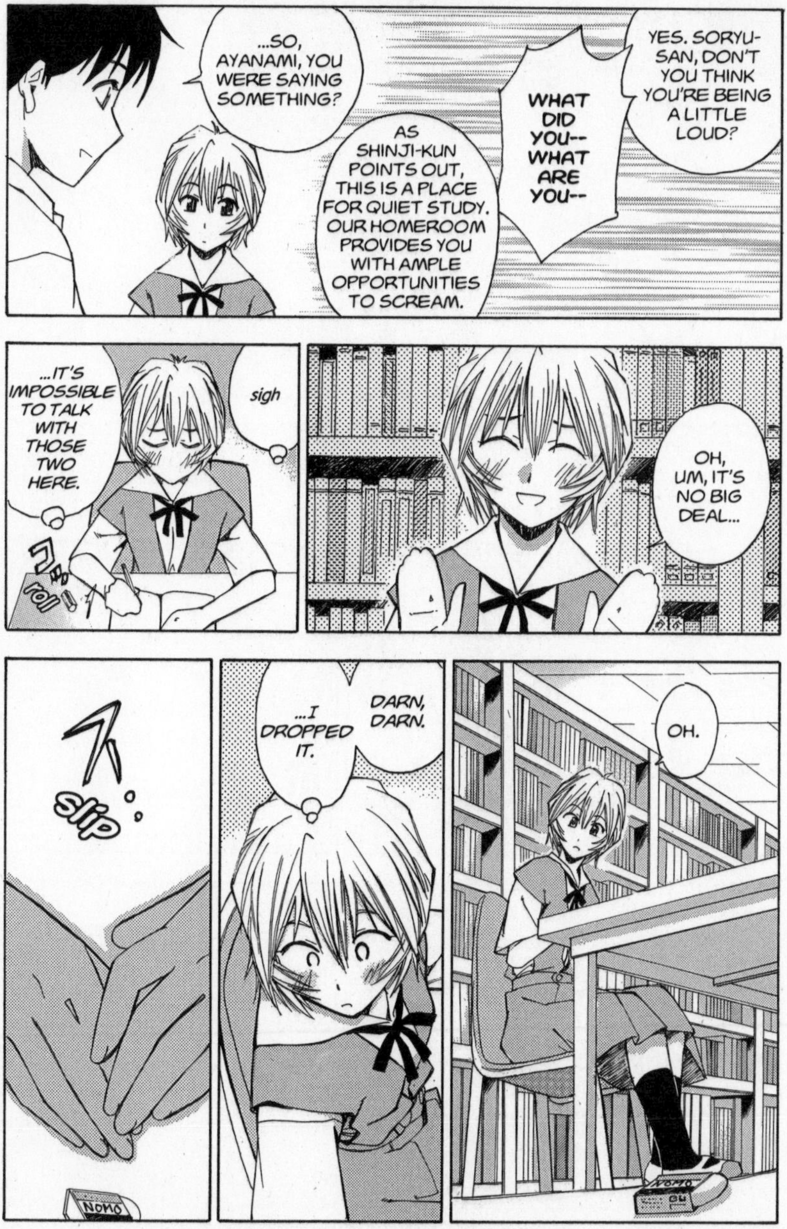
YES. SORYU-SAN, DON'T YOU THINK YOU'RE BEING A LITTLE LOUD?
WHAT DID YOU-- WHAT ARE YOU--
AS SHINJI-KUN POINTS OUT, THIS IS A PLACE FOR QUIET STUDY. OUR HOMEROOM PROVIDES YOU WITH AMPLE OPPORTUNITIES TO SCREAM.
...SO, AYANAMI, YOU WERE SAYING SOMETHING?
OH, UM, IT'S NO BIG DEAL...
sigh
...IT'S IMPOSSIBLE TO TALK WITH THOSE TWO HERE.
roll
OH.
DARN, DARN.
...I DROPPED IT.
slip
NONO

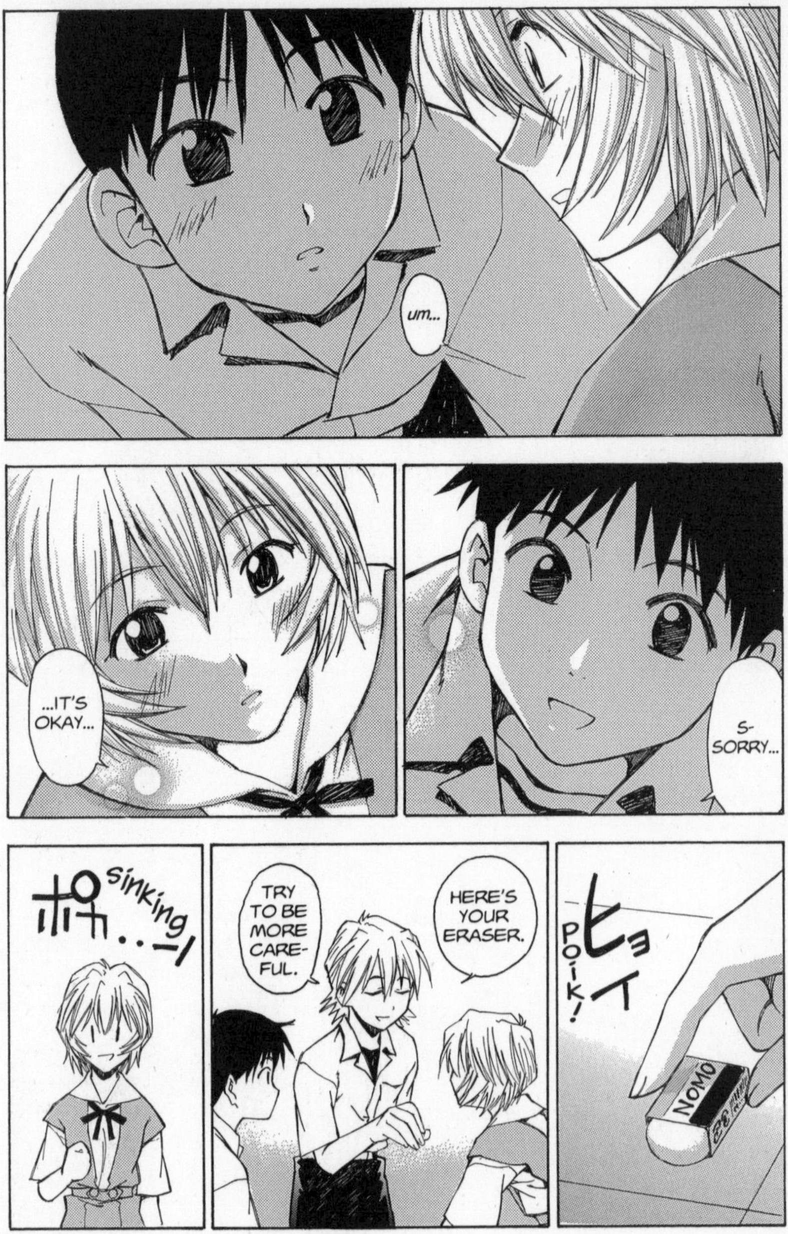
um...
S-SORRY...
...IT'S OKAY...
ヒョイ
POIK!
NOMO
HERE'S YOUR ERASER.
TRY TO BE MORE CAREFUL.
sinking!

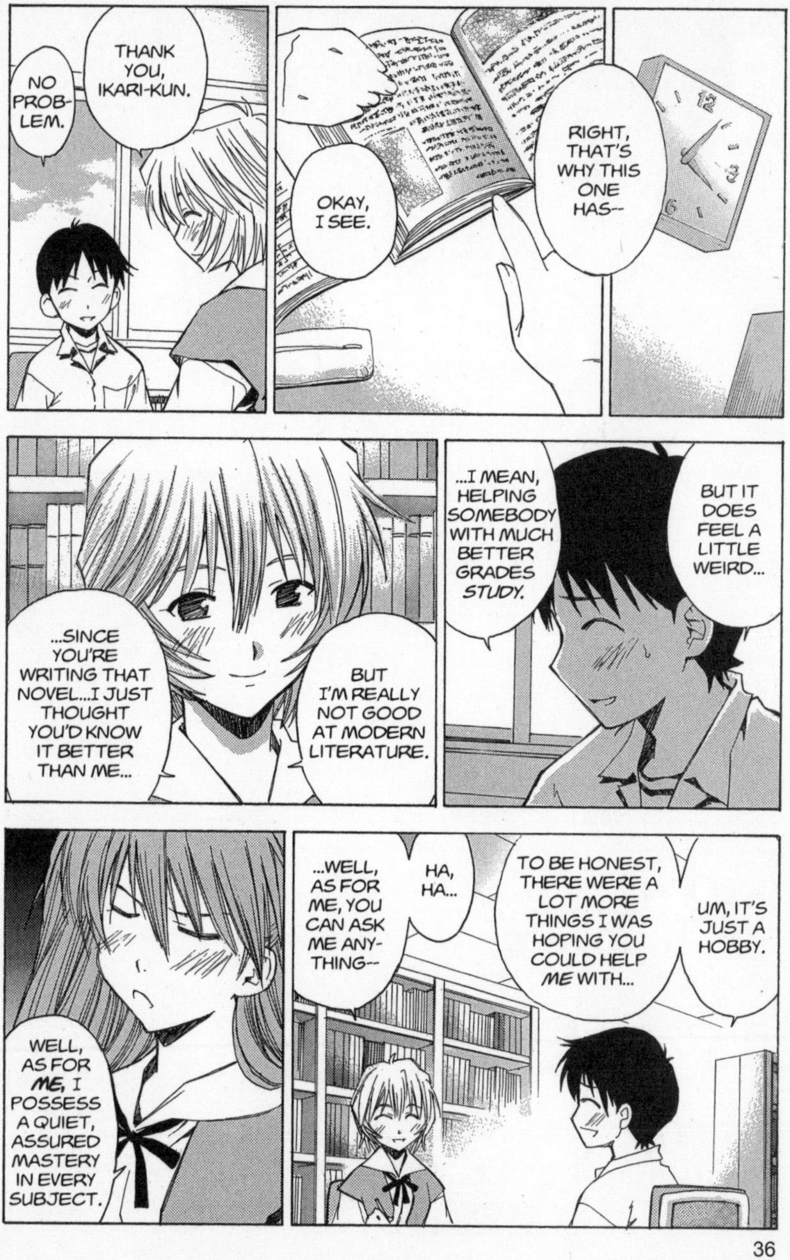
RIGHT, THAT'S WHY THIS ONE HAS--
OKAY, I SEE.
THANK YOU, IKARI-KUN.
NO PROBLEM.
BUT IT DOES FEEL A LITTLE WEIRD...
...I MEAN, HELPING SOMEBODY WITH MUCH BETTER GRADES *STUDY.*
BUT I'M REALLY NOT GOOD AT MODERN LITERATURE.
...SINCE YOU'RE WRITING THAT NOVEL...I JUST THOUGHT YOU'D KNOW IT BETTER THAN ME...
UM, IT'S JUST A HOBBY.
TO BE HONEST, THERE WERE A LOT MORE THINGS I WAS HOPING YOU COULD HELP *ME* WITH...
HA, HA...
...WELL, AS FOR ME, YOU CAN ASK ME ANY-THING--
WELL, AS FOR ***ME,*** I POSSESS A QUIET, ASSURED MASTERY IN EVERY SUBJECT.

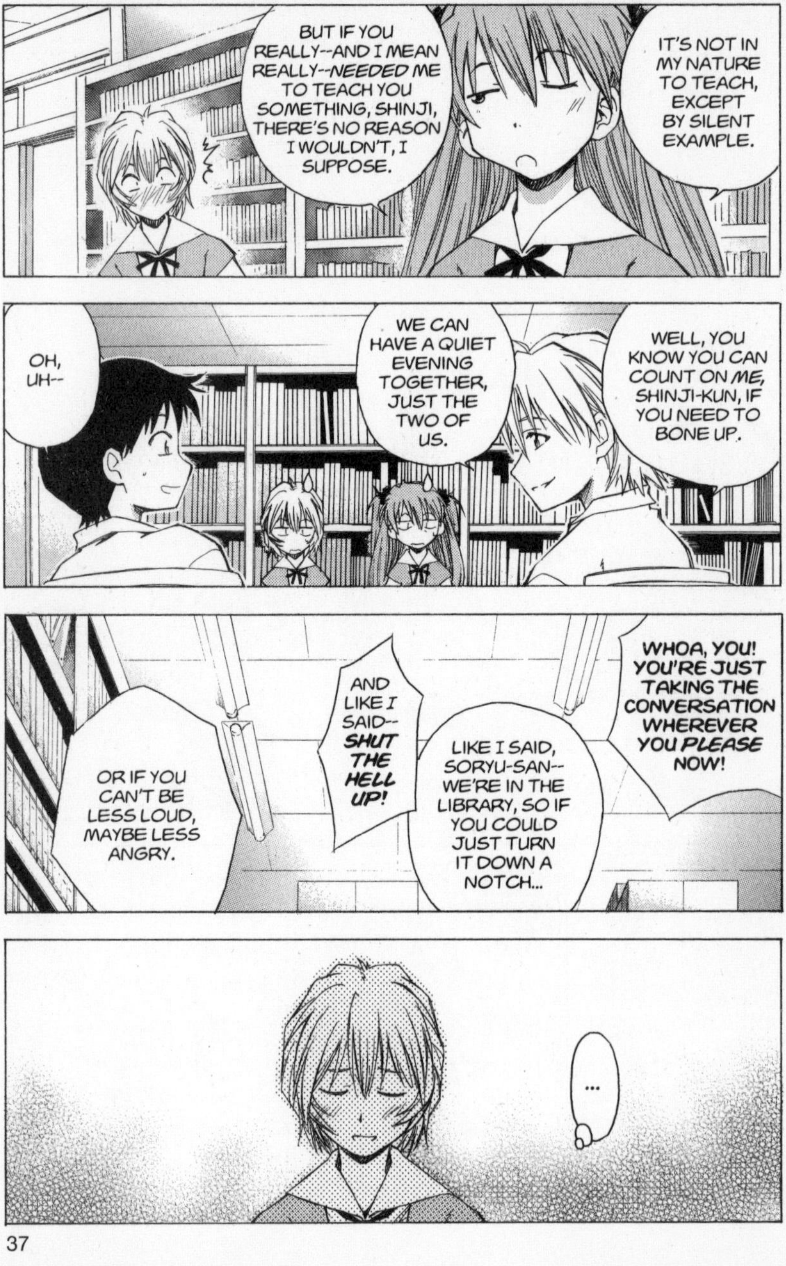
IT'S NOT IN MY NATURE TO TEACH, EXCEPT BY SILENT EXAMPLE.
BUT IF YOU REALLY--AND I MEAN REALLY--*NEEDED* ME TO TEACH YOU SOMETHING, SHINJI, THERE'S NO REASON I WOULDN'T, I SUPPOSE.
WELL, YOU KNOW YOU CAN COUNT ON *ME*, SHINJI-KUN, IF YOU NEED TO BONE UP.
WE CAN HAVE A QUIET EVENING TOGETHER, JUST THE TWO OF US.
OH, UH--
WHOA, YOU! YOU'RE JUST TAKING THE CONVERSATION WHEREVER YOU *PLEASE* NOW!
LIKE I SAID, SORYU-SAN--WE'RE IN THE LIBRARY, SO IF YOU COULD JUST TURN IT DOWN A NOTCH...
AND LIKE I SAID--***SHUT THE HELL UP!***
OR IF YOU CAN'T BE LESS LOUD, MAYBE LESS ANGRY.
...

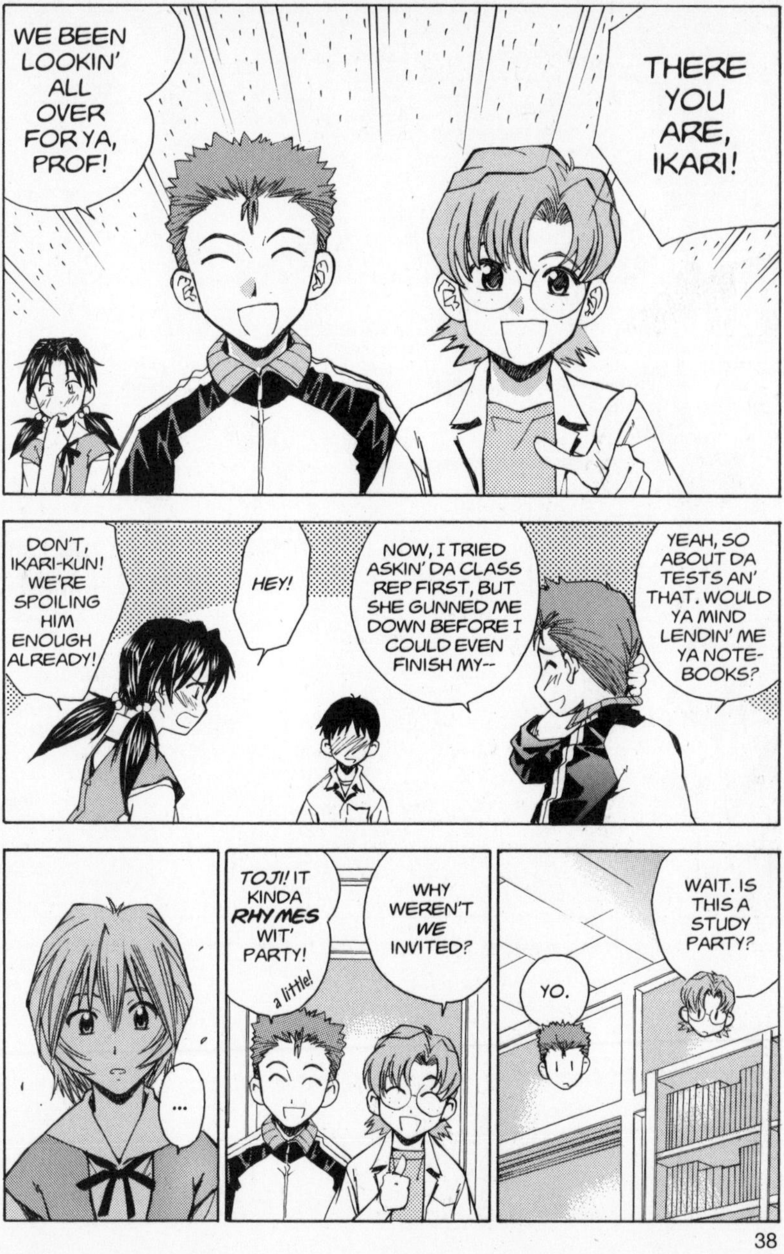
THERE YOU ARE, IKARI!
WE BEEN LOOKIN' ALL OVER FOR YA, PROF!
YEAH, SO ABOUT DA TESTS AN' THAT. WOULD YA MIND LENDIN' ME YA NOTE-BOOKS?
NOW, I TRIED ASKIN' DA CLASS REP FIRST, BUT SHE GUNNED ME DOWN BEFORE I COULD EVEN FINISH MY--
HEY!
DON'T, IKARI-KUN! WE'RE SPOILING HIM ENOUGH ALREADY!
WAIT. IS THIS A STUDY PARTY?
YO.
WHY WEREN'T WE INVITED?
TOJI! IT KINDA RHYMES WIT' PARTY!
a little!
...

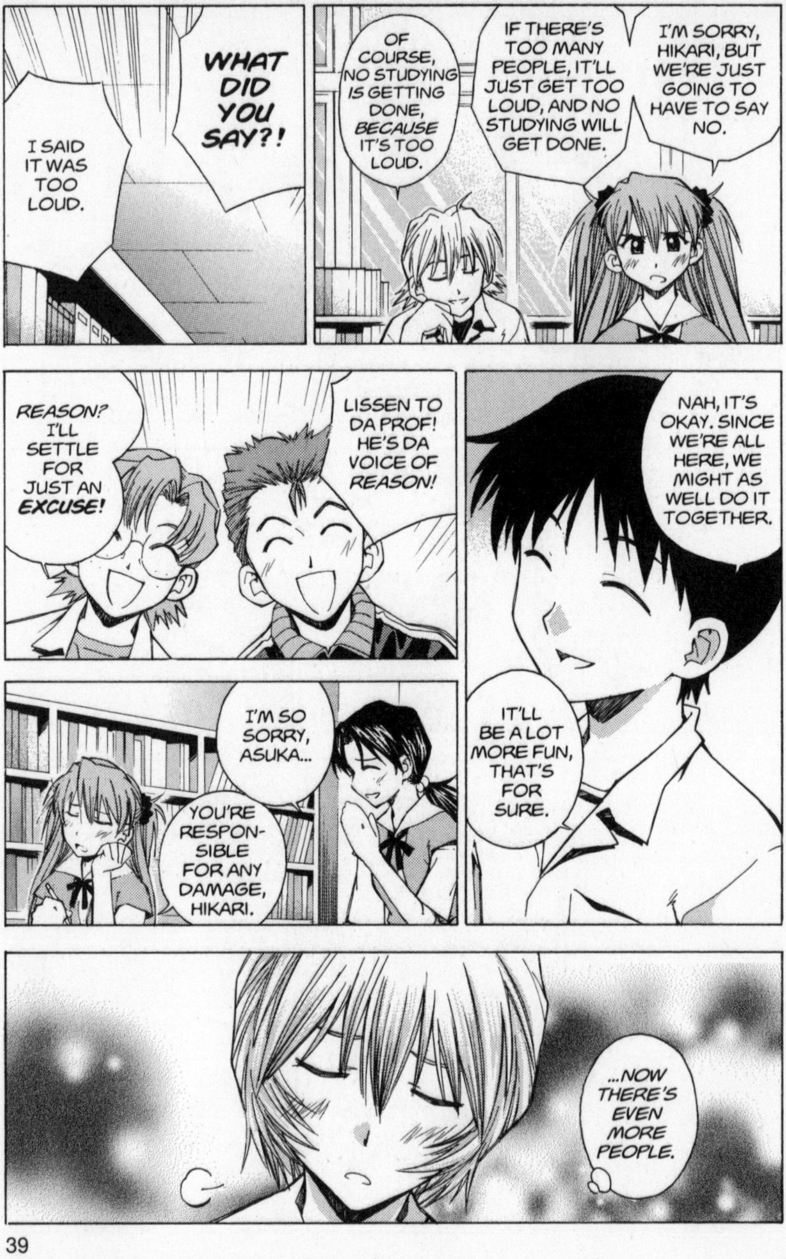
I'M SORRY, HIKARI, BUT WE'RE JUST GOING TO HAVE TO SAY NO.
IF THERE'S TOO MANY PEOPLE, IT'LL JUST GET TOO LOUD, AND NO STUDYING WILL GET DONE.
OF COURSE, NO STUDYING IS GETTING DONE, *BECAUSE* IT'S TOO LOUD.
WHAT DID YOU SAY?!
I SAID IT WAS TOO LOUD.
NAH, IT'S OKAY. SINCE WE'RE ALL HERE, WE MIGHT AS WELL DO IT TOGETHER.
IT'LL BE A LOT MORE FUN, THAT'S FOR SURE.
LISSEN TO DA PROF! HE'S DA VOICE OF *REASON!*
REASON? I'LL SETTLE FOR JUST AN ***EXCUSE!***
I'M SO SORRY, ASUKA...
YOU'RE RESPON-SIBLE FOR ANY DAMAGE, HIKARI.
...NOW THERE'S EVEN MORE PEOPLE.

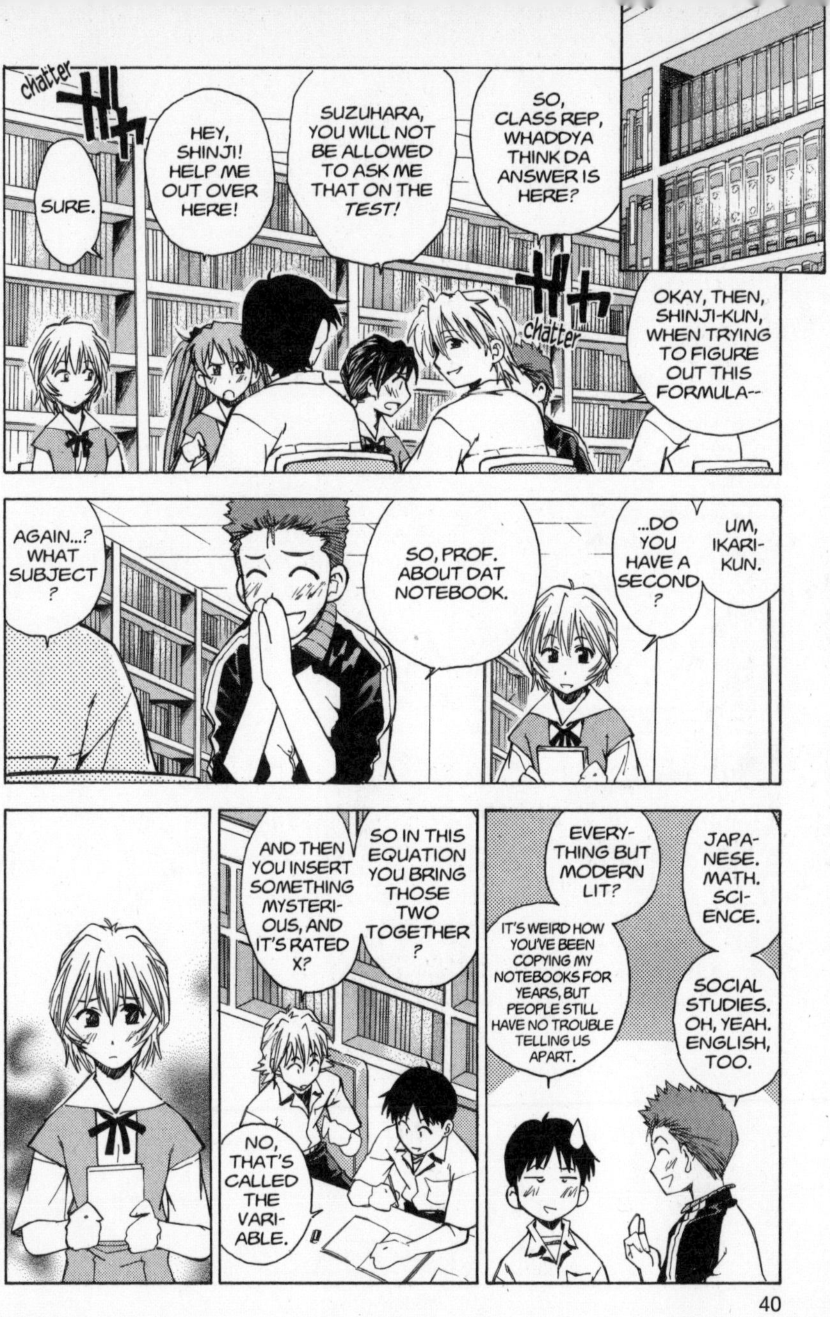
SO, CLASS REP, WHADDYA THINK DA ANSWER IS HERE?
SUZUHARA, YOU WILL NOT BE ALLOWED TO ASK ME THAT ON THE *TEST!*
chatter
OKAY, THEN, SHINJI-KUN, WHEN TRYING TO FIGURE OUT THIS FORMULA--
chatter
HEY, SHINJI! HELP ME OUT OVER HERE!
SURE.
UM, IKARI-KUN.
...DO YOU HAVE A SECOND?
SO, PROF. ABOUT DAT NOTEBOOK.
AGAIN...? WHAT SUBJECT?
JAPANESE. MATH. SCIENCE.
EVERYTHING BUT MODERN LIT?
SOCIAL STUDIES. OH, YEAH. ENGLISH, TOO.
IT'S WEIRD HOW YOU'VE BEEN COPYING MY NOTEBOOKS FOR YEARS, BUT PEOPLE STILL HAVE NO TROUBLE TELLING US APART.
SO IN THIS EQUATION YOU BRING THOSE TWO TOGETHER?
AND THEN YOU INSERT SOMETHING MYSTERIOUS, AND IT'S RATED X?
NO, THAT'S CALLED THE VARIABLE.

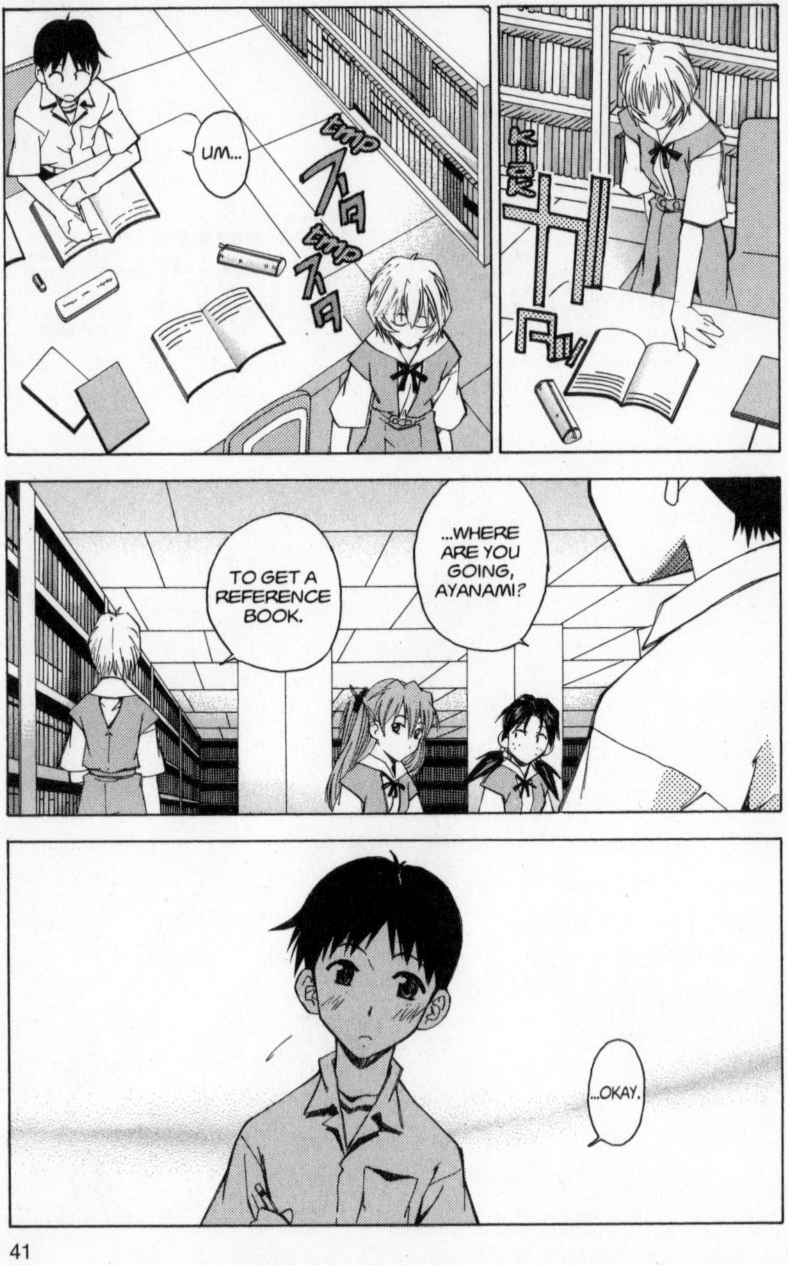
kree
UM...
tmp
tmp
...WHERE ARE YOU GOING, AYANAMI?
TO GET A REFERENCE BOOK.
...OKAY.

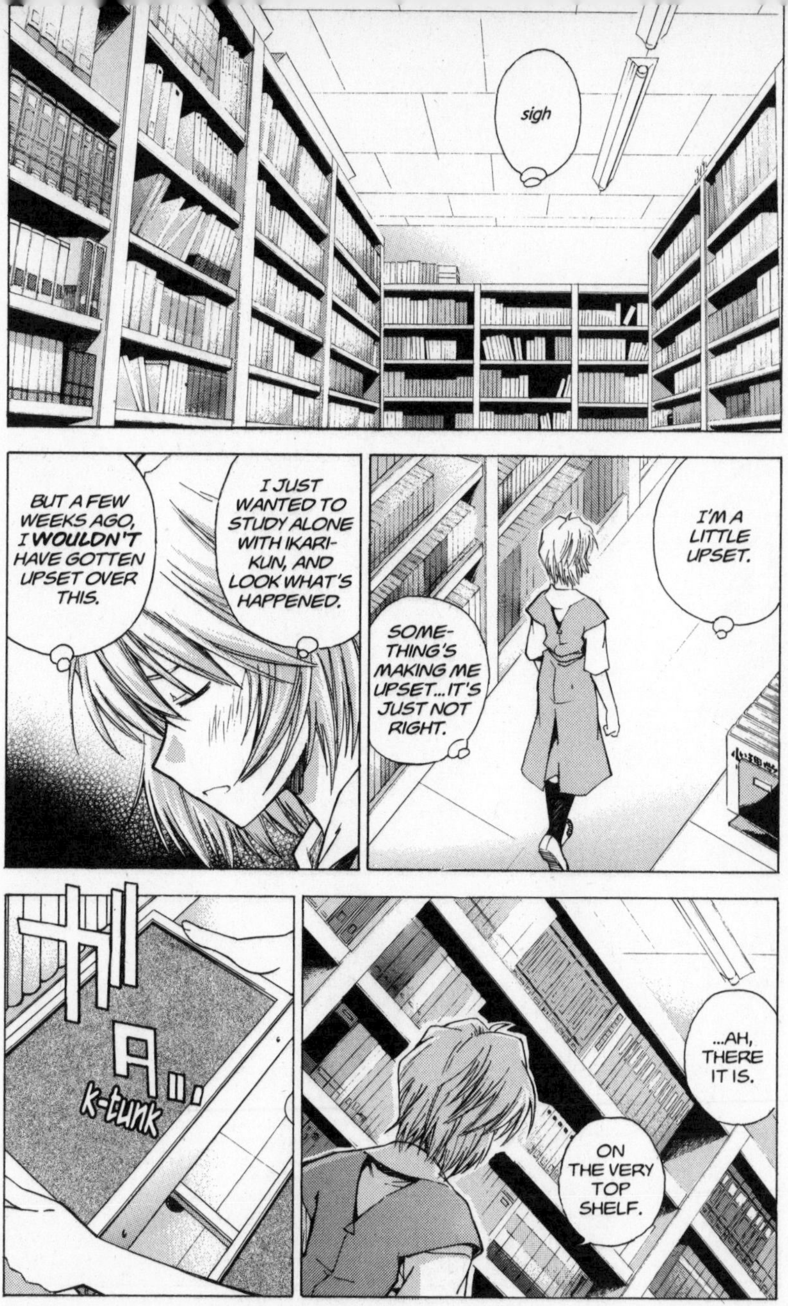
sigh
I'M A LITTLE UPSET.
SOMETHING'S MAKING ME UPSET...IT'S JUST NOT RIGHT.
I JUST WANTED TO STUDY ALONE WITH IKARI-KUN, AND LOOK WHAT'S HAPPENED.
BUT A FEW WEEKS AGO, I **WOULDN'T** HAVE GOTTEN UPSET OVER THIS.
...AH, THERE IT IS.
ON THE VERY TOP SHELF.
k-tunk

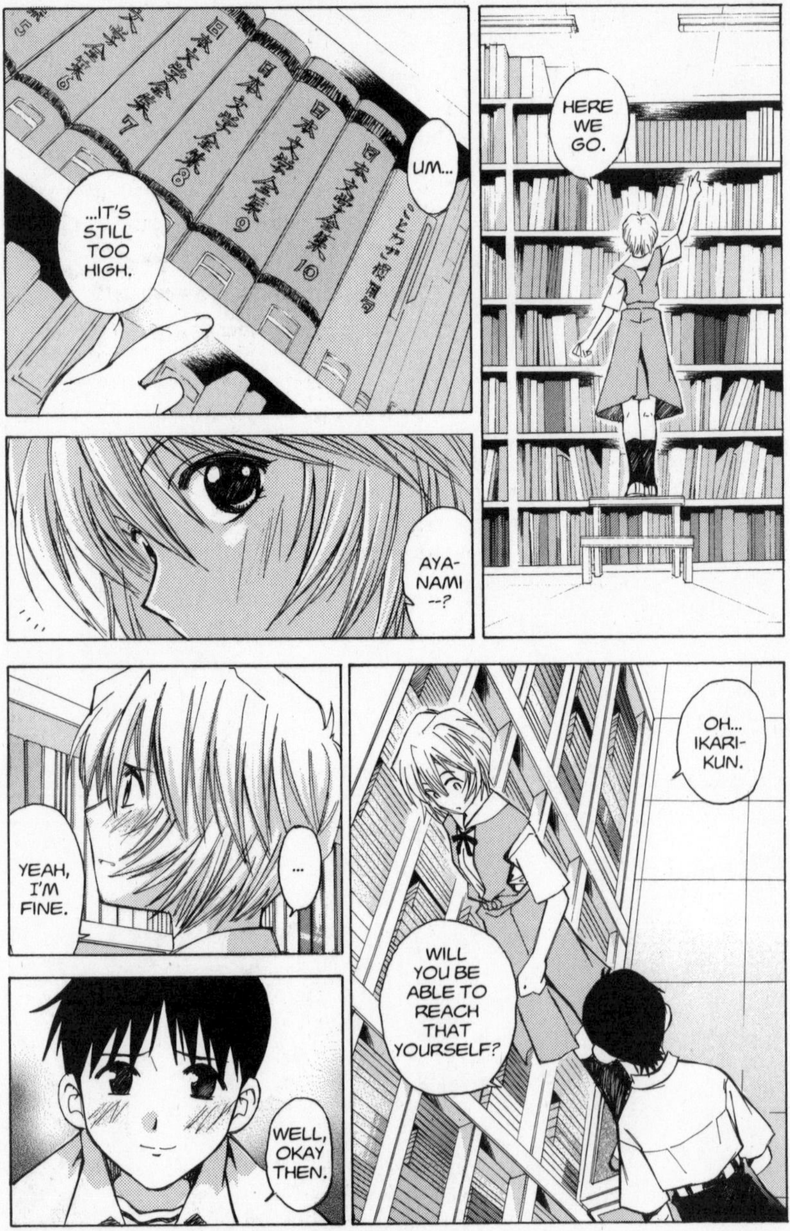
HERE WE GO.
UM...
...IT'S STILL TOO HIGH.
AYA-NAMI --?
OH... IKARI-KUN.
WILL YOU BE ABLE TO REACH THAT YOURSELF?
...
YEAH, I'M FINE.
WELL, OKAY THEN.

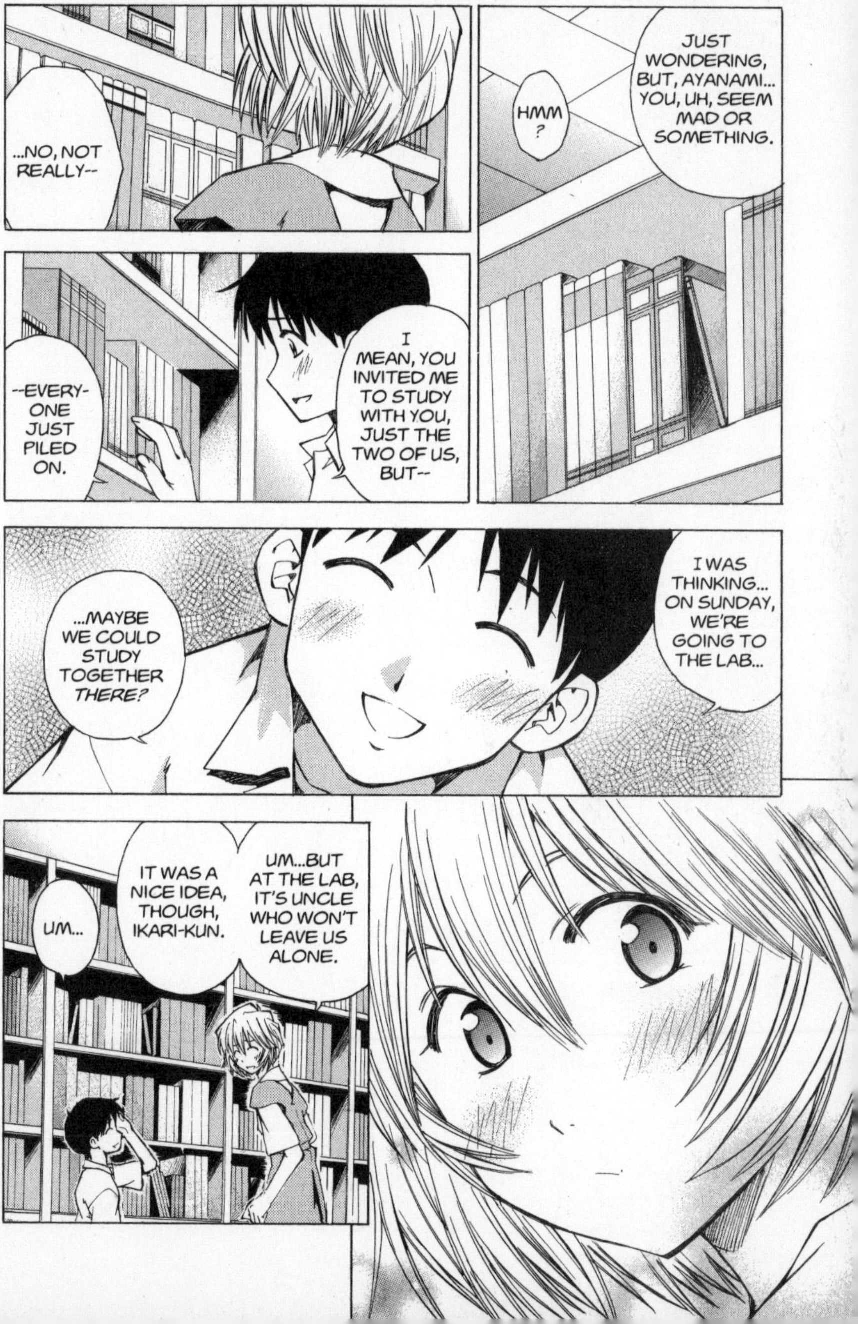
JUST WONDERING, BUT, AYANAMI... YOU, UH, SEEM MAD OR SOMETHING.
HMM?
...NO, NOT REALLY--
I MEAN, YOU INVITED ME TO STUDY WITH YOU, JUST THE TWO OF US, BUT--
--EVERY-ONE JUST PILED ON.
I WAS THINKING... ON SUNDAY, WE'RE GOING TO THE LAB...
...MAYBE WE COULD STUDY TOGETHER *THERE?*
UM...BUT AT THE LAB, IT'S UNCLE WHO WON'T LEAVE US ALONE.
IT WAS A NICE IDEA, THOUGH, IKARI-KUN.
UM...

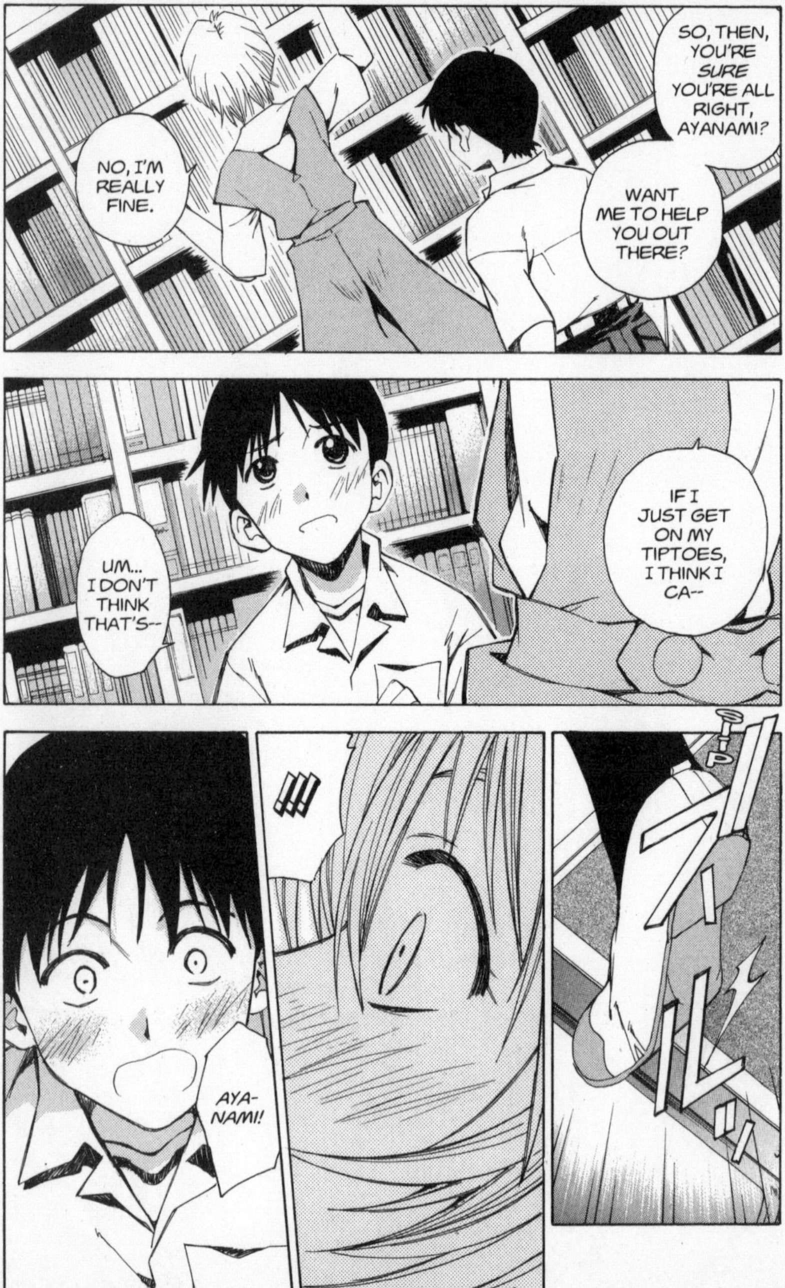

SO, THEN, YOU'RE *SURE* YOU'RE ALL RIGHT, AYANAMI?
WANT ME TO HELP YOU OUT THERE?
NO, I'M REALLY FINE.
IF I JUST GET ON MY TIPTOES, I THINK I CA--
UM... I DON'T THINK THAT'S--
SLIP
!!!
AYA-NAMI!

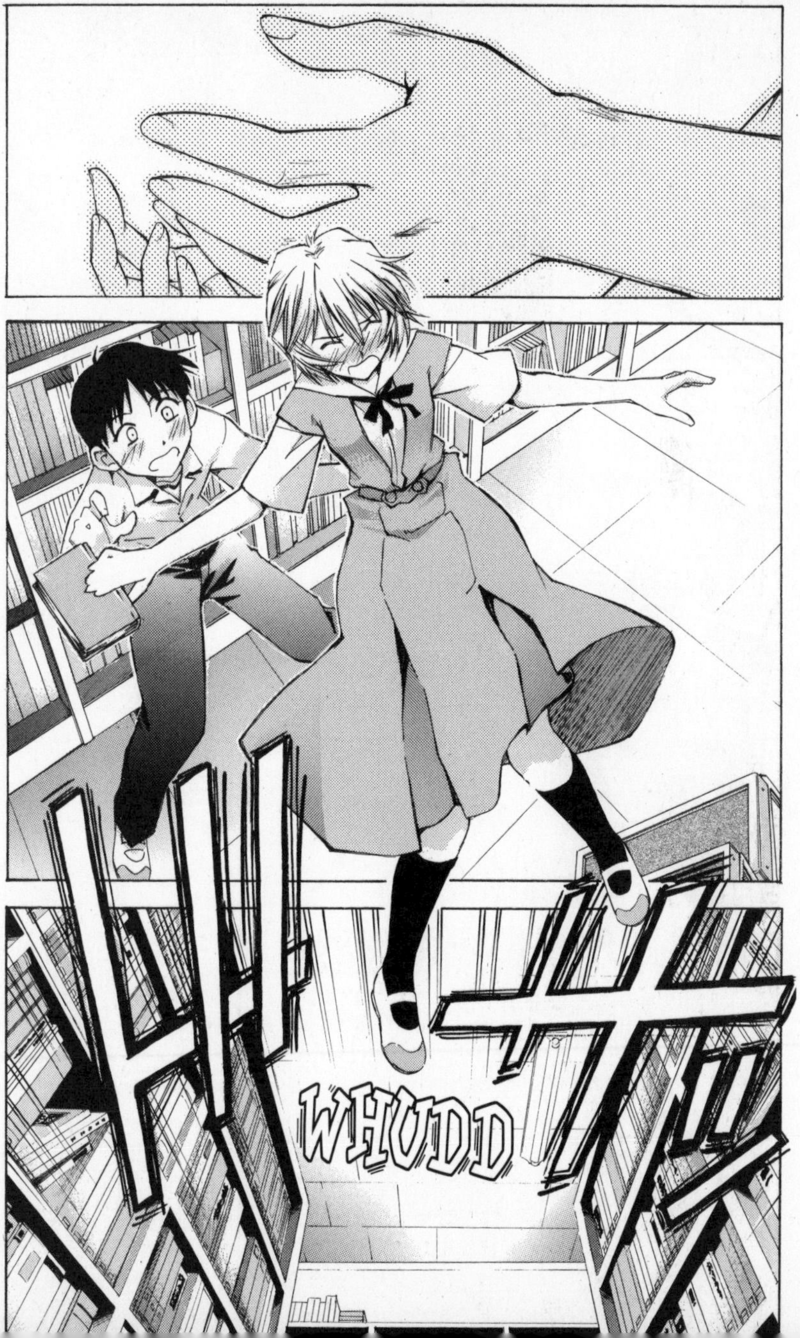
WHUDD

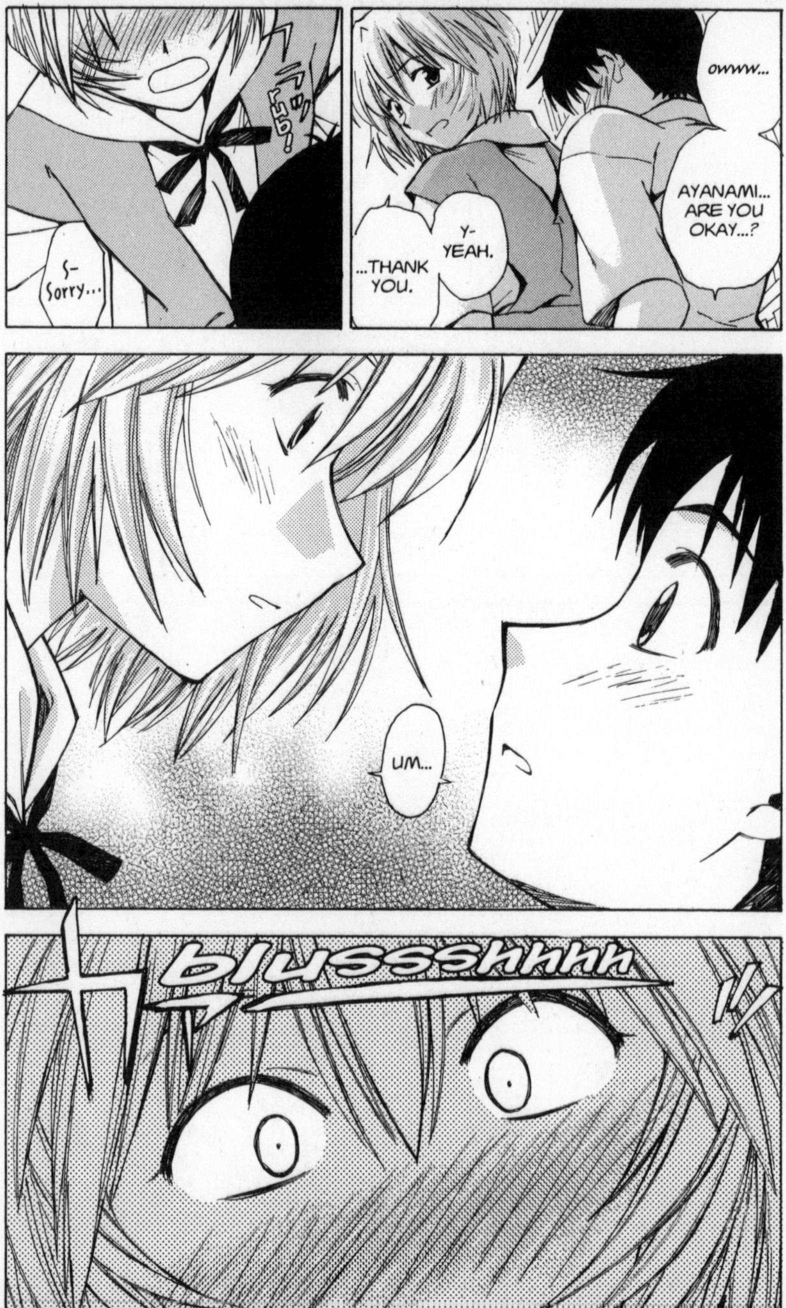
owww...
AYANAMI... ARE YOU OKAY...?
Y- YEAH.
...THANK YOU.
S- Sorry...
UM...
blussshhhh

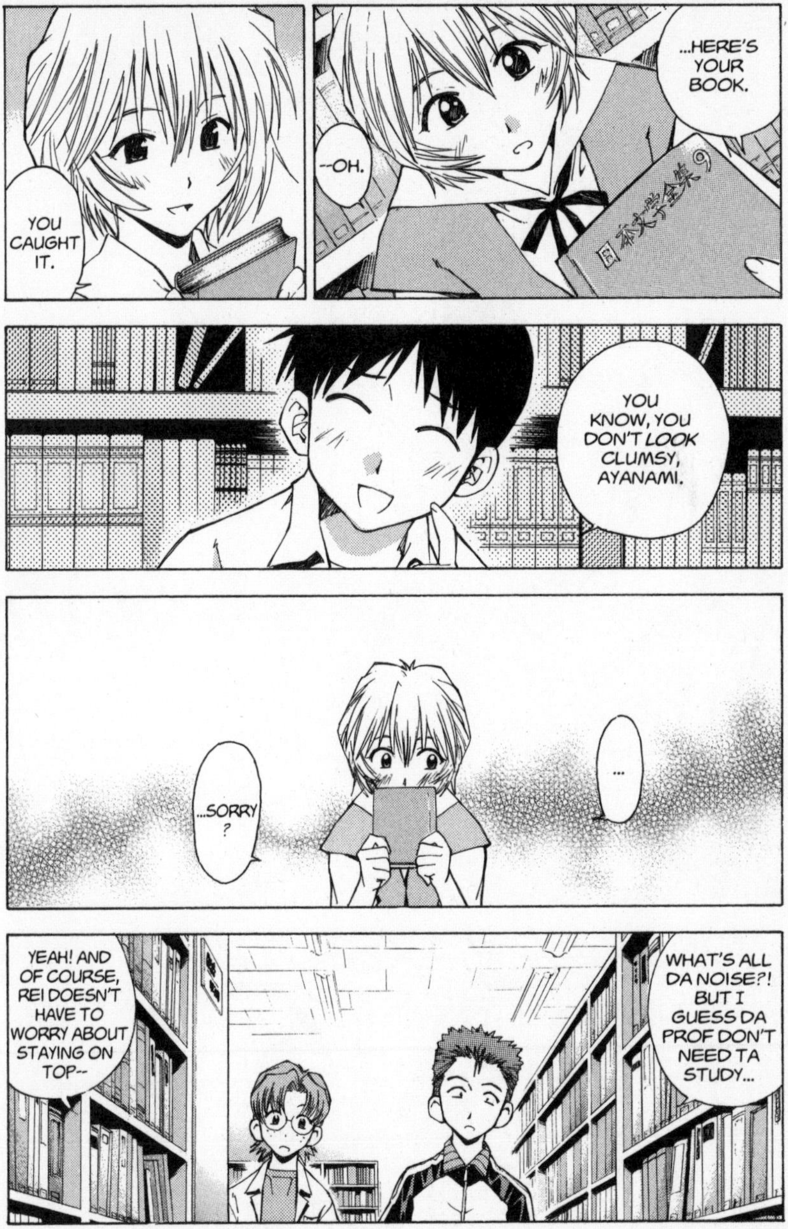
...HERE'S YOUR BOOK.
--OH.
YOU CAUGHT IT.
YOU KNOW, YOU DON'T LOOK CLUMSY, AYANAMI.
...
...SORRY?
WHAT'S ALL DA NOISE?! BUT I GUESS DA PROF DON'T NEED TA STUDY...
YEAH! AND OF COURSE, REI DOESN'T HAVE TO WORRY ABOUT STAYING ON TOP--

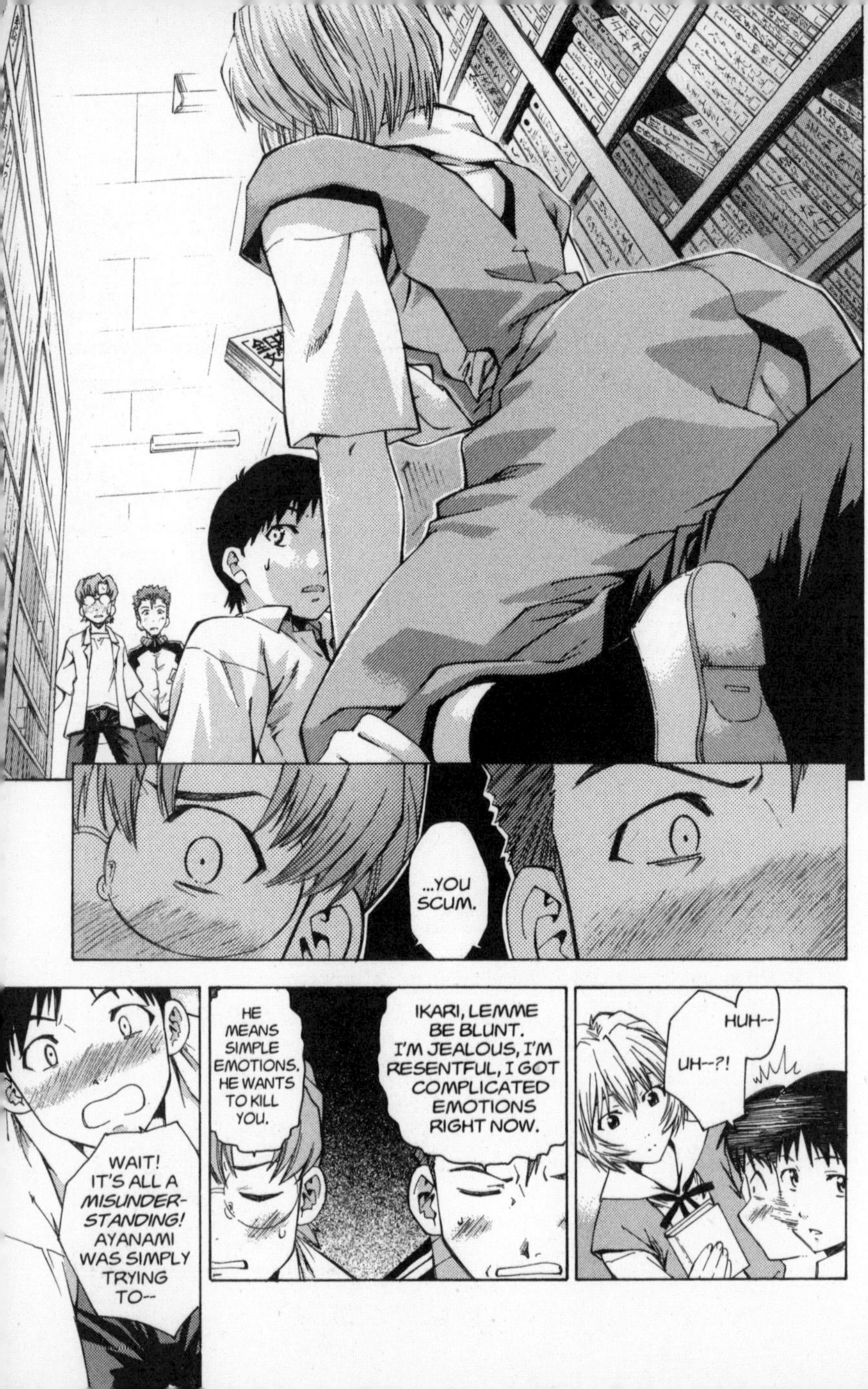
...YOU SCUM.
HUH--
UH--?!
IKARI, LEMME BE BLUNT. I'M JEALOUS, I'M RESENTFUL, I GOT COMPLICATED EMOTIONS RIGHT NOW.
HE MEANS SIMPLE EMOTIONS. HE WANTS TO KILL YOU.
WAIT! IT'S ALL A MISUNDER-STANDING! AYANAMI WAS SIMPLY TRYING TO--

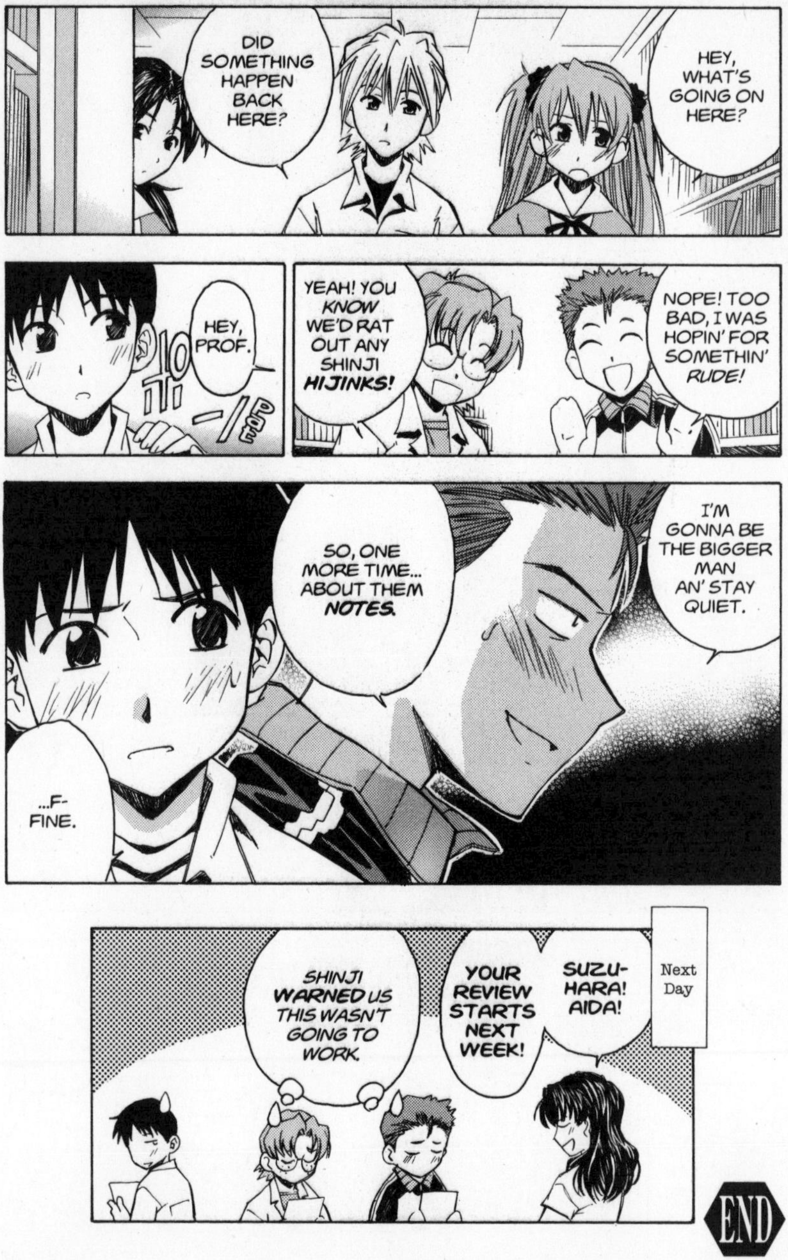
HEY, WHAT'S GOING ON HERE?
DID SOMETHING HAPPEN BACK HERE?
NOPE! TOO BAD, I WAS HOPIN' FOR SOMETHIN' *RUDE!*
YEAH! YOU *KNOW* WE'D RAT OUT ANY SHINJI **HIJINKS!**
HEY, PROF.
I'M GONNA BE THE BIGGER MAN AN' STAY QUIET.
SO, ONE MORE TIME... ABOUT THEM **NOTES.**
...F- FINE.
Next Day
SUZU-HARA! AIDA!
YOUR REVIEW STARTS NEXT WEEK!
SHINJI WARNED US THIS WASN'T GOING TO WORK.
END

STAGE 17

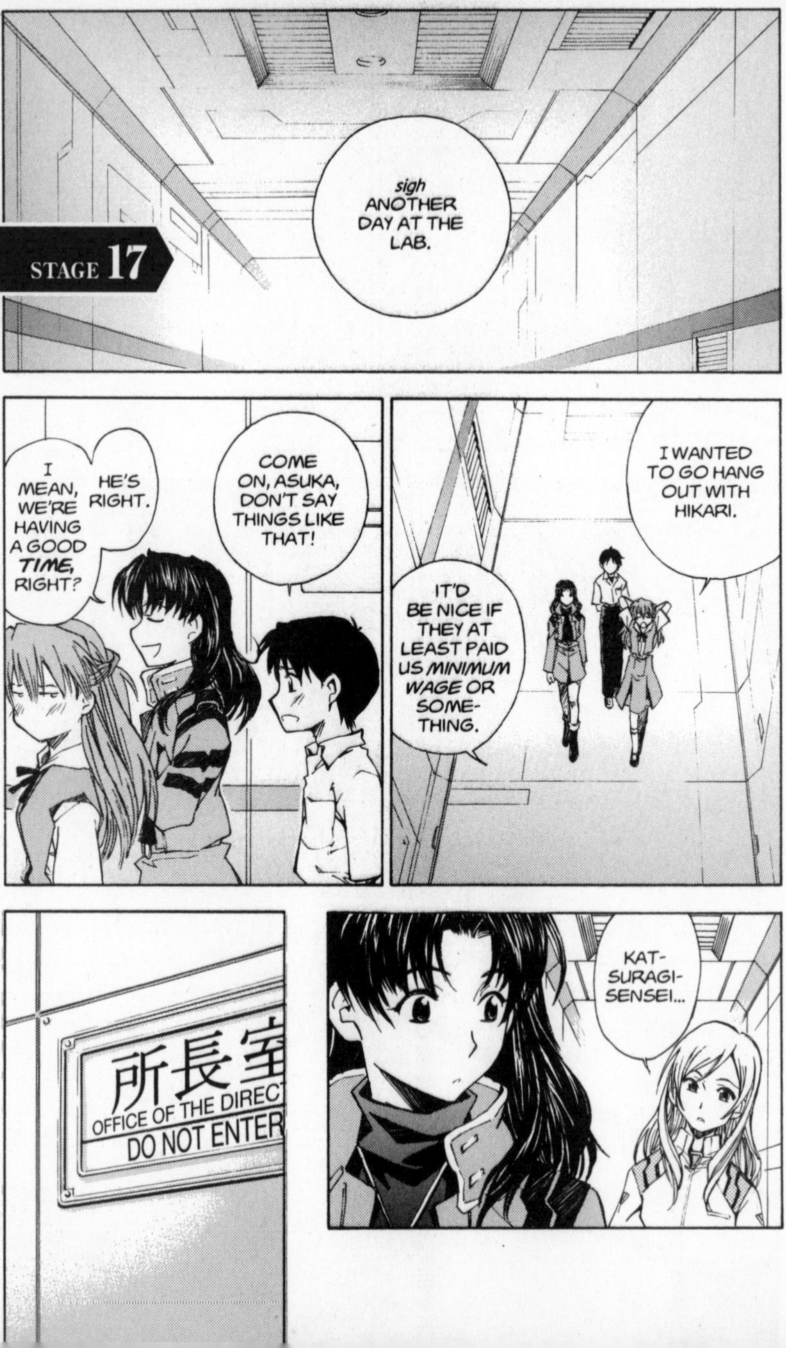
sigh ANOTHER DAY AT THE LAB.
I WANTED TO GO HANG OUT WITH HIKARI.
IT'D BE NICE IF THEY AT LEAST PAID US *MINIMUM WAGE* OR SOME-THING.
COME ON, ASUKA, DON'T SAY THINGS LIKE THAT!
HE'S RIGHT.
I MEAN, WE'RE HAVING A GOOD ***TIME,*** RIGHT?
KAT-SURAGI-SENSEI...
所長室
OFFICE OF THE DIRECT
DO NOT ENTER

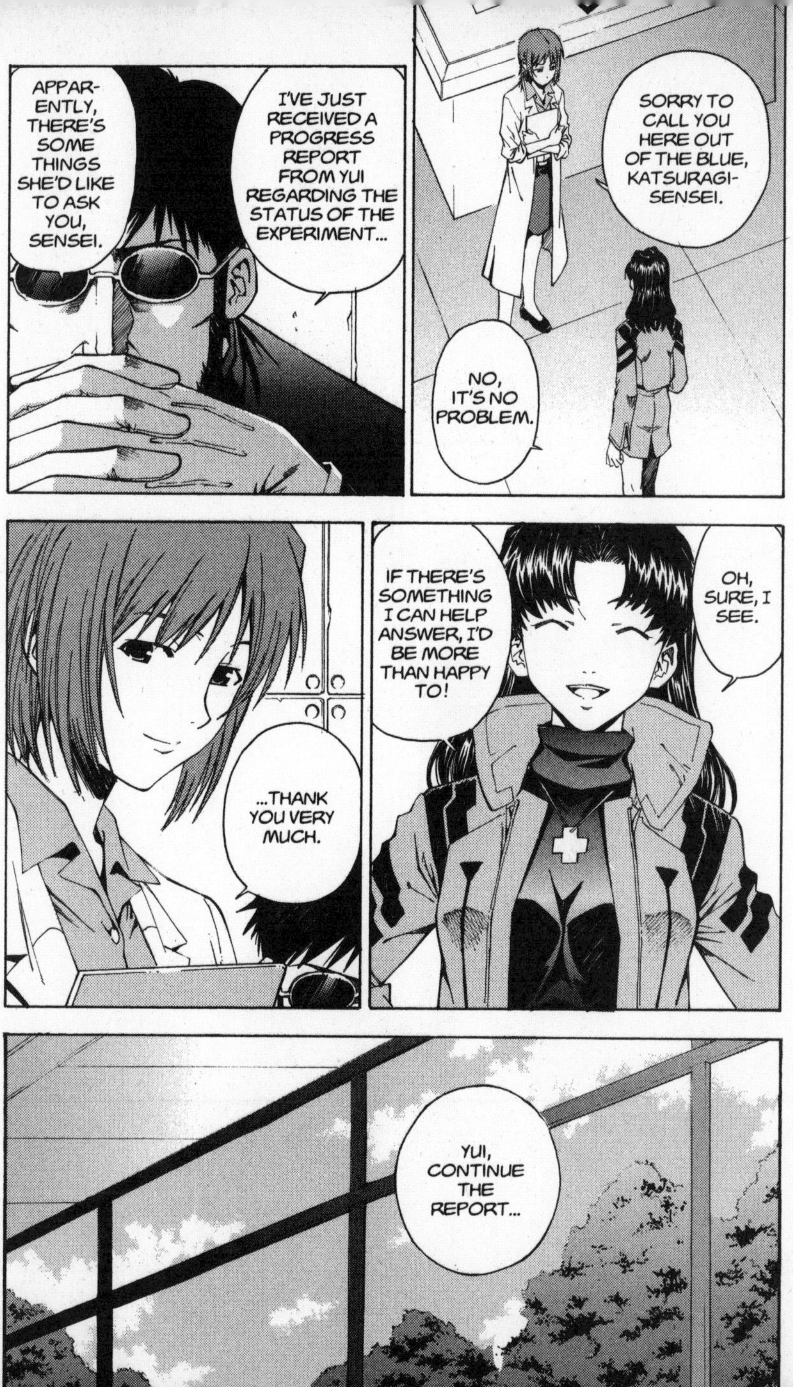
SORRY TO CALL YOU HERE OUT OF THE BLUE, KATSURAGI-SENSEI.
NO, IT'S NO PROBLEM.
I'VE JUST RECEIVED A PROGRESS REPORT FROM YUI REGARDING THE STATUS OF THE EXPERIMENT...
APPAR-ENTLY, THERE'S SOME THINGS SHE'D LIKE TO ASK YOU, SENSEI.
OH, SURE, I SEE.
IF THERE'S SOMETHING I CAN HELP ANSWER, I'D BE MORE THAN HAPPY TO!
...THANK YOU VERY MUCH.
YUI, CONTINUE THE REPORT...

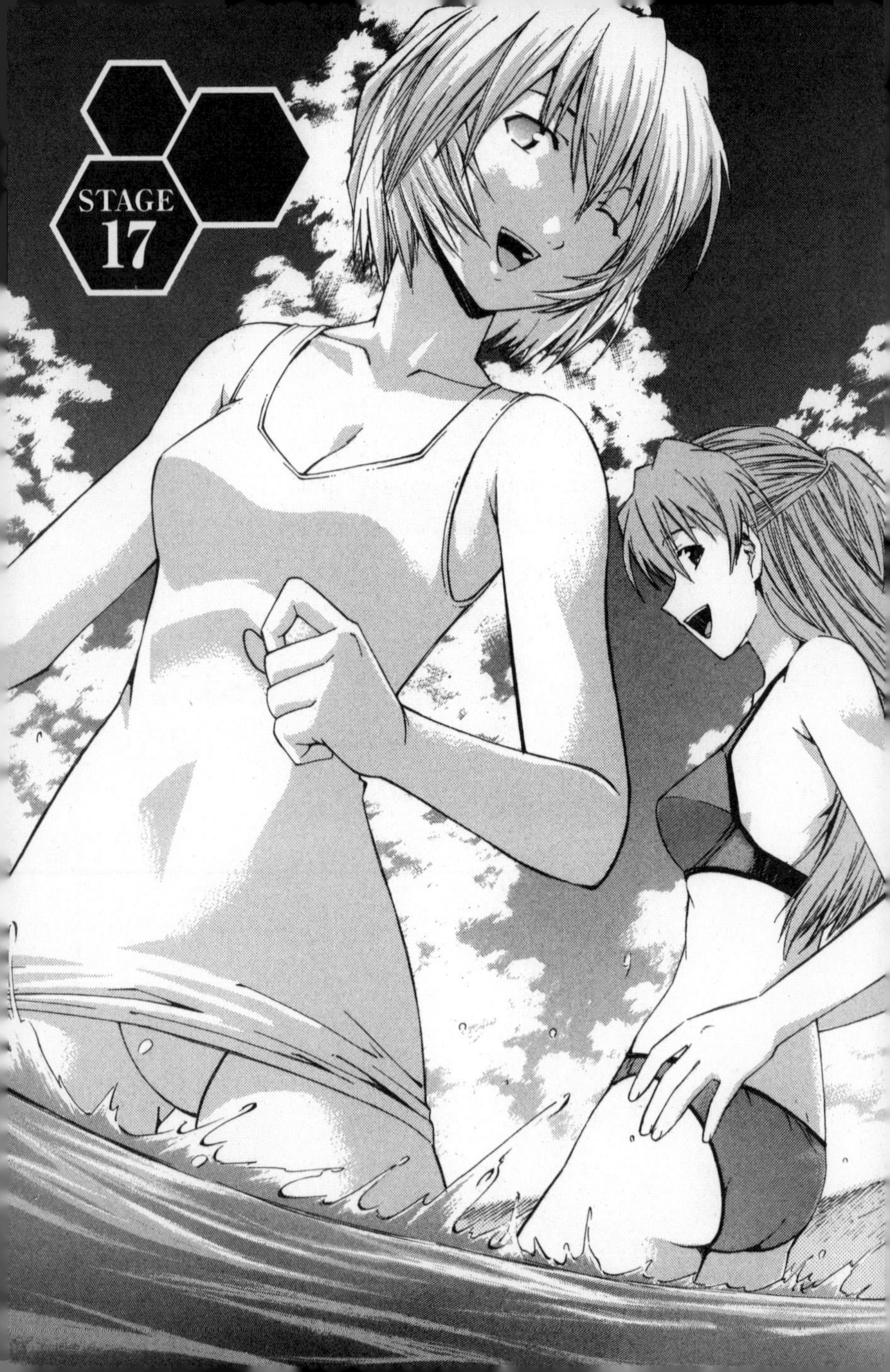
STAGE
17

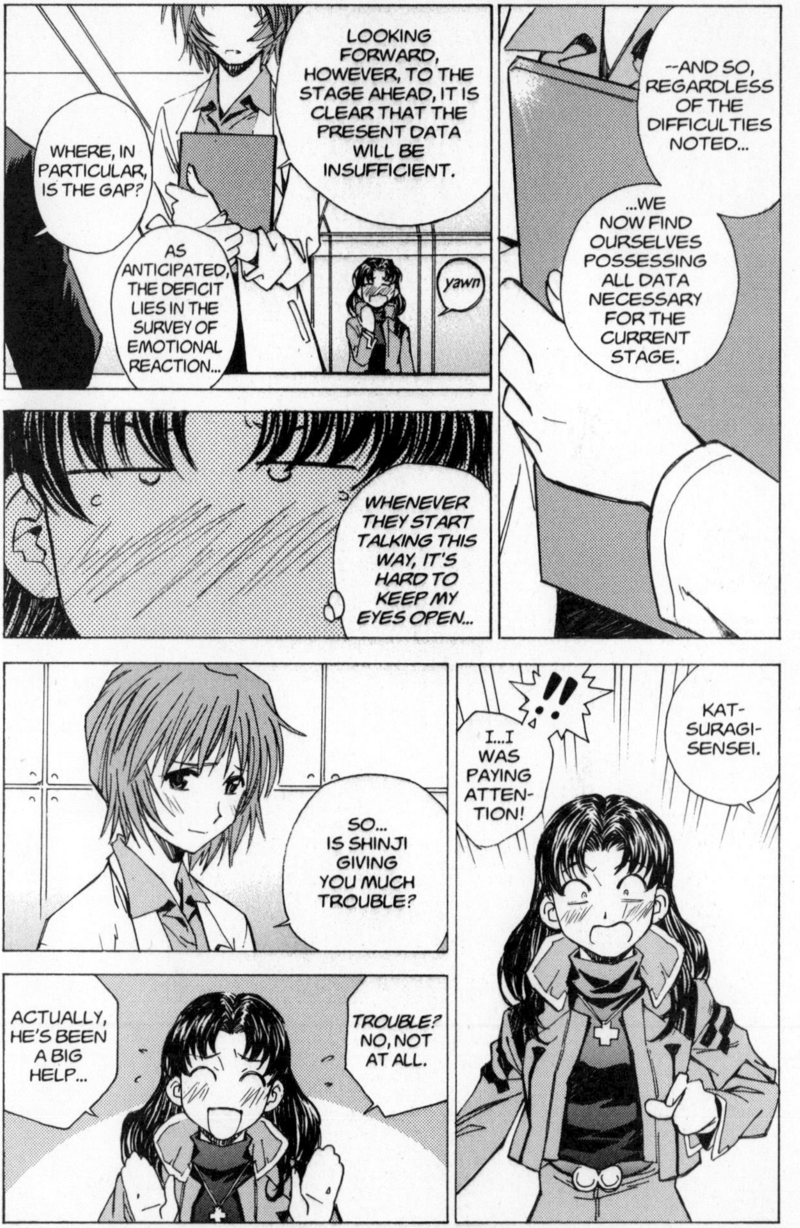
--AND SO, REGARDLESS OF THE DIFFICULTIES NOTED...
...WE NOW FIND OURSELVES POSSESSING ALL DATA NECESSARY FOR THE CURRENT STAGE.
LOOKING FORWARD, HOWEVER, TO THE STAGE AHEAD, IT IS CLEAR THAT THE PRESENT DATA WILL BE INSUFFICIENT.
WHERE, IN PARTICULAR, IS THE GAP?
AS ANTICIPATED, THE DEFICIT LIES IN THE SURVEY OF EMOTIONAL REACTION...
yawn
WHENEVER THEY START TALKING THIS WAY, IT'S HARD TO KEEP MY EYES OPEN...
KAT-SURAGI-SENSEI.
!!
I...I WAS PAYING ATTEN-TION!
SO... IS SHINJI GIVING YOU MUCH TROUBLE?
TROUBLE? NO, NOT AT ALL.
ACTUALLY, HE'S BEEN A BIG HELP...

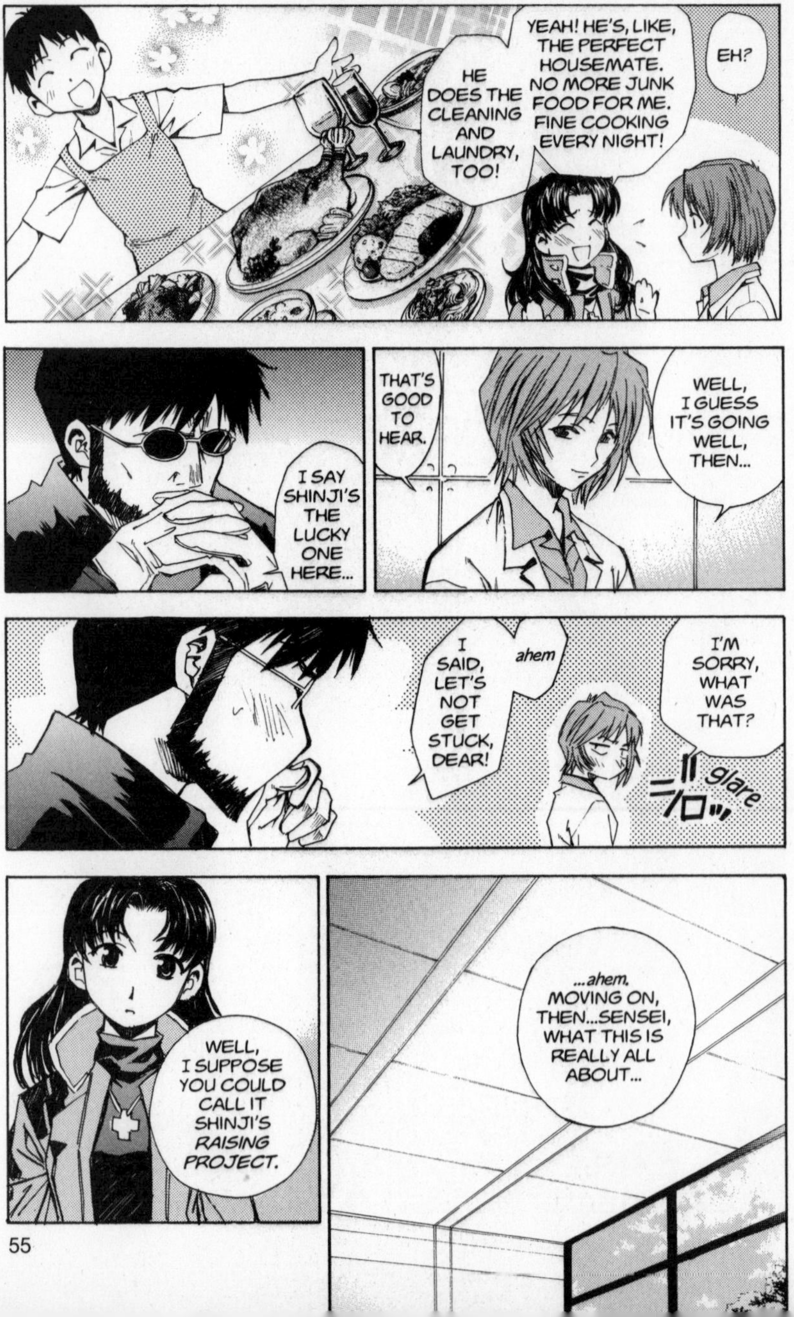
EH?
YEAH! HE'S, LIKE, THE PERFECT HOUSEMATE. NO MORE JUNK FOOD FOR ME. FINE COOKING EVERY NIGHT!
HE DOES THE CLEANING AND LAUNDRY, TOO!
WELL, I GUESS IT'S GOING WELL, THEN...
THAT'S GOOD TO HEAR.
I SAY SHINJI'S THE LUCKY ONE HERE...
I'M SORRY, WHAT WAS THAT?
glare
ahem
I SAID, LET'S NOT GET STUCK, DEAR!
...ahem. MOVING ON, THEN...SENSEI, WHAT THIS IS REALLY ALL ABOUT...
WELL, I SUPPOSE YOU COULD CALL IT SHINJI'S RAISING PROJECT.

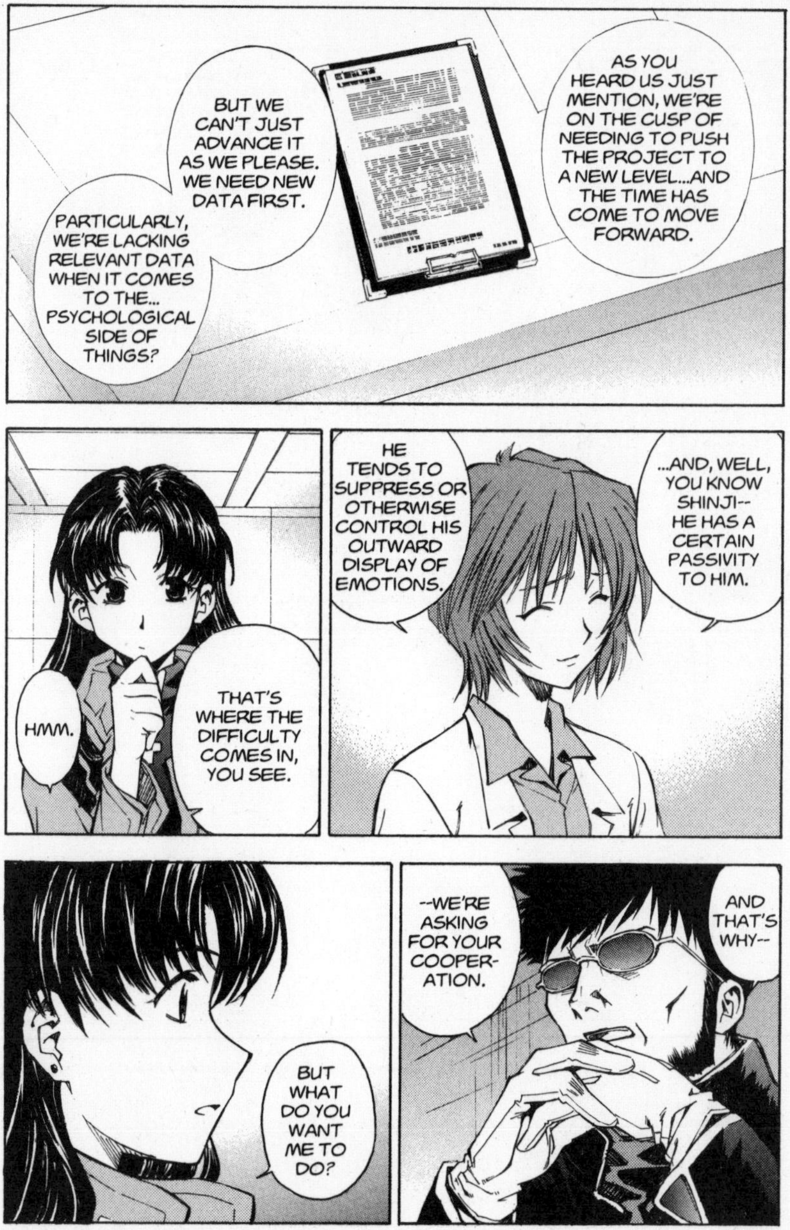
AS YOU HEARD US JUST MENTION, WE'RE ON THE CUSP OF NEEDING TO PUSH THE PROJECT TO A NEW LEVEL...AND THE TIME HAS COME TO MOVE FORWARD.
BUT WE CAN'T JUST ADVANCE IT AS WE PLEASE. WE NEED NEW DATA FIRST.
PARTICULARLY, WE'RE LACKING RELEVANT DATA WHEN IT COMES TO THE... PSYCHOLOGICAL SIDE OF THINGS?
...AND, WELL, YOU KNOW SHINJI-- HE HAS A CERTAIN PASSIVITY TO HIM.
HE TENDS TO SUPPRESS OR OTHERWISE CONTROL HIS OUTWARD DISPLAY OF EMOTIONS.
THAT'S WHERE THE DIFFICULTY COMES IN, YOU SEE.
HMM.
AND THAT'S WHY--
--WE'RE ASKING FOR YOUR COOPER-ATION.
BUT WHAT DO YOU WANT ME TO DO?

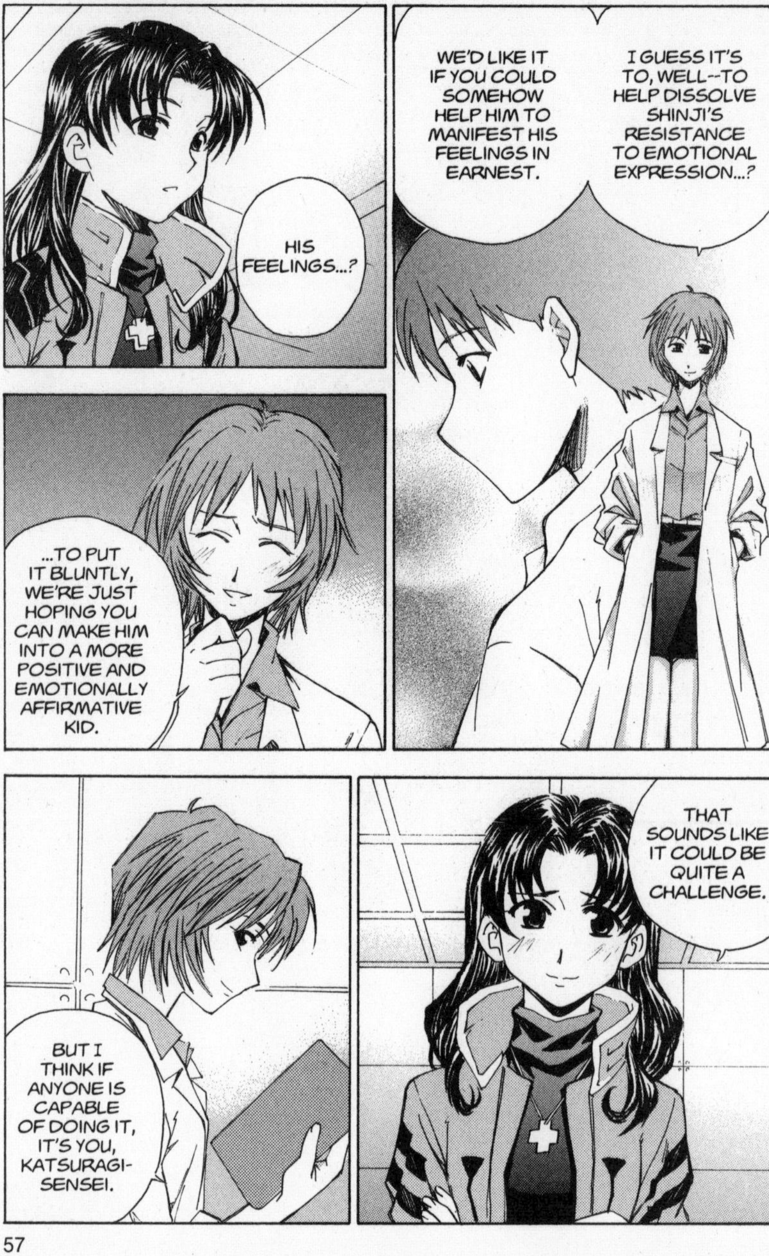
I GUESS IT'S TO, WELL--TO HELP DISSOLVE SHINJI'S RESISTANCE TO EMOTIONAL EXPRESSION...?
WE'D LIKE IT IF YOU COULD SOMEHOW HELP HIM TO MANIFEST HIS FEELINGS IN EARNEST.
HIS FEELINGS...?
...TO PUT IT BLUNTLY, WE'RE JUST HOPING YOU CAN MAKE HIM INTO A MORE POSITIVE AND EMOTIONALLY AFFIRMATIVE KID.
THAT SOUNDS LIKE IT COULD BE QUITE A CHALLENGE.
BUT I THINK IF ANYONE IS CAPABLE OF DOING IT, IT'S YOU, KATSURAGI-SENSEI.

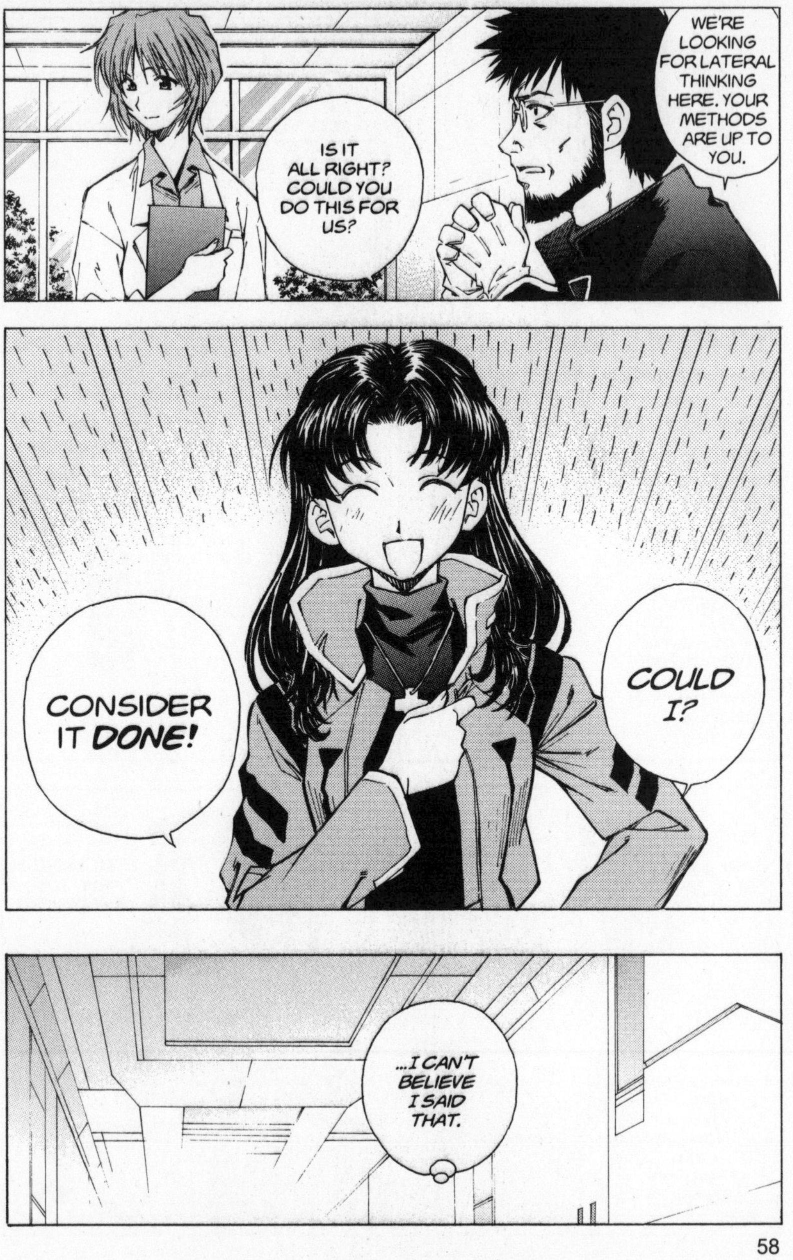
WE'RE LOOKING FOR LATERAL THINKING HERE. YOUR METHODS ARE UP TO YOU.
IS IT ALL RIGHT? COULD YOU DO THIS FOR US?
COULD I?
CONSIDER IT DONE!
...I CAN'T BELIEVE I SAID THAT.

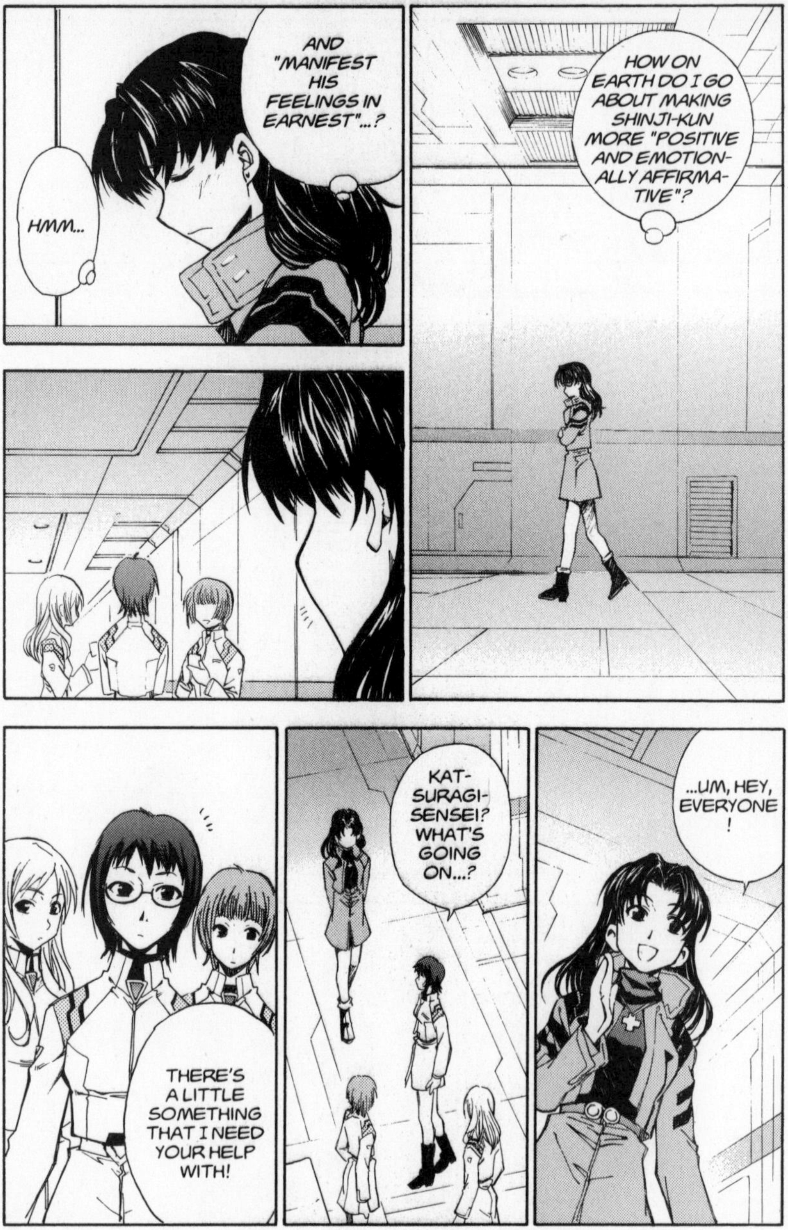
HOW ON EARTH DO I GO ABOUT MAKING SHINJI-KUN MORE "POSITIVE AND EMOTION-ALLY AFFIRMA-TIVE"?
AND "MANIFEST HIS FEELINGS IN EARNEST"...?
HMM...
...UM, HEY, EVERYONE!
KAT-SURAGI-SENSEI? WHAT'S GOING ON...?
THERE'S A LITTLE SOMETHING THAT I NEED YOUR HELP WITH!

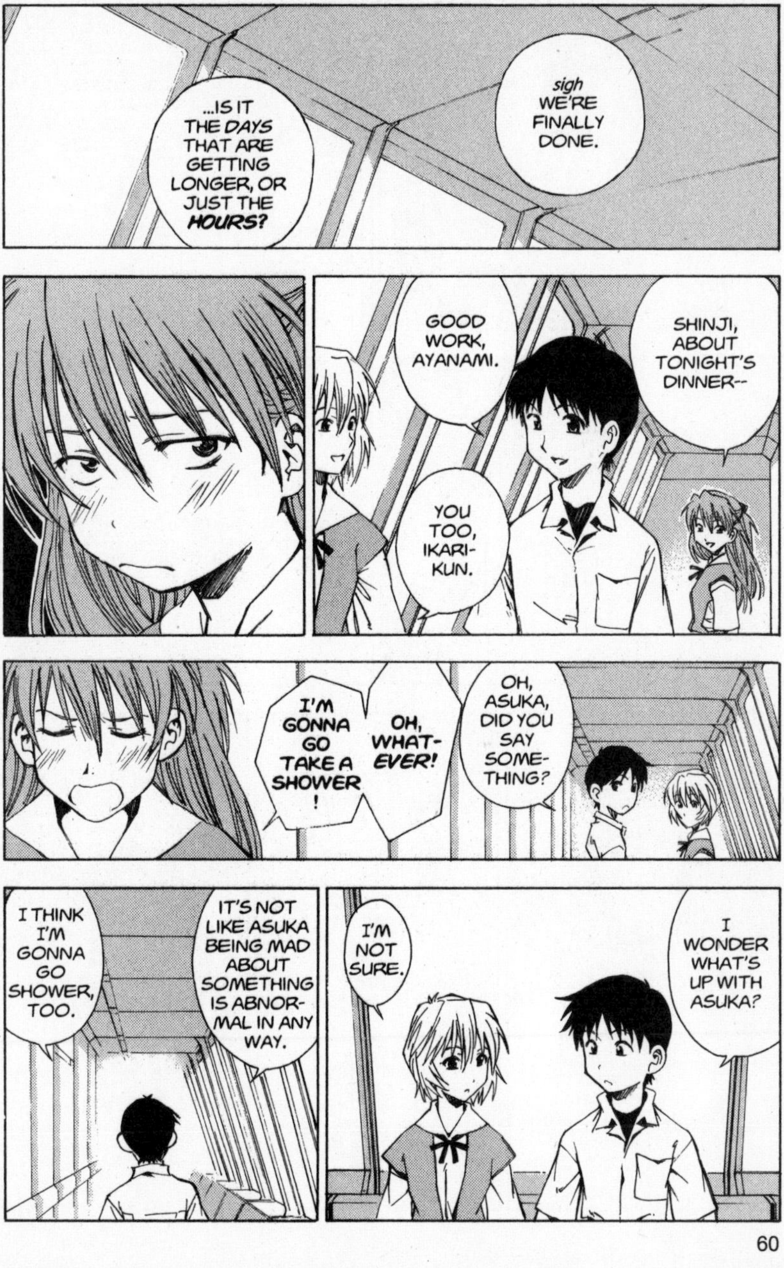
sigh WE'RE FINALLY DONE.
...IS IT THE DAYS THAT ARE GETTING LONGER, OR JUST THE HOURS?
SHINJI, ABOUT TONIGHT'S DINNER--
GOOD WORK, AYANAMI.
YOU TOO, IKARI-KUN.
OH, ASUKA, DID YOU SAY SOMETHING?
OH, WHATEVER!
I'M GONNA GO TAKE A SHOWER!
I WONDER WHAT'S UP WITH ASUKA?
I'M NOT SURE.
IT'S NOT LIKE ASUKA BEING MAD ABOUT SOMETHING IS ABNORMAL IN ANY WAY.
I THINK I'M GONNA GO SHOWER, TOO.

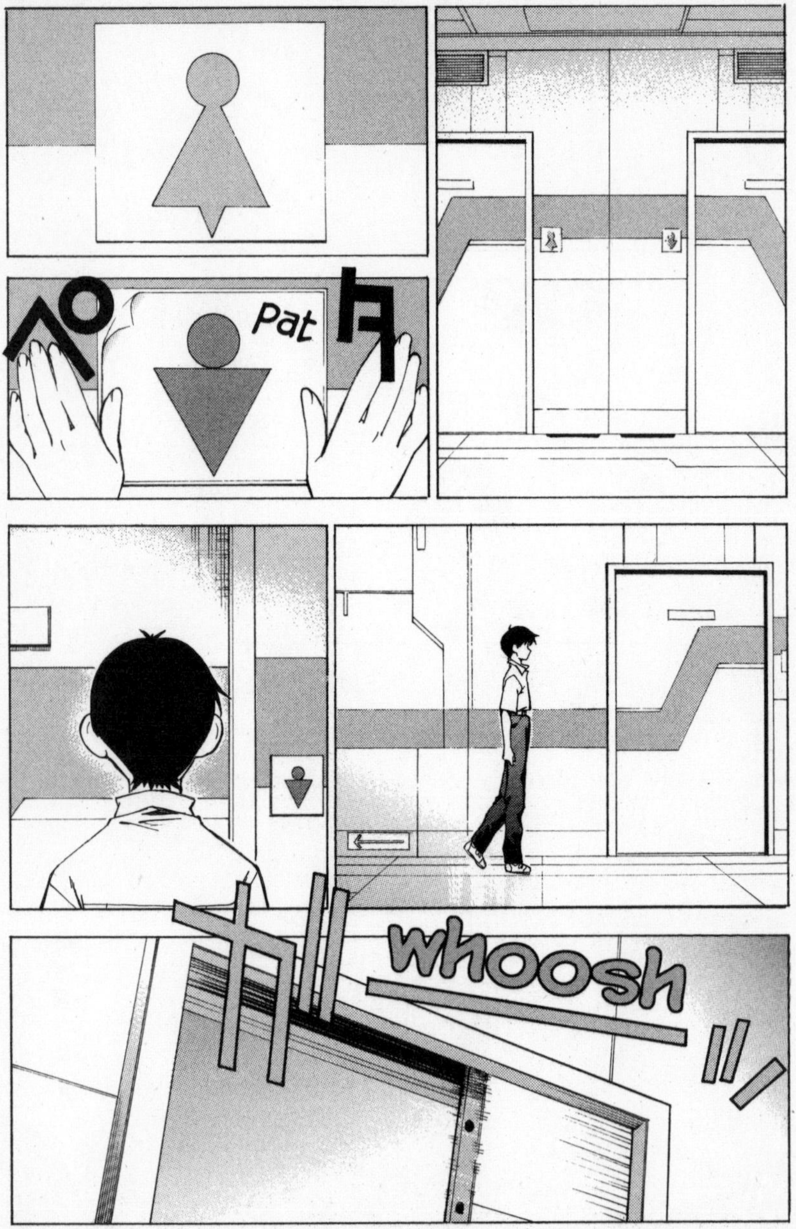
pat
whoosh

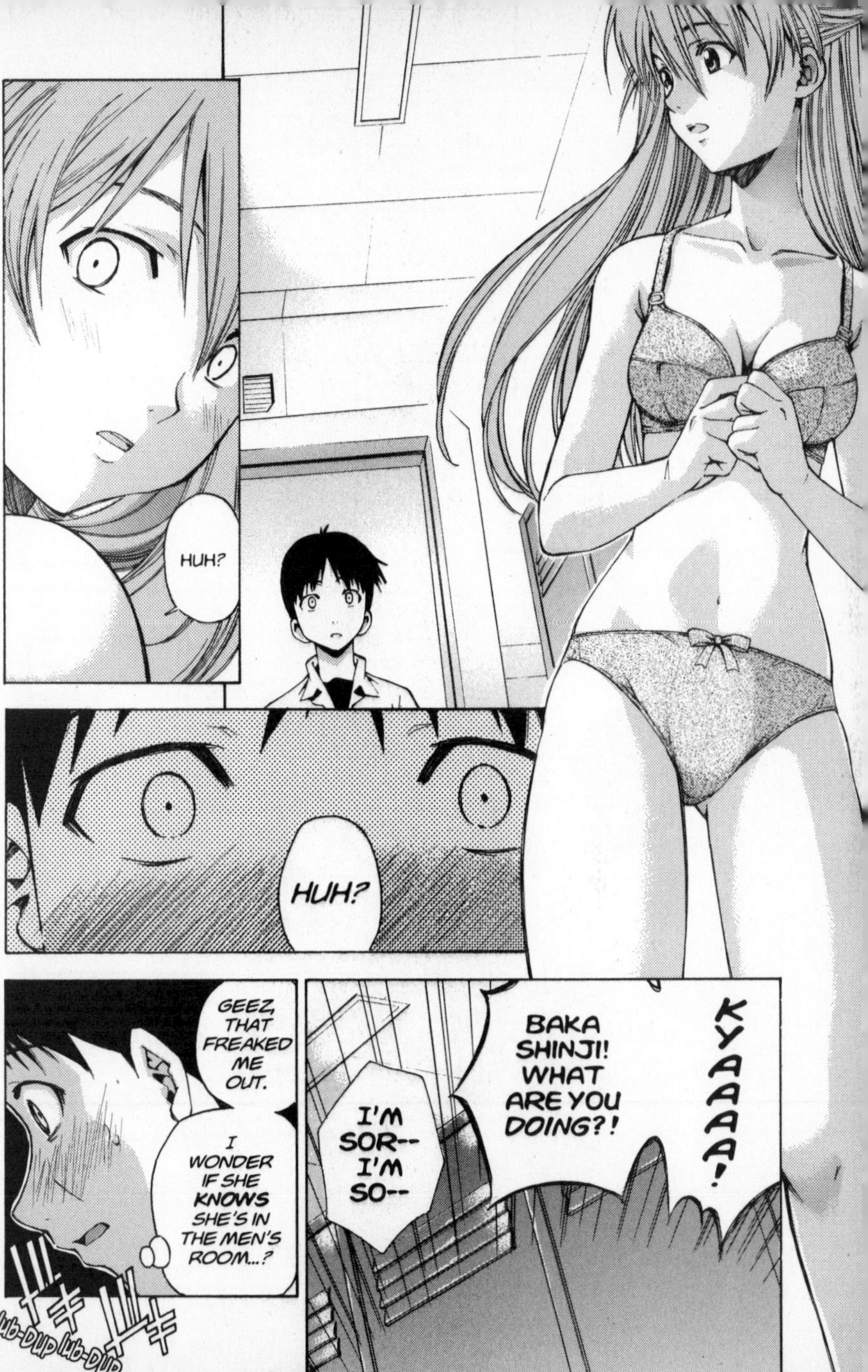
HUH?
HUH?
KYAAAA!
BAKA SHINJI! WHAT ARE YOU DOING?!
I'M SOR-- I'M SO--
GEEZ, THAT FREAKED ME OUT.
I WONDER IF SHE KNOWS SHE'S IN THE MEN'S ROOM...?
lub-dup lub-dup

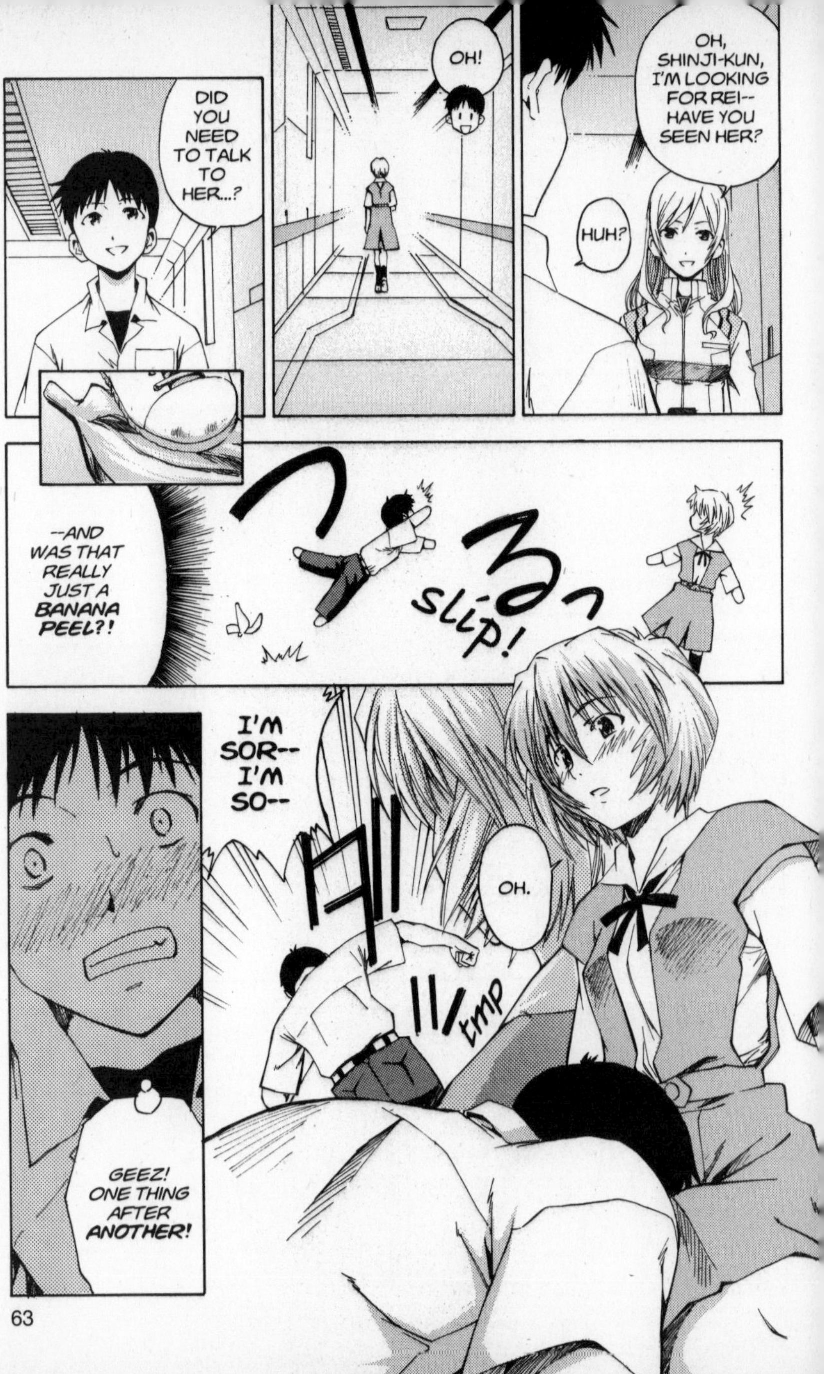
OH, SHINJI-KUN, I'M LOOKING FOR REI-- HAVE YOU SEEN HER?
HUH?
OH!
DID YOU NEED TO TALK TO HER...?
SLIP!
--AND WAS THAT REALLY JUST A BANANA PEEL?!
I'M SOR-- I'M SO--
OH.
TMP
GEEZ! ONE THING AFTER ANOTHER!

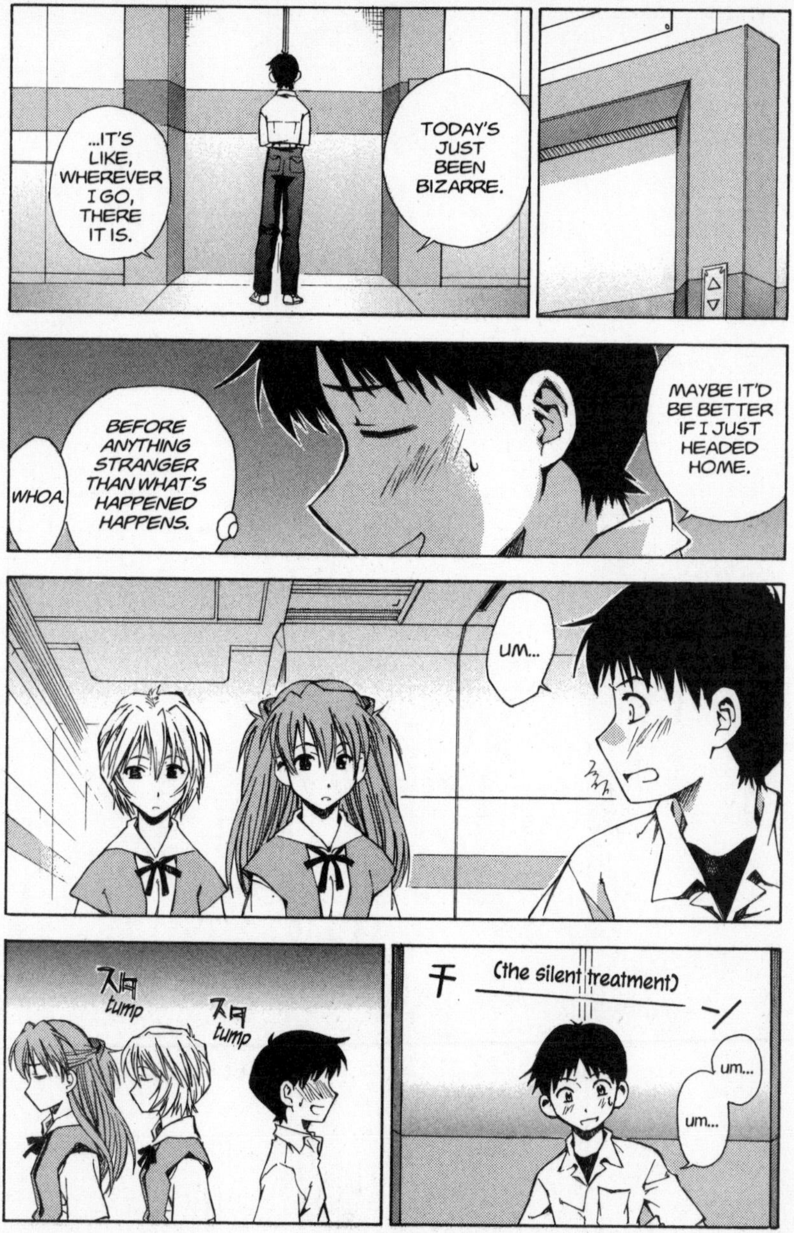
TODAY'S JUST BEEN BIZARRE.
...IT'S LIKE, WHEREVER I GO, THERE IT IS.
MAYBE IT'D BE BETTER IF I JUST HEADED HOME.
BEFORE ANYTHING STRANGER THAN WHAT'S HAPPENED HAPPENS.
WHOA.
UM...
(the silent treatment)
um...
um...
tump
tump

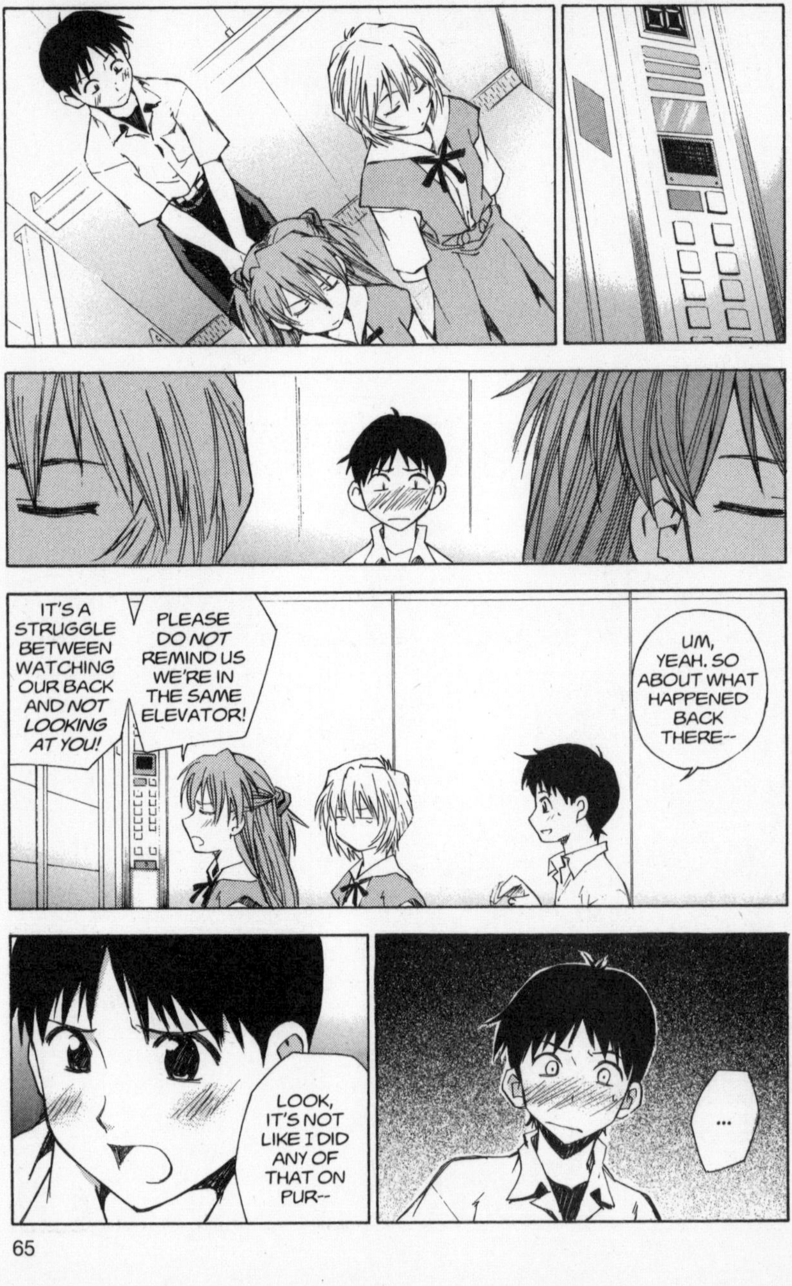
UM, YEAH. SO ABOUT WHAT HAPPENED BACK THERE--
PLEASE DO NOT REMIND US WE'RE IN THE SAME ELEVATOR!
IT'S A STRUGGLE BETWEEN WATCHING OUR BACK AND NOT LOOKING AT YOU!
...
LOOK, IT'S NOT LIKE I DID ANY OF THAT ON PUR--

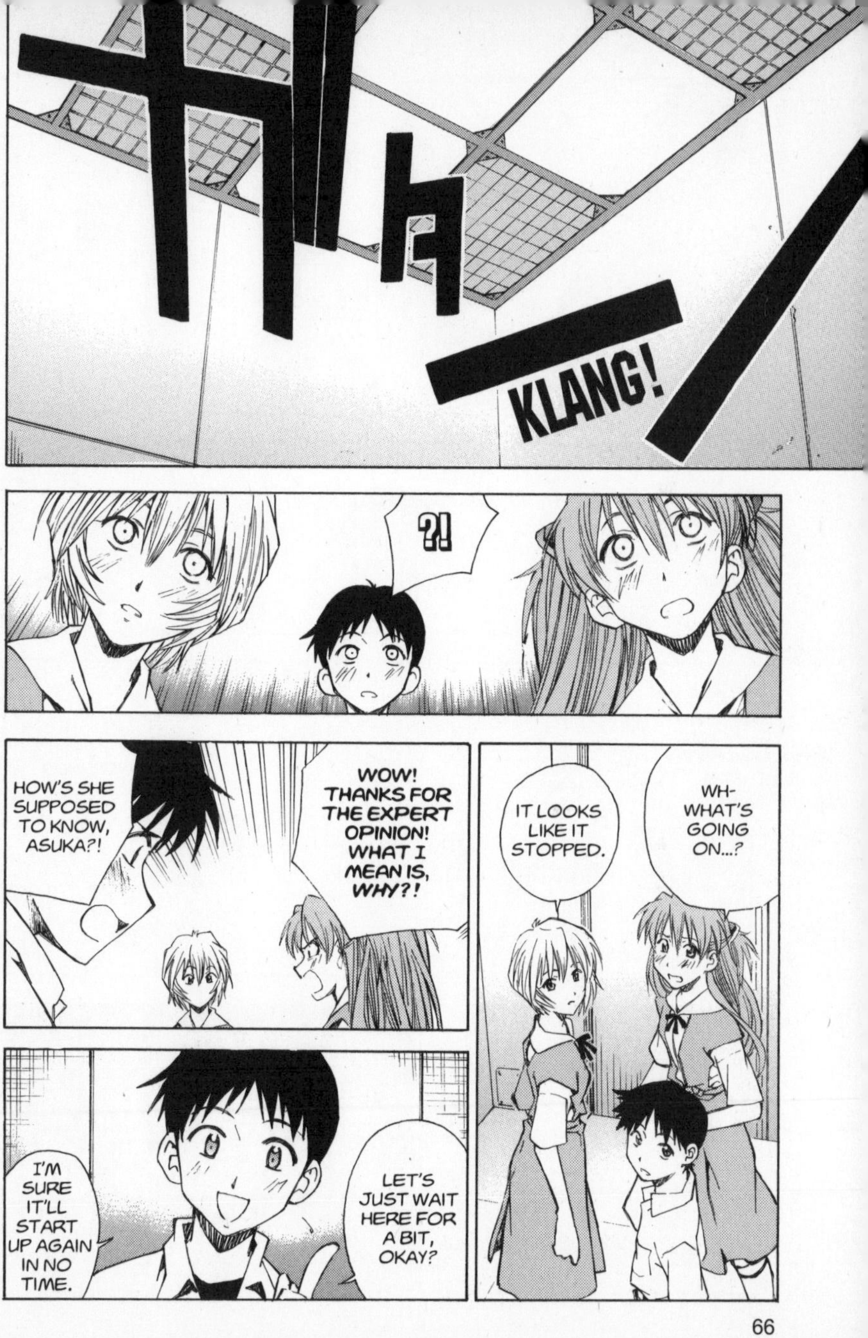
KLANG!
?!
WH- WHAT'S GOING ON...?
IT LOOKS LIKE IT STOPPED.
WOW! THANKS FOR THE EXPERT OPINION! WHAT I MEAN IS, WHY?!
HOW'S SHE SUPPOSED TO KNOW, ASUKA?!
LET'S JUST WAIT HERE FOR A BIT, OKAY?
I'M SURE IT'LL START UP AGAIN IN NO TIME.

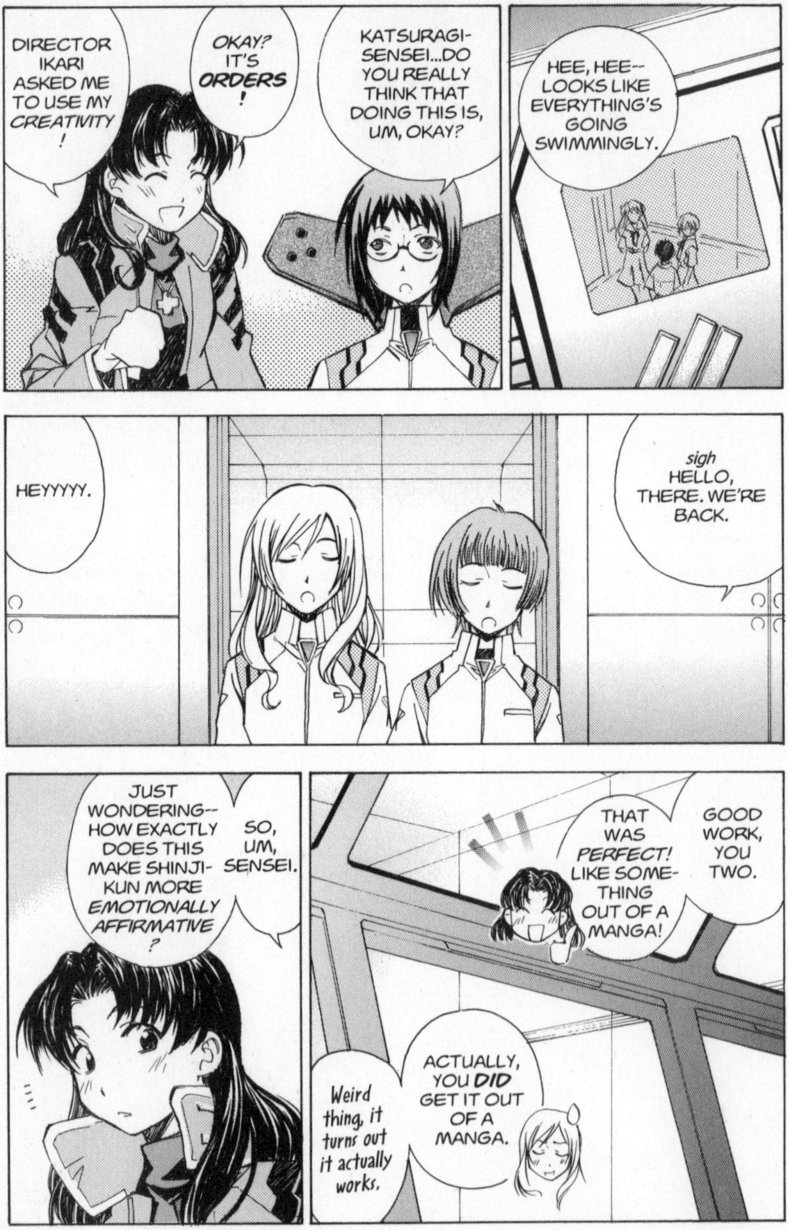
HEE, HEE-- LOOKS LIKE EVERYTHING'S GOING SWIMMINGLY.
KATSURAGI-SENSEI...DO YOU REALLY THINK THAT DOING THIS IS, UM, OKAY?
DIRECTOR IKARI ASKED ME TO USE MY *CREATIVITY*!
OKAY? IT'S ***ORDERS***!
sigh HELLO, THERE. WE'RE BACK.
HEYYYYY.
GOOD WORK, YOU TWO.
THAT WAS *PERFECT!* LIKE SOMETHING OUT OF A MANGA!
ACTUALLY, YOU ***DID*** GET IT OUT OF A MANGA.
Weird thing, it turns out it actually works.
SO, UM, SENSEI.
JUST WONDERING-- HOW EXACTLY DOES THIS MAKE SHINJI-KUN MORE *EMOTIONALLY AFFIRMATIVE*?

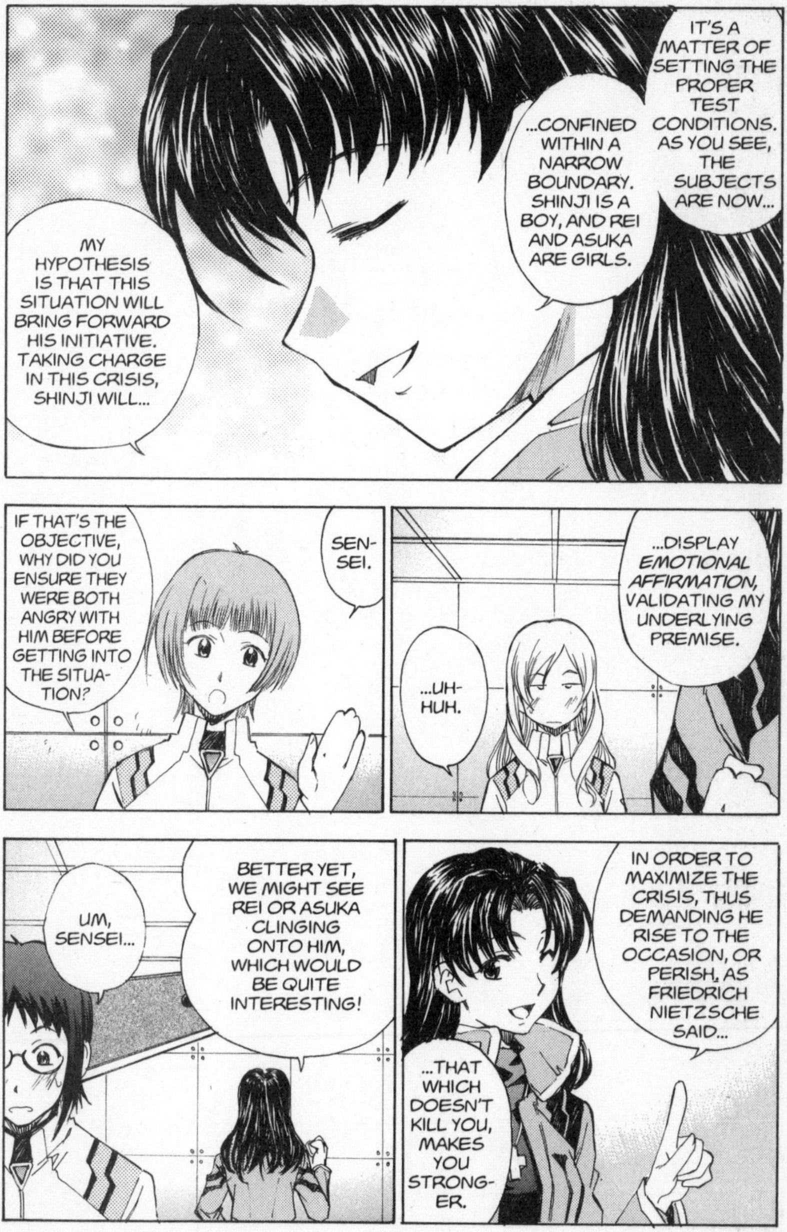
IT'S A MATTER OF SETTING THE PROPER TEST CONDITIONS. AS YOU SEE, THE SUBJECTS ARE NOW...
...CONFINED WITHIN A NARROW BOUNDARY. SHINJI IS A BOY, AND REI AND ASUKA ARE GIRLS.
MY HYPOTHESIS IS THAT THIS SITUATION WILL BRING FORWARD HIS INITIATIVE. TAKING CHARGE IN THIS CRISIS, SHINJI WILL...
...DISPLAY *EMOTIONAL AFFIRMATION*, VALIDATING MY UNDERLYING PREMISE.
...UH-HUH.
SEN-SEI.
IF THAT'S THE OBJECTIVE, WHY DID YOU ENSURE THEY WERE BOTH ANGRY WITH HIM BEFORE GETTING INTO THE SITUA-TION?
IN ORDER TO MAXIMIZE THE CRISIS, THUS DEMANDING HE RISE TO THE OCCASION, OR PERISH, AS FRIEDRICH NIETZSCHE SAID...
...THAT WHICH DOESN'T KILL YOU, MAKES YOU STRONG-ER.
BETTER YET, WE MIGHT SEE REI OR ASUKA CLINGING ONTO HIM, WHICH WOULD BE QUITE INTERESTING!
UM, SENSEI...

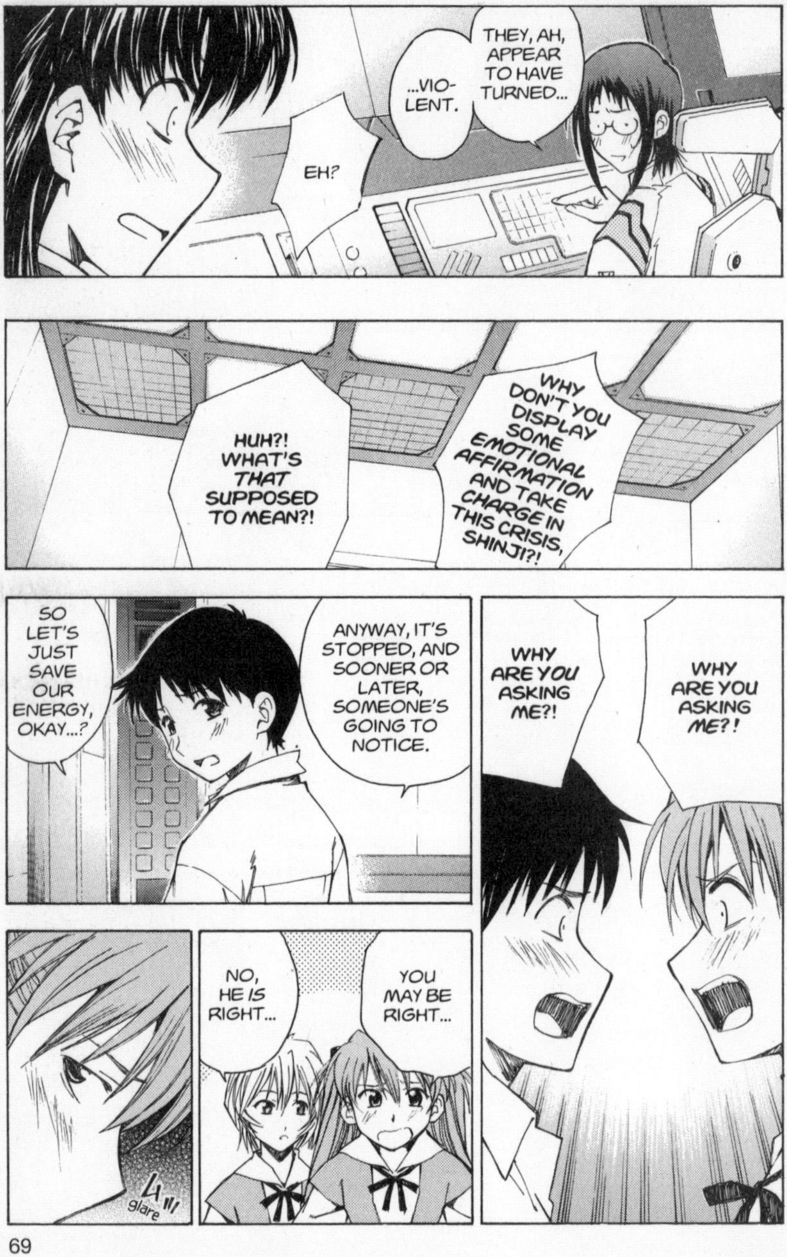
THEY, AH, APPEAR TO HAVE TURNED...
...VIO-LENT.
EH?
WHY DON'T YOU DISPLAY SOME EMOTIONAL AFFIRMATION AND TAKE CHARGE IN THIS CRISIS, SHINJI?!
HUH?! WHAT'S *THAT* SUPPOSED TO MEAN?!
WHY ARE YOU ASKING *ME*?!
WHY ARE *YOU* ASKING ME?!
ANYWAY, IT'S STOPPED, AND SOONER OR LATER, SOMEONE'S GOING TO NOTICE.
SO LET'S JUST SAVE OUR ENERGY, OKAY...?
YOU MAY BE RIGHT...
NO, HE *IS* RIGHT...
glare

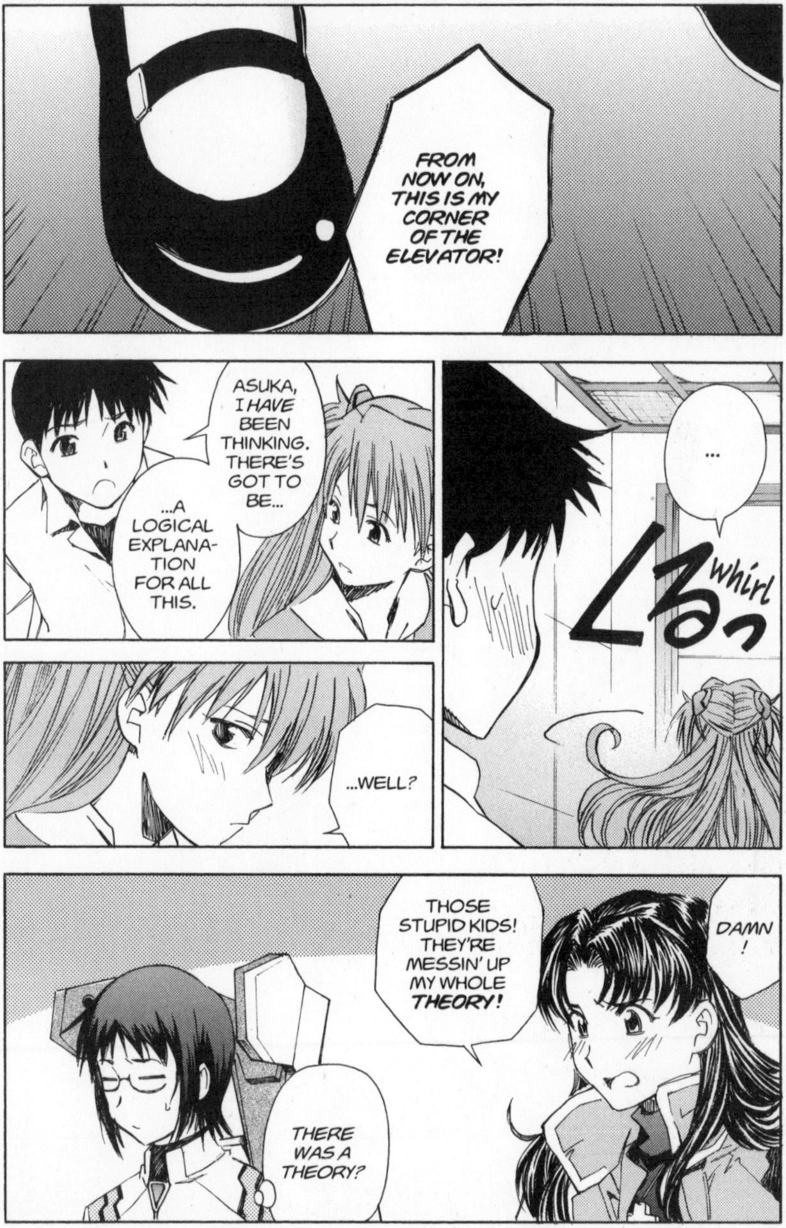
FROM NOW ON, THIS IS MY CORNER OF THE ELEVATOR!
...
くるっ
whirl
ASUKA, I HAVE BEEN THINKING. THERE'S GOT TO BE...
...A LOGICAL EXPLANATION FOR ALL THIS.
...WELL?
DAMN!
THOSE STUPID KIDS! THEY'RE MESSIN' UP MY WHOLE THEORY!
THERE WAS A THEORY?

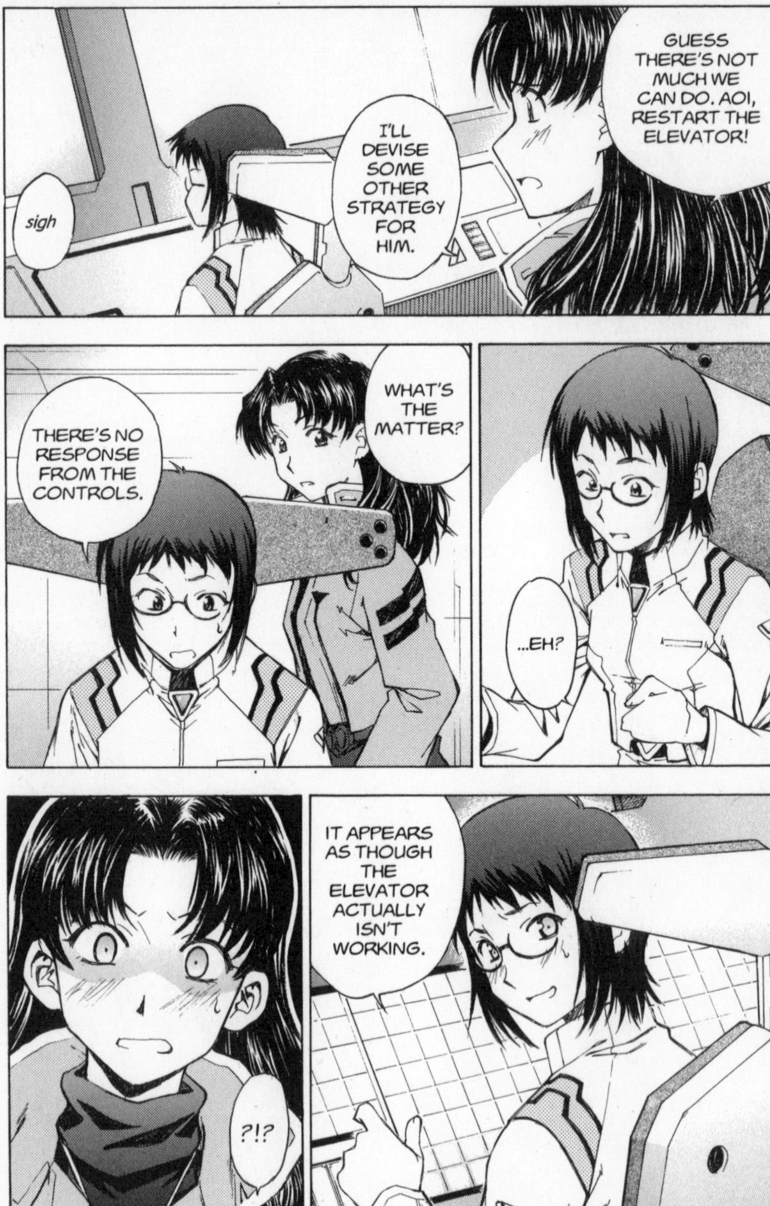
GUESS THERE'S NOT MUCH WE CAN DO. AOI, RESTART THE ELEVATOR!
I'LL DEVISE SOME OTHER STRATEGY FOR HIM.
sigh
...EH?
WHAT'S THE MATTER?
THERE'S NO RESPONSE FROM THE CONTROLS.
IT APPEARS AS THOUGH THE ELEVATOR ACTUALLY ISN'T WORKING.
?!?

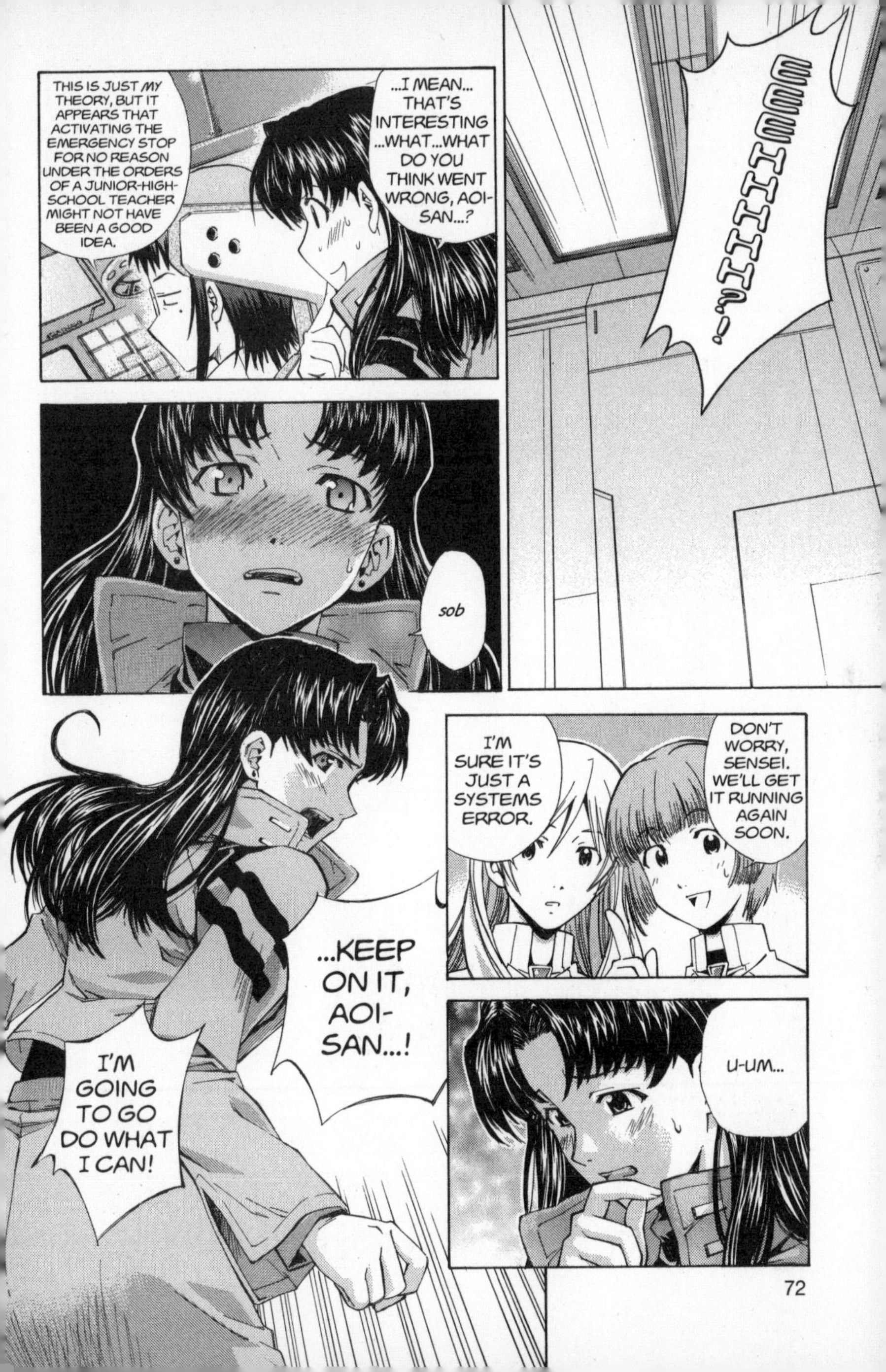
EEEEHHHHH?!
...I MEAN... THAT'S INTERESTING ...WHAT...WHAT DO YOU THINK WENT WRONG, AOI-SAN...?
THIS IS JUST MY THEORY, BUT IT APPEARS THAT ACTIVATING THE EMERGENCY STOP FOR NO REASON UNDER THE ORDERS OF A JUNIOR-HIGH-SCHOOL TEACHER MIGHT NOT HAVE BEEN A GOOD IDEA.
sob
DON'T WORRY, SENSEI. WE'LL GET IT RUNNING AGAIN SOON.
I'M SURE IT'S JUST A SYSTEMS ERROR.
U-UM...
...KEEP ON IT, AOI-SAN...!
I'M GOING TO GO DO WHAT I CAN!

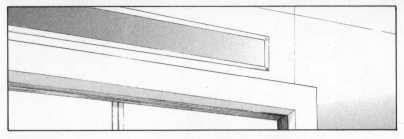

hahh
haa
I...
...I'M SO SORRY, SHINJI-KUN!
bow
IT'S ALL MY FAULT YOU'RE IN THIS MESS... IF I HADN'T STOPPED THE ELEVATOR...
IF I-I HADN'T SWITCHED THE BATHROOM SIGNS...IF I HADN'T MADE YOU T-TRIP INTO REI...
...WELL, YOU WERE RIGHT, SHINJI.
NOW THERE'S ONLY ONE THING TO ASK MISATO-SENSEI...
ding!

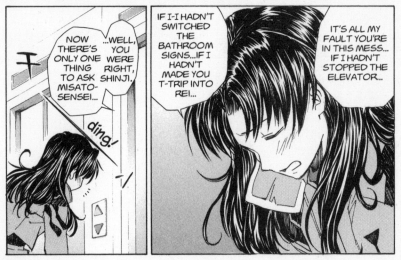

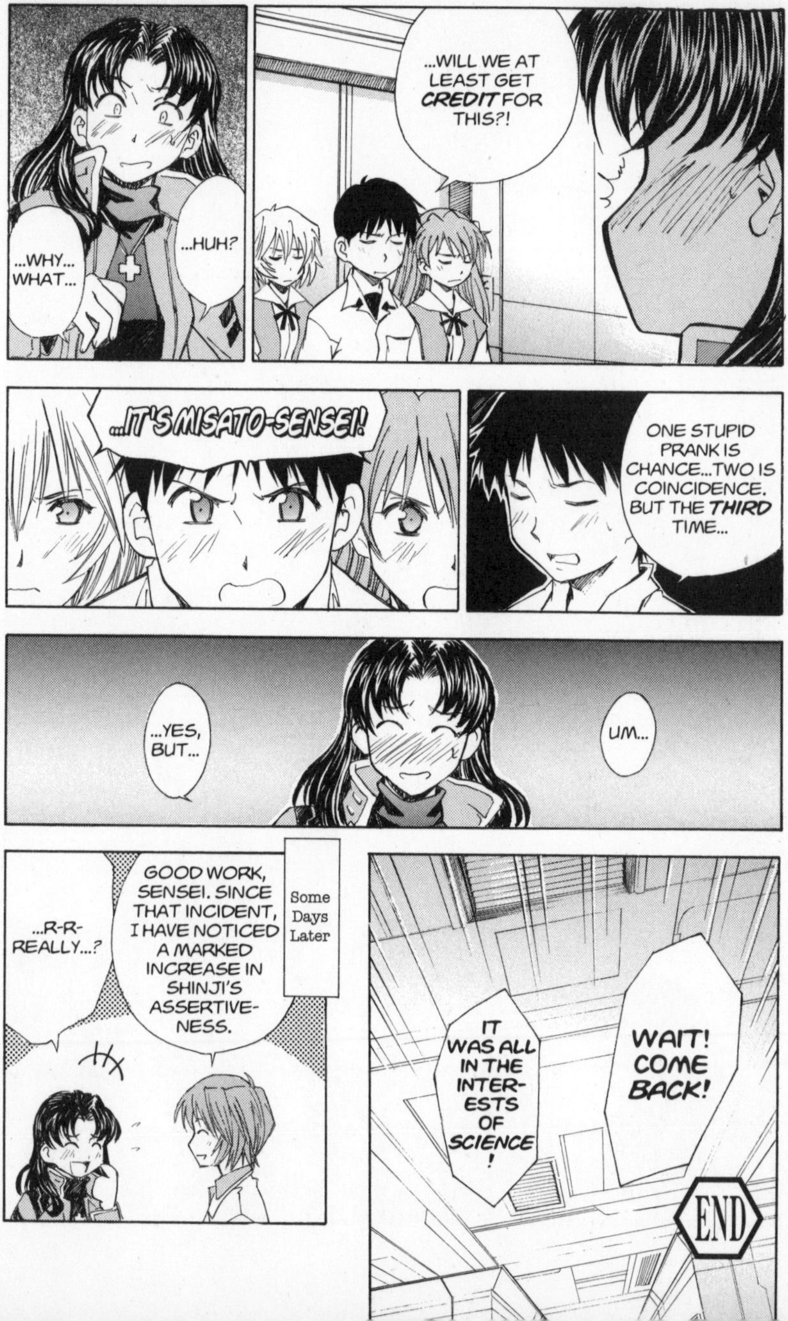
...WILL WE AT LEAST GET CREDIT FOR THIS?!
...HUH?
...WHY... WHAT...
ONE STUPID PRANK IS CHANCE...TWO IS COINCIDENCE. BUT THE THIRD TIME...
...IT'S MISATO-SENSEI!
UM...
...YES, BUT...
WAIT! COME BACK!
IT WAS ALL IN THE INTERESTS OF SCIENCE!
END
Some Days Later
GOOD WORK, SENSEI. SINCE THAT INCIDENT, I HAVE NOTICED A MARKED INCREASE IN SHINJI'S ASSERTIVENESS.
...R-R-REALLY...?

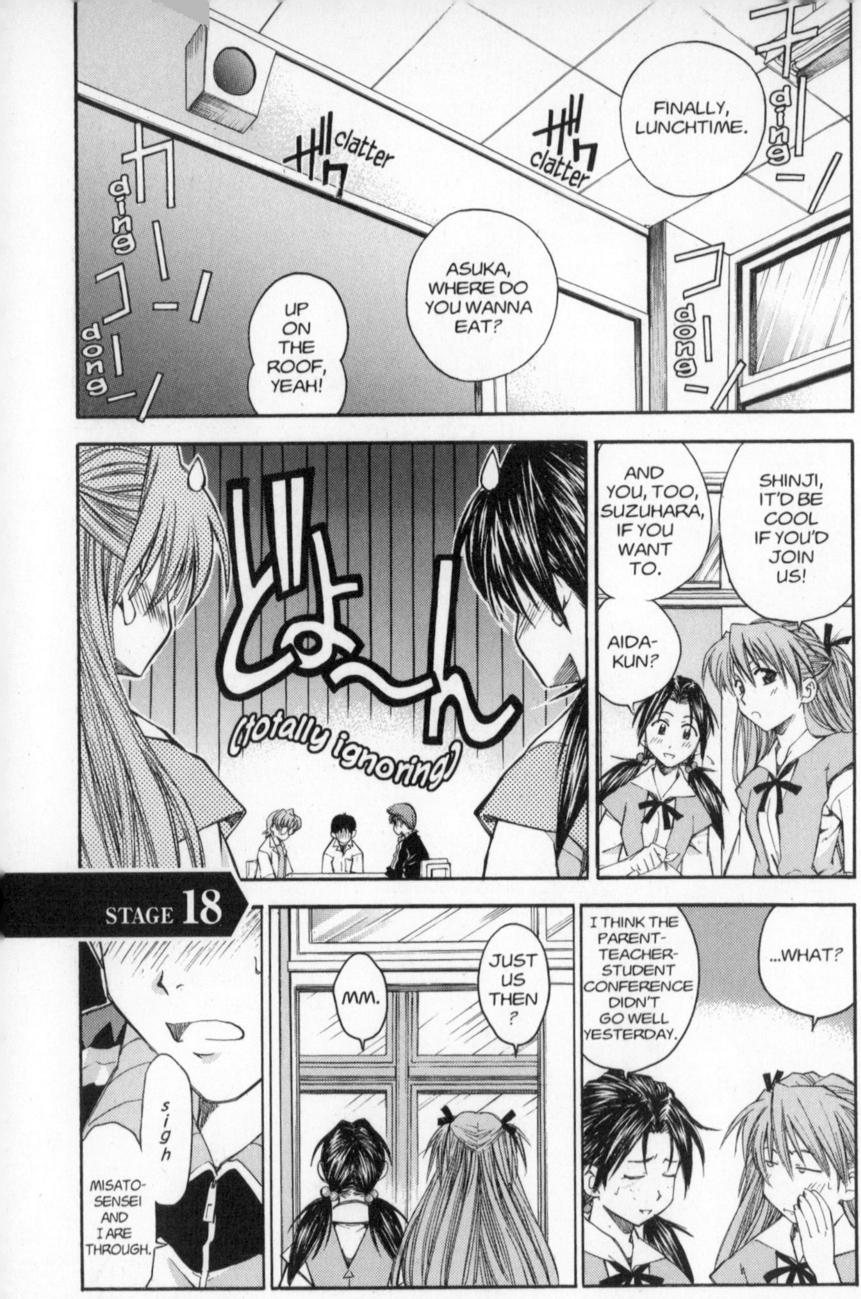
ding—
FINALLY, LUNCHTIME.
clatter
clatter
ASUKA, WHERE DO YOU WANNA EAT?
UP ON THE ROOF, YEAH!
ding—
dong—
dong—
SHINJI, IT'D BE COOL IF YOU'D JOIN US!
AND YOU, TOO, SUZUHARA, IF YOU WANT TO.
AIDA-KUN?
(totally ignoring)
STAGE 18
...WHAT?
I THINK THE PARENT-TEACHER-STUDENT CONFERENCE DIDN'T GO WELL YESTERDAY.
JUST US THEN?
MM.
sigh
MISATO-SENSEI AND I ARE THROUGH.

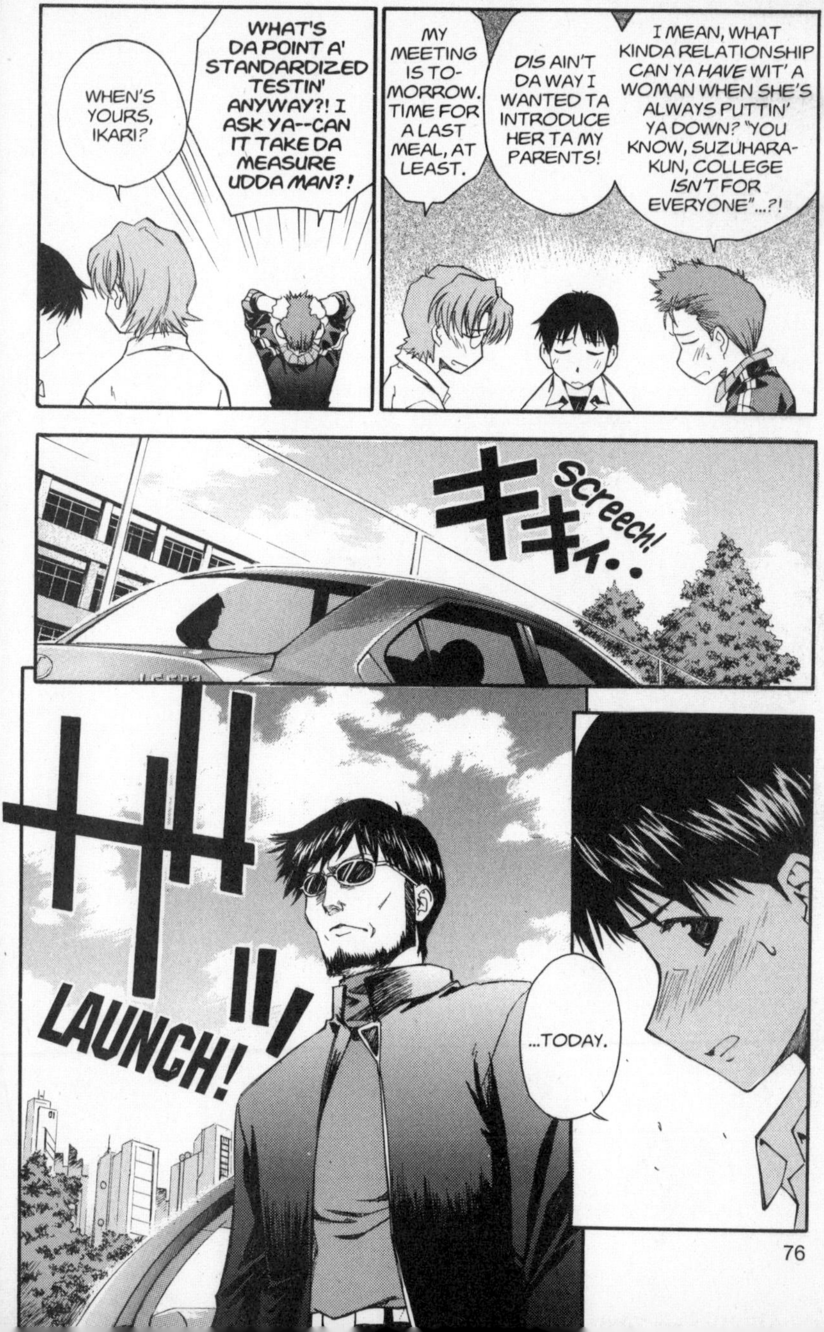
I MEAN, WHAT KINDA RELATIONSHIP CAN YA HAVE WIT' A WOMAN WHEN SHE'S ALWAYS PUTTIN' YA DOWN? "YOU KNOW, SUZUHARA-KUN, COLLEGE ISN'T FOR EVERYONE"...?!
DIS AIN'T DA WAY I WANTED TA INTRODUCE HER TA MY PARENTS!
MY MEETING IS TO-MORROW. TIME FOR A LAST MEAL, AT LEAST.
WHAT'S DA POINT A' STANDARDIZED TESTIN' ANYWAY?! I ASK YA--CAN IT TAKE DA MEASURE UDDA MAN?!
WHEN'S YOURS, IKARI?
キキィ・・
Screech!
...TODAY.
LAUNCH!

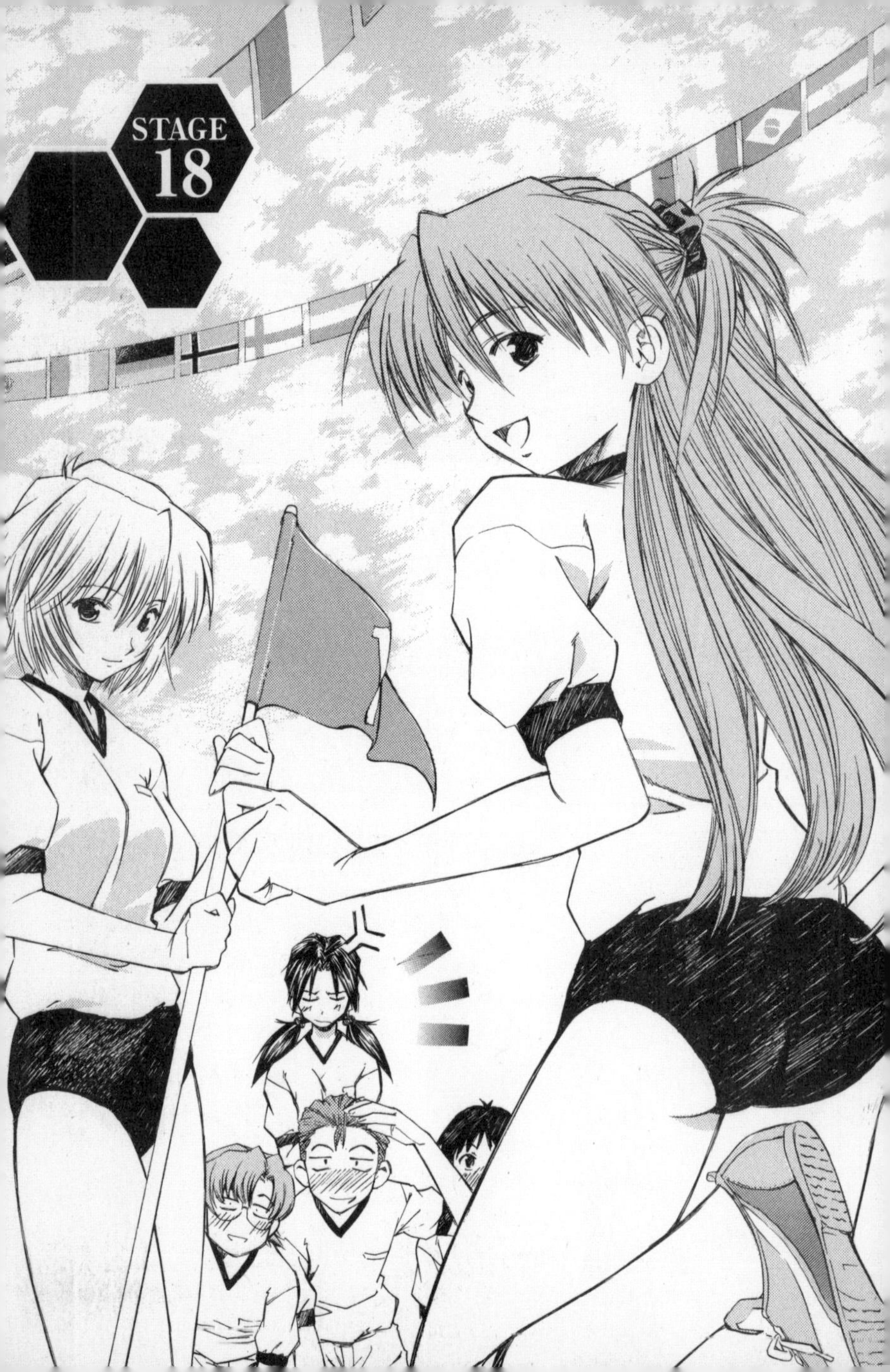
STAGE
18

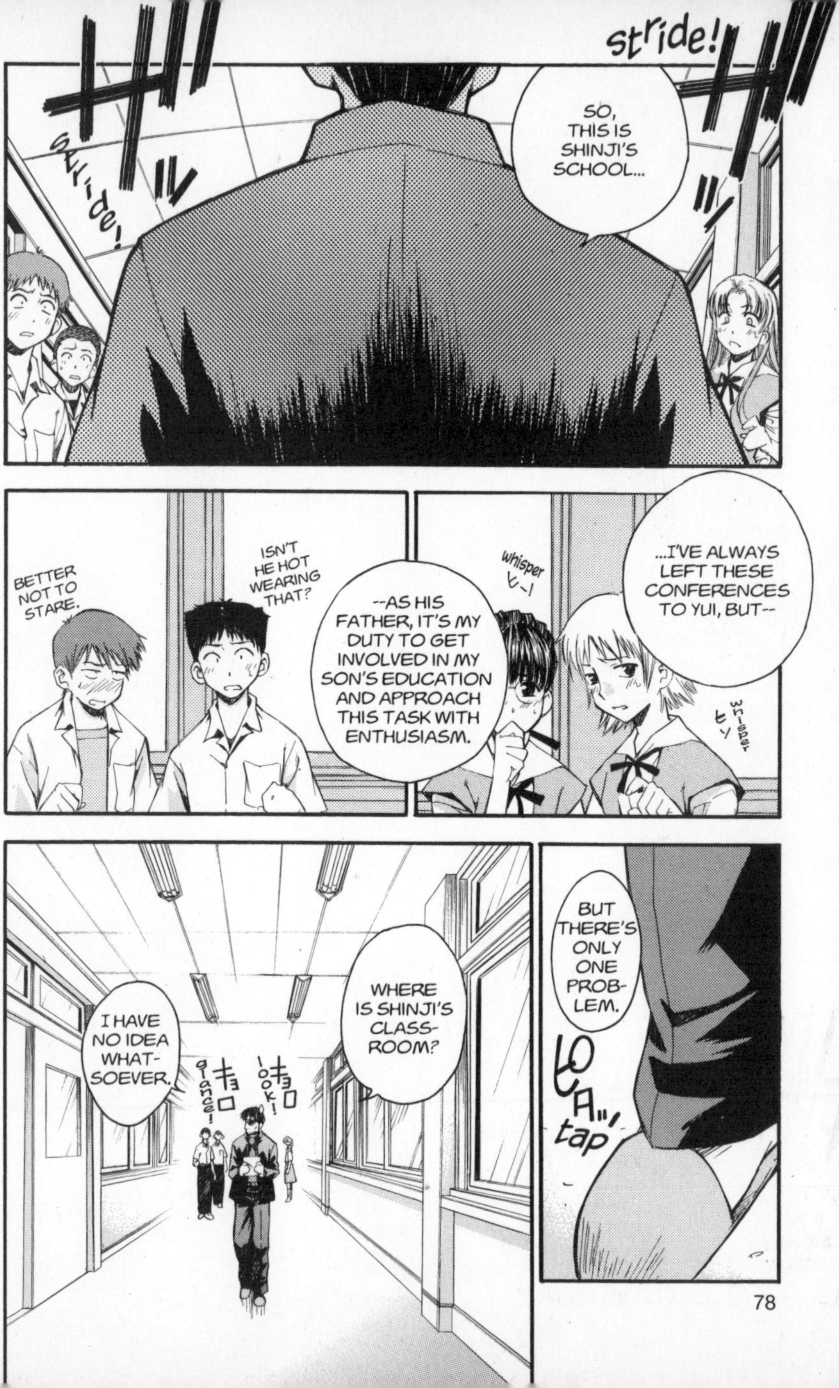
stride!
stride!
SO, THIS IS SHINJI'S SCHOOL...
...I'VE ALWAYS LEFT THESE CONFERENCES TO YUI, BUT--
whisper
whisper
--AS HIS FATHER, IT'S MY DUTY TO GET INVOLVED IN MY SON'S EDUCATION AND APPROACH THIS TASK WITH ENTHUSIASM.
ISN'T HE HOT WEARING THAT?
BETTER NOT TO STARE.
BUT THERE'S ONLY ONE PROB-LEM.
tap
WHERE IS SHINJI'S CLASS-ROOM?
look!
glance!
I HAVE NO IDEA WHAT-SOEVER.

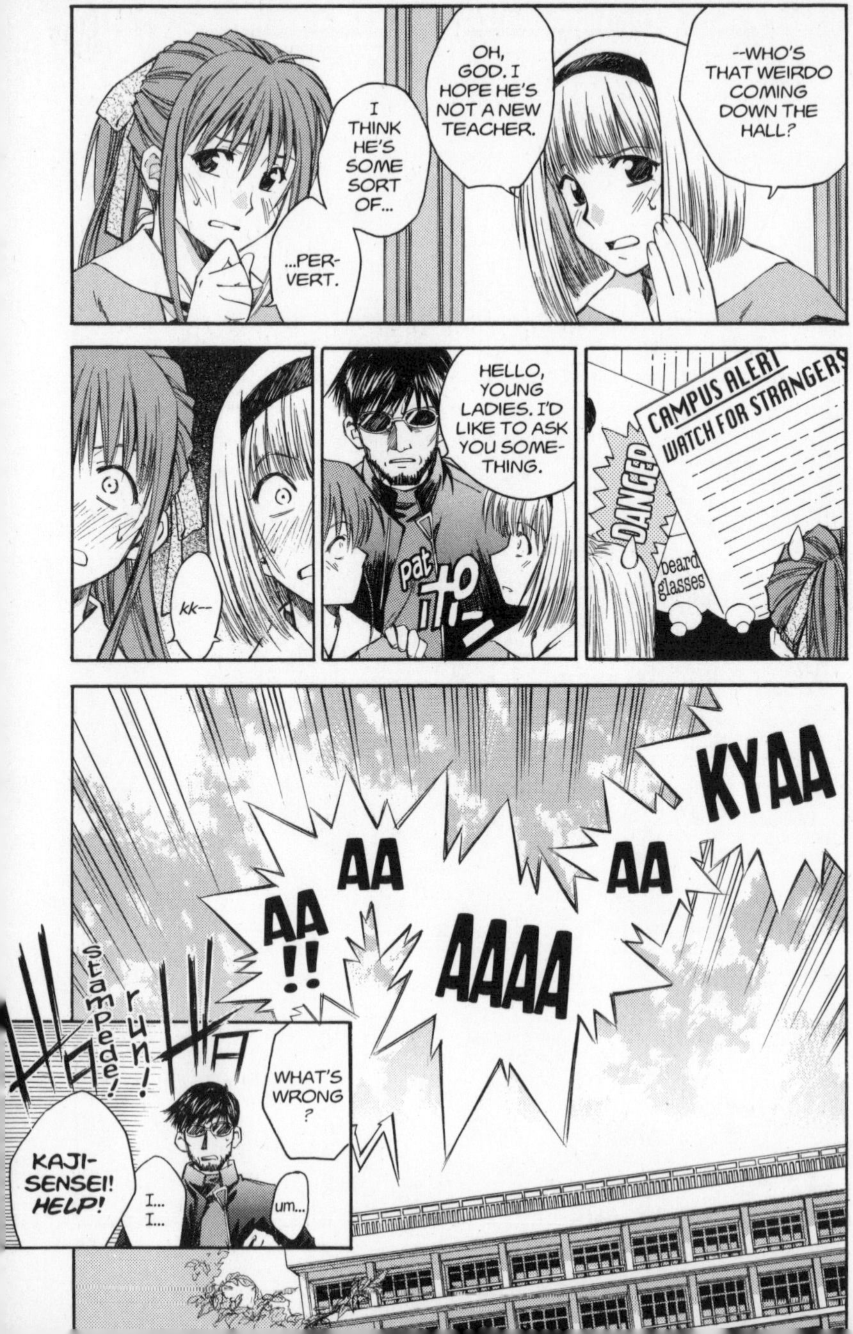
--WHO'S THAT WEIRDO COMING DOWN THE HALL?
OH, GOD. I HOPE HE'S NOT A NEW TEACHER.
I THINK HE'S SOME SORT OF...
...PER-VERT.
CAMPUS ALERT
WATCH FOR STRANGERS
beard glasses
HELLO, YOUNG LADIES. I'D LIKE TO ASK YOU SOME-THING.
pat
kk--
KYAA
AA
AA
AA!!
AAAA
WHAT'S WRONG?
um...
I... I...
KAJI-SENSEI! HELP!
run!
stampede!

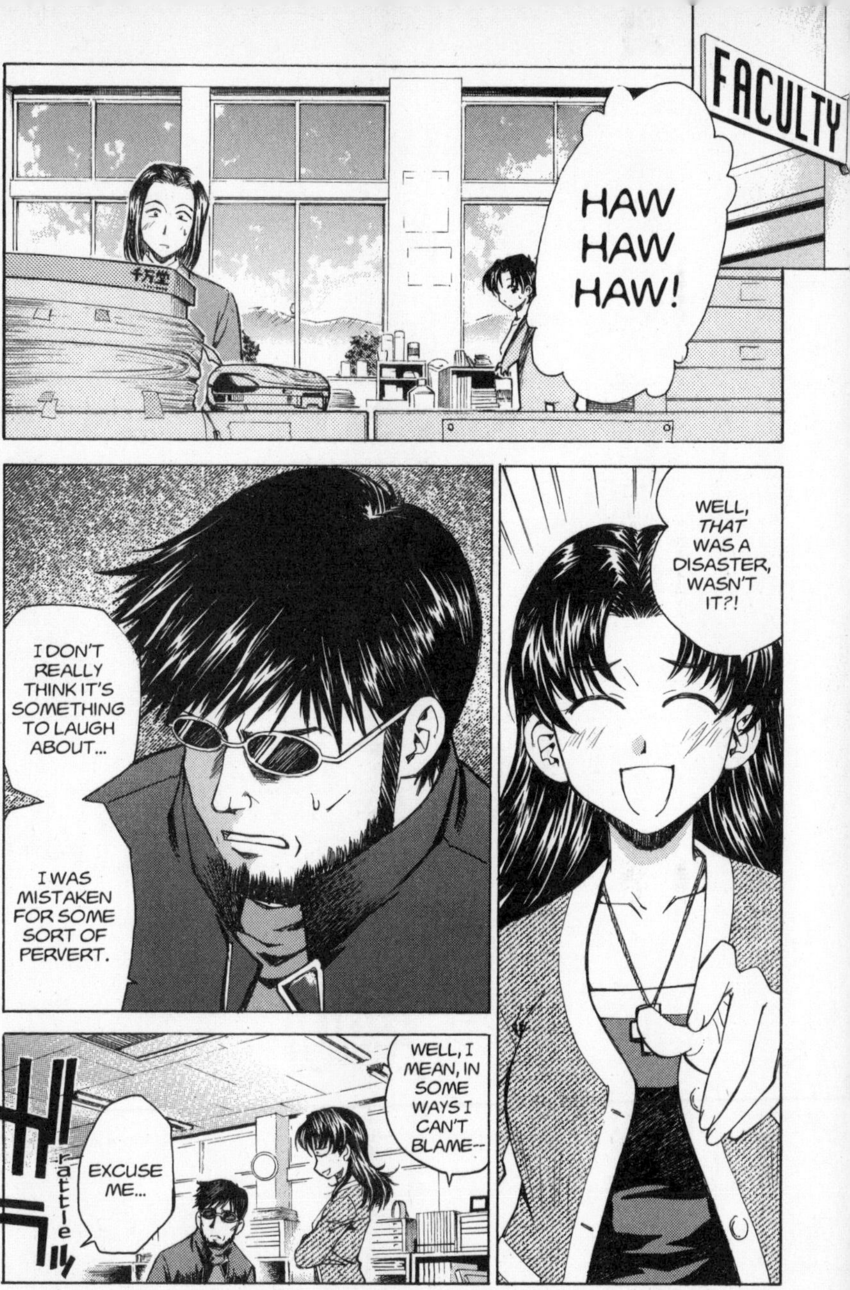
FACULTY
HAW HAW HAW!
WELL, THAT WAS A DISASTER, WASN'T IT?!
I DON'T REALLY THINK IT'S SOMETHING TO LAUGH ABOUT...
I WAS MISTAKEN FOR SOME SORT OF PERVERT.
WELL, I MEAN, IN SOME WAYS I CAN'T BLAME--
EXCUSE ME...
rattle

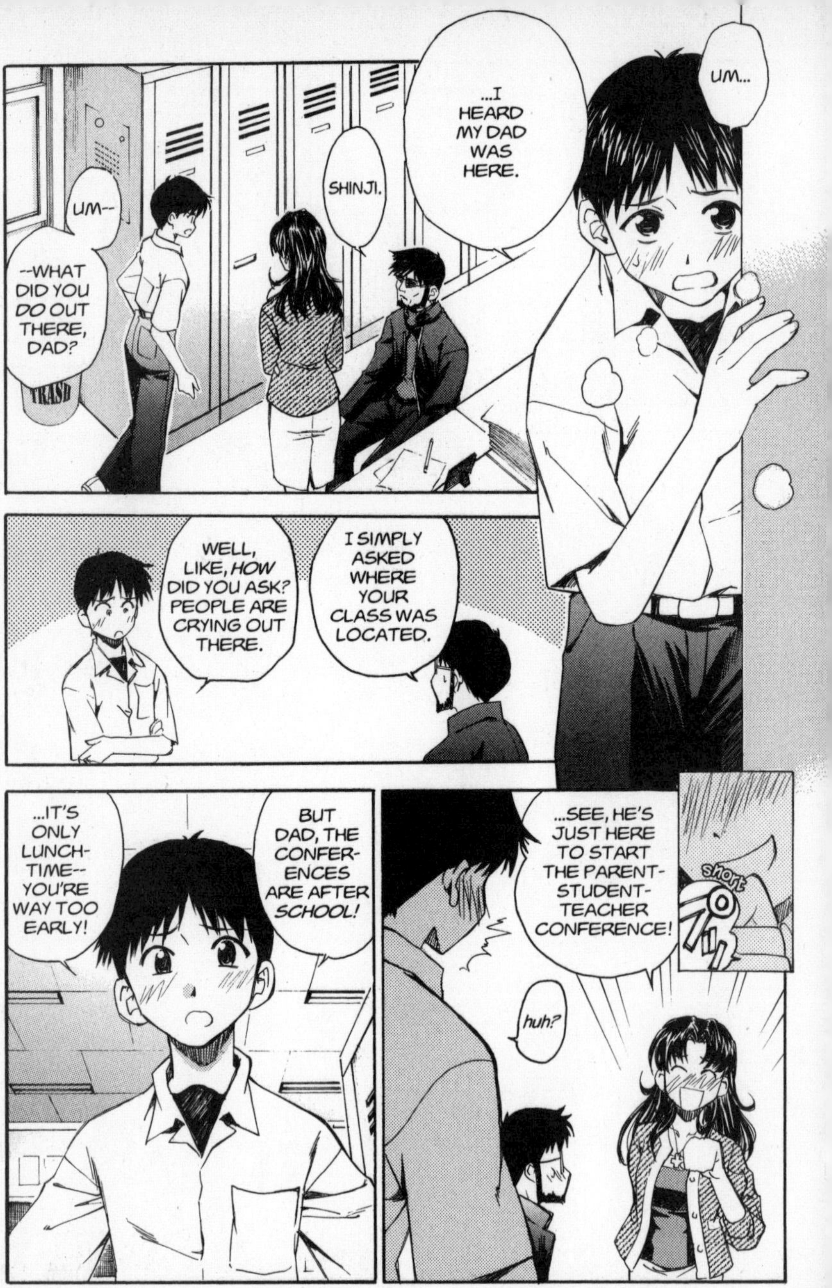
UM...
...I HEARD MY DAD WAS HERE.
SHINJI.
UM--
--WHAT DID YOU *DO* OUT THERE, DAD?
TRASH
I SIMPLY ASKED WHERE YOUR CLASS WAS LOCATED.
WELL, LIKE, *HOW* DID YOU ASK? PEOPLE ARE CRYING OUT THERE.
short
...SEE, HE'S JUST HERE TO START THE PARENT-STUDENT-TEACHER CONFERENCE!
huh?
BUT DAD, THE CONFER-ENCES ARE AFTER *SCHOOL*!
...IT'S ONLY LUNCH-TIME-- YOU'RE WAY TOO EARLY!

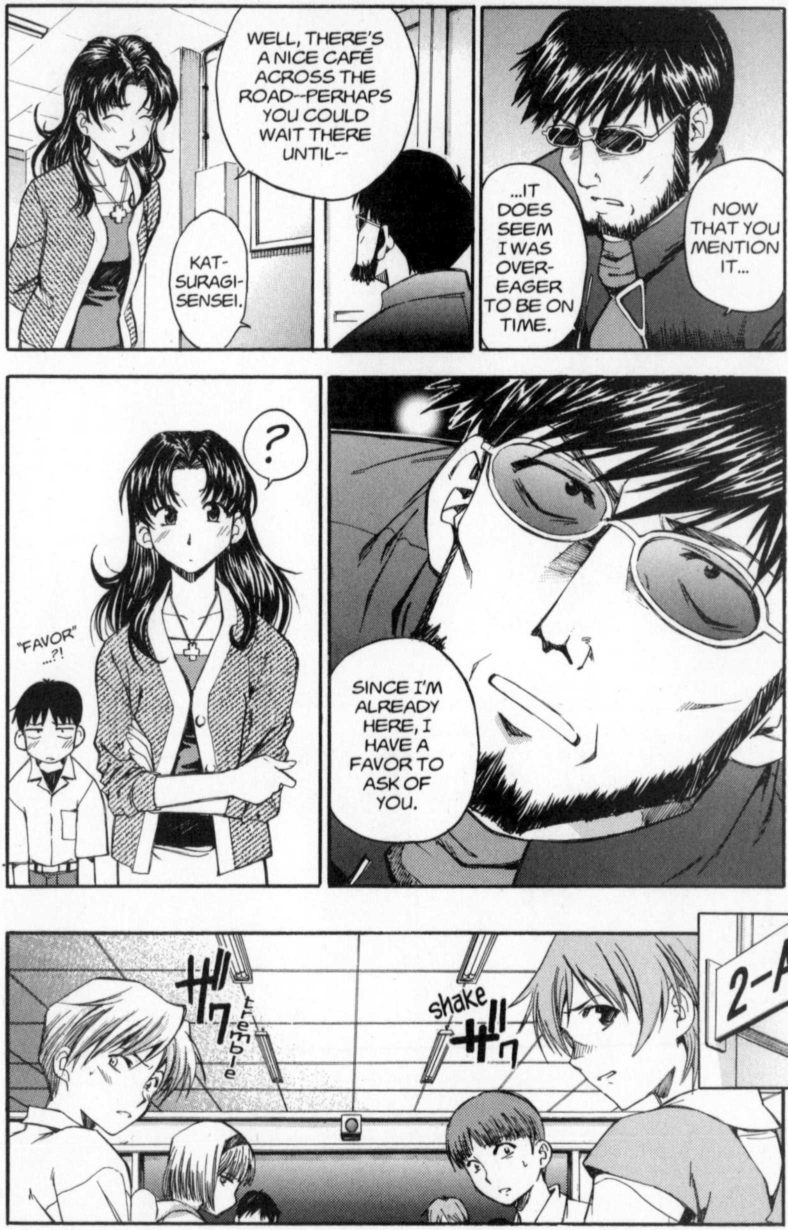
NOW THAT YOU MENTION IT...
...IT DOES SEEM I WAS OVER-EAGER TO BE ON TIME.
WELL, THERE'S A NICE CAFÉ ACROSS THE ROAD--PERHAPS YOU COULD WAIT THERE UNTIL--
KAT-SURAGI-SENSEI.
SINCE I'M ALREADY HERE, I HAVE A FAVOR TO ASK OF YOU.
?
"FAVOR" ...?!
2-A
shake
ザワ
ザワ
tremble

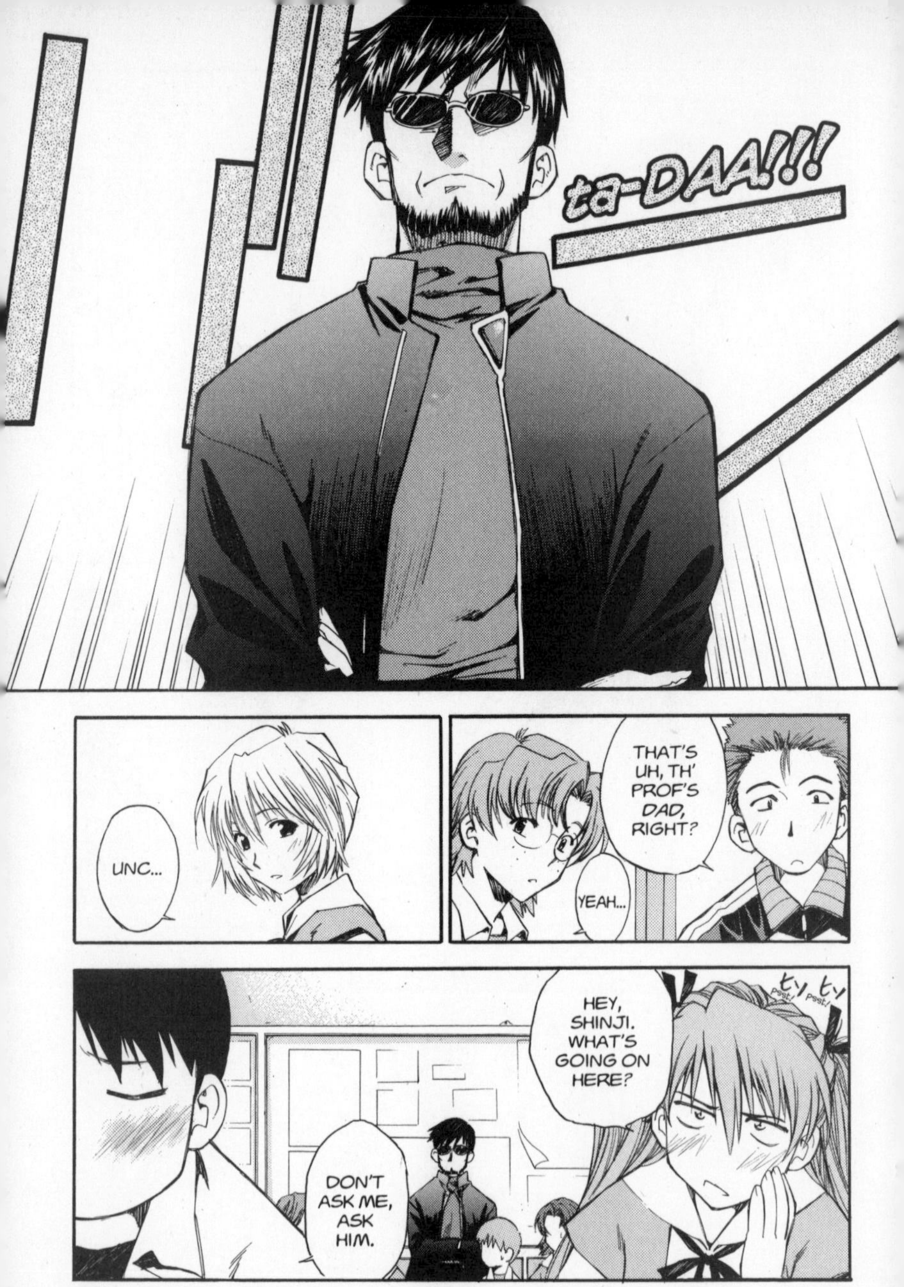
ta-DAA!!!
THAT'S UH, TH' PROF'S DAD, RIGHT?
YEAH...
UNC...
psst! psst!
HEY, SHINJI. WHAT'S GOING ON HERE?
DON'T ASK ME, ASK HIM.

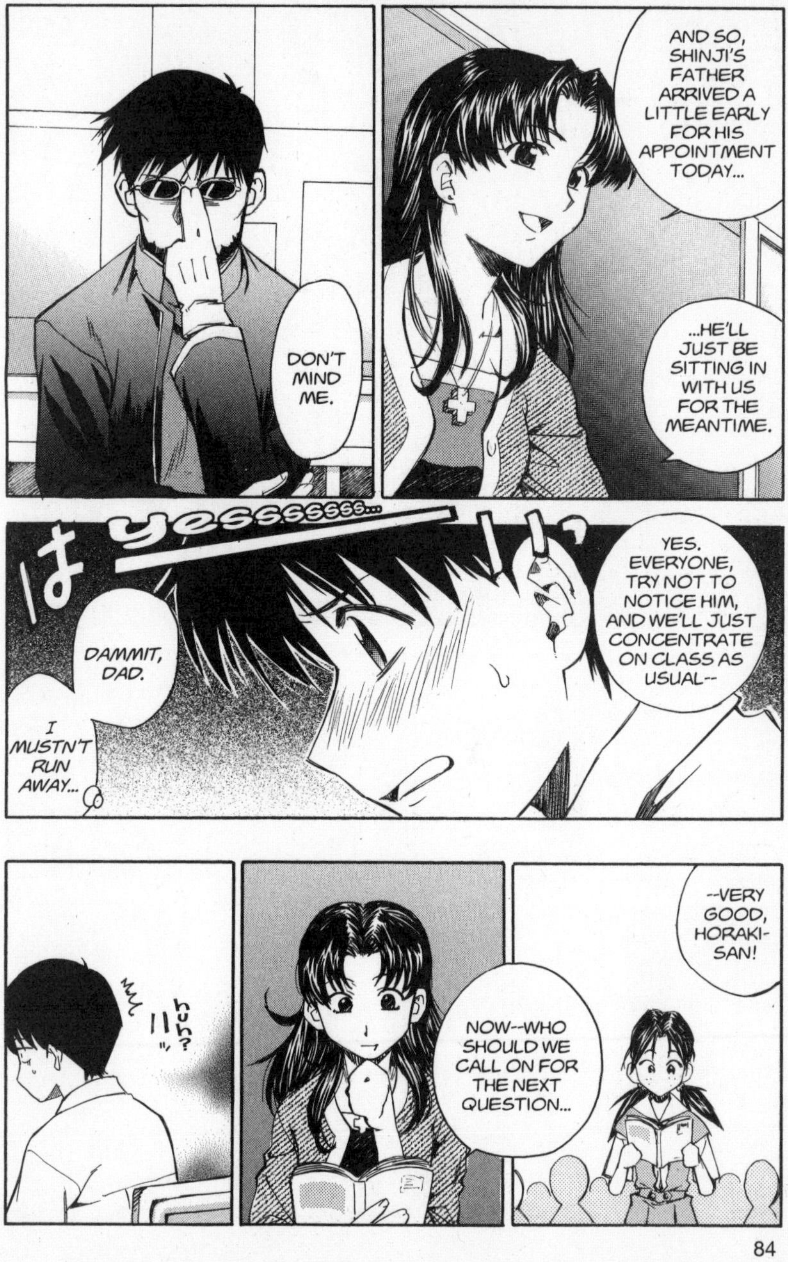
AND SO, SHINJI'S FATHER ARRIVED A LITTLE EARLY FOR HIS APPOINTMENT TODAY...
...HE'LL JUST BE SITTING IN WITH US FOR THE MEANTIME.
DON'T MIND ME.
YES. EVERYONE, TRY NOT TO NOTICE HIM, AND WE'LL JUST CONCENTRATE ON CLASS AS USUAL--
はい
yessssssss...
DAMMIT, DAD.
I MUSTN'T RUN AWAY...
--VERY GOOD, HORAKI-SAN!
NOW--WHO SHOULD WE CALL ON FOR THE NEXT QUESTION...
ハッ
huh?

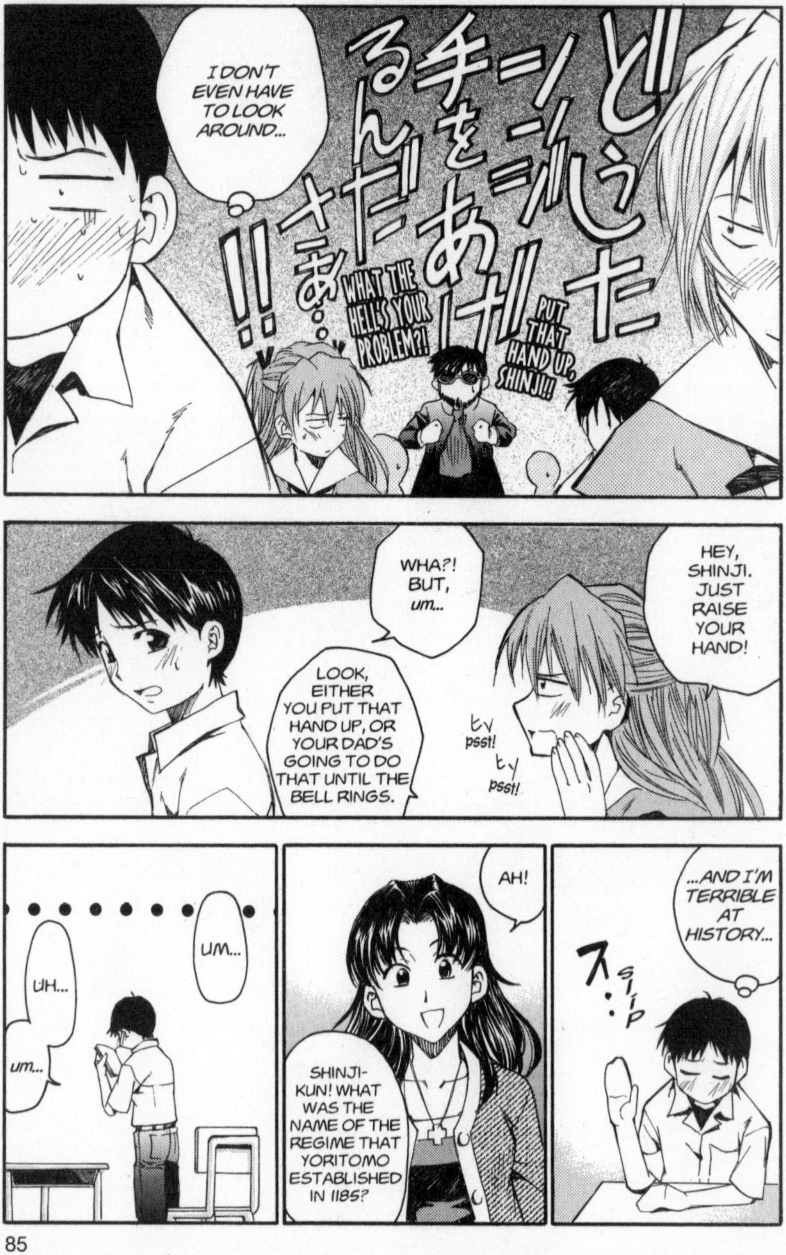
PUT THAT HAND UP, SHINJI!!
WHAT THE HELL'S YOUR PROBLEM?!
I DON'T EVEN HAVE TO LOOK AROUND...
HEY, SHINJI. JUST RAISE YOUR HAND!
ヒソ pssst!
ヒソ psst!
WHA?! BUT, um...
LOOK, EITHER YOU PUT THAT HAND UP, OR YOUR DAD'S GOING TO DO THAT UNTIL THE BELL RINGS.
...AND I'M TERRIBLE AT HISTORY...
ス slip
AH!
SHINJI-KUN! WHAT WAS THE NAME OF THE REGIME THAT YORITOMO ESTABLISHED IN 1185?
um...
UH...
um...

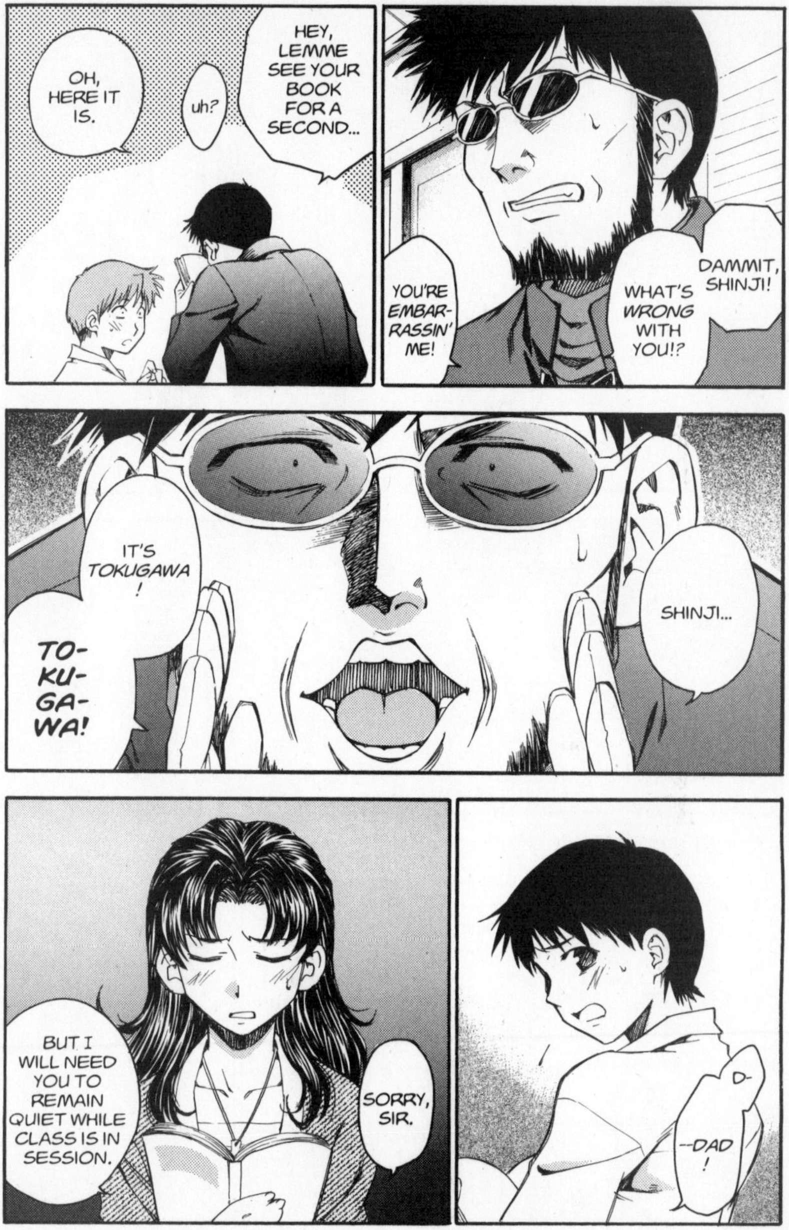
DAMMIT, SHINJI!
WHAT'S WRONG WITH YOU!?
YOU'RE EMBAR-RASSIN' ME!
HEY, LEMME SEE YOUR BOOK FOR A SECOND...
uh?
OH, HERE IT IS.
SHINJI...
IT'S TOKUGAWA!
TO-KU-GA-WA!
D-
--DAD!
SORRY, SIR.
BUT I WILL NEED YOU TO REMAIN QUIET WHILE CLASS IS IN SESSION.

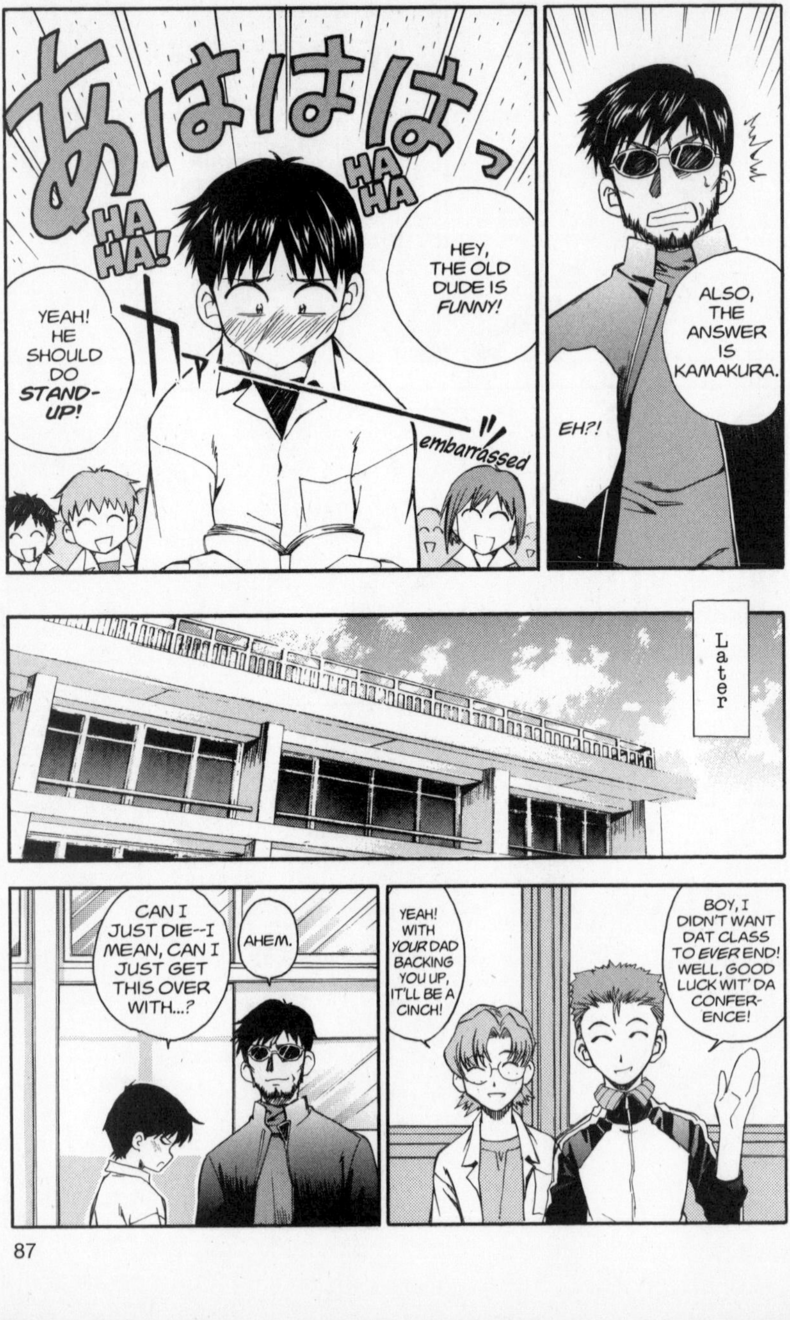
ALSO, THE ANSWER IS KAMAKURA.
EH?!
あはははっ
HA HA
HA HA!
HEY, THE OLD DUDE IS FUNNY!
YEAH! HE SHOULD DO STAND-UP!
embarrassed
Later
BOY, I DIDN'T WANT DAT CLASS TO EVER END! WELL, GOOD LUCK WIT' DA CONFERENCE!
YEAH! WITH YOUR DAD BACKING YOU UP, IT'LL BE A CINCH!
AHEM.
CAN I JUST DIE--I MEAN, CAN I JUST GET THIS OVER WITH...?

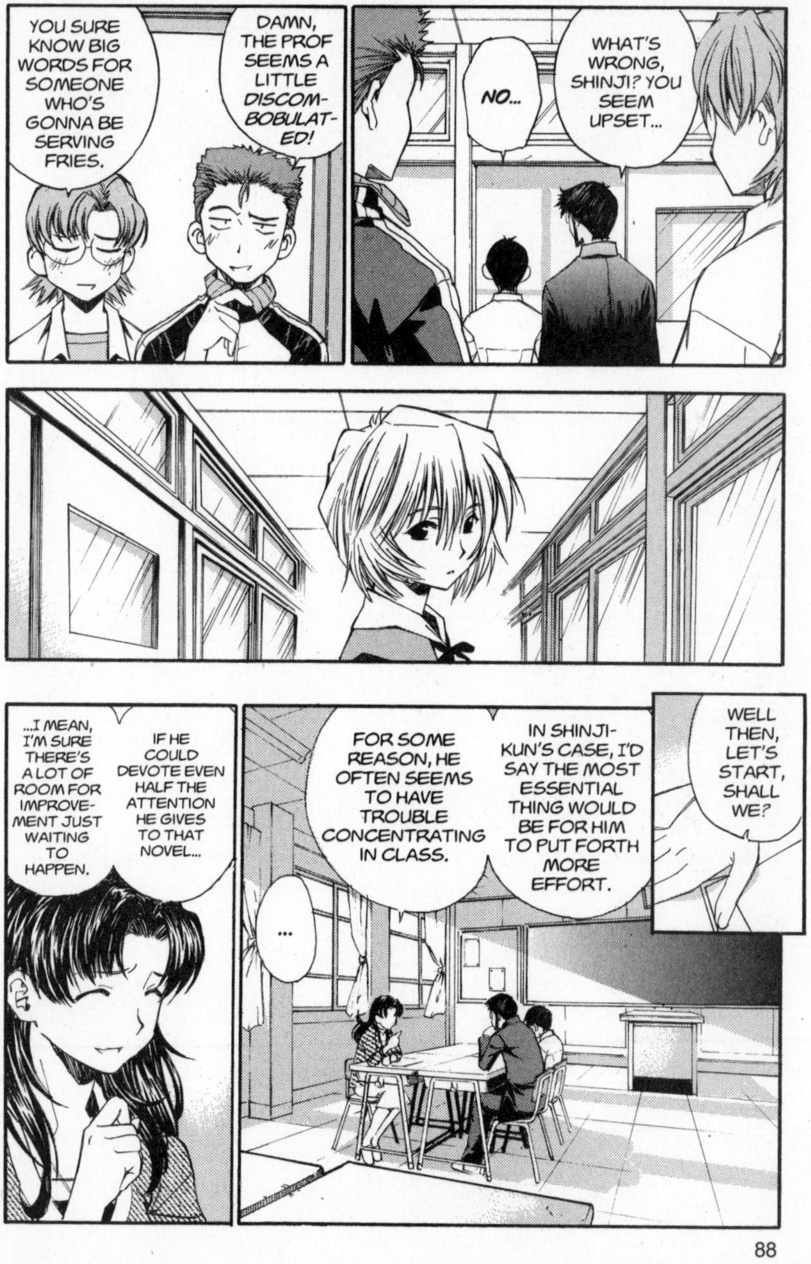
WHAT'S WRONG, SHINJI? YOU SEEM UPSET...
NO...
DAMN, THE PROF SEEMS A LITTLE DISCOMBOBULATED!
YOU SURE KNOW BIG WORDS FOR SOMEONE WHO'S GONNA BE SERVING FRIES.
WELL THEN, LET'S START, SHALL WE?
IN SHINJI-KUN'S CASE, I'D SAY THE MOST ESSENTIAL THING WOULD BE FOR HIM TO PUT FORTH MORE EFFORT.
FOR SOME REASON, HE OFTEN SEEMS TO HAVE TROUBLE CONCENTRATING IN CLASS.
...
IF HE COULD DEVOTE EVEN HALF THE ATTENTION HE GIVES TO THAT NOVEL...
...I MEAN, I'M SURE THERE'S A LOT OF ROOM FOR IMPROVEMENT JUST WAITING TO HAPPEN.

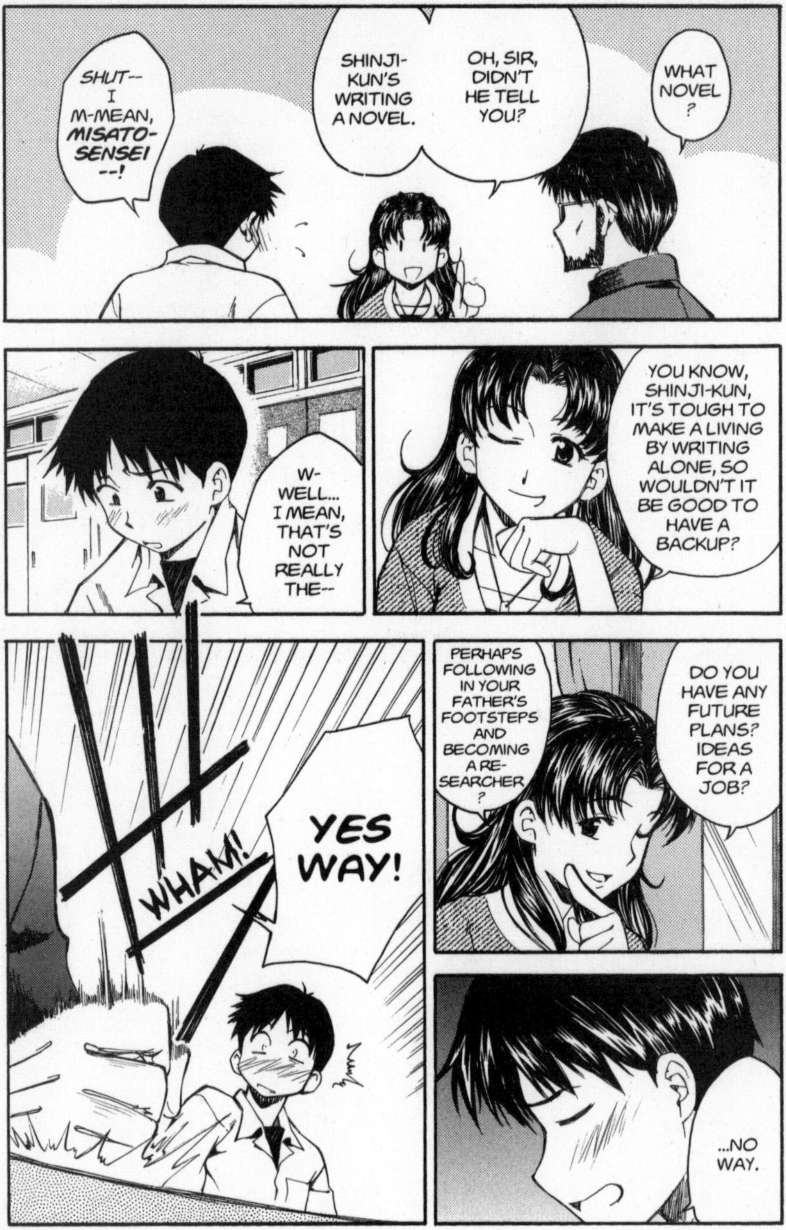
WHAT NOVEL?
OH, SIR, DIDN'T HE TELL YOU?
SHINJI-KUN'S WRITING A NOVEL.
SHUT-- I M-MEAN, MISATO-SENSEI--!
YOU KNOW, SHINJI-KUN, IT'S TOUGH TO MAKE A LIVING BY WRITING ALONE, SO WOULDN'T IT BE GOOD TO HAVE A BACKUP?
W-WELL... I MEAN, THAT'S NOT REALLY THE--
DO YOU HAVE ANY FUTURE PLANS? IDEAS FOR A JOB?
PERHAPS FOLLOWING IN YOUR FATHER'S FOOTSTEPS AND BECOMING A RE-SEARCHER?
...NO WAY.
YES WAY!
WHAM!

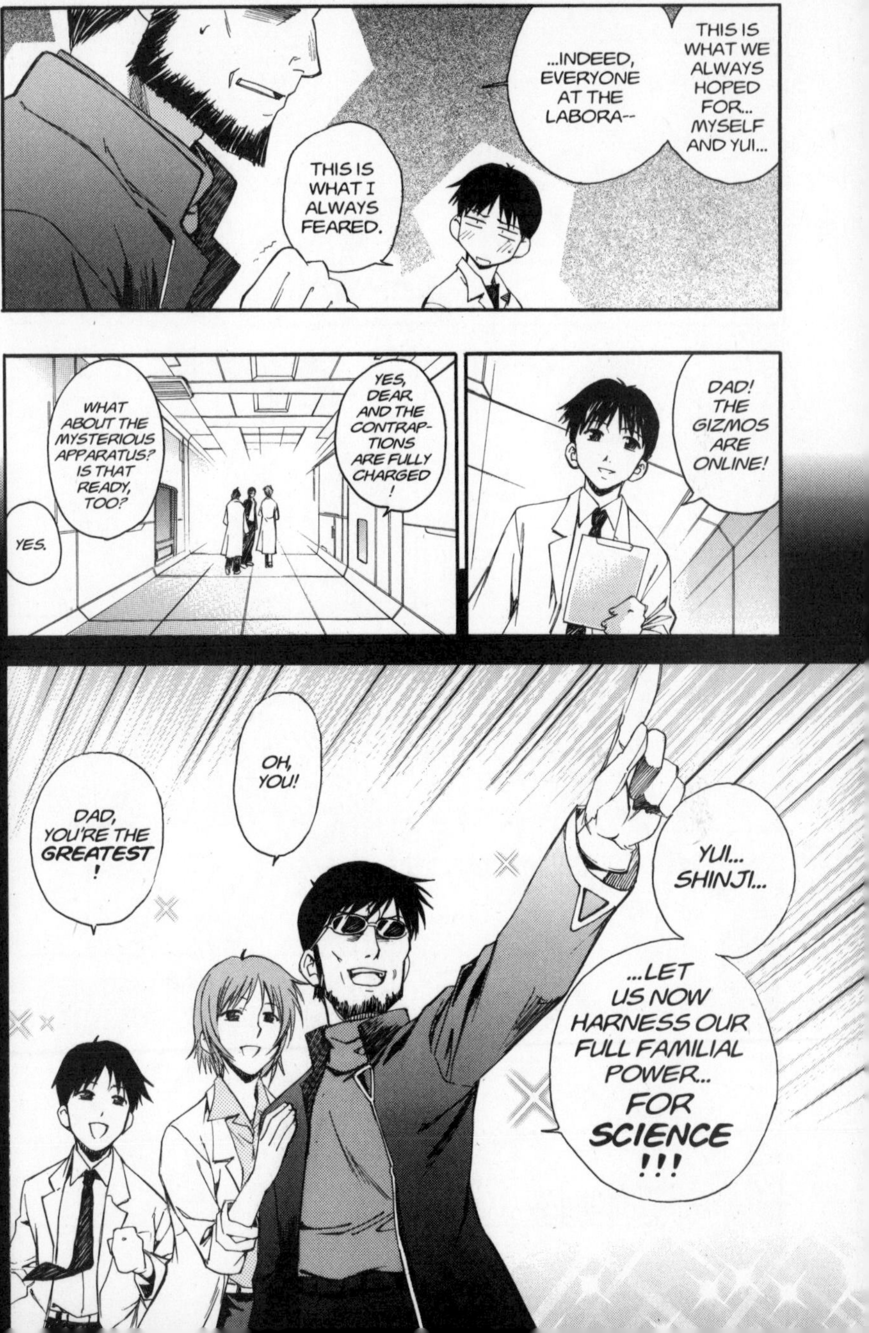
THIS IS WHAT WE ALWAYS HOPED FOR... MYSELF AND YUI...
...INDEED, EVERYONE AT THE LABORA--
THIS IS WHAT I ALWAYS FEARED.
DAD! THE GIZMOS ARE ONLINE!
YES, DEAR, AND THE CONTRAPTIONS ARE FULLY CHARGED!
WHAT ABOUT THE MYSTERIOUS APPARATUS? IS THAT READY, TOO?
YES.
YUI... SHINJI...
...LET US NOW HARNESS OUR FULL FAMILIAL POWER... FOR SCIENCE!!!
OH, YOU!
DAD, YOU'RE THE GREATEST!

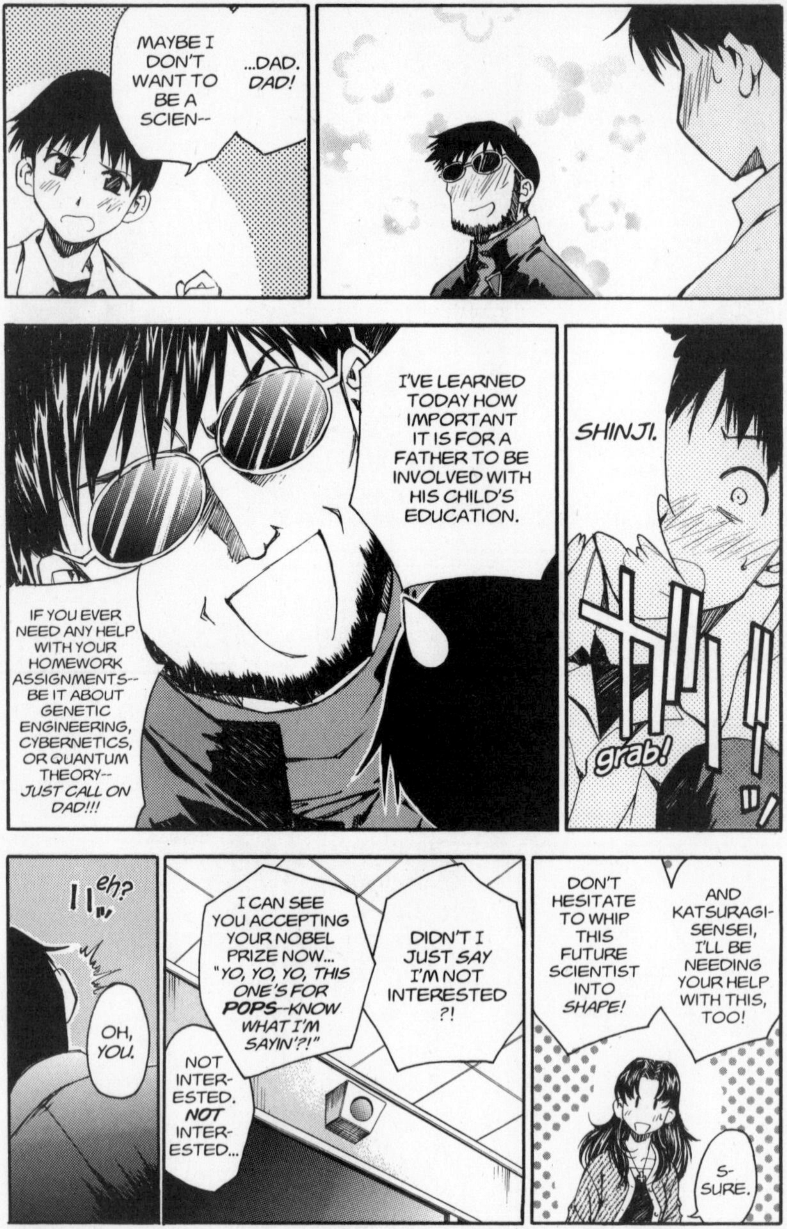
MAYBE I DON'T WANT TO BE A SCIEN--
...DAD. DAD!
SHINJI.
grab!
I'VE LEARNED TODAY HOW IMPORTANT IT IS FOR A FATHER TO BE INVOLVED WITH HIS CHILD'S EDUCATION.
IF YOU EVER NEED ANY HELP WITH YOUR HOMEWORK ASSIGNMENTS--BE IT ABOUT GENETIC ENGINEERING, CYBERNETICS, OR QUANTUM THEORY--JUST CALL ON DAD!!!
AND KATSURAGI-SENSEI, I'LL BE NEEDING YOUR HELP WITH THIS, TOO!
DON'T HESITATE TO WHIP THIS FUTURE SCIENTIST INTO SHAPE!
S-SURE.
DIDN'T I JUST SAY I'M NOT INTERESTED?!
I CAN SEE YOU ACCEPTING YOUR NOBEL PRIZE NOW... "YO, YO, YO, THIS ONE'S FOR POPS--KNOW WHAT I'M SAYIN'?!"
NOT INTER-ESTED. NOT INTER-ESTED...
eh?
OH, YOU.

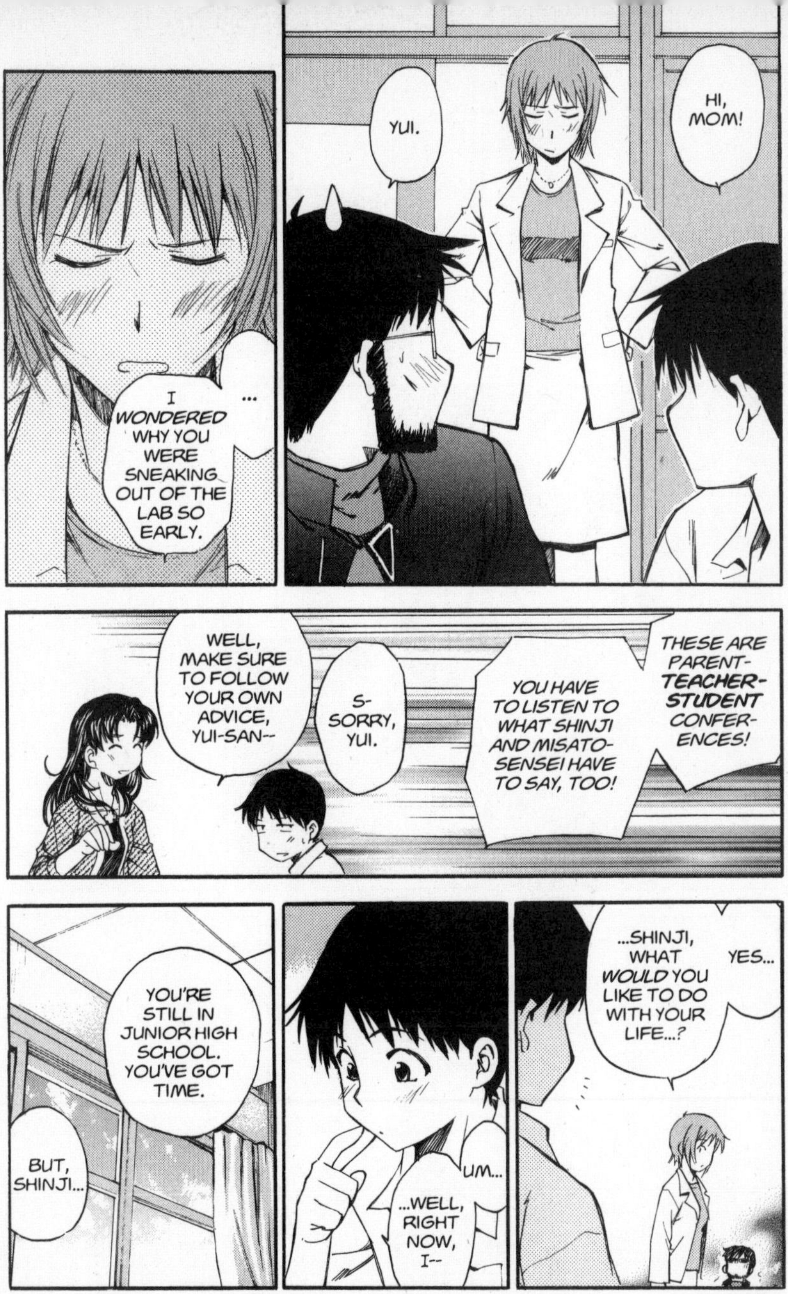
HI, MOM!
YUI.
...
I WONDERED WHY YOU WERE SNEAKING OUT OF THE LAB SO EARLY.
THESE ARE PARENT-TEACHER-STUDENT CONFERENCES!
YOU HAVE TO LISTEN TO WHAT SHINJI AND MISATO-SENSEI HAVE TO SAY, TOO!
S-SORRY, YUI.
WELL, MAKE SURE TO FOLLOW YOUR OWN ADVICE, YUI-SAN--
YES...
...SHINJI, WHAT WOULD YOU LIKE TO DO WITH YOUR LIFE...?
UM...
...WELL, RIGHT NOW, I--
YOU'RE STILL IN JUNIOR HIGH SCHOOL. YOU'VE GOT TIME.
BUT, SHINJI...

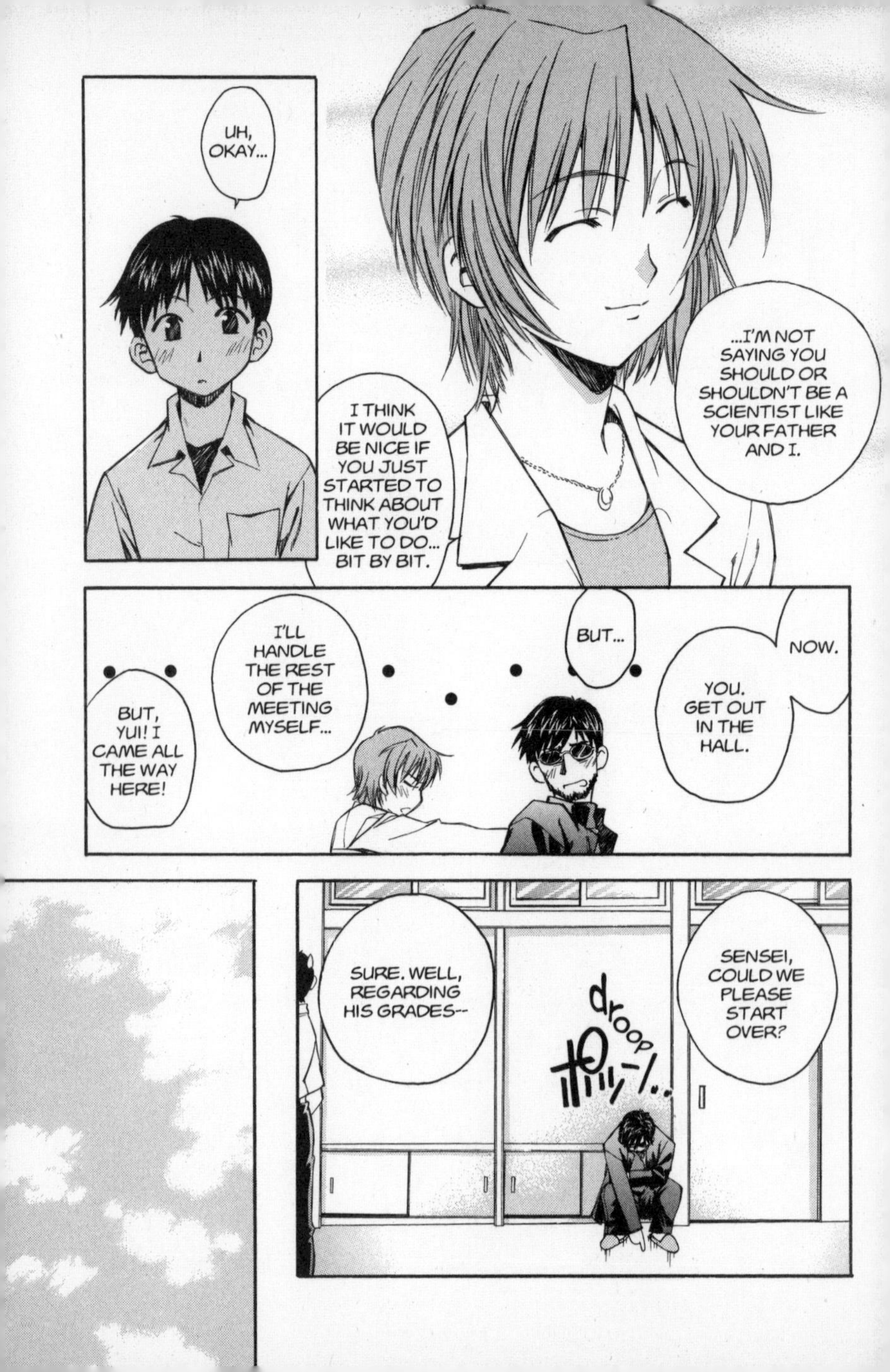
...I'M NOT SAYING YOU SHOULD OR SHOULDN'T BE A SCIENTIST LIKE YOUR FATHER AND I.
I THINK IT WOULD BE NICE IF YOU JUST STARTED TO THINK ABOUT WHAT YOU'D LIKE TO DO... BIT BY BIT.
UH, OKAY...
NOW.
YOU. GET OUT IN THE HALL.
BUT...
I'LL HANDLE THE REST OF THE MEETING MYSELF...
BUT, YUI! I CAME ALL THE WAY HERE!
SENSEI, COULD WE PLEASE START OVER?
droop
SURE. WELL, REGARDING HIS GRADES--

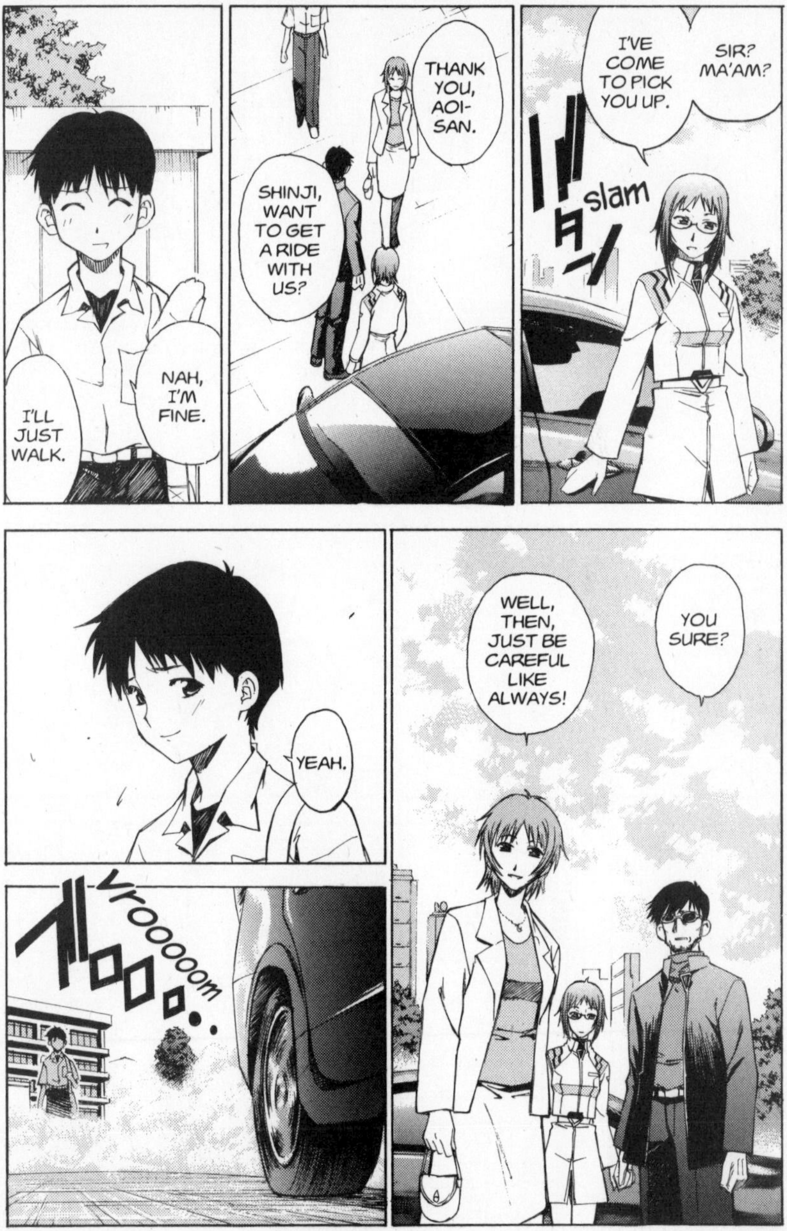
SIR? MA'AM?
I'VE COME TO PICK YOU UP.
slam
THANK YOU, AOI-SAN.
SHINJI, WANT TO GET A RIDE WITH US?
NAH, I'M FINE.
I'LL JUST WALK.
YOU SURE?
WELL, THEN, JUST BE CAREFUL LIKE ALWAYS!
YEAH.
vroooooom...

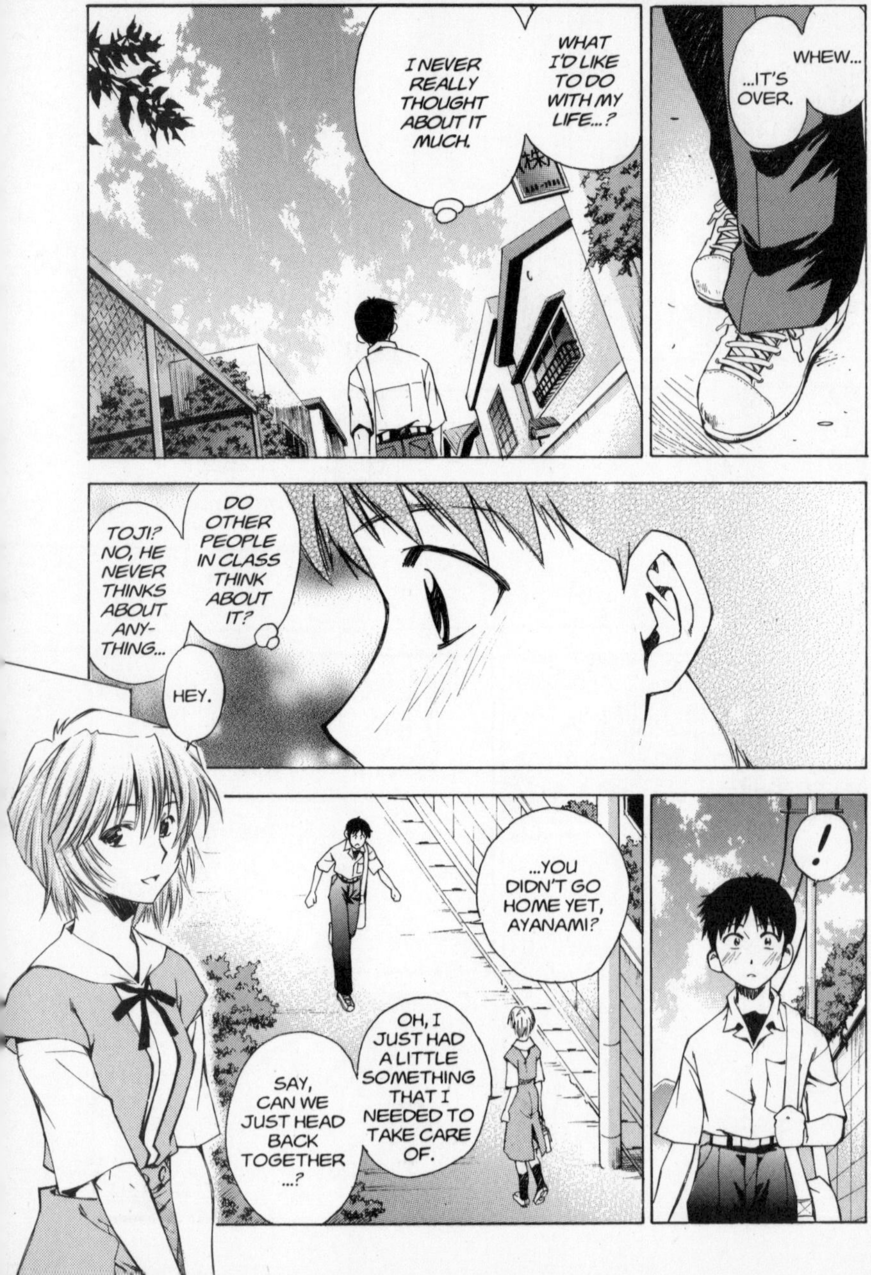
WHEW...
...IT'S OVER.
WHAT I'D LIKE TO DO WITH MY LIFE...?
I NEVER REALLY THOUGHT ABOUT IT MUCH.
DO OTHER PEOPLE IN CLASS THINK ABOUT IT?
TOJI? NO, HE NEVER THINKS ABOUT ANY-THING...
HEY.
!
...YOU DIDN'T GO HOME YET, AYANAMI?
OH, I JUST HAD A LITTLE SOMETHING THAT I NEEDED TO TAKE CARE OF.
SAY, CAN WE JUST HEAD BACK TOGETHER ...?

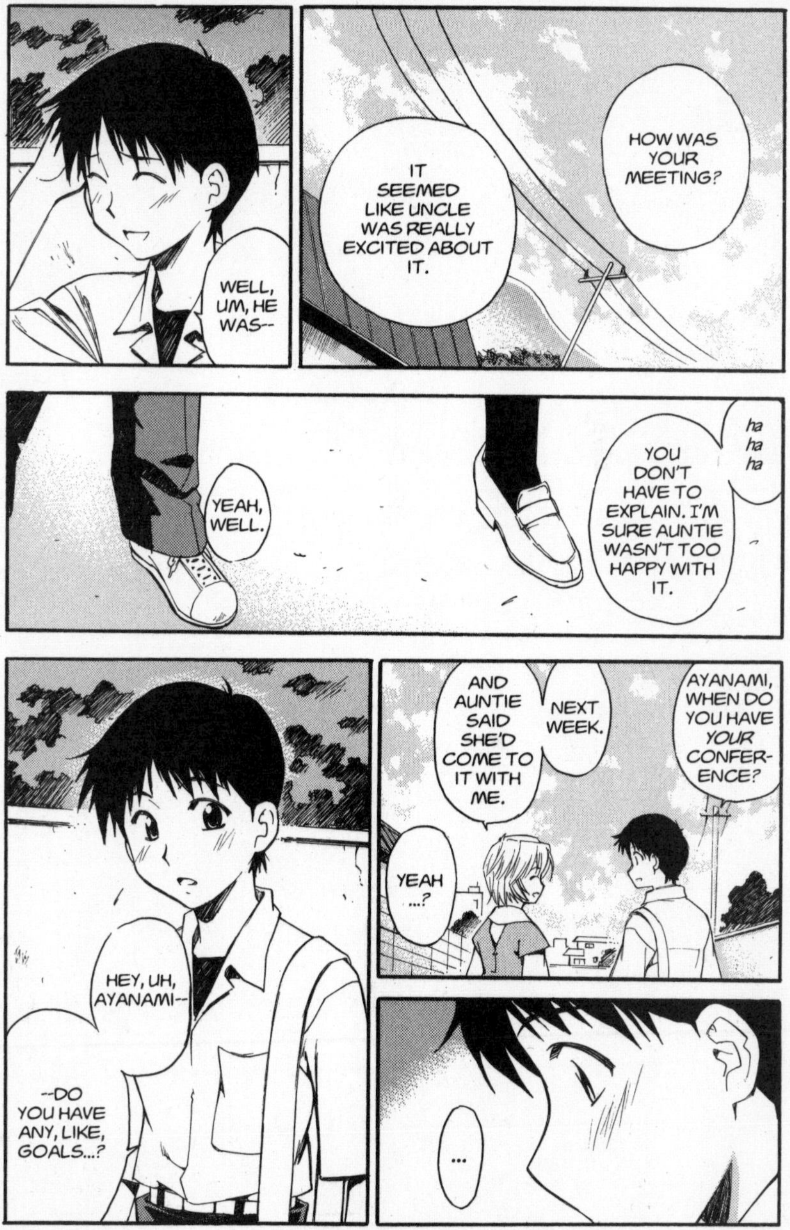
HOW WAS YOUR MEETING?
IT SEEMED LIKE UNCLE WAS REALLY EXCITED ABOUT IT.
WELL, UM, HE WAS--
ha ha ha
YOU DON'T HAVE TO EXPLAIN. I'M SURE AUNTIE WASN'T TOO HAPPY WITH IT.
YEAH, WELL.
AYANAMI, WHEN DO YOU HAVE *YOUR* CONFERENCE?
NEXT WEEK.
AND AUNTIE SAID SHE'D COME TO IT WITH ME.
YEAH ...?
...
HEY, UH, AYANAMI--
--DO YOU HAVE ANY, LIKE, GOALS...?

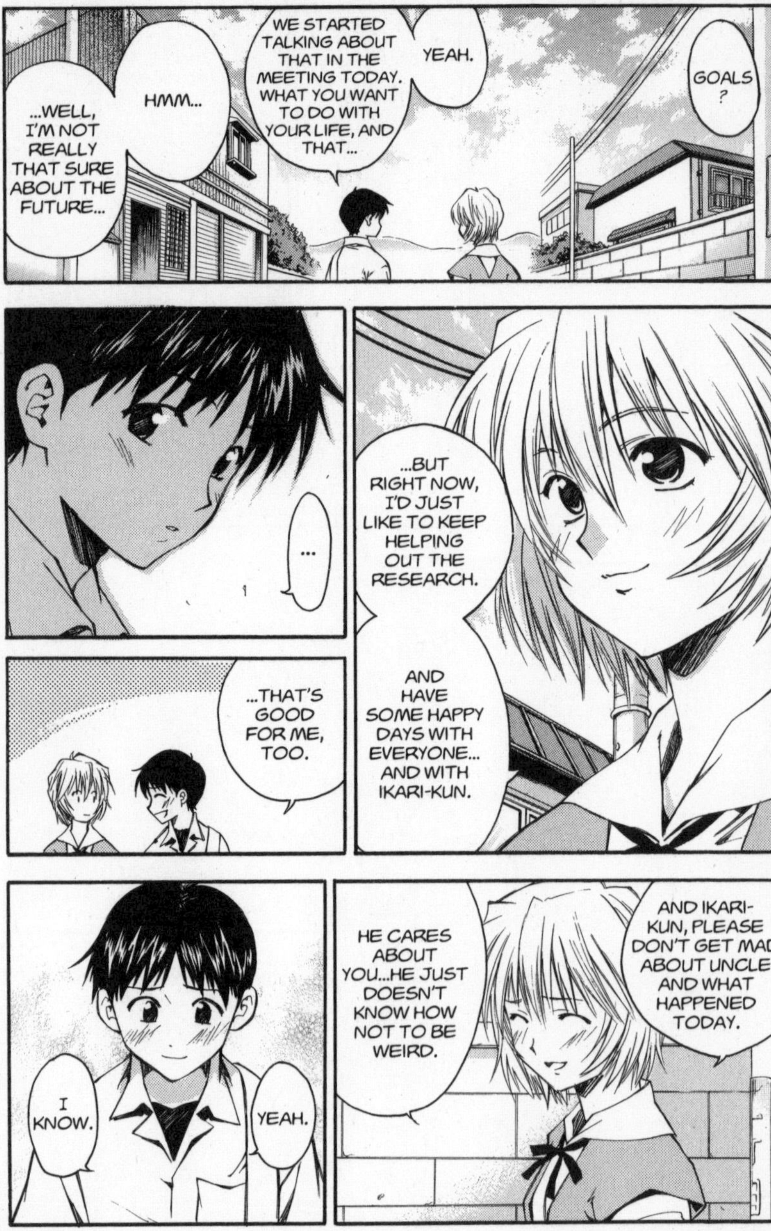
GOALS?
YEAH.
WE STARTED TALKING ABOUT THAT IN THE MEETING TODAY. WHAT YOU WANT TO DO WITH YOUR LIFE, AND THAT...
HMM...
...WELL, I'M NOT REALLY THAT SURE ABOUT THE FUTURE...
...BUT RIGHT NOW, I'D JUST LIKE TO KEEP HELPING OUT THE RESEARCH.
AND HAVE SOME HAPPY DAYS WITH EVERYONE... AND WITH IKARI-KUN.
...
...THAT'S GOOD FOR ME, TOO.
AND IKARI-KUN, PLEASE DON'T GET MAD ABOUT UNCLE AND WHAT HAPPENED TODAY.
HE CARES ABOUT YOU...HE JUST DOESN'T KNOW HOW NOT TO BE WEIRD.
YEAH.
I KNOW.

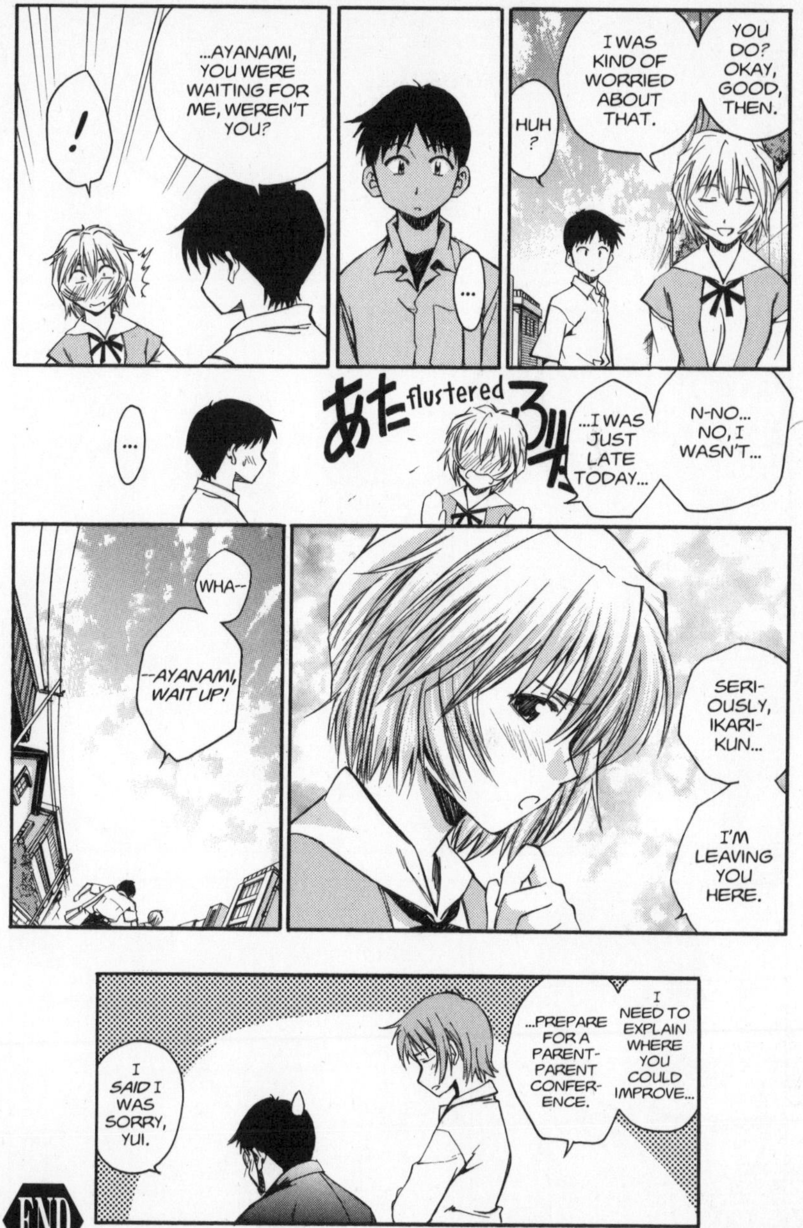
YOU DO? OKAY, GOOD, THEN.
I WAS KIND OF WORRIED ABOUT THAT.
HUH?
...
...AYANAMI, YOU WERE WAITING FOR ME, WEREN'T YOU?
!
N-NO... NO, I WASN'T...
...I WAS JUST LATE TODAY...
あた flustered
...
SERI-OUSLY, IKARI-KUN...
I'M LEAVING YOU HERE.
WHA--
--AYANAMI, WAIT UP!
I NEED TO EXPLAIN WHERE YOU COULD IMPROVE...
...PREPARE FOR A PARENT-PARENT CONFERENCE.
I SAID I WAS SORRY, YUI.
END

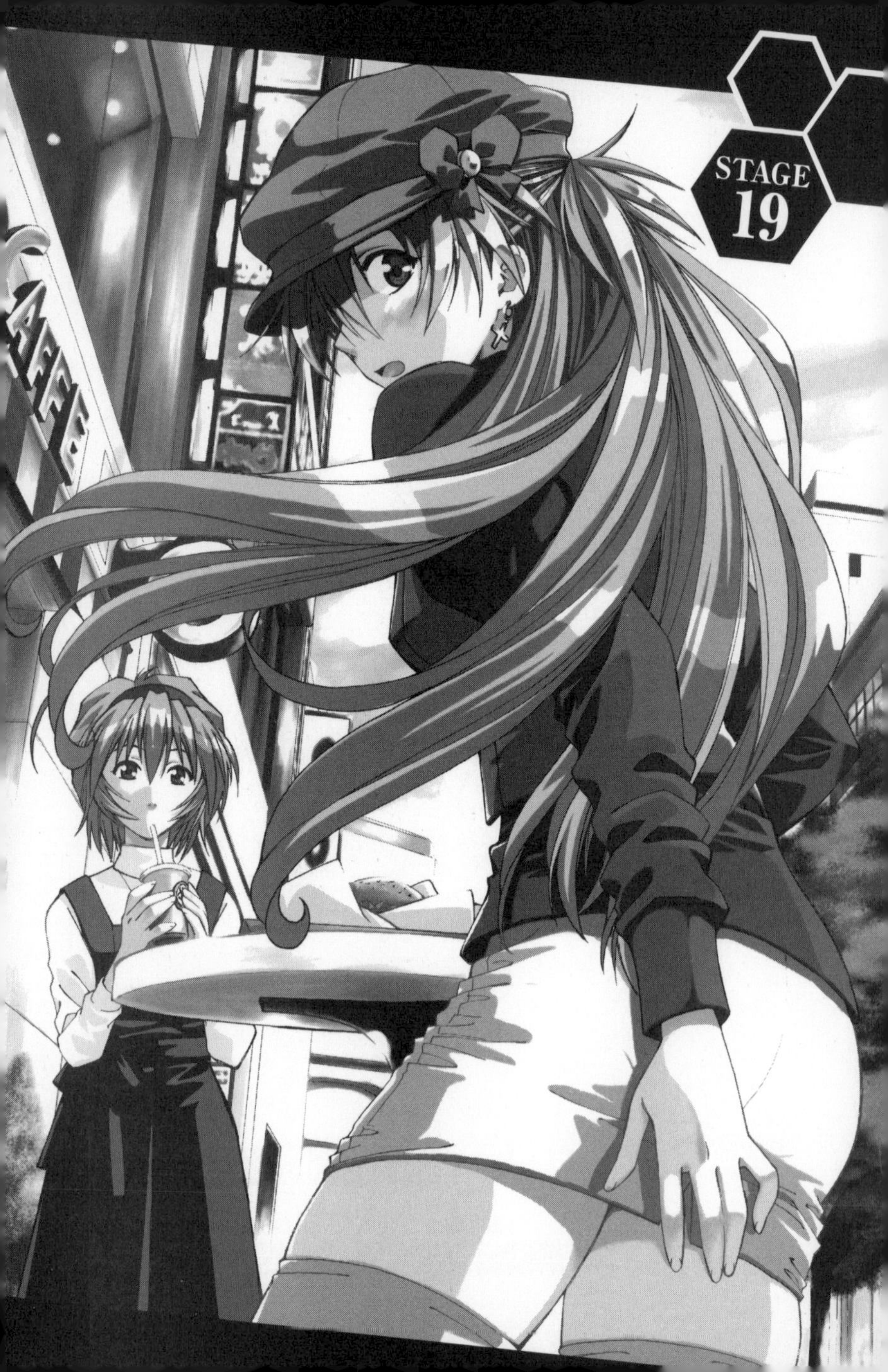
STAGE
19

NEON GENESIS
EVANGELION
THE SHINJI IKARI RAISING PROJECT

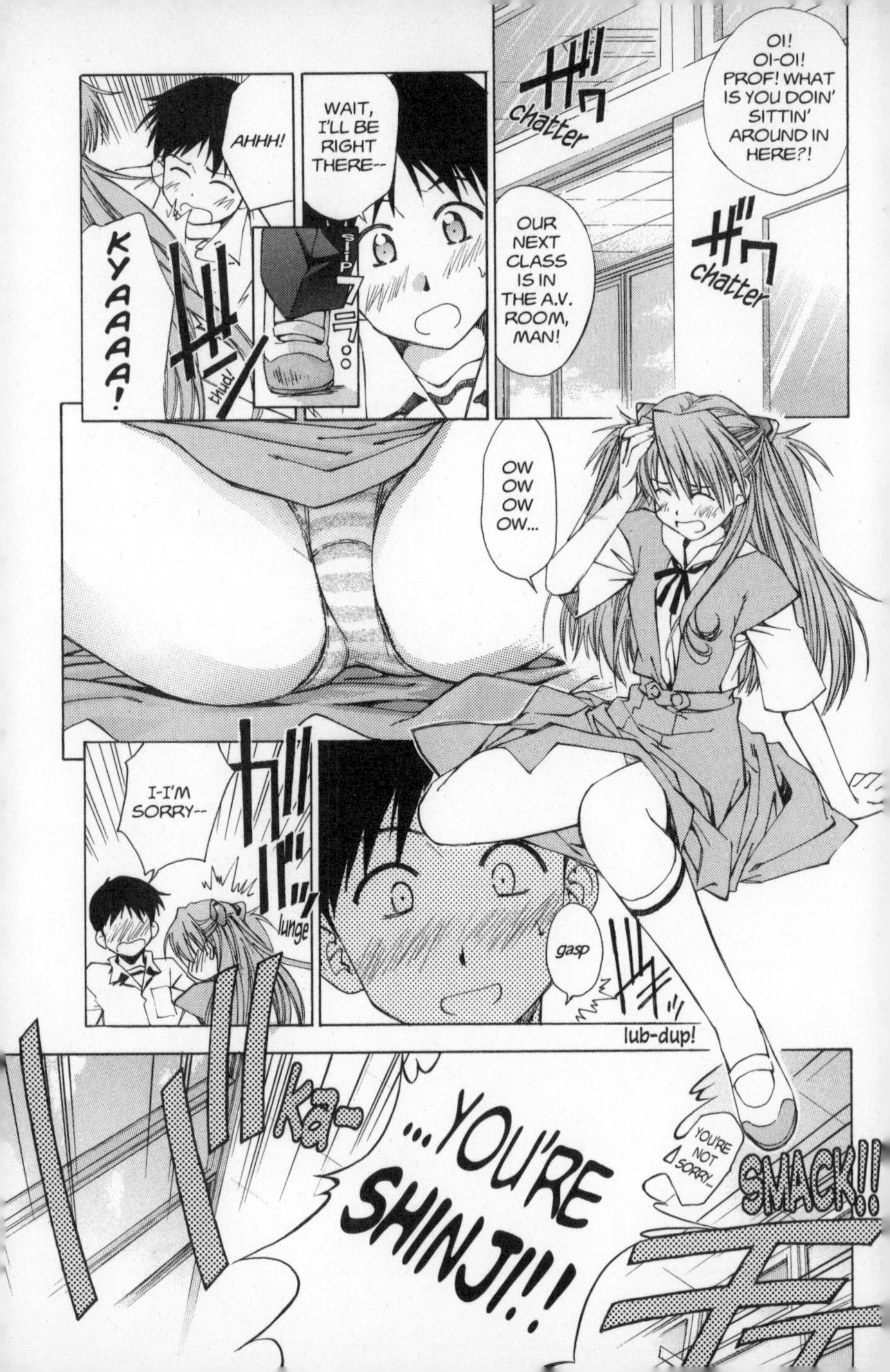

chatter
OI! OI-OI! PROF! WHAT IS YOU DOIN' SITTIN' AROUND IN HERE?!
chatter
OUR NEXT CLASS IS IN THE A.V. ROOM, MAN!
WAIT, I'LL BE RIGHT THERE--
SLIP
AHHH!
KYAAAAA!
thud!
OW OW OW OW...
gasp
lub-dup!
I-I'M SORRY--
lunge
YOU'RE NOT SORRY...
SMACK!!
ka-
...YOU'RE SHINJI!!

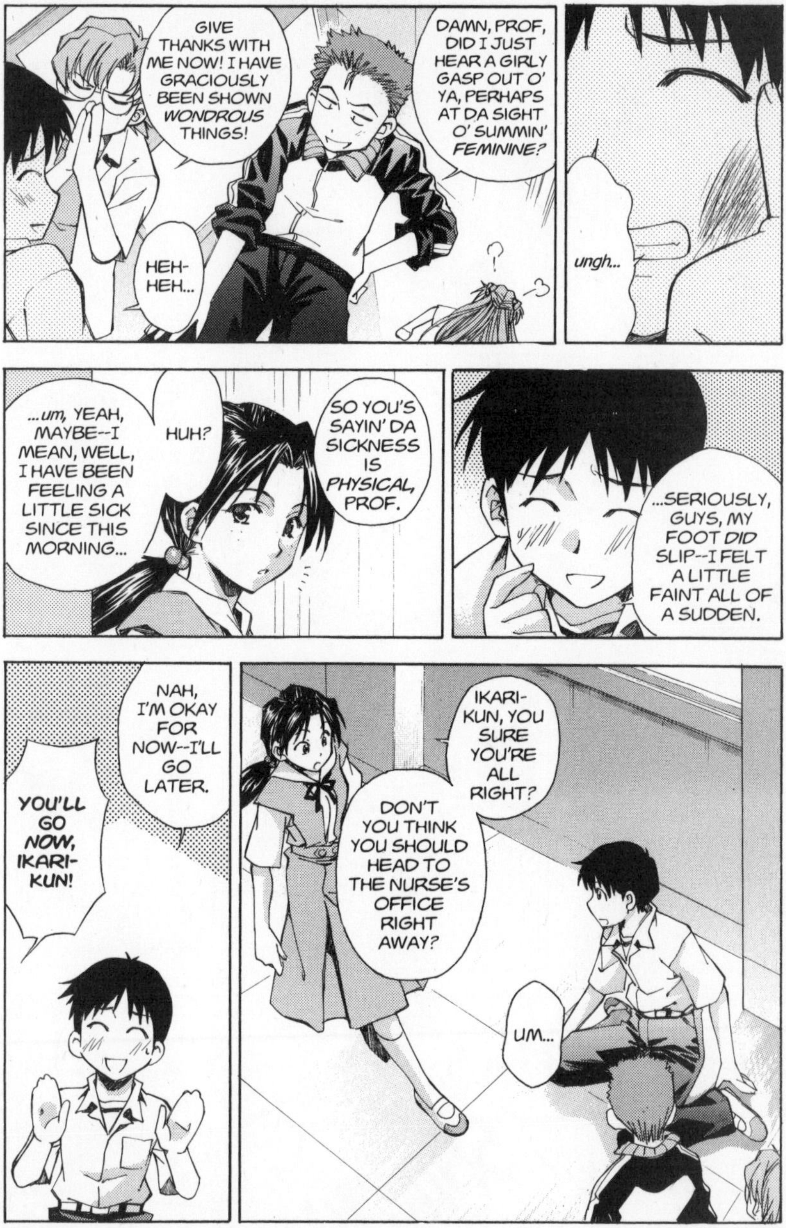
ungh...
DAMN, PROF, DID I JUST HEAR A GIRLY GASP OUT O' YA, PERHAPS AT DA SIGHT O' SUMMIN' *FEMININE?*
GIVE THANKS WITH ME NOW! I HAVE GRACIOUSLY BEEN SHOWN *WONDROUS* THINGS!
HEH-HEH...
...SERIOUSLY, GUYS, MY FOOT *DID* SLIP--I FELT A LITTLE FAINT ALL OF A SUDDEN.
SO YOU'S SAYIN' DA SICKNESS IS *PHYSICAL,* PROF.
HUH?
...um, YEAH, MAYBE--I MEAN, WELL, I HAVE BEEN FEELING A LITTLE SICK SINCE THIS MORNING...
IKARI-KUN, YOU SURE YOU'RE ALL RIGHT?
DON'T YOU THINK YOU SHOULD HEAD TO THE NURSE'S OFFICE RIGHT AWAY?
UM...
NAH, I'M OKAY FOR NOW--I'LL GO LATER.
YOU'LL GO *NOW,* IKARI-KUN!

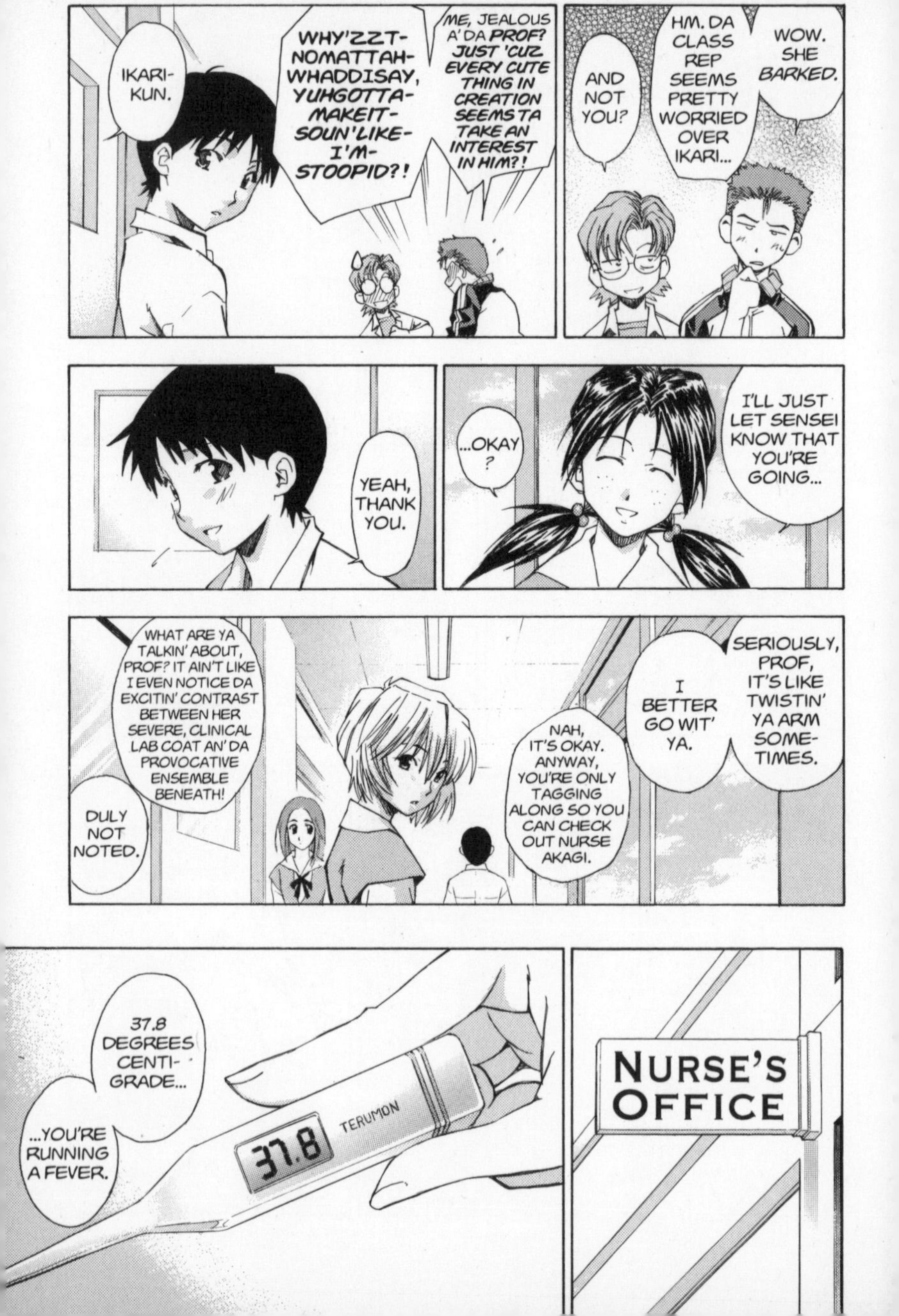
WOW. SHE BARKED.
HM. DA CLASS REP SEEMS PRETTY WORRIED OVER IKARI...
AND NOT YOU?
ME, JEALOUS A' DA PROF? JUST 'CUZ EVERY CUTE THING IN CREATION SEEMS TA TAKE AN INTEREST IN HIM?!
WHY'ZZT-NOMATTAH-WHADDISAY, YUHGOTTA-MAKEIT-SOUN'LIKE-I'M-STOOPID?!
IKARI-KUN.
I'LL JUST LET SENSEI KNOW THAT YOU'RE GOING...
...OKAY?
YEAH, THANK YOU.
SERIOUSLY, PROF, IT'S LIKE TWISTIN' YA ARM SOMETIMES.
I BETTER GO WIT' YA.
NAH, IT'S OKAY. ANYWAY, YOU'RE ONLY TAGGING ALONG SO YOU CAN CHECK OUT NURSE AKAGI.
WHAT ARE YA TALKIN' ABOUT, PROF? IT AIN'T LIKE I EVEN NOTICE DA EXCITIN' CONTRAST BETWEEN HER SEVERE, CLINICAL LAB COAT AN'DA PROVOCATIVE ENSEMBLE BENEATH!
DULY NOT NOTED.
NURSE'S OFFICE
37.8 DEGREES CENTIGRADE...
37.8
TERUMON
...YOU'RE RUNNING A FEVER.

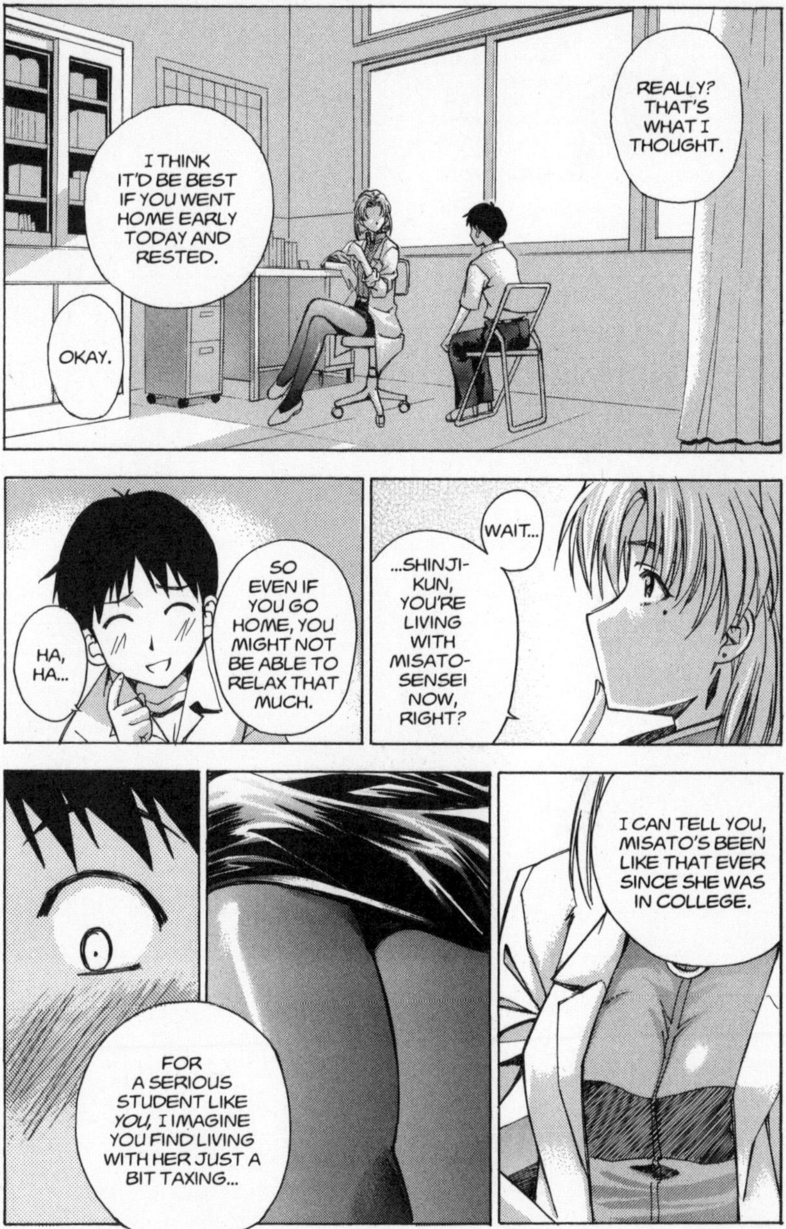
REALLY? THAT'S WHAT I THOUGHT.
I THINK IT'D BE BEST IF YOU WENT HOME EARLY TODAY AND RESTED.
OKAY.
WAIT...
...SHINJI-KUN, YOU'RE LIVING WITH MISATO-SENSEI NOW, RIGHT?
SO EVEN IF YOU GO HOME, YOU MIGHT NOT BE ABLE TO RELAX THAT MUCH.
HA, HA...
I CAN TELL YOU, MISATO'S BEEN LIKE THAT EVER SINCE SHE WAS IN COLLEGE.
FOR A SERIOUS STUDENT LIKE *YOU*, I IMAGINE YOU FIND LIVING WITH HER JUST A BIT TAXING...

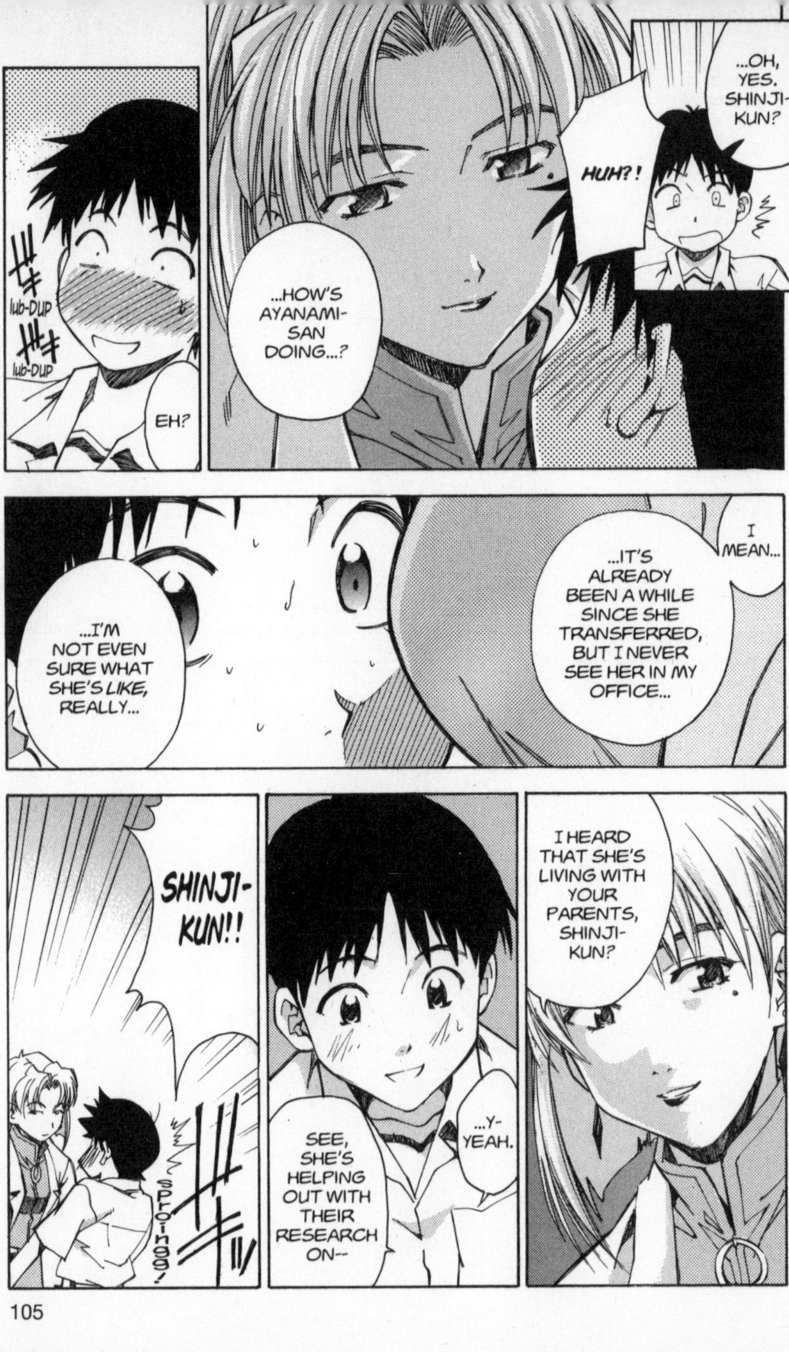

...OH, YES. SHINJI-KUN?
HUH?!
...HOW'S AYANAMI-SAN DOING...?
EH?
lub-DUP
lub-DUP
I MEAN...
...IT'S ALREADY BEEN A WHILE SINCE SHE TRANSFERRED, BUT I NEVER SEE HER IN MY OFFICE...
...I'M NOT EVEN SURE WHAT SHE'S *LIKE*, REALLY...
I HEARD THAT SHE'S LIVING WITH YOUR PARENTS, SHINJI-KUN?
...Y-YEAH.
SEE, SHE'S HELPING OUT WITH THEIR RESEARCH ON--
SHINJI-KUN!!
sproingg!

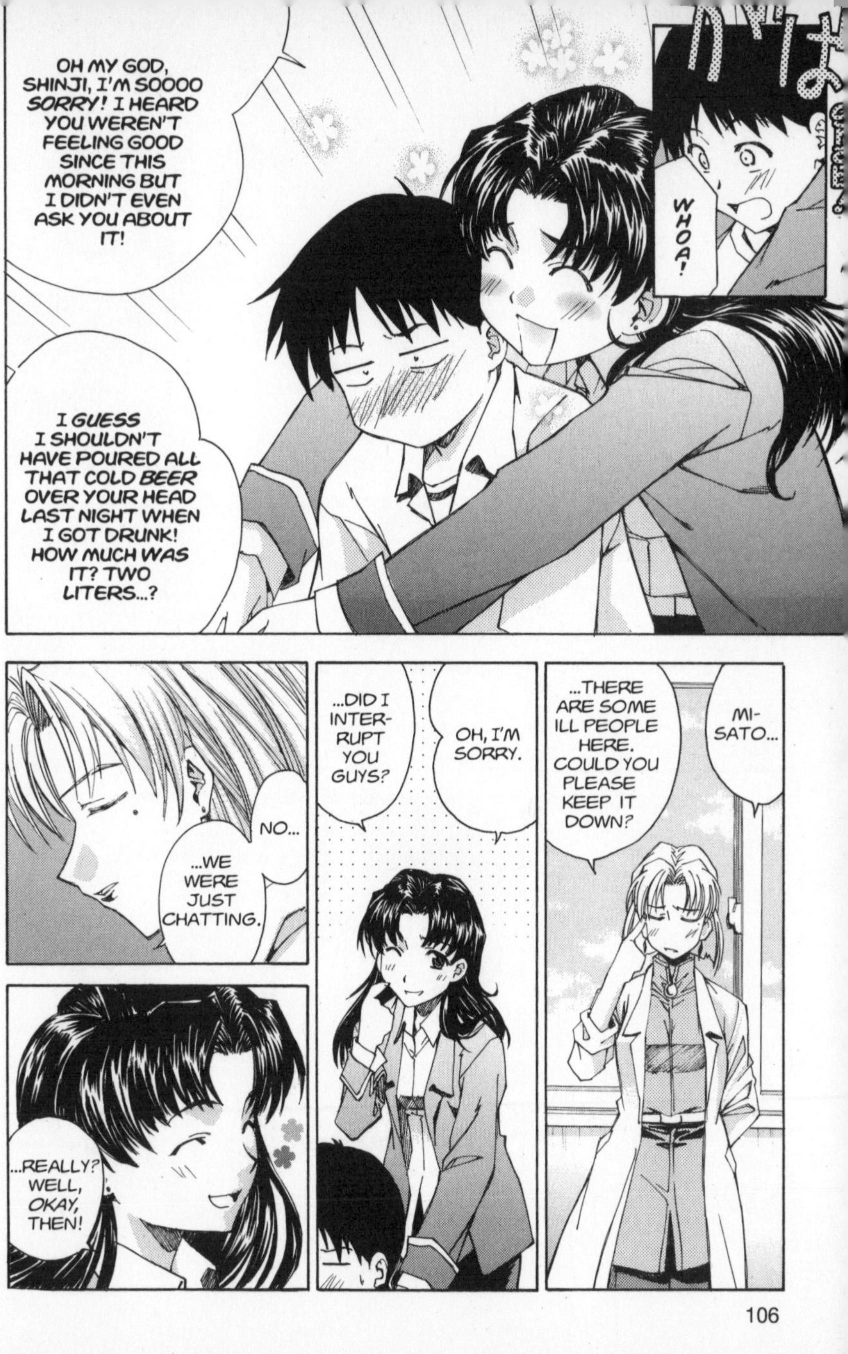
WHOA!
OH MY GOD, SHINJI, I'M SOOOO SORRY! I HEARD YOU WEREN'T FEELING GOOD SINCE THIS MORNING BUT I DIDN'T EVEN ASK YOU ABOUT IT!
I GUESS I SHOULDN'T HAVE POURED ALL THAT COLD BEER OVER YOUR HEAD LAST NIGHT WHEN I GOT DRUNK! HOW MUCH WAS IT? TWO LITERS...?
MI-SATO...
...THERE ARE SOME ILL PEOPLE HERE. COULD YOU PLEASE KEEP IT DOWN?
OH, I'M SORRY.
...DID I INTERRUPT YOU GUYS?
NO...
...WE WERE JUST CHATTING.
...REALLY? WELL, OKAY, THEN!

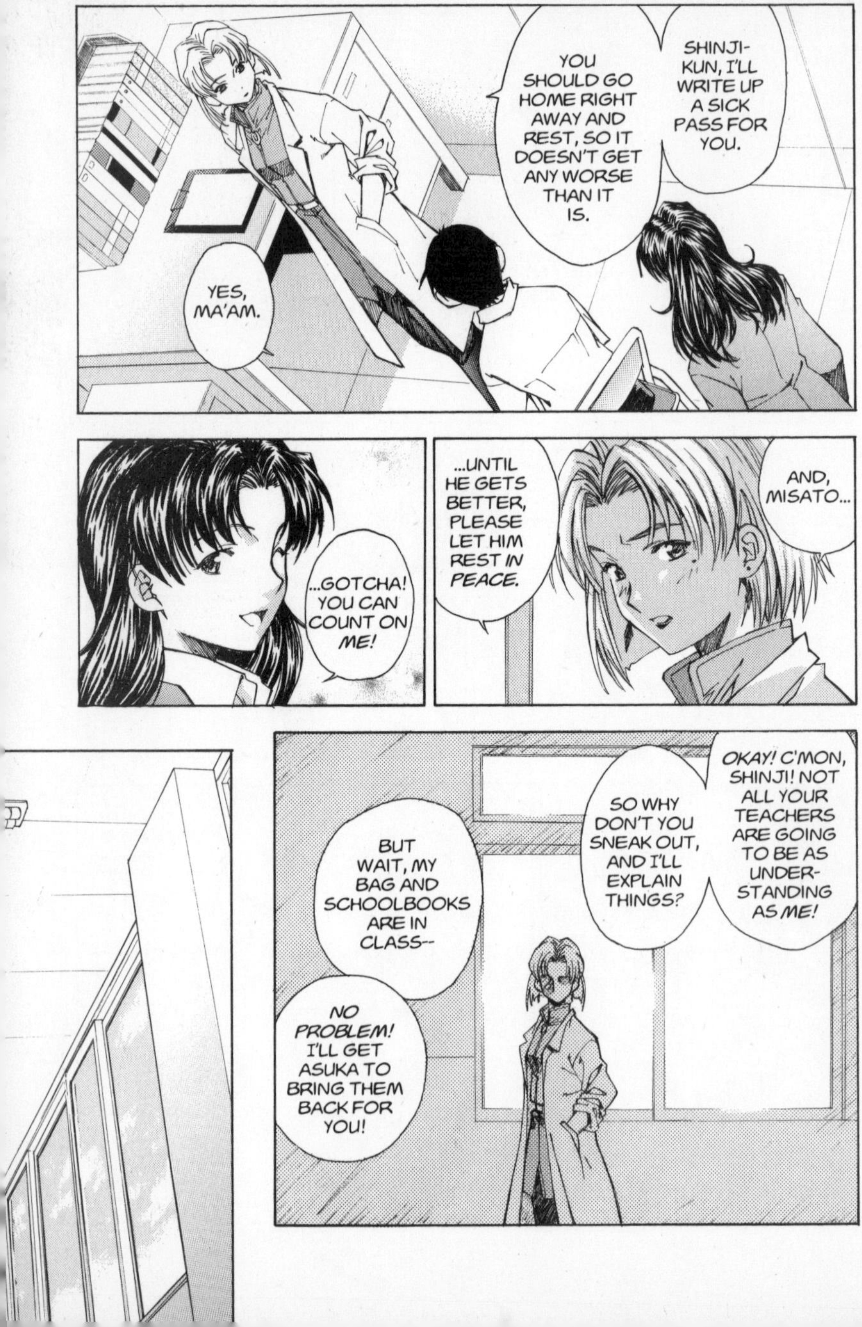
SHINJI-KUN, I'LL WRITE UP A SICK PASS FOR YOU.
YOU SHOULD GO HOME RIGHT AWAY AND REST, SO IT DOESN'T GET ANY WORSE THAN IT IS.
YES, MA'AM.
AND, MISATO...
...UNTIL HE GETS BETTER, PLEASE LET HIM REST IN *PEACE*.
...GOTCHA! YOU CAN COUNT ON *ME!*
OKAY! C'MON, SHINJI! NOT ALL YOUR TEACHERS ARE GOING TO BE AS UNDER-STANDING AS *ME!*
SO WHY DON'T YOU SNEAK OUT, AND I'LL EXPLAIN THINGS?
BUT WAIT, MY BAG AND SCHOOLBOOKS ARE IN CLASS--
NO PROBLEM! I'LL GET ASUKA TO BRING THEM BACK FOR YOU!

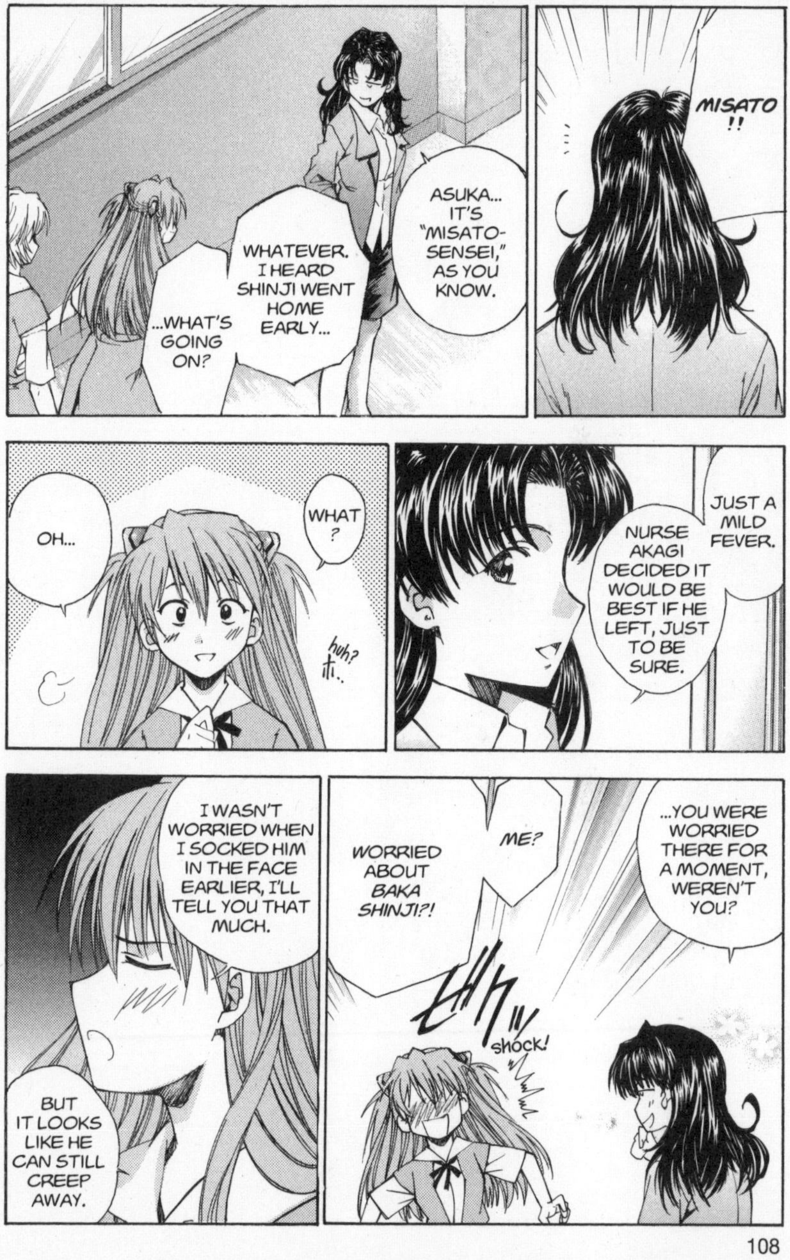
MISATO !!
ASUKA... IT'S "MISATO-SENSEI," AS YOU KNOW.
WHATEVER. I HEARD SHINJI WENT HOME EARLY...
...WHAT'S GOING ON?
JUST A MILD FEVER.
NURSE AKAGI DECIDED IT WOULD BE BEST IF HE LEFT, JUST TO BE SURE.
WHAT?
huh?
OH...
...YOU WERE WORRIED THERE FOR A MOMENT, WEREN'T YOU?
ME?
WORRIED ABOUT BAKA SHINJI?!
shock!
I WASN'T WORRIED WHEN I SOCKED HIM IN THE FACE EARLIER, I'LL TELL YOU THAT MUCH.
BUT IT LOOKS LIKE HE CAN STILL CREEP AWAY.

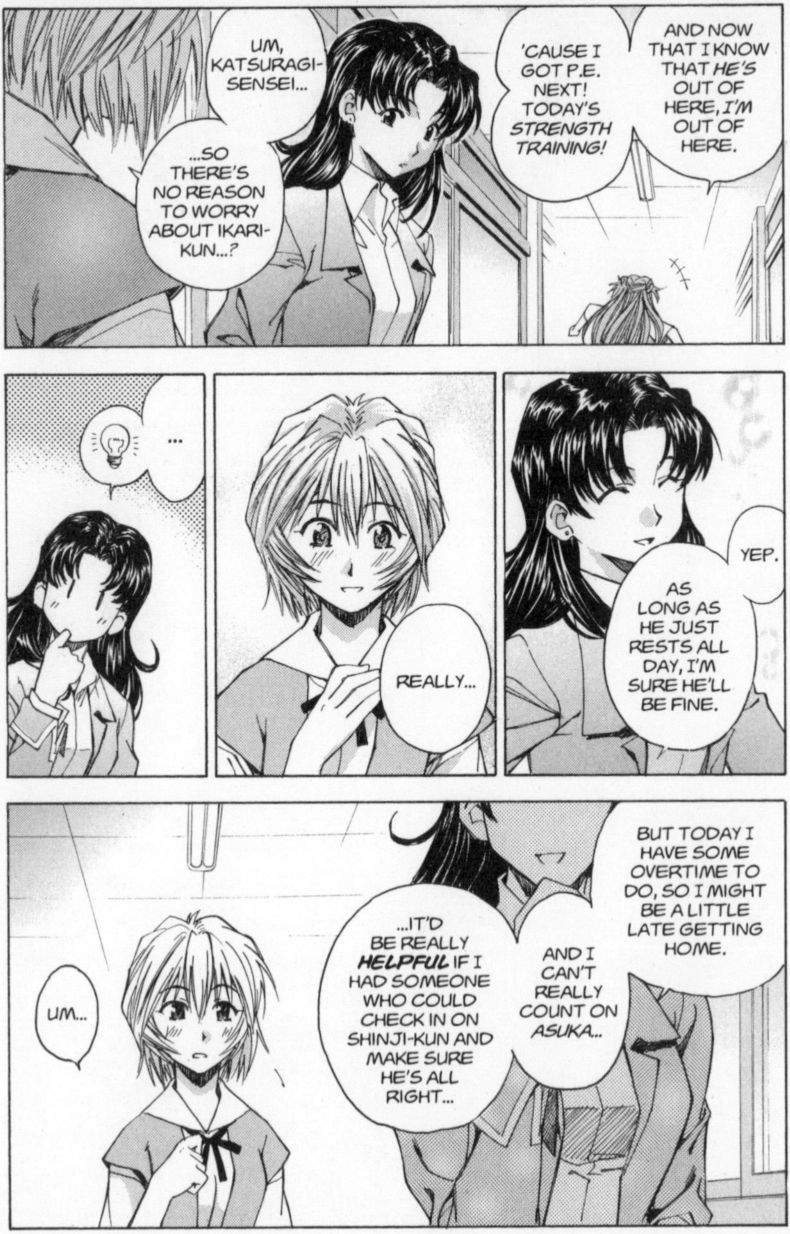
AND NOW THAT I KNOW THAT HE'S OUT OF HERE, I'M OUT OF HERE.
'CAUSE I GOT P.E. NEXT! TODAY'S STRENGTH TRAINING!
UM, KATSURAGI-SENSEI...
...SO THERE'S NO REASON TO WORRY ABOUT IKARI-KUN...?
YEP.
AS LONG AS HE JUST RESTS ALL DAY, I'M SURE HE'LL BE FINE.
REALLY...
...
BUT TODAY I HAVE SOME OVERTIME TO DO, SO I MIGHT BE A LITTLE LATE GETTING HOME.
AND I CAN'T REALLY COUNT ON ASUKA...
...IT'D BE REALLY HELPFUL IF I HAD SOMEONE WHO COULD CHECK IN ON SHINJI-KUN AND MAKE SURE HE'S ALL RIGHT...
UM...

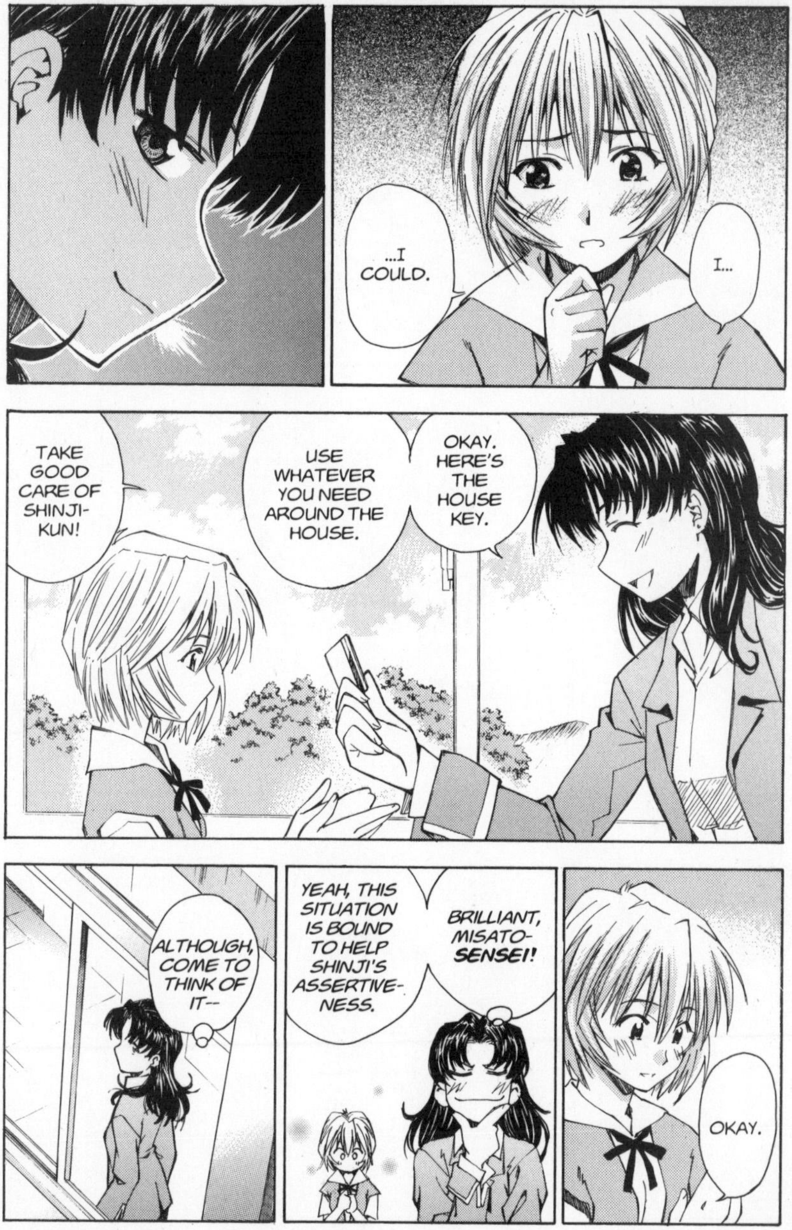
I...
...I COULD.
OKAY. HERE'S THE HOUSE KEY.
USE WHATEVER YOU NEED AROUND THE HOUSE.
TAKE GOOD CARE OF SHINJI-KUN!
OKAY.
BRILLIANT, MISATO-SENSEI!
YEAH, THIS SITUATION IS BOUND TO HELP SHINJI'S ASSERTIVE-NESS.
ALTHOUGH, COME TO THINK OF IT--

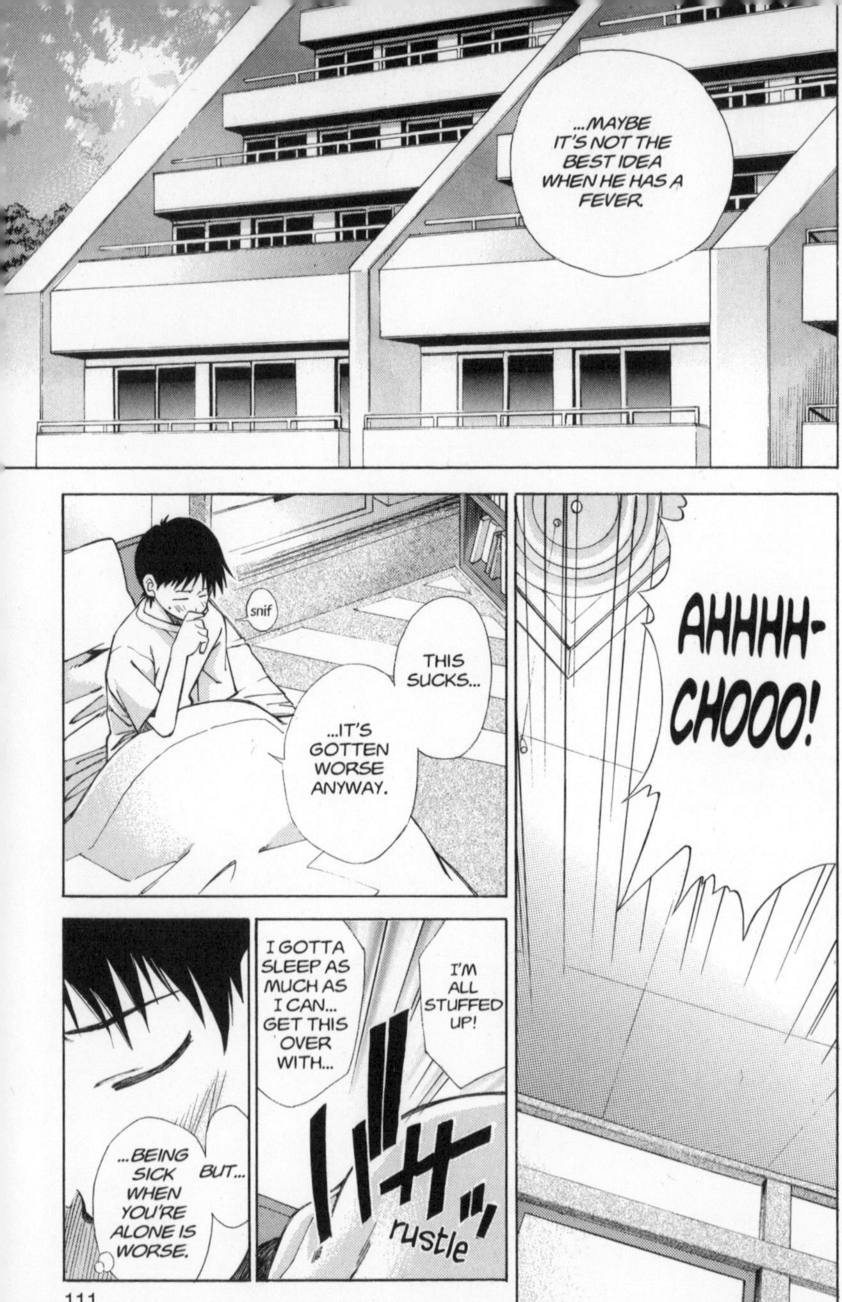
...MAYBE IT'S NOT THE BEST IDEA WHEN HE HAS A FEVER.
AHHHH-CHOOO!
snif
THIS SUCKS...
...IT'S GOTTEN WORSE ANYWAY.
I'M ALL STUFFED UP!
I GOTTA SLEEP AS MUCH AS I CAN... GET THIS OVER WITH...
rustle
BUT...
...BEING SICK WHEN YOU'RE ALONE IS WORSE.

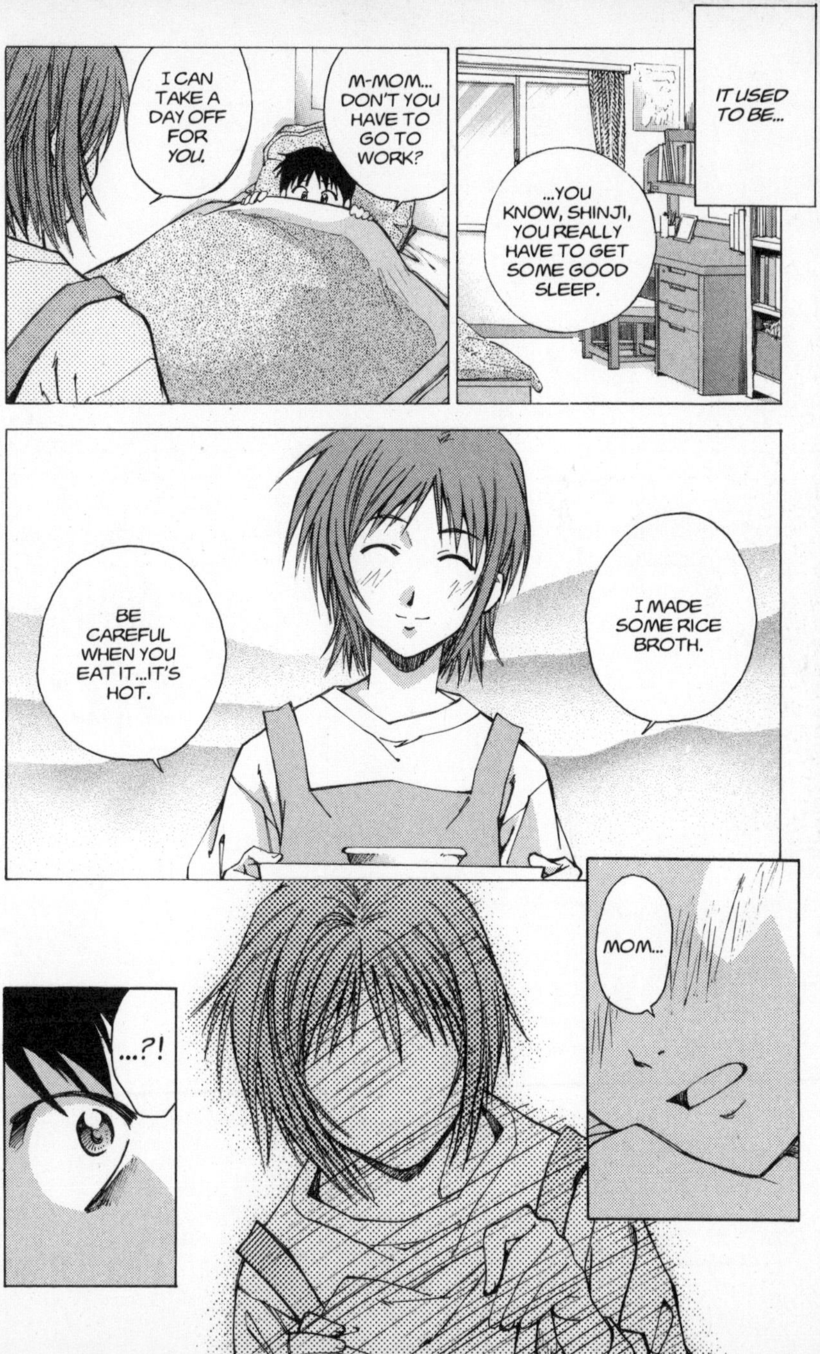
IT USED TO BE...
...YOU KNOW, SHINJI, YOU REALLY HAVE TO GET SOME GOOD SLEEP.
M-MOM... DON'T YOU HAVE TO GO TO WORK?
I CAN TAKE A DAY OFF FOR YOU.
I MADE SOME RICE BROTH.
BE CAREFUL WHEN YOU EAT IT...IT'S HOT.
MOM...
...?!

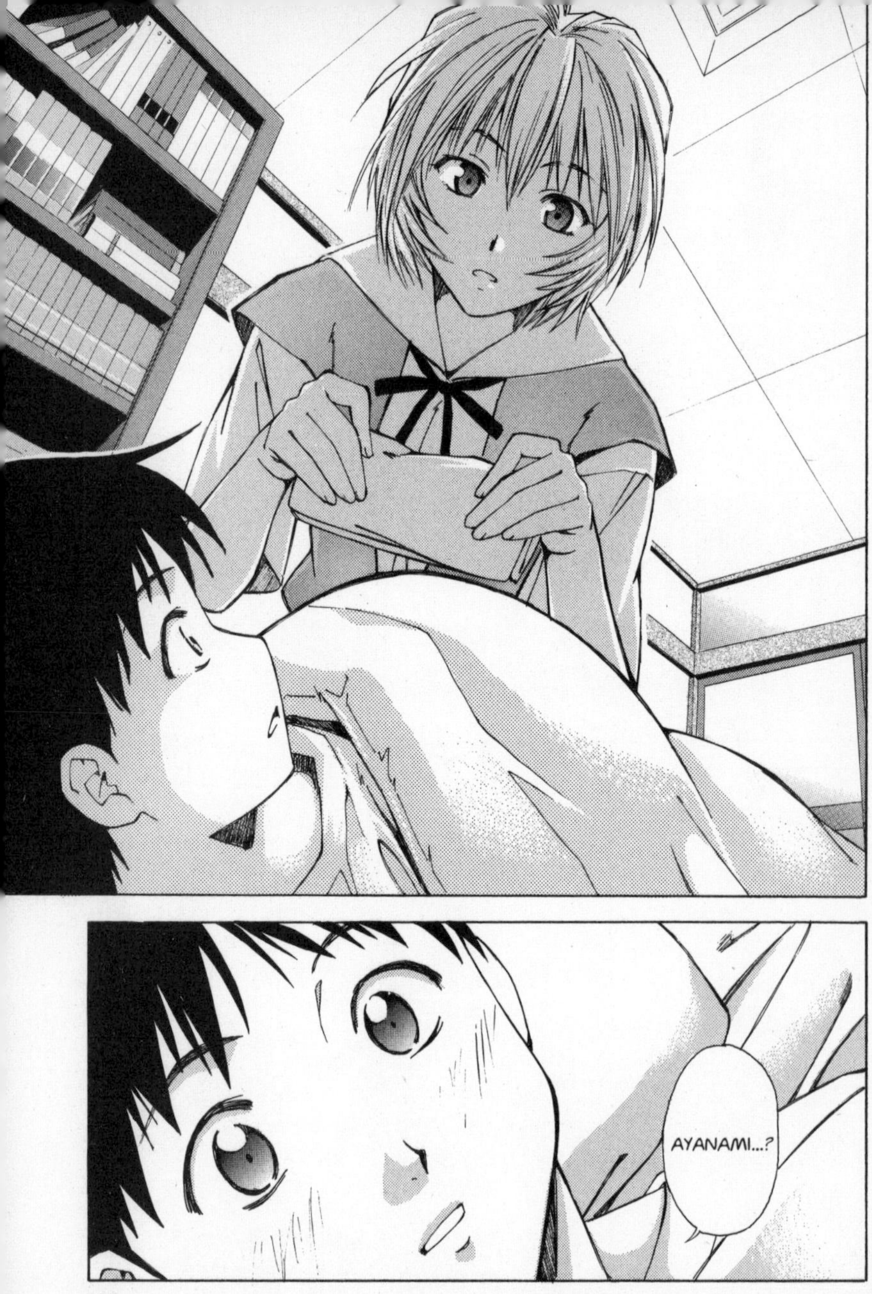
AYANAMI...?

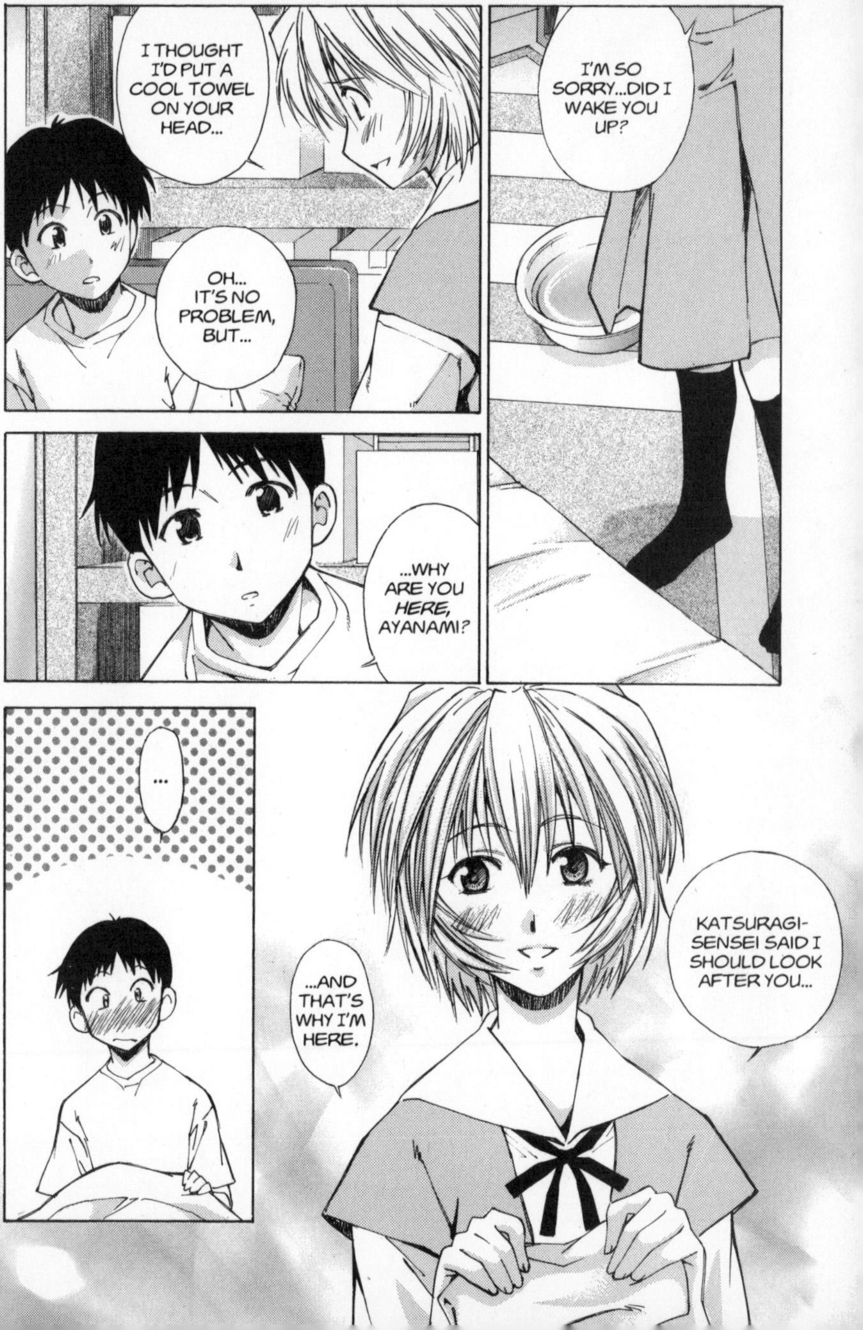
I'M SO SORRY...DID I WAKE YOU UP?
I THOUGHT I'D PUT A COOL TOWEL ON YOUR HEAD...
OH... IT'S NO PROBLEM, BUT...
...WHY ARE YOU *HERE,* AYANAMI?
KATSURAGI-SENSEI SAID I SHOULD LOOK AFTER YOU...
...AND THAT'S WHY I'M HERE.
...

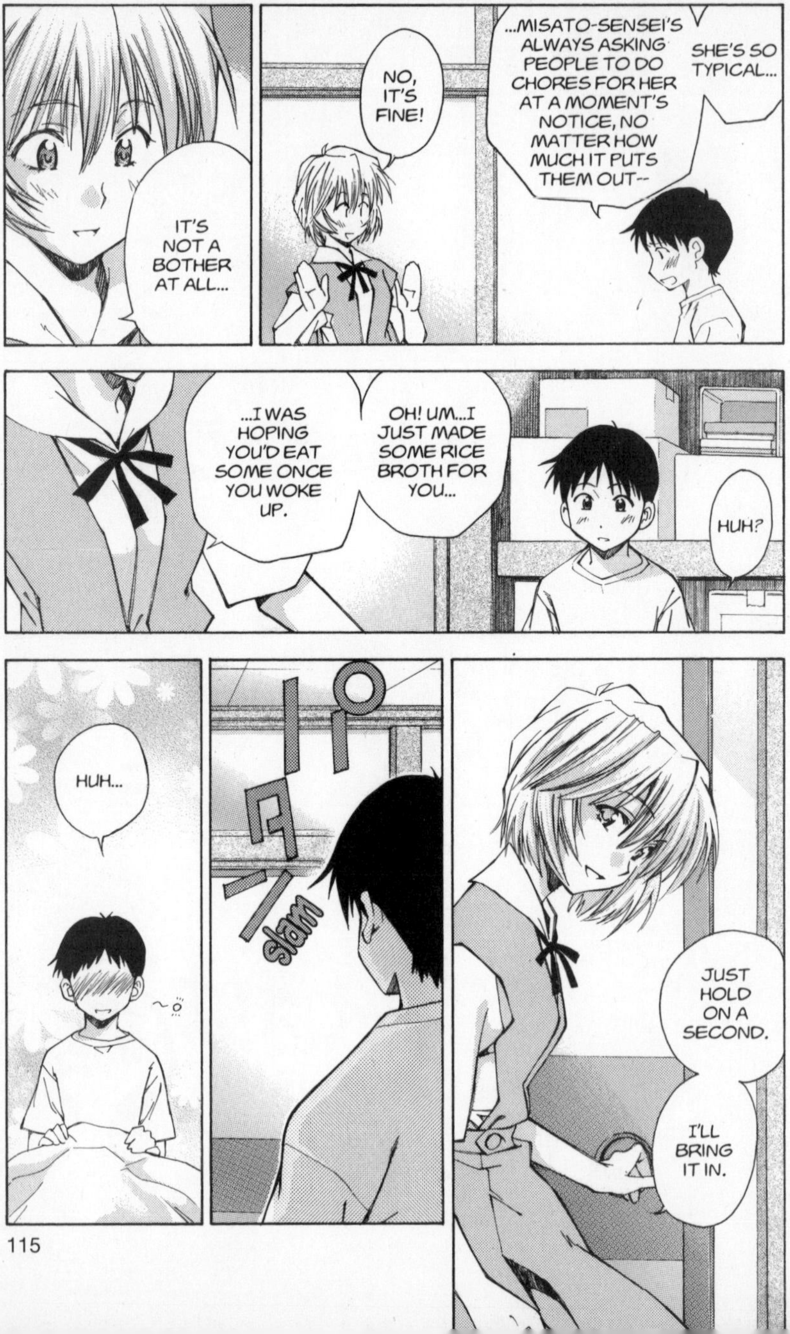
SHE'S SO TYPICAL...
...MISATO-SENSEI'S ALWAYS ASKING PEOPLE TO DO CHORES FOR HER AT A MOMENT'S NOTICE, NO MATTER HOW MUCH IT PUTS THEM OUT--
NO, IT'S FINE!
IT'S NOT A BOTHER AT ALL...
HUH?
OH! UM...I JUST MADE SOME RICE BROTH FOR YOU...
...I WAS HOPING YOU'D EAT SOME ONCE YOU WOKE UP.
JUST HOLD ON A SECOND.
I'LL BRING IT IN.
slam
HUH...

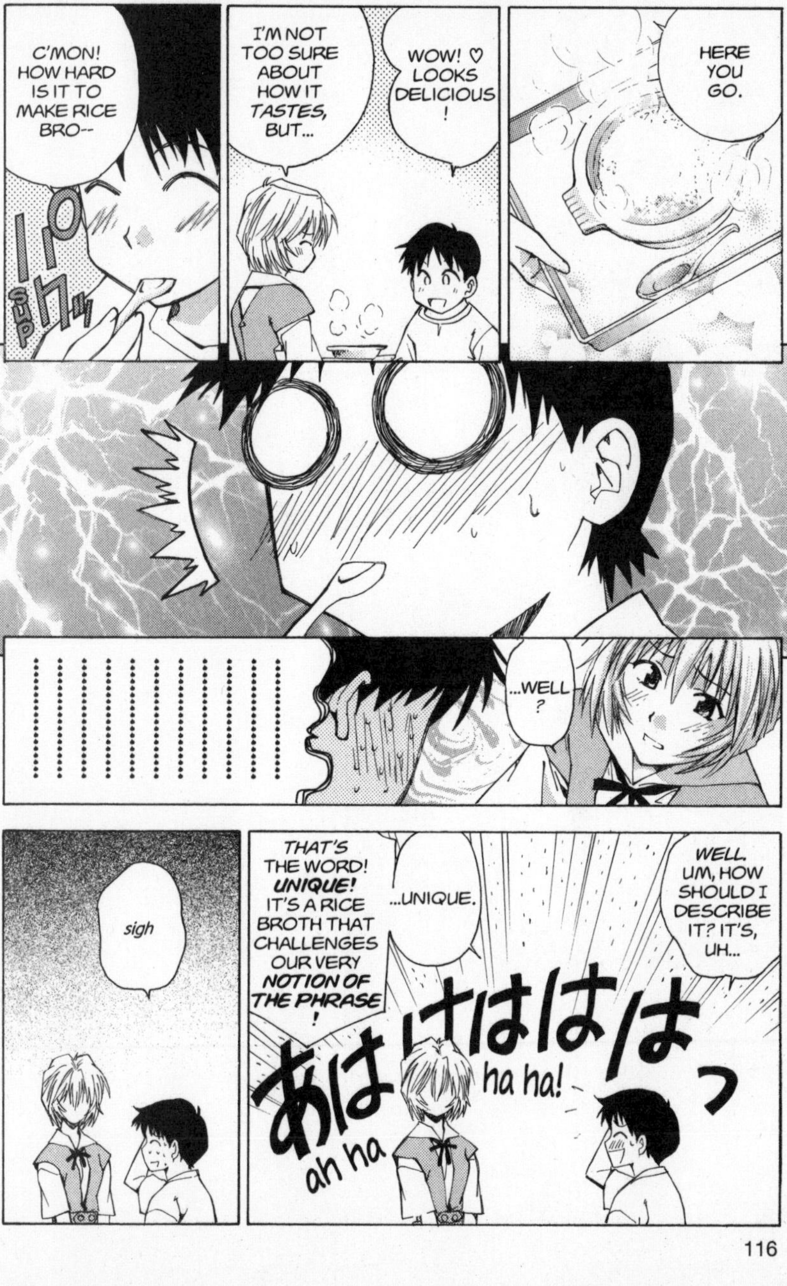
HERE YOU GO.
WOW! ♡ LOOKS DELICIOUS!
I'M NOT TOO SURE ABOUT HOW IT *TASTES,* BUT...
C'MON! HOW HARD IS IT TO MAKE RICE BRO--
SUP
...WELL?
WELL. UM, HOW SHOULD I DESCRIBE IT? IT'S, UH...
...UNIQUE.
THAT'S THE WORD! ***UNIQUE!*** IT'S A RICE BROTH THAT CHALLENGES OUR VERY ***NOTION OF THE PHRASE!***
ah ha ha ha!
sigh

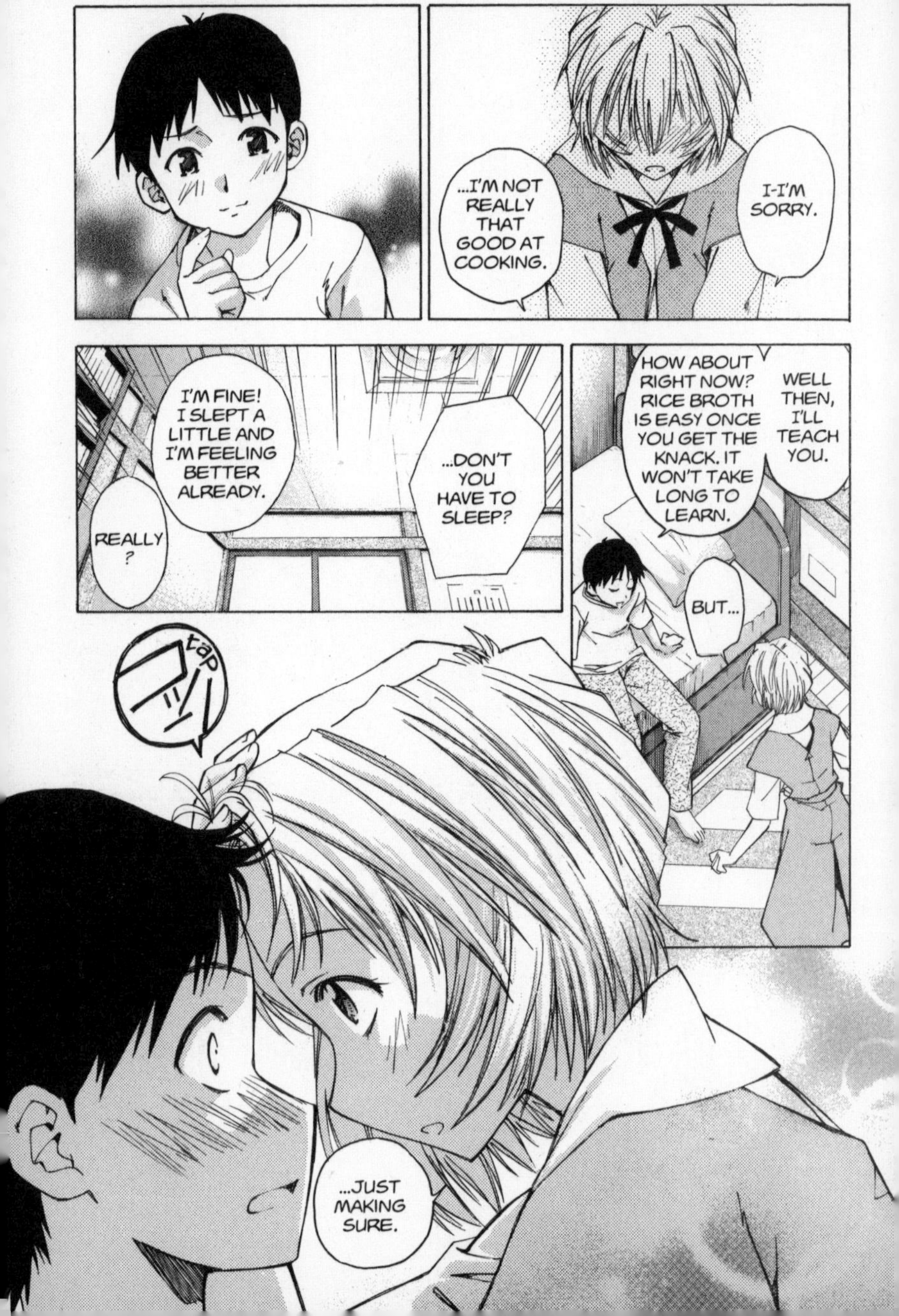
I-I'M SORRY.
...I'M NOT REALLY THAT GOOD AT COOKING.
WELL THEN, I'LL TEACH YOU.
HOW ABOUT RIGHT NOW? RICE BROTH IS EASY ONCE YOU GET THE KNACK. IT WON'T TAKE LONG TO LEARN.
BUT...
...DON'T YOU HAVE TO SLEEP?
I'M FINE! I SLEPT A LITTLE AND I'M FEELING BETTER ALREADY.
REALLY?
tap
...JUST MAKING SURE.

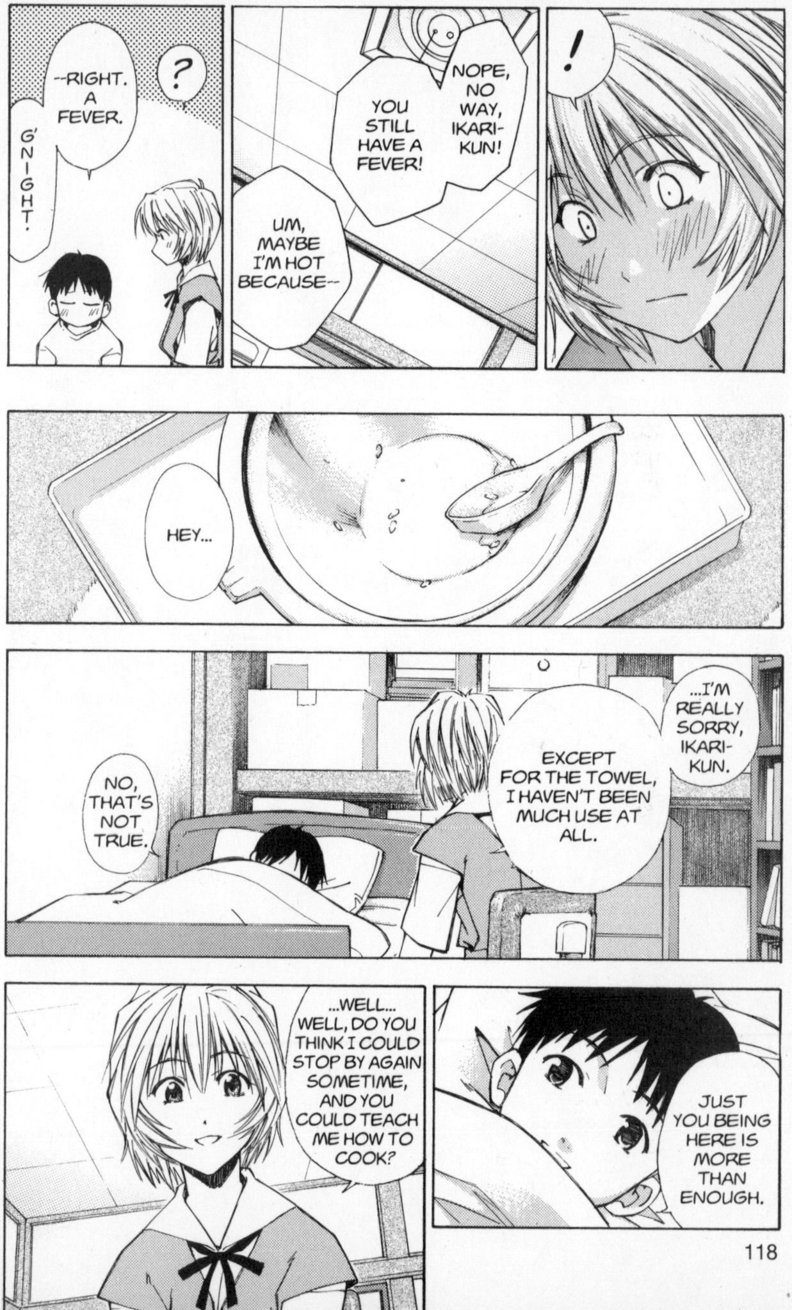
!
NOPE, NO WAY, IKARI-KUN!
YOU STILL HAVE A FEVER!
UM, MAYBE I'M HOT BECAUSE--
?
--RIGHT. A FEVER.
G'NIGHT.
HEY...
...I'M REALLY SORRY, IKARI-KUN.
EXCEPT FOR THE TOWEL, I HAVEN'T BEEN MUCH USE AT ALL.
NO, THAT'S NOT TRUE.
JUST YOU BEING HERE IS MORE THAN ENOUGH.
...WELL... WELL, DO YOU THINK I COULD STOP BY AGAIN SOMETIME, AND YOU COULD TEACH ME HOW TO COOK?

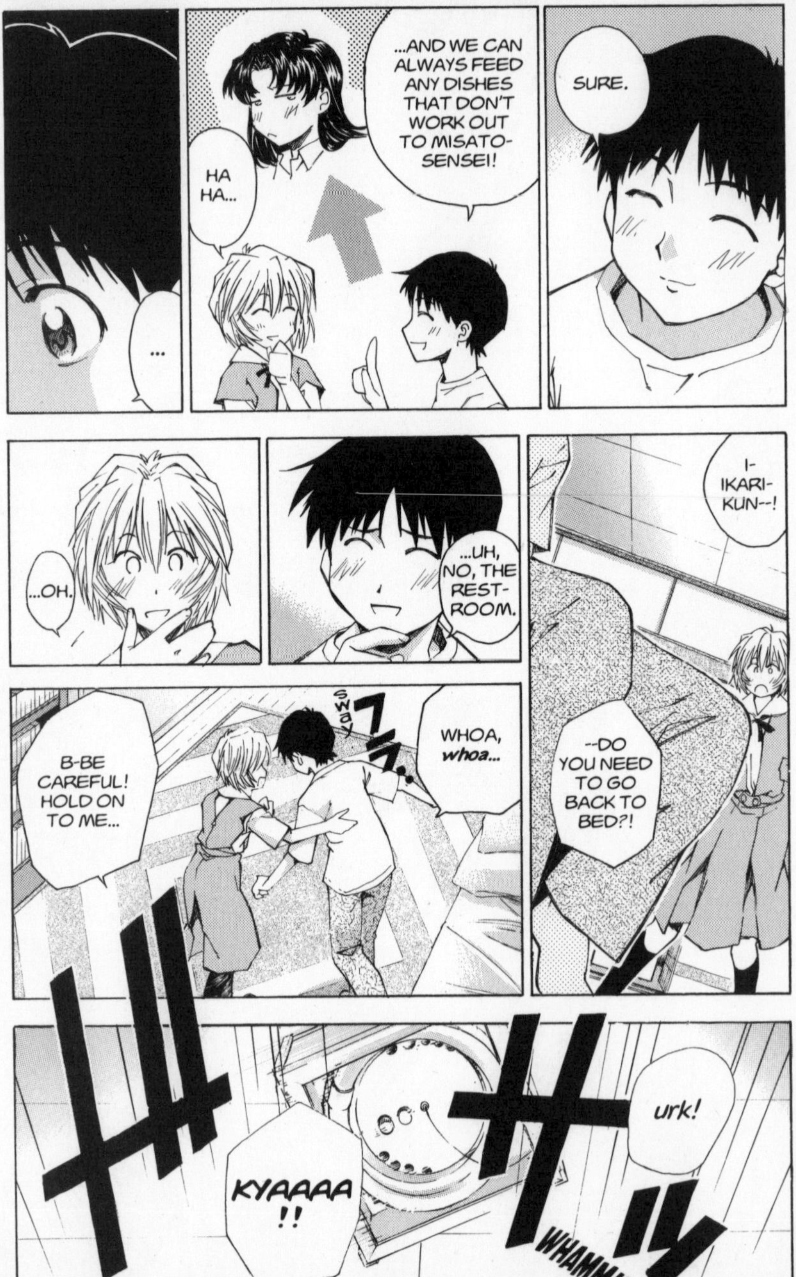
SURE.
...AND WE CAN ALWAYS FEED ANY DISHES THAT DON'T WORK OUT TO MISATO-SENSEI!
HA HA...
...
I- IKARI-KUN--!
--DO YOU NEED TO GO BACK TO BED?!
...UH, NO, THE REST-ROOM.
...OH.
WHOA, *whoa...*
sway
B-BE CAREFUL! HOLD ON TO ME...
urk!
WHAMM!!
KYAAAA !!

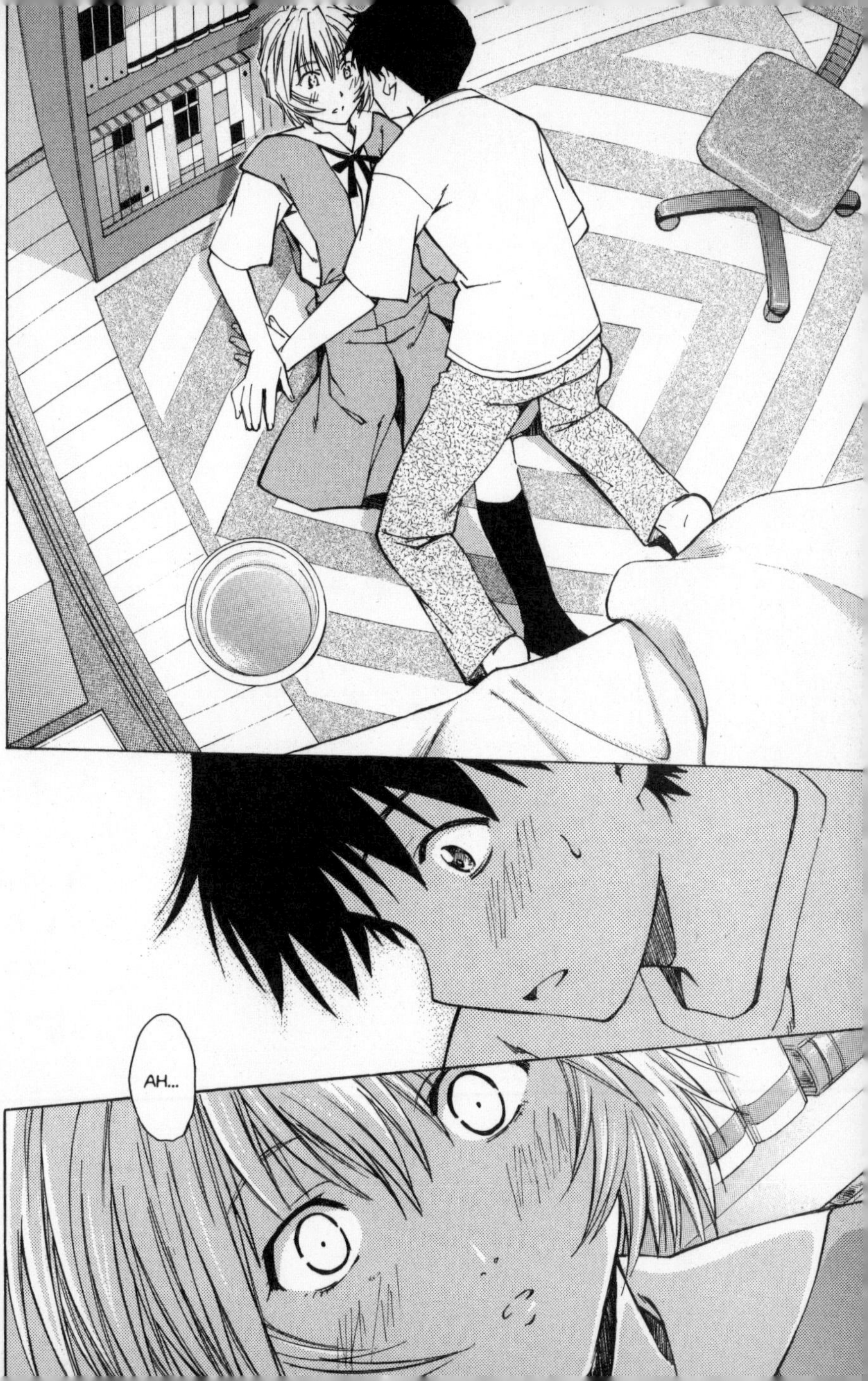
AH...

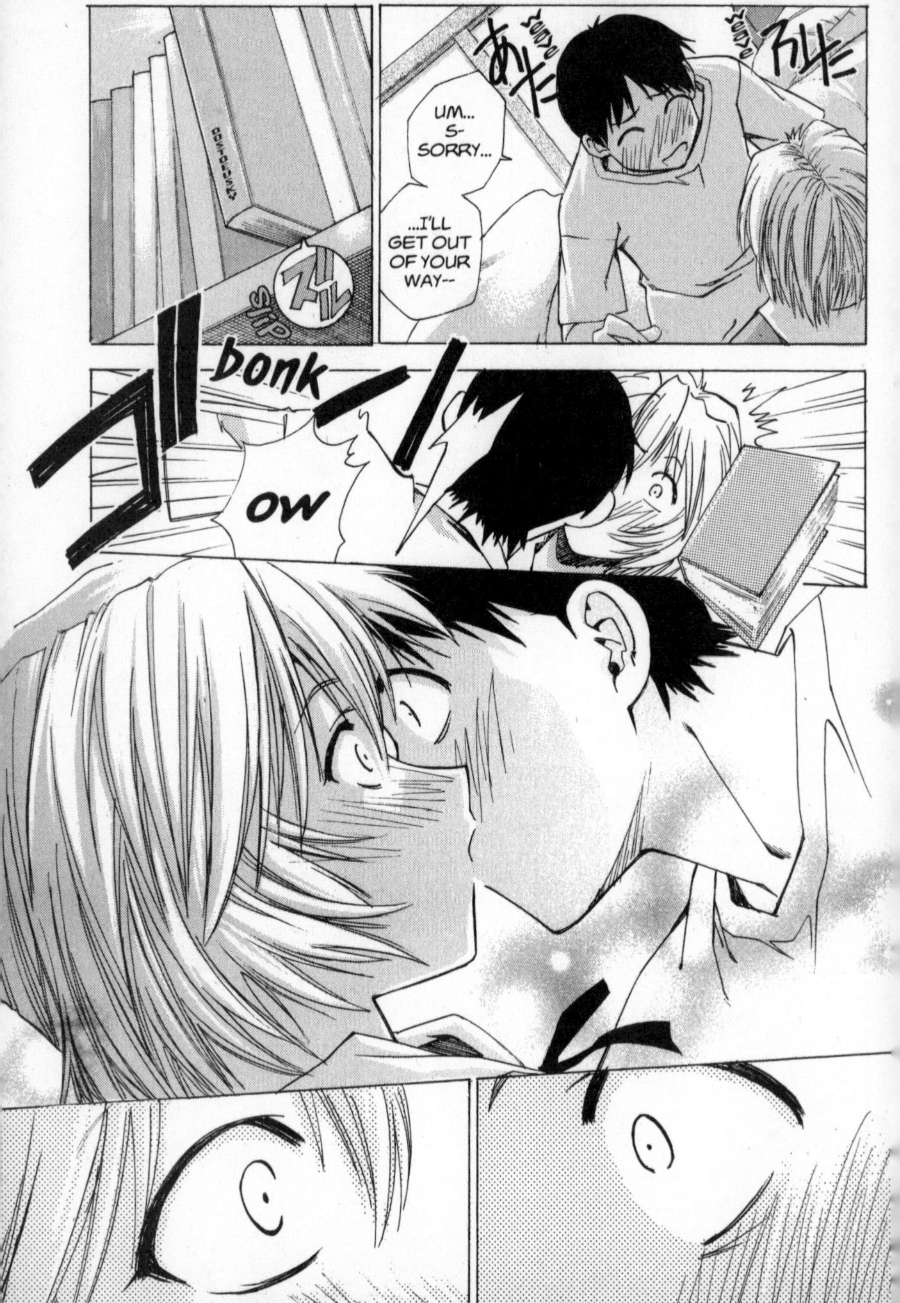
swerve
swerve
UM... S-SORRY...
...I'LL GET OUT OF YOUR WAY--
DOSTOEVSKY
slip
bonk
OW

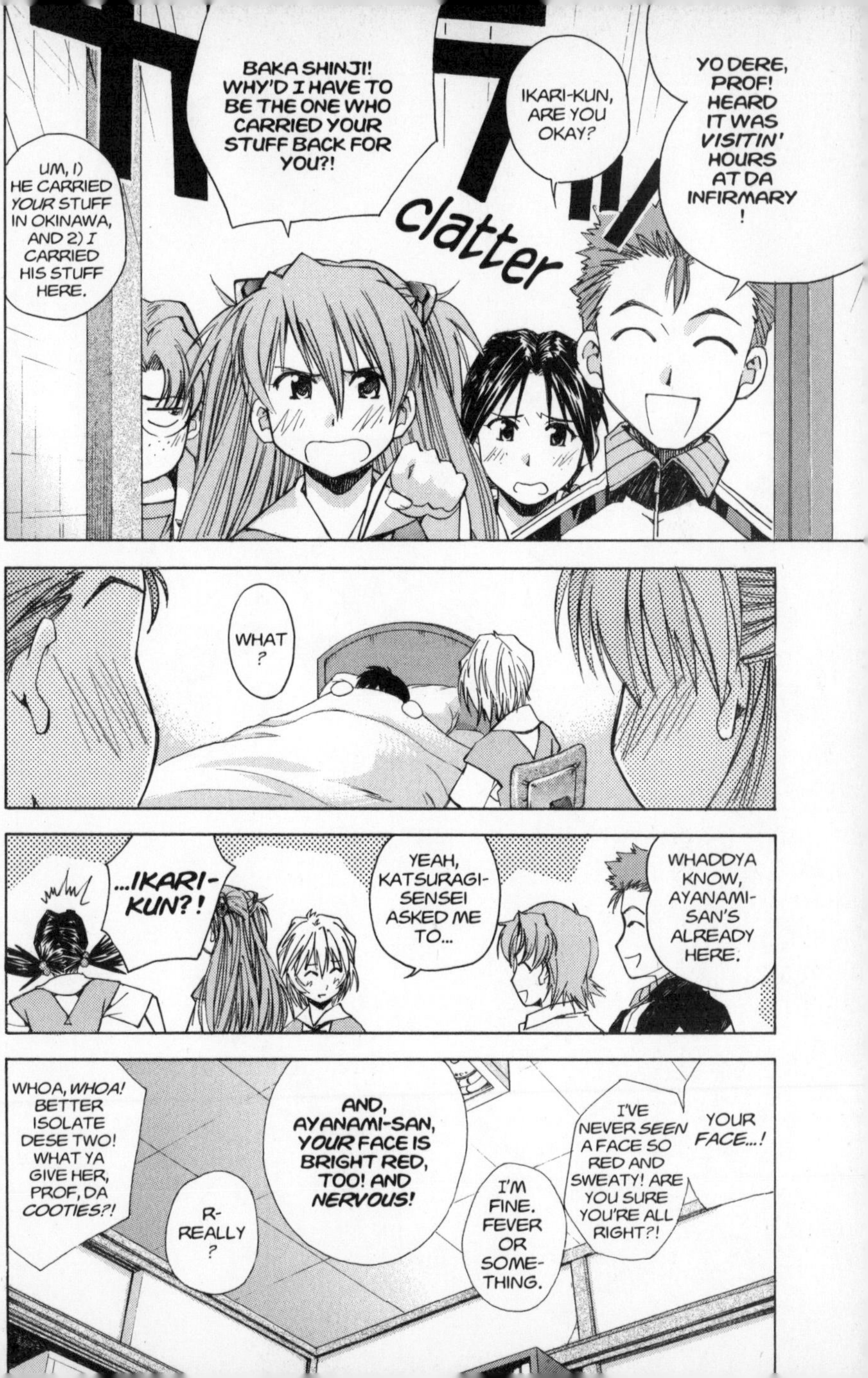
YO DERE, PROF! HEARD IT WAS VISITIN' HOURS AT DA INFIRMARY!
IKARI-KUN, ARE YOU OKAY?
clatter
BAKA SHINJI! WHY'D I HAVE TO BE THE ONE WHO CARRIED YOUR STUFF BACK FOR YOU?!
UM, 1) HE CARRIED YOUR STUFF IN OKINAWA, AND 2) I CARRIED HIS STUFF HERE.
WHAT?
WHADDYA KNOW, AYANAMI-SAN'S ALREADY HERE.
YEAH, KATSURAGI-SENSEI ASKED ME TO...
...IKARI-KUN?!
YOUR FACE...!
I'VE NEVER SEEN A FACE SO RED AND SWEATY! ARE YOU SURE YOU'RE ALL RIGHT?!
I'M FINE. FEVER OR SOMETHING.
AND, AYANAMI-SAN, YOUR FACE IS BRIGHT RED, TOO! AND NERVOUS!
R-REALLY?
WHOA, WHOA! BETTER ISOLATE DESE TWO! WHAT YA GIVE HER, PROF, DA COOTIES?!

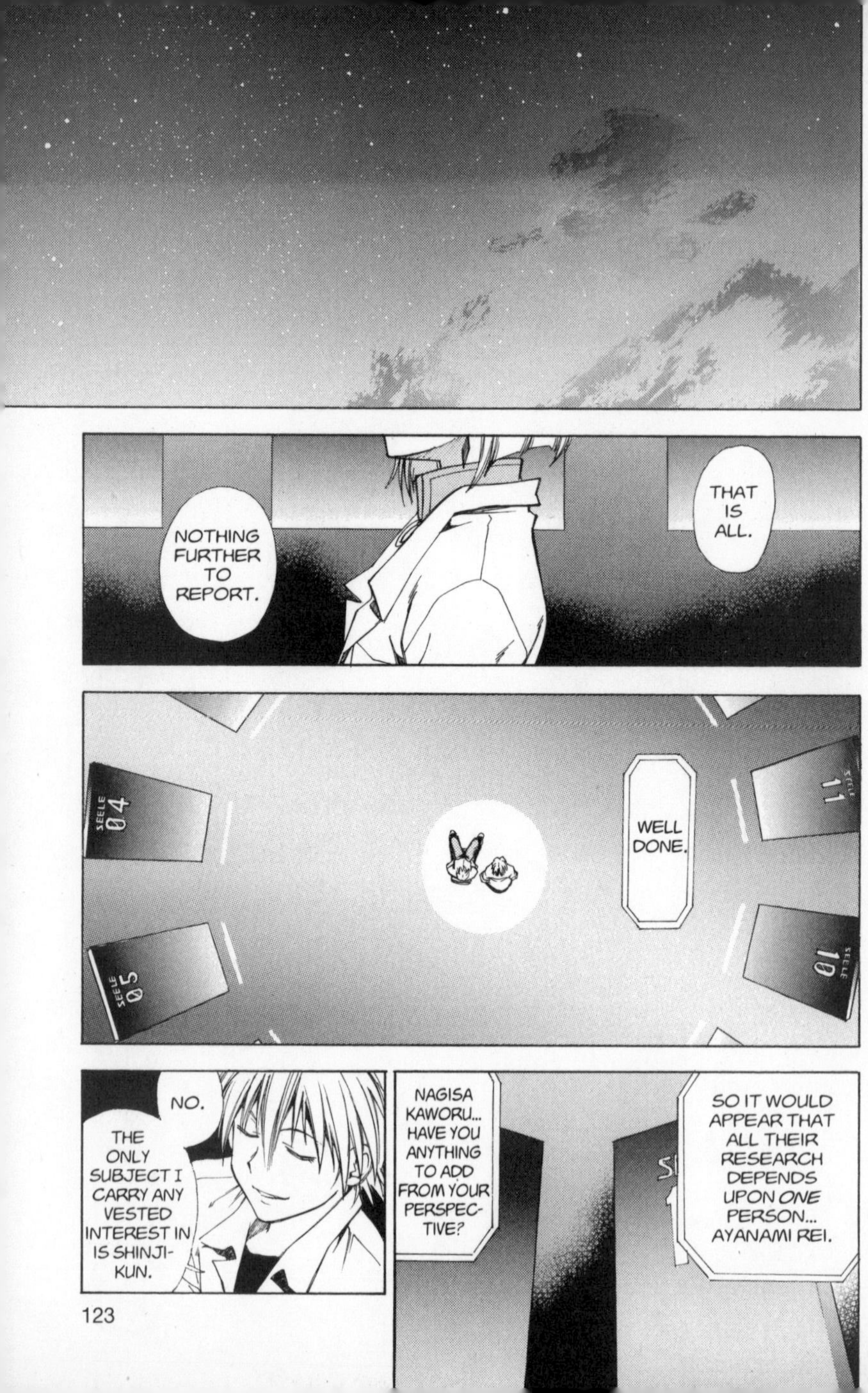
THAT IS ALL.
NOTHING FURTHER TO REPORT.
WELL DONE.
SEELE 11
SEELE 04
SEELE 10
SEELE 05
SO IT WOULD APPEAR THAT ALL THEIR RESEARCH DEPENDS UPON *ONE* PERSON... AYANAMI REI.
NAGISA KAWORU... HAVE YOU ANYTHING TO ADD FROM YOUR PERSPEC-TIVE?
NO.
THE ONLY SUBJECT I CARRY ANY VESTED INTEREST IN IS SHINJI-KUN.

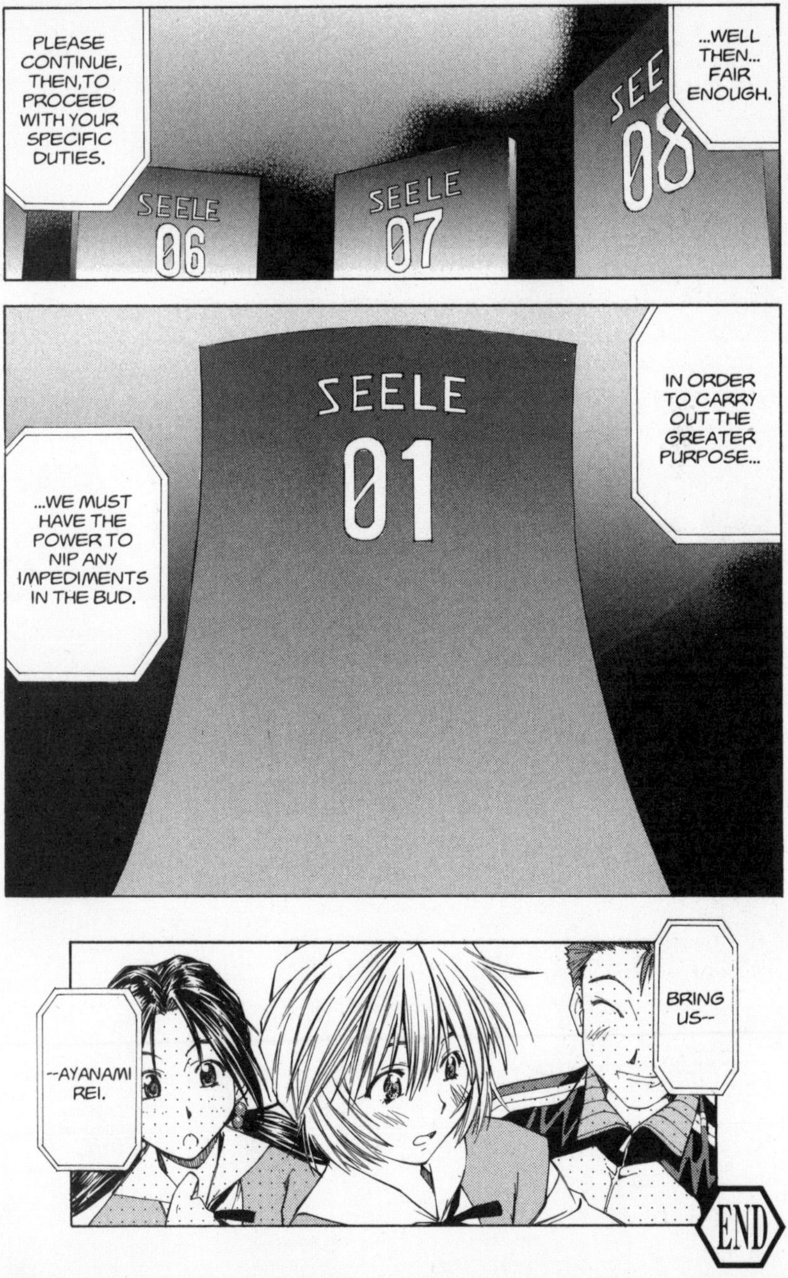
...WELL THEN... FAIR ENOUGH.
PLEASE CONTINUE, THEN,TO PROCEED WITH YOUR SPECIFIC DUTIES.
SEELE 08
SEELE 07
SEELE 06
IN ORDER TO CARRY OUT THE GREATER PURPOSE...
SEELE 01
...WE MUST HAVE THE POWER TO NIP ANY IMPEDIMENTS IN THE BUD.
BRING US--
--AYANAMI REI.
END

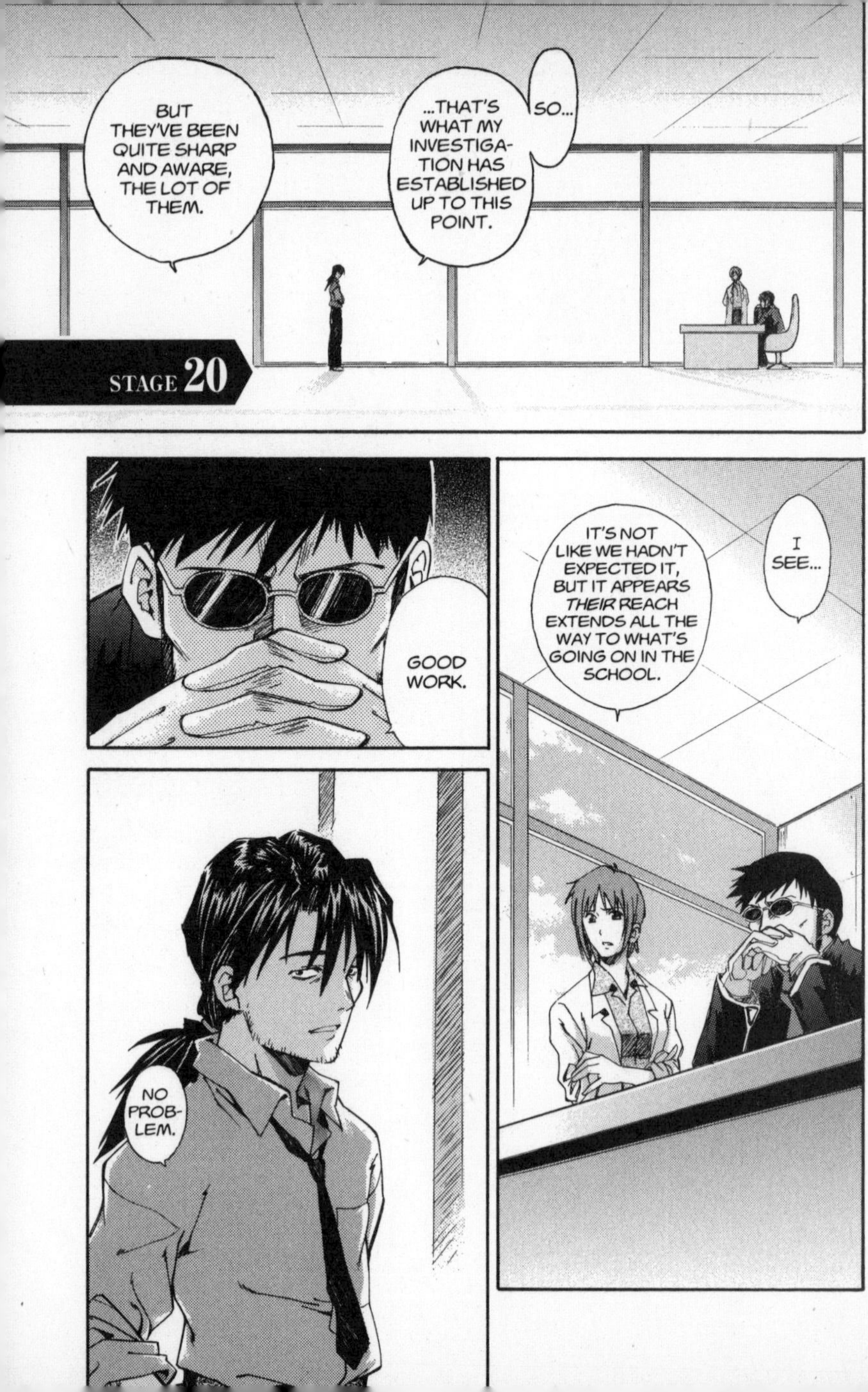
SO...
...THAT'S WHAT MY INVESTIGATION HAS ESTABLISHED UP TO THIS POINT.
BUT THEY'VE BEEN QUITE SHARP AND AWARE, THE LOT OF THEM.
STAGE 20
I SEE...
IT'S NOT LIKE WE HADN'T EXPECTED IT, BUT IT APPEARS *THEIR* REACH EXTENDS ALL THE WAY TO WHAT'S GOING ON IN THE SCHOOL.
GOOD WORK.
NO PROBLEM.

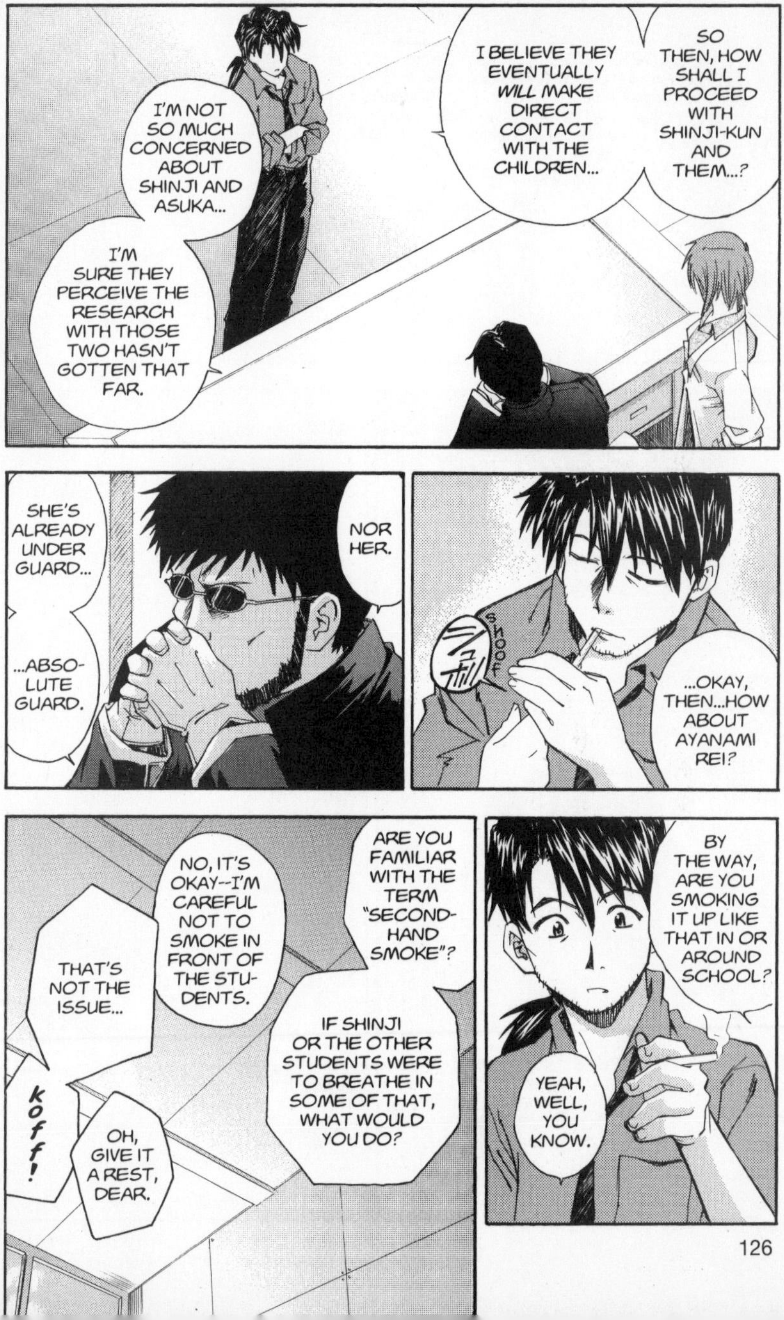
SO THEN, HOW SHALL I PROCEED WITH SHINJI-KUN AND THEM...?
I BELIEVE THEY EVENTUALLY *WILL* MAKE DIRECT CONTACT WITH THE CHILDREN...
I'M NOT SO MUCH CONCERNED ABOUT SHINJI AND ASUKA...
I'M SURE THEY PERCEIVE THE RESEARCH WITH THOSE TWO HASN'T GOTTEN THAT FAR.
SHOOF
...OKAY, THEN...HOW ABOUT AYANAMI REI?
NOR HER.
SHE'S ALREADY UNDER GUARD...
...ABSO-LUTE GUARD.
BY THE WAY, ARE YOU SMOKING IT UP LIKE THAT IN OR AROUND SCHOOL?
YEAH, WELL, YOU KNOW.
ARE YOU FAMILIAR WITH THE TERM "SECOND-HAND SMOKE"?
NO, IT'S OKAY--I'M CAREFUL NOT TO SMOKE IN FRONT OF THE STU-DENTS.
THAT'S NOT THE ISSUE...
IF SHINJI OR THE OTHER STUDENTS WERE TO BREATHE IN SOME OF THAT, WHAT WOULD YOU DO?
KOFF!
OH, GIVE IT A REST, DEAR.

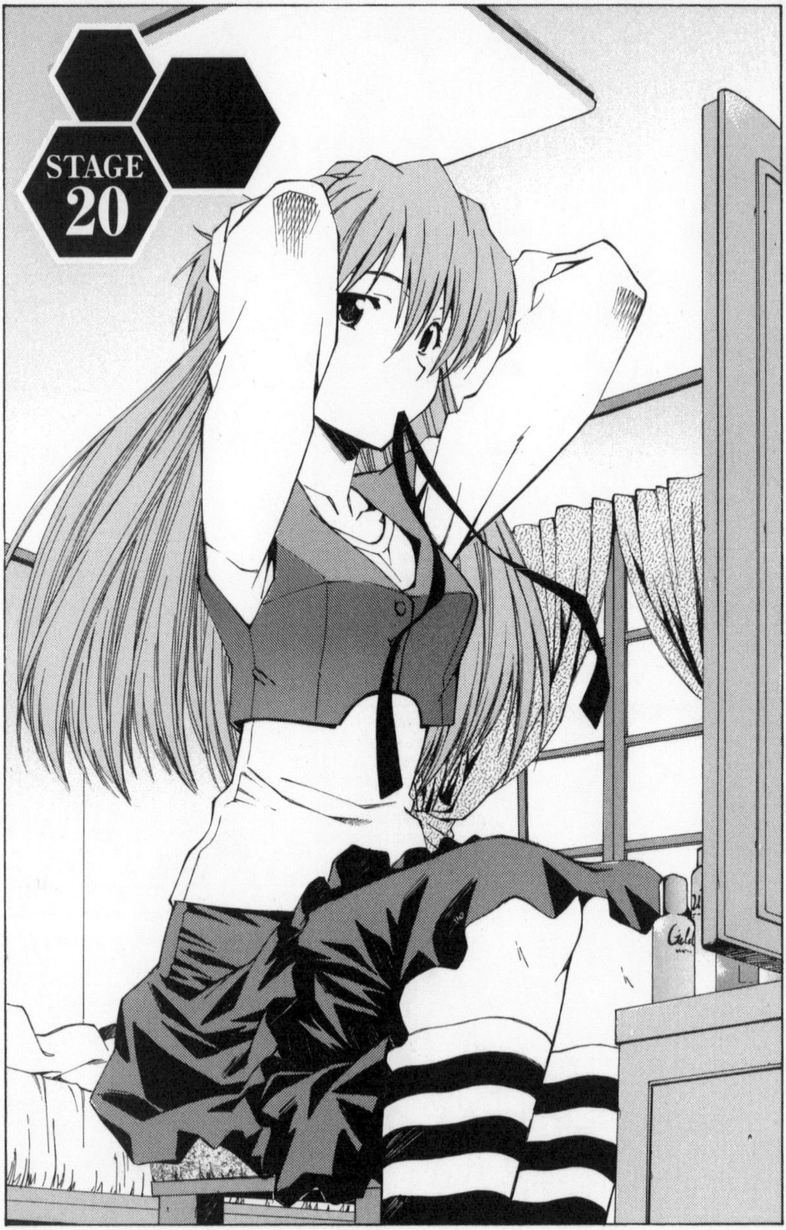
STAGE
20

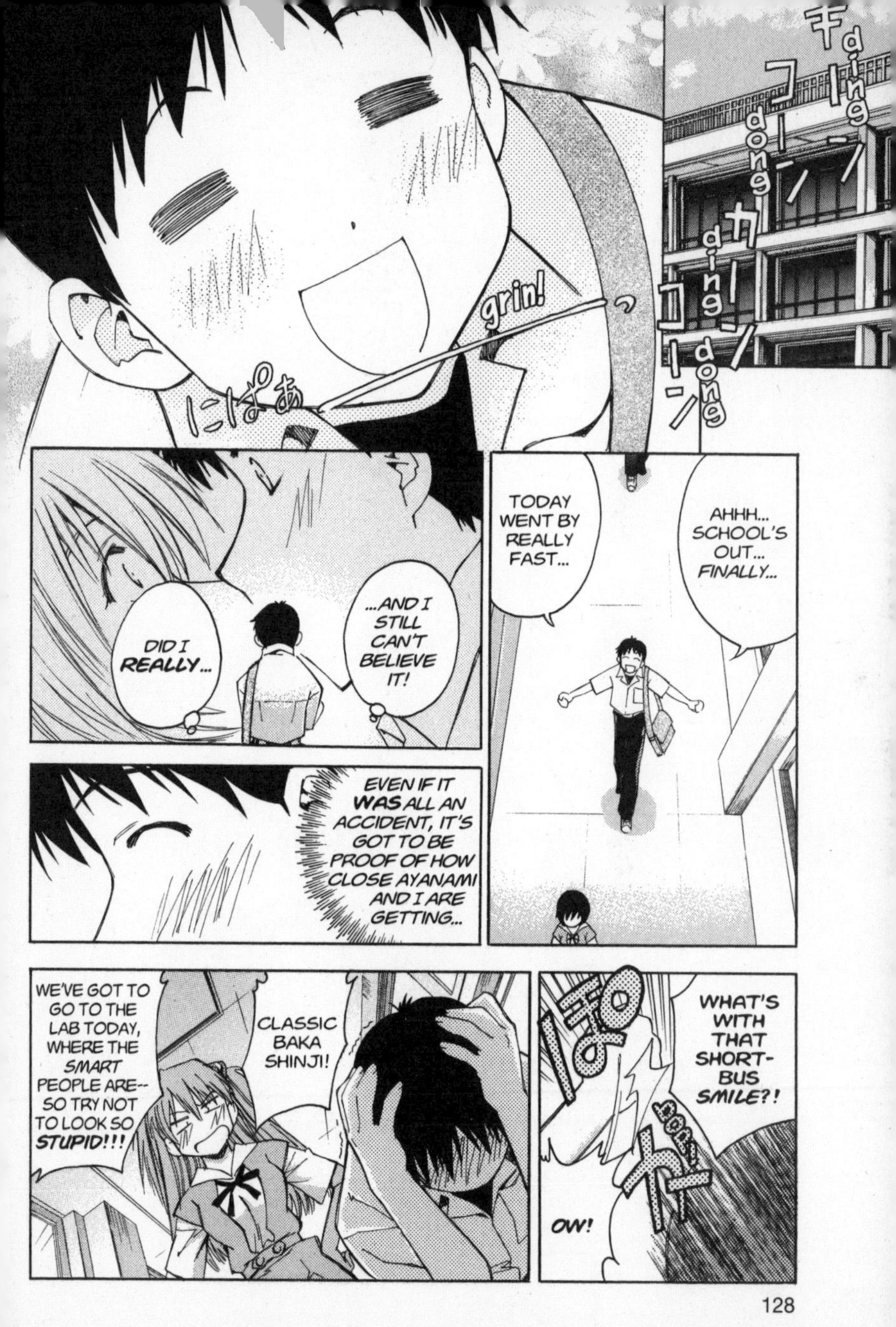

ding-dong
ding-dong
キーンコーンカーンコーン
grin!
にぱあ
AHHH... SCHOOL'S OUT... FINALLY...
TODAY WENT BY REALLY FAST...
...AND I STILL CAN'T BELIEVE IT!
DID I REALLY...
EVEN IF IT WAS ALL AN ACCIDENT, IT'S GOT TO BE PROOF OF HOW CLOSE AYANAMI AND I ARE GETTING...
WHAT'S WITH THAT SHORT-BUS SMILE?!
ぽ
bonk!
OW!
CLASSIC BAKA SHINJI!
WE'VE GOT TO GO TO THE LAB TODAY, WHERE THE SMART PEOPLE ARE-- SO TRY NOT TO LOOK SO STUPID!!!

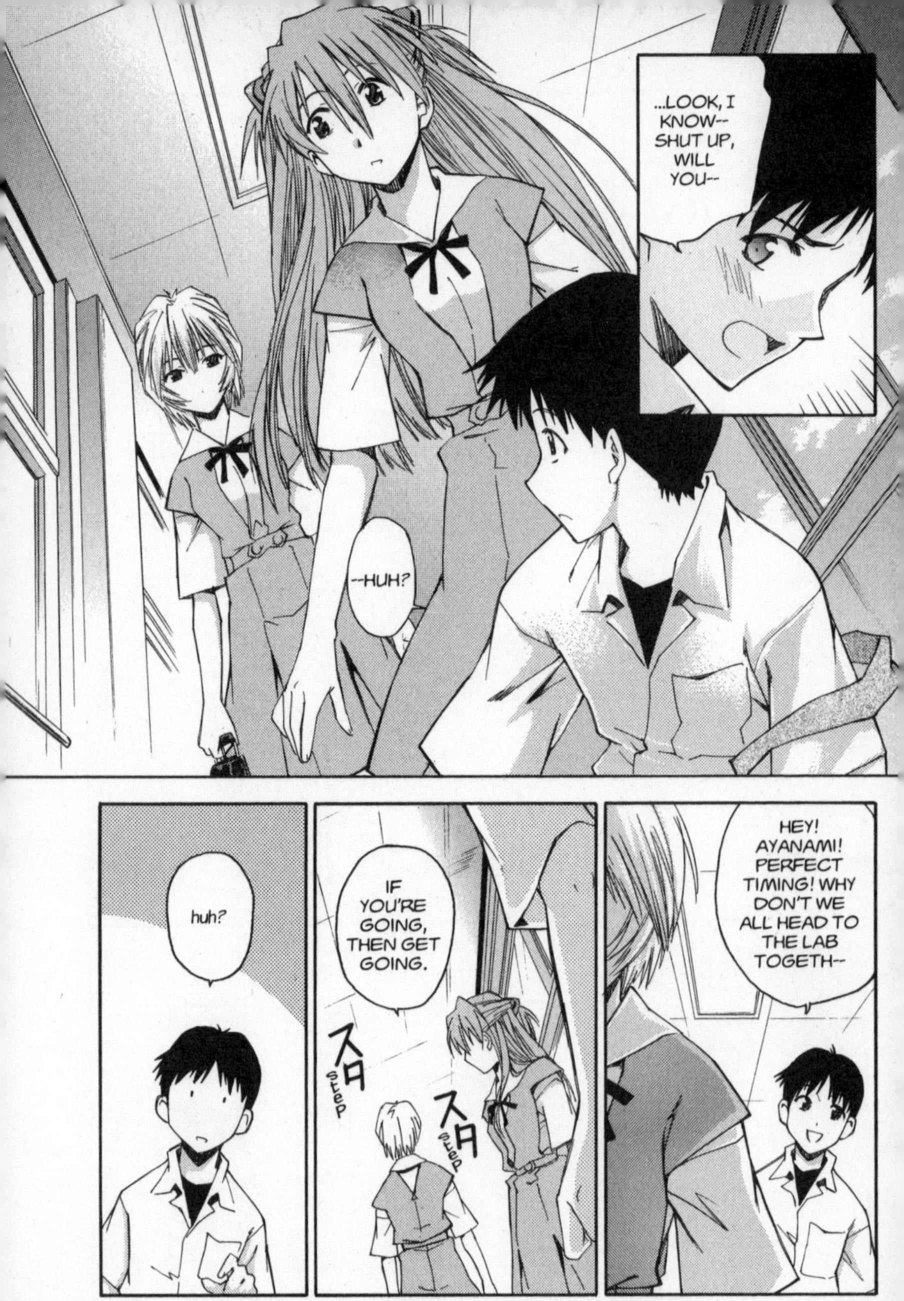
...LOOK, I KNOW-- SHUT UP, WILL YOU--
--HUH?
HEY! AYANAMI! PERFECT TIMING! WHY DON'T WE ALL HEAD TO THE LAB TOGETH--
IF YOU'RE GOING, THEN GET GOING.
スタ STEP
スタ STEP
huh?

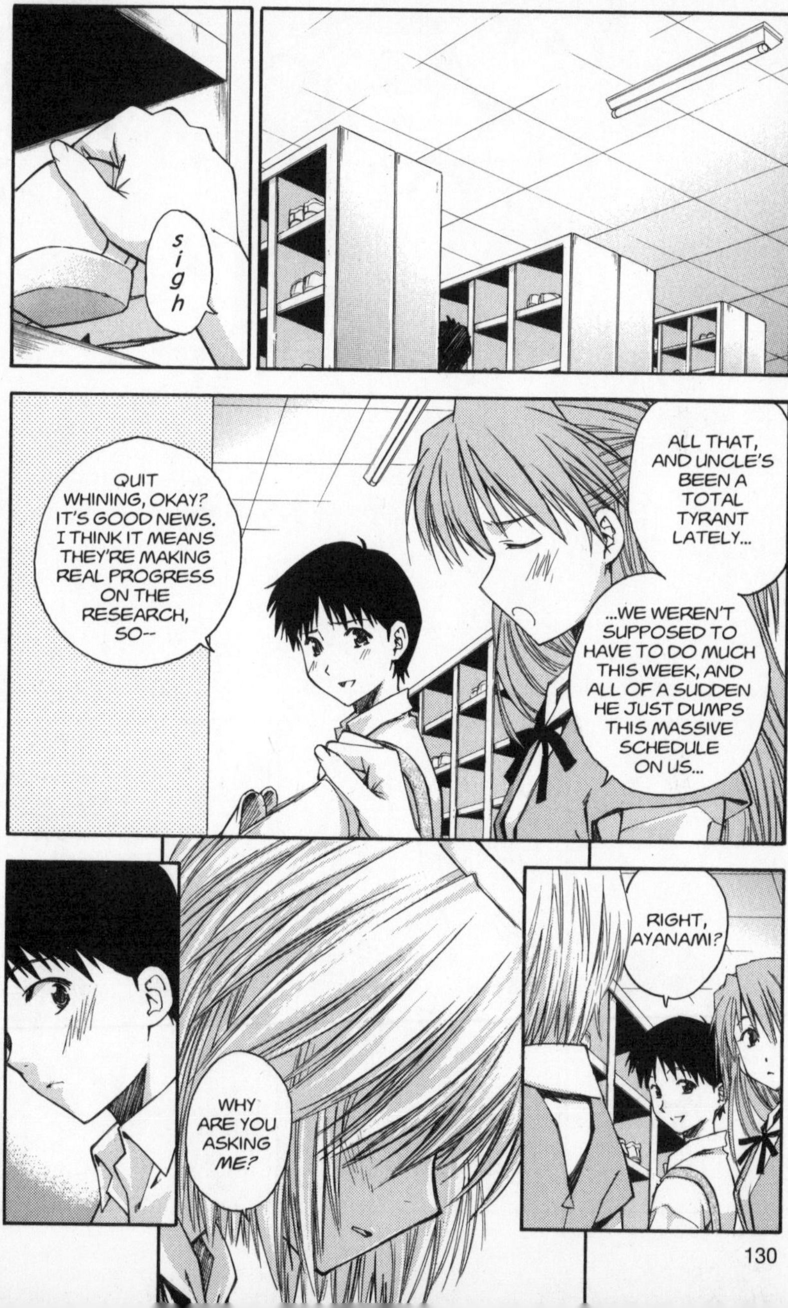
sigh
ALL THAT, AND UNCLE'S BEEN A TOTAL TYRANT LATELY...
...WE WEREN'T SUPPOSED TO HAVE TO DO MUCH THIS WEEK, AND ALL OF A SUDDEN HE JUST DUMPS THIS MASSIVE SCHEDULE ON US...
QUIT WHINING, OKAY? IT'S GOOD NEWS. I THINK IT MEANS THEY'RE MAKING REAL PROGRESS ON THE RESEARCH, SO--
RIGHT, AYANAMI?
WHY ARE YOU ASKING *ME?*

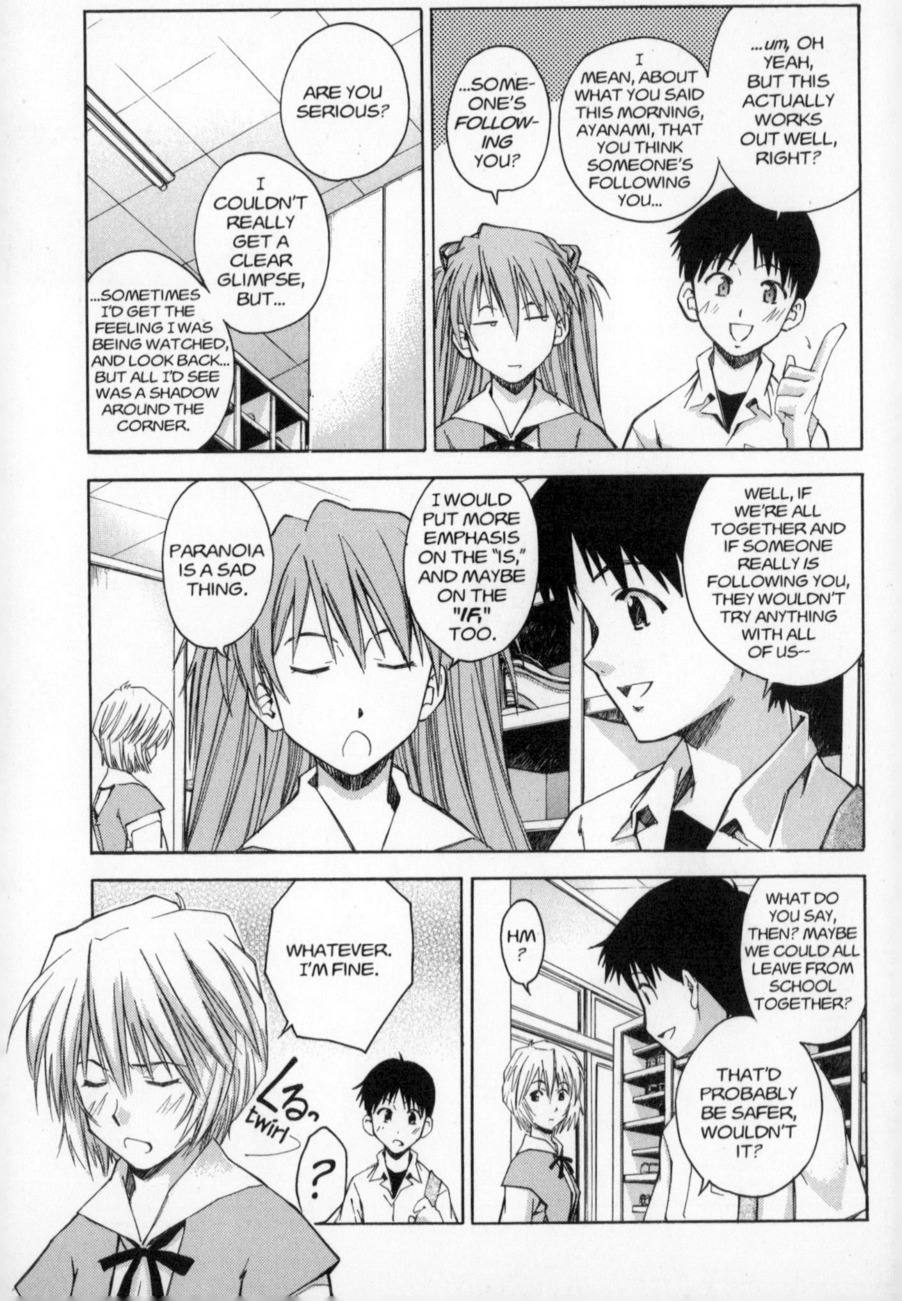
...um, OH YEAH, BUT THIS ACTUALLY WORKS OUT WELL, RIGHT?
I MEAN, ABOUT WHAT YOU SAID THIS MORNING, AYANAMI, THAT YOU THINK SOMEONE'S FOLLOWING YOU...
...SOME-ONE'S FOLLOW-ING YOU?
ARE YOU SERIOUS?
I COULDN'T REALLY GET A CLEAR GLIMPSE, BUT...
...SOMETIMES I'D GET THE FEELING I WAS BEING WATCHED, AND LOOK BACK... BUT ALL I'D SEE WAS A SHADOW AROUND THE CORNER.
WELL, IF WE'RE ALL TOGETHER AND IF SOMEONE REALLY IS FOLLOWING YOU, THEY WOULDN'T TRY ANYTHING WITH ALL OF US--
I WOULD PUT MORE EMPHASIS ON THE "IS," AND MAYBE ON THE "IF," TOO.
PARANOIA IS A SAD THING.
WHAT DO YOU SAY, THEN? MAYBE WE COULD ALL LEAVE FROM SCHOOL TOGETHER?
HM?
THAT'D PROBABLY BE SAFER, WOULDN'T IT?
WHATEVER. I'M FINE.
twirl
?

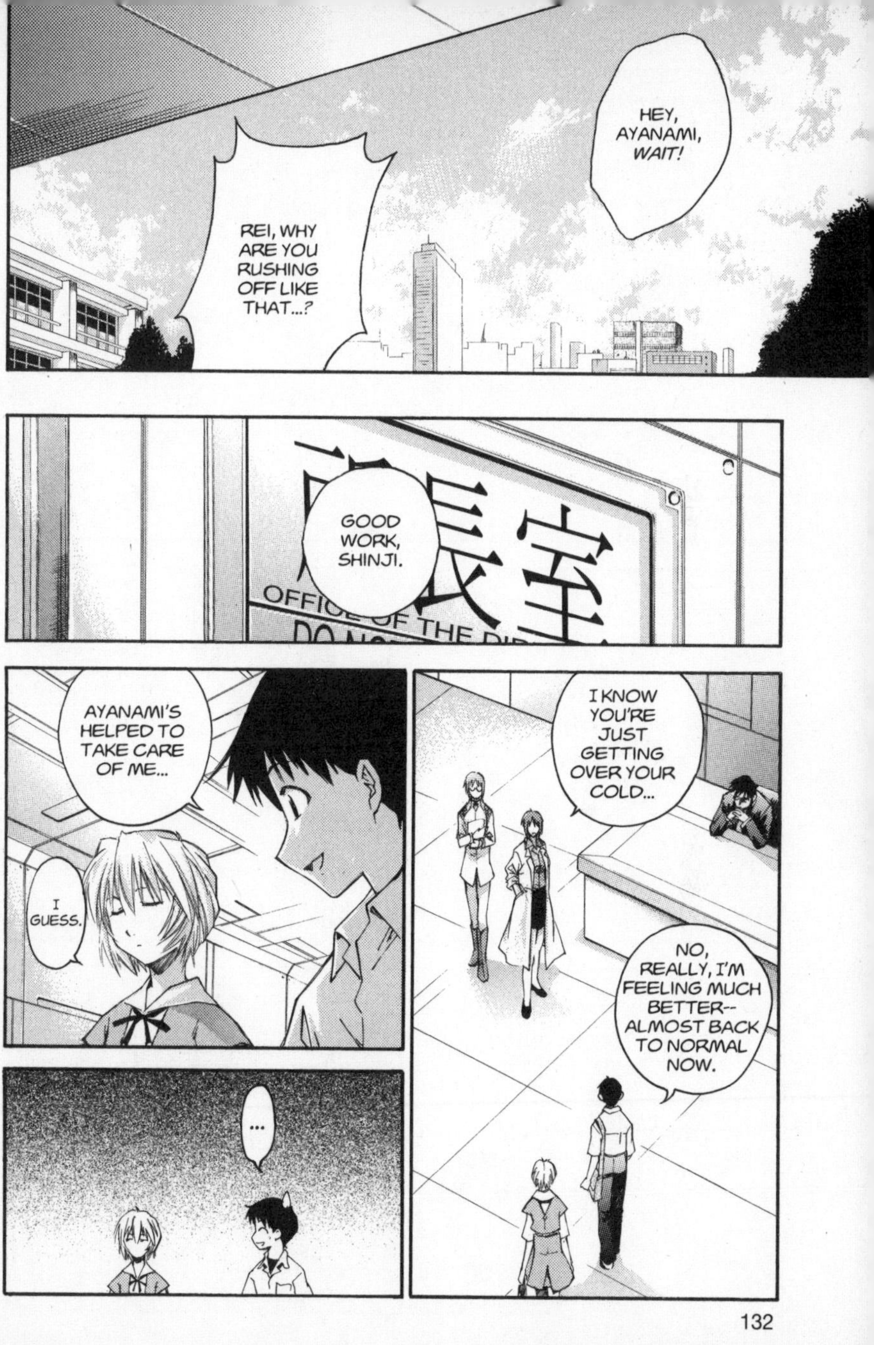
HEY, AYANAMI, WAIT!
REI, WHY ARE YOU RUSHING OFF LIKE THAT...?
GOOD WORK, SHINJI.
I KNOW YOU'RE JUST GETTING OVER YOUR COLD...
NO, REALLY, I'M FEELING MUCH BETTER-- ALMOST BACK TO NORMAL NOW.
AYANAMI'S HELPED TO TAKE CARE OF ME...
I GUESS.
...

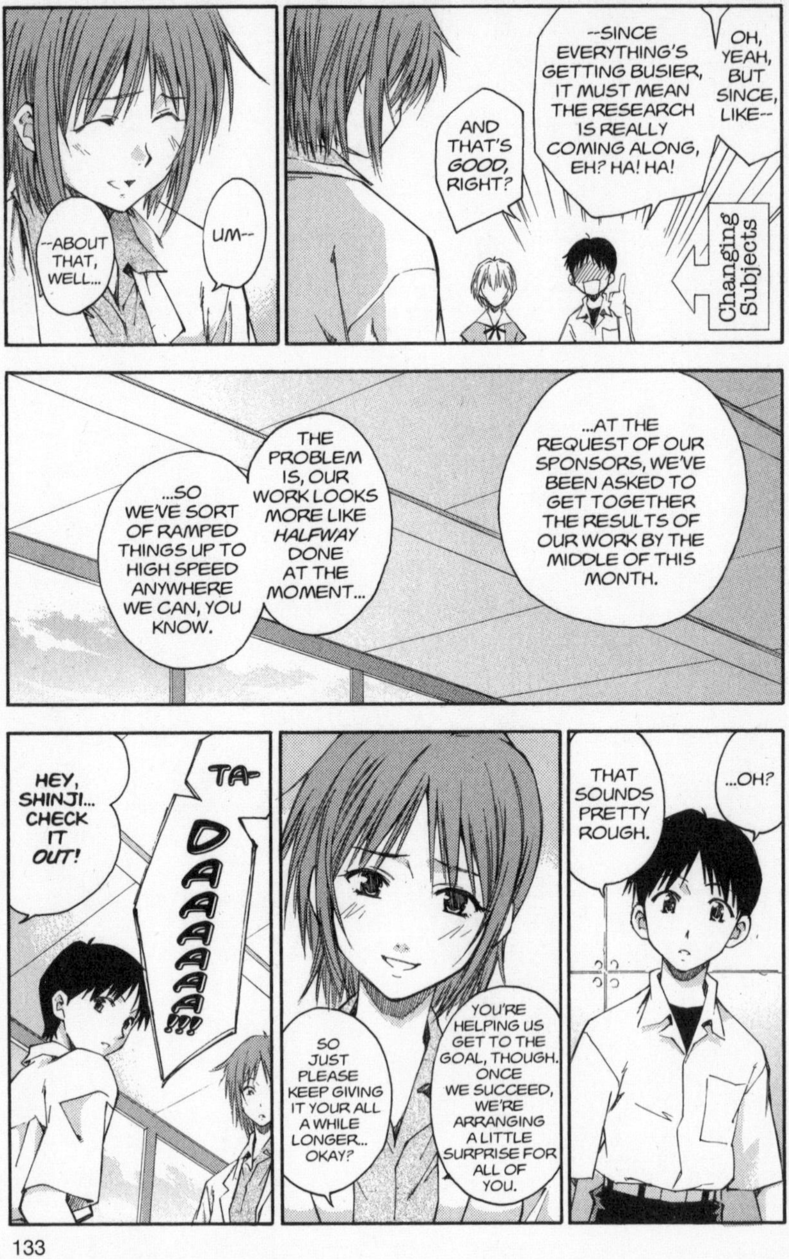
OH, YEAH, BUT SINCE, LIKE--
--SINCE EVERYTHING'S GETTING BUSIER, IT MUST MEAN THE RESEARCH IS REALLY COMING ALONG, EH? HA! HA!
AND THAT'S GOOD, RIGHT?
Changing Subjects
UM--
--ABOUT THAT, WELL...
...AT THE REQUEST OF OUR SPONSORS, WE'VE BEEN ASKED TO GET TOGETHER THE RESULTS OF OUR WORK BY THE MIDDLE OF THIS MONTH.
THE PROBLEM IS, OUR WORK LOOKS MORE LIKE HALFWAY DONE AT THE MOMENT...
...SO WE'VE SORT OF RAMPED THINGS UP TO HIGH SPEED ANYWHERE WE CAN, YOU KNOW.
...OH?
THAT SOUNDS PRETTY ROUGH.
YOU'RE HELPING US GET TO THE GOAL, THOUGH. ONCE WE SUCCEED, WE'RE ARRANGING A LITTLE SURPRISE FOR ALL OF YOU.
SO JUST PLEASE KEEP GIVING IT YOUR ALL A WHILE LONGER... OKAY?
TA-DAAAAAAAA!!!
HEY, SHINJI... CHECK IT OUT!

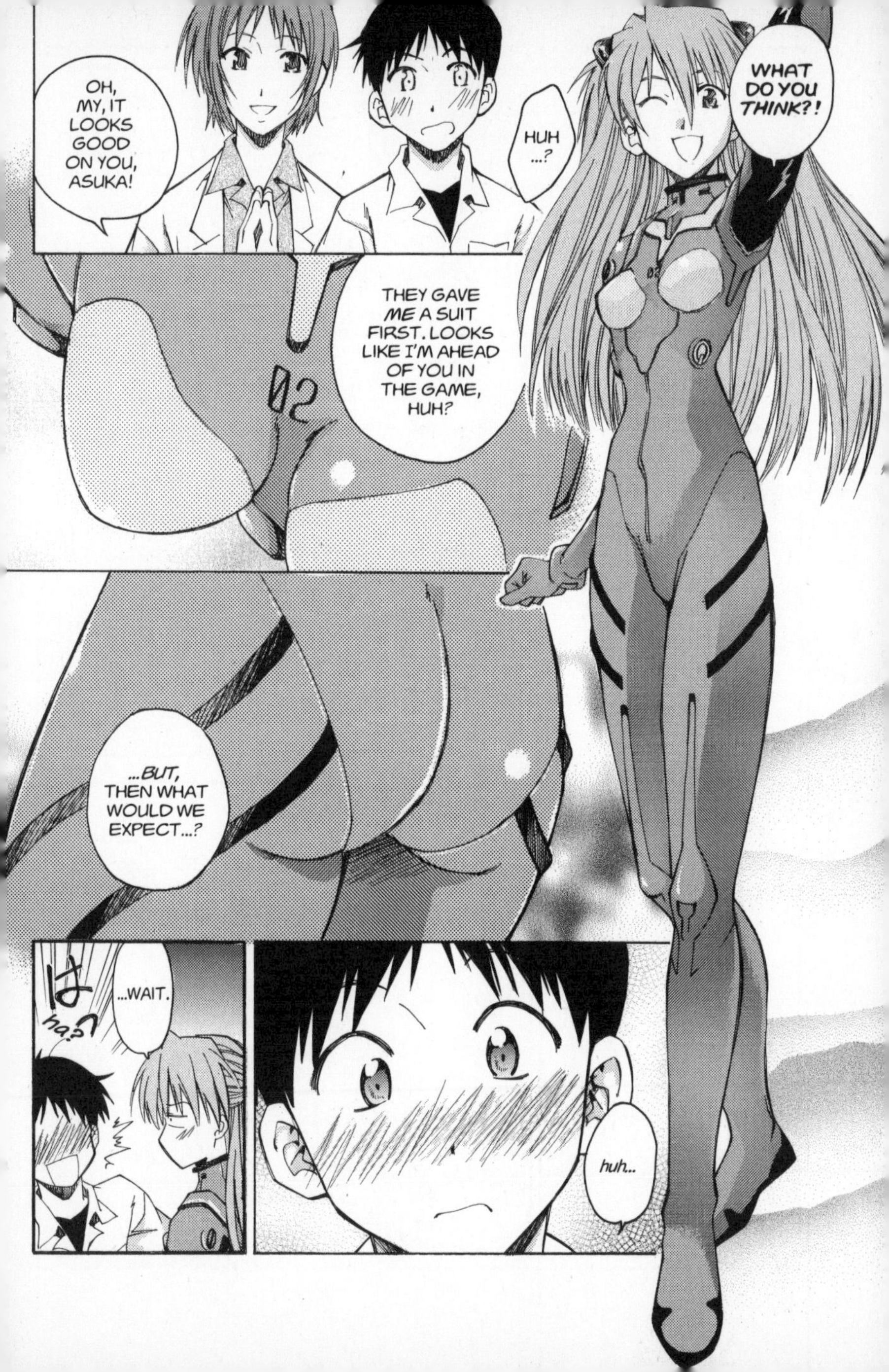
WHAT DO YOU THINK?!
HUH ...?
OH, MY, IT LOOKS GOOD ON YOU, ASUKA!
THEY GAVE *ME* A SUIT FIRST. LOOKS LIKE I'M AHEAD OF YOU IN THE GAME, HUH?
...*BUT*, THEN WHAT WOULD WE EXPECT...?
huh...
...WAIT.
は
ha?

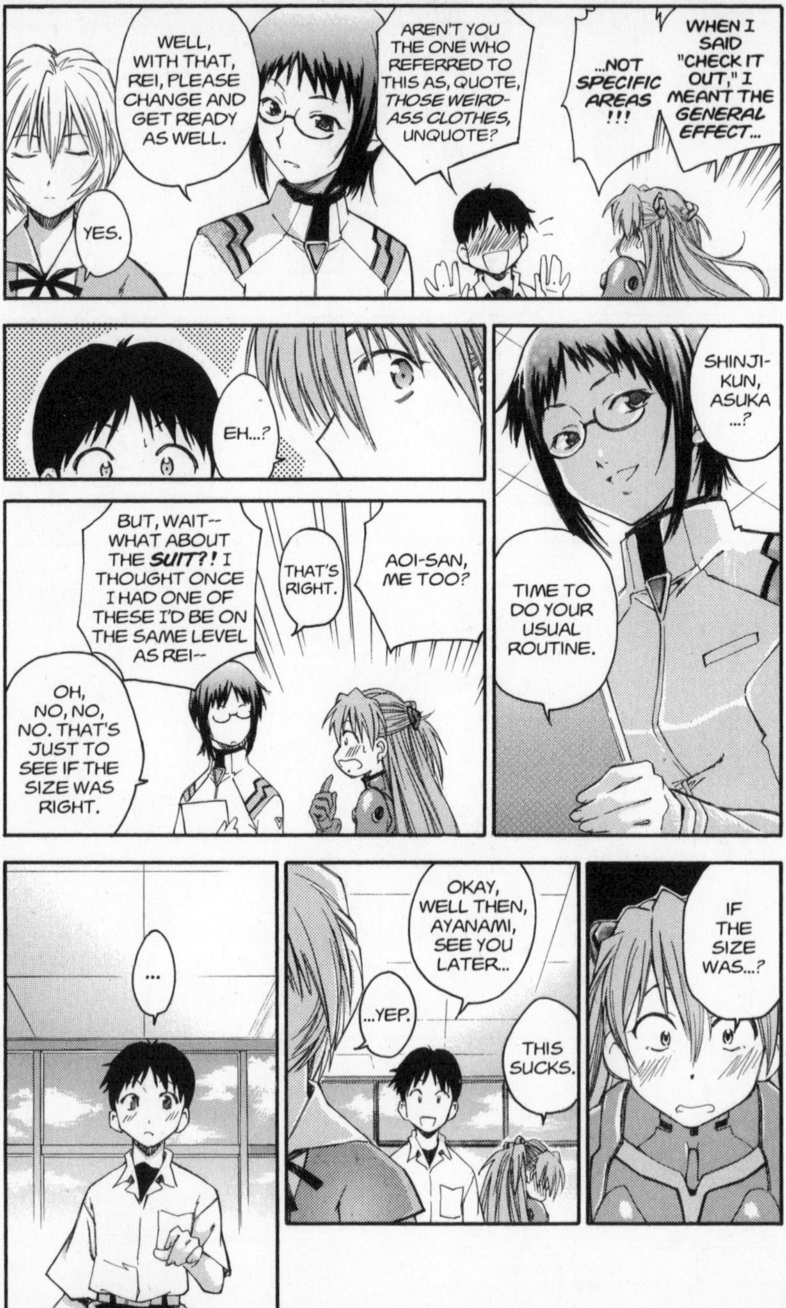
WHEN I SAID "CHECK IT OUT," I MEANT THE GENERAL EFFECT...
...NOT SPECIFIC AREAS !!!
AREN'T YOU THE ONE WHO REFERRED TO THIS AS, QUOTE, THOSE WEIRD-ASS CLOTHES, UNQUOTE?
WELL, WITH THAT, REI, PLEASE CHANGE AND GET READY AS WELL.
YES.
SHINJI-KUN, ASUKA ...?
TIME TO DO YOUR USUAL ROUTINE.
EH...?
AOI-SAN, ME TOO?
THAT'S RIGHT.
BUT, WAIT-- WHAT ABOUT THE SUIT?! I THOUGHT ONCE I HAD ONE OF THESE I'D BE ON THE SAME LEVEL AS REI--
OH, NO, NO, NO. THAT'S JUST TO SEE IF THE SIZE WAS RIGHT.
IF THE SIZE WAS...?
OKAY, WELL THEN, AYANAMI, SEE YOU LATER...
...YEP.
THIS SUCKS.
...

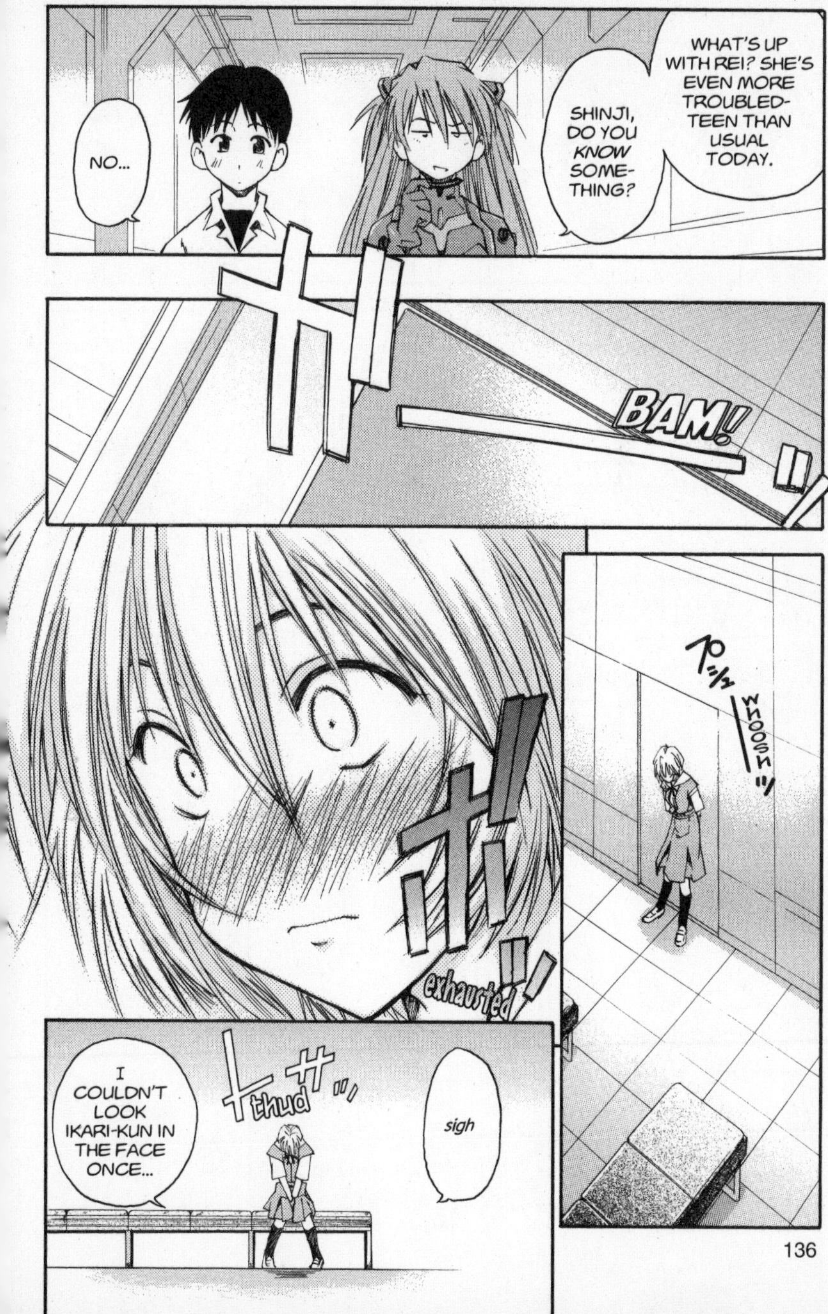

WHAT'S UP WITH REI? SHE'S EVEN MORE TROUBLED-TEEN THAN USUAL TODAY.
SHINJI, DO YOU KNOW SOME-THING?
NO...
BAM!
WHOOSH
exhausted
sigh
thud
I COULDN'T LOOK IKARI-KUN IN THE FACE ONCE...

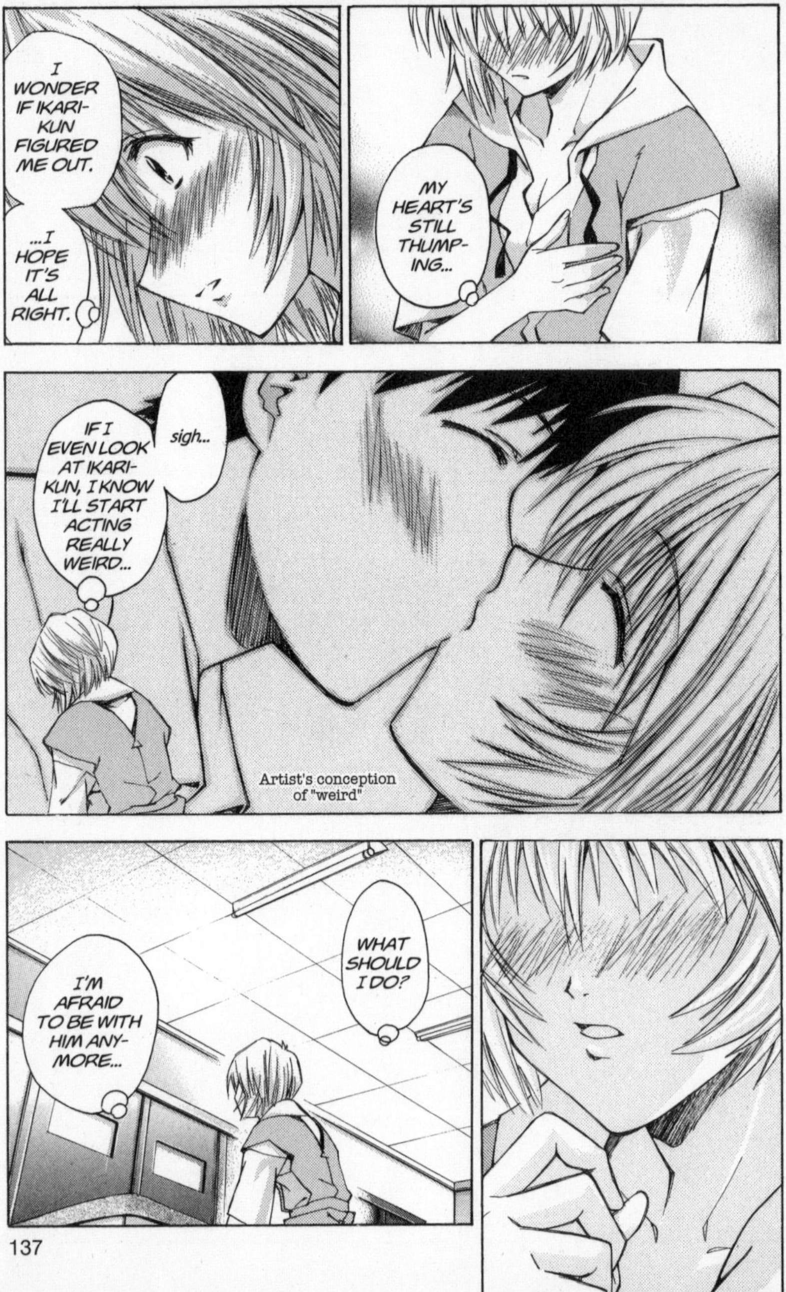
MY HEART'S STILL THUMPING...
I WONDER IF IKARI-KUN FIGURED ME OUT.
...I HOPE IT'S ALL RIGHT.
sigh...
IF I EVEN LOOK AT IKARI-KUN, I KNOW I'LL START ACTING REALLY WEIRD...
Artist's conception of "weird"
WHAT SHOULD I DO?
I'M AFRAID TO BE WITH HIM ANY-MORE...

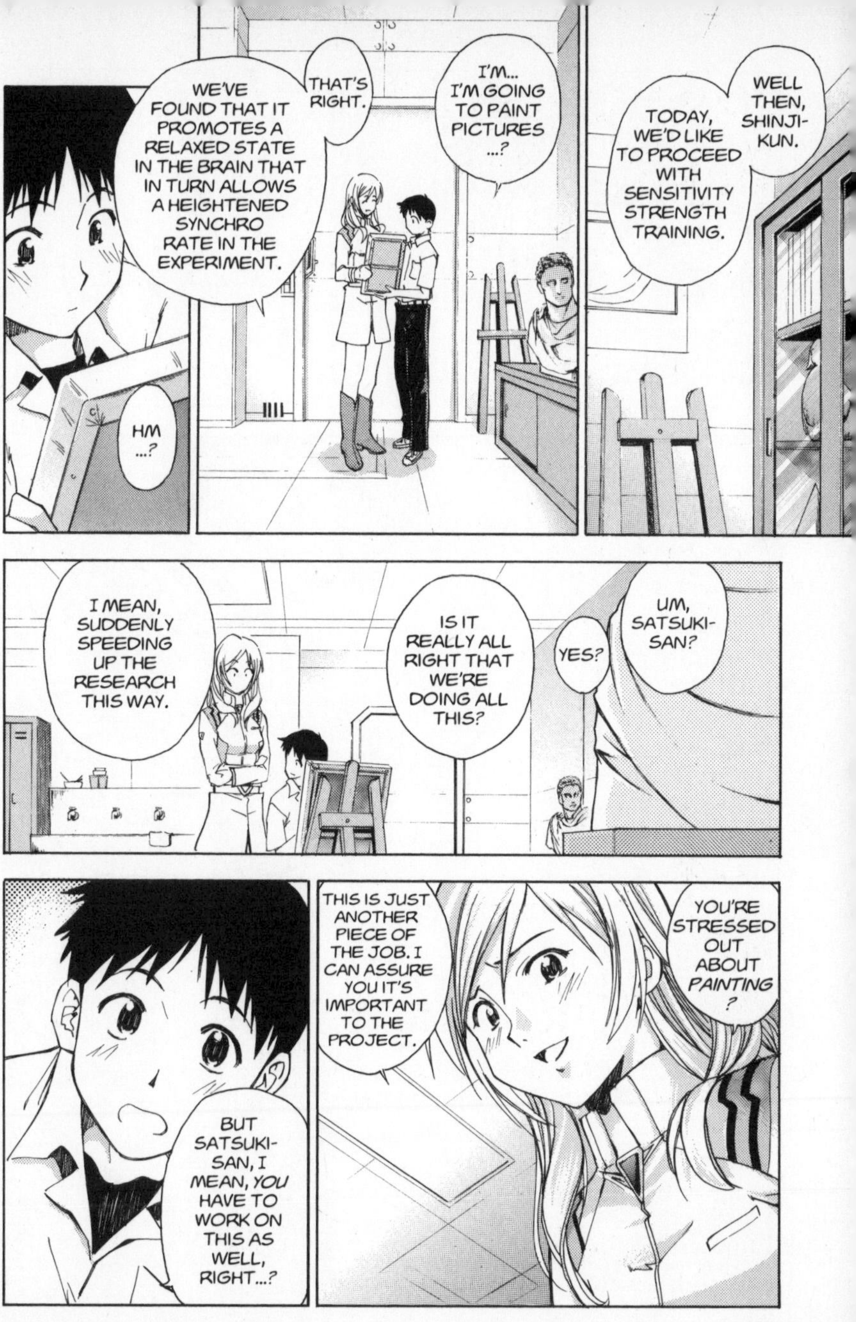

WELL THEN, SHINJI-KUN.
TODAY, WE'D LIKE TO PROCEED WITH SENSITIVITY STRENGTH TRAINING.
I'M... I'M GOING TO PAINT PICTURES ...?
THAT'S RIGHT.
WE'VE FOUND THAT IT PROMOTES A RELAXED STATE IN THE BRAIN THAT IN TURN ALLOWS A HEIGHTENED SYNCHRO RATE IN THE EXPERIMENT.
HM ...?
UM, SATSUKI-SAN?
YES?
IS IT REALLY ALL RIGHT THAT WE'RE DOING ALL THIS?
I MEAN, SUDDENLY SPEEDING UP THE RESEARCH THIS WAY.
YOU'RE STRESSED OUT ABOUT *PAINTING* ?
THIS IS JUST ANOTHER PIECE OF THE JOB. I CAN ASSURE YOU IT'S IMPORTANT TO THE PROJECT.
BUT SATSUKI-SAN, I MEAN, *YOU* HAVE TO WORK ON THIS AS WELL, RIGHT...?

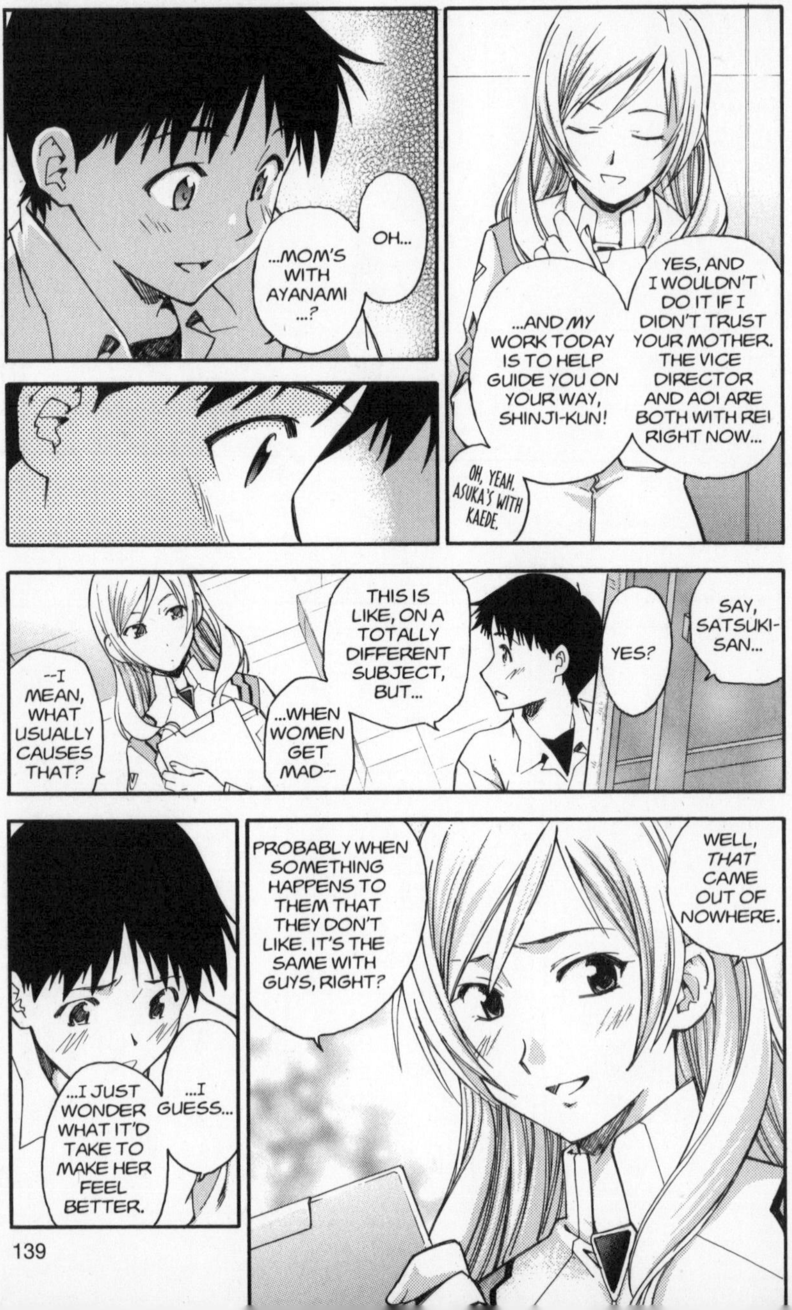
YES, AND I WOULDN'T DO IT IF I DIDN'T TRUST YOUR MOTHER. THE VICE DIRECTOR AND AOI ARE BOTH WITH REI RIGHT NOW...
...AND MY WORK TODAY IS TO HELP GUIDE YOU ON YOUR WAY, SHINJI-KUN!
OH, YEAH. ASUKA'S WITH KAEDE.
OH...
...MOM'S WITH AYANAMI ...?
SAY, SATSUKI-SAN...
YES?
THIS IS LIKE, ON A TOTALLY DIFFERENT SUBJECT, BUT...
...WHEN WOMEN GET MAD--
--I MEAN, WHAT USUALLY CAUSES THAT?
WELL, *THAT* CAME OUT OF NOWHERE.
PROBABLY WHEN SOMETHING HAPPENS TO THEM THAT THEY DON'T LIKE. IT'S THE SAME WITH GUYS, RIGHT?
...I GUESS...
...I JUST WONDER WHAT IT'D TAKE TO MAKE HER FEEL BETTER.

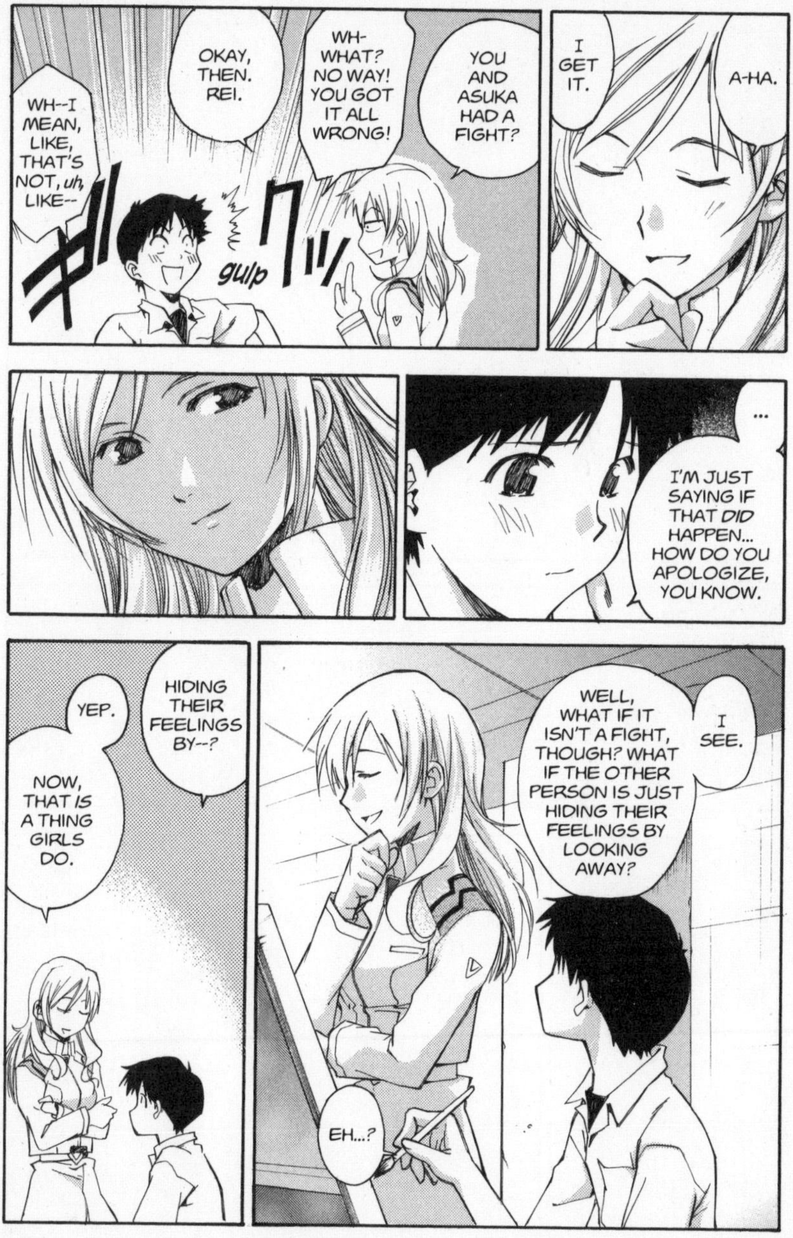
A-HA.
I GET IT.
YOU AND ASUKA HAD A FIGHT?
WH- WHAT? NO WAY! YOU GOT IT ALL WRONG!
OKAY, THEN. REI.
WH--I MEAN, LIKE, THAT'S NOT, *uh*, LIKE--
gulp
...
I'M JUST SAYING IF THAT *DID* HAPPEN... HOW DO YOU APOLOGIZE, YOU KNOW.
I SEE.
WELL, WHAT IF IT ISN'T A FIGHT, THOUGH? WHAT IF THE OTHER PERSON IS JUST HIDING THEIR FEELINGS BY LOOKING AWAY?
EH...?
HIDING THEIR FEELINGS BY--?
YEP.
NOW, THAT *IS* A THING GIRLS DO.

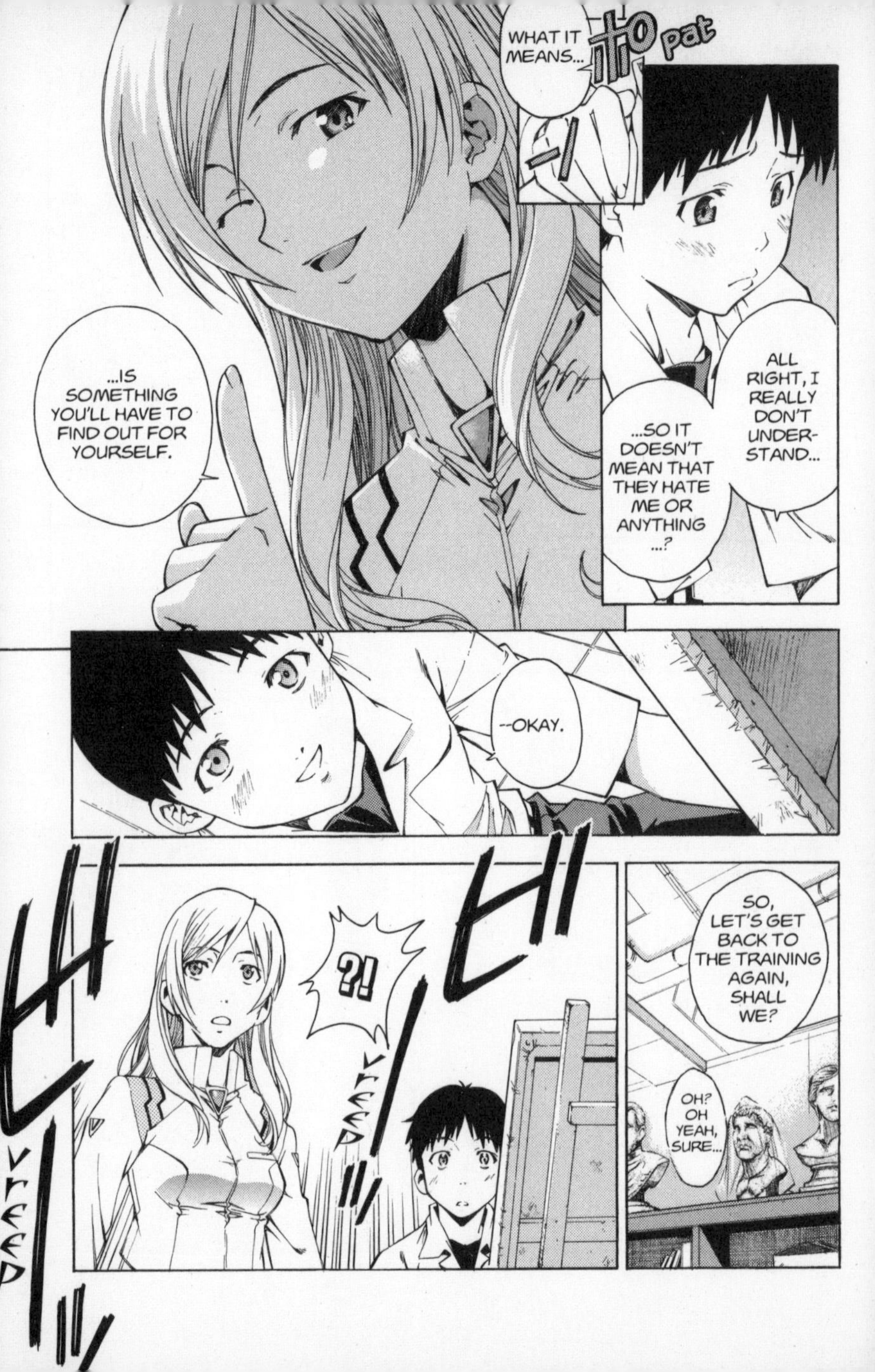
ALL RIGHT, I REALLY DON'T UNDER-STAND...
...SO IT DOESN'T MEAN THAT THEY HATE ME OR ANYTHING ...?
WHAT IT MEANS...
pat
...IS SOMETHING YOU'LL HAVE TO FIND OUT FOR YOURSELF.
--OKAY.
SO, LET'S GET BACK TO THE TRAINING AGAIN, SHALL WE?
OH? OH YEAH, SURE...
VREEP
?!
VREEP

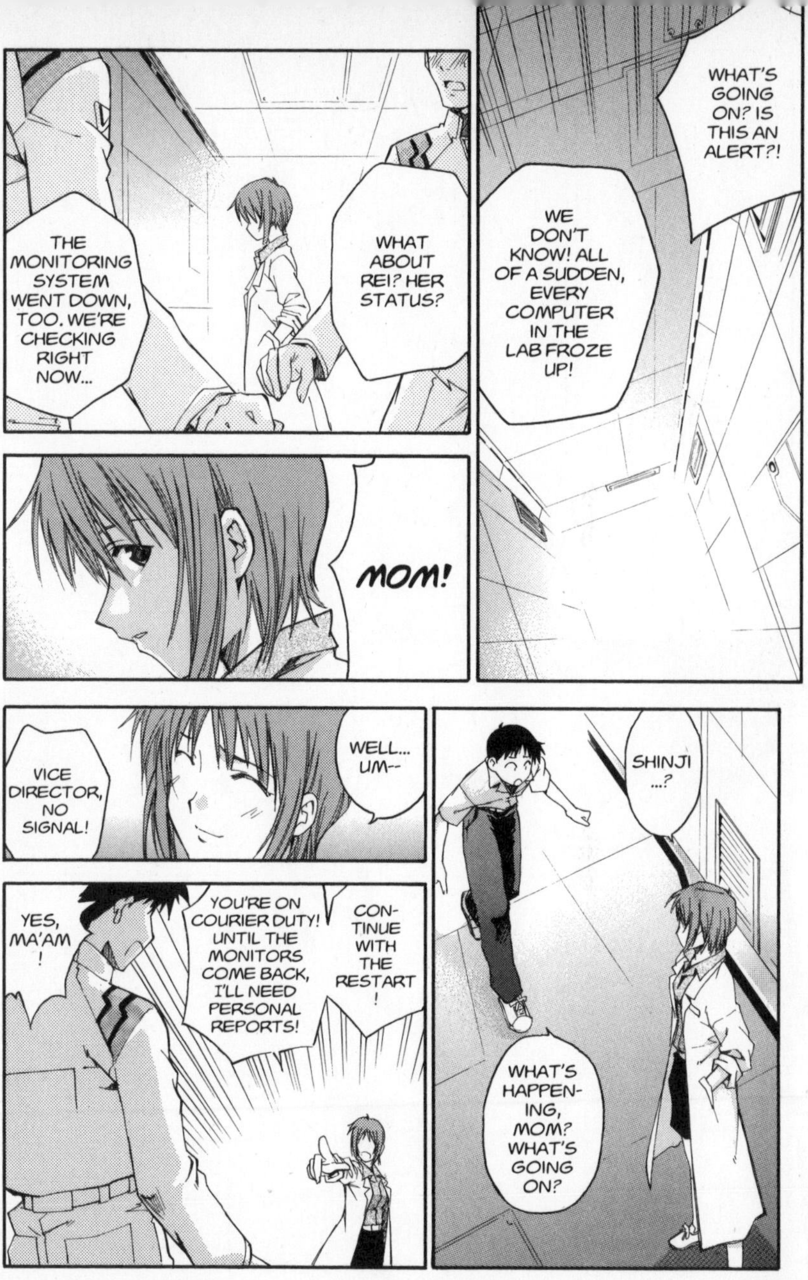
WHAT'S GOING ON? IS THIS AN ALERT?!
WE DON'T KNOW! ALL OF A SUDDEN, EVERY COMPUTER IN THE LAB FROZE UP!
WHAT ABOUT REI? HER STATUS?
THE MONITORING SYSTEM WENT DOWN, TOO. WE'RE CHECKING RIGHT NOW...
MOM!
SHINJI ...?
WHAT'S HAPPENING, MOM? WHAT'S GOING ON?
WELL... UM--
VICE DIRECTOR, NO SIGNAL!
CONTINUE WITH THE RESTART!
YOU'RE ON COURIER DUTY! UNTIL THE MONITORS COME BACK, I'LL NEED PERSONAL REPORTS!
YES, MA'AM!

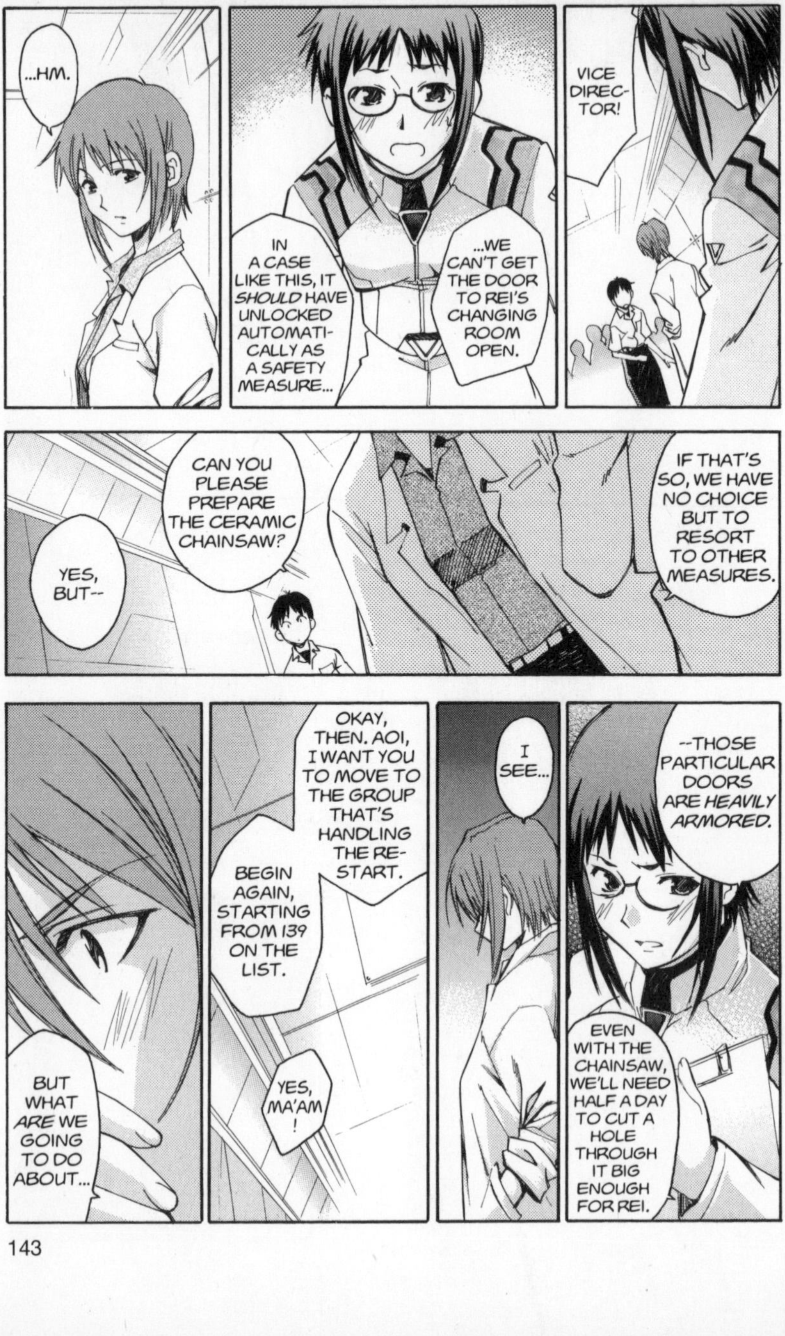
VICE DIRECTOR!
...WE CAN'T GET THE DOOR TO REI'S CHANGING ROOM OPEN.
IN A CASE LIKE THIS, IT *SHOULD* HAVE UNLOCKED AUTOMATICALLY AS A SAFETY MEASURE...
...HM.
IF THAT'S SO, WE HAVE NO CHOICE BUT TO RESORT TO OTHER MEASURES.
CAN YOU PLEASE PREPARE THE CERAMIC CHAINSAW?
YES, BUT--
--THOSE PARTICULAR DOORS ARE *HEAVILY ARMORED.*
EVEN WITH THE CHAINSAW, WE'LL NEED HALF A DAY TO CUT A HOLE THROUGH IT BIG ENOUGH FOR REI.
I SEE...
OKAY, THEN. AOI, I WANT YOU TO MOVE TO THE GROUP THAT'S HANDLING THE RE-START.
BEGIN AGAIN, STARTING FROM 139 ON THE LIST.
YES, MA'AM!
BUT WHAT *ARE* WE GOING TO DO ABOUT...

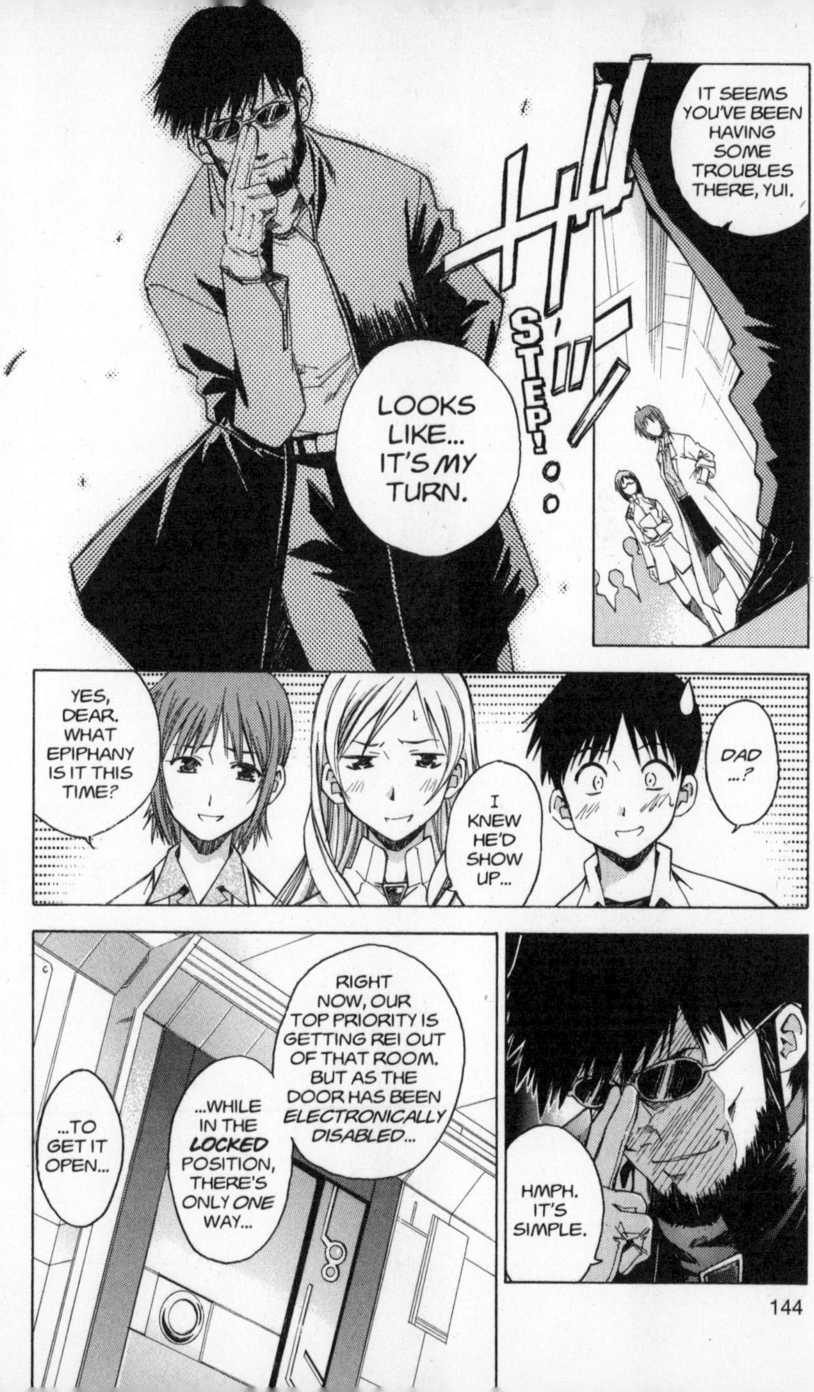
IT SEEMS YOU'VE BEEN HAVING SOME TROUBLES THERE, YUI.
STEP!
LOOKS LIKE... IT'S *MY* TURN.
DAD ...?
I KNEW HE'D SHOW UP...
YES, DEAR. WHAT EPIPHANY IS IT THIS TIME?
HMPH. IT'S SIMPLE.
RIGHT NOW, OUR TOP PRIORITY IS GETTING REI OUT OF THAT ROOM. BUT AS THE DOOR HAS BEEN *ELECTRONICALLY DISABLED*...
...WHILE IN THE ***LOCKED*** POSITION, THERE'S ONLY *ONE* WAY...
...TO GET IT OPEN...

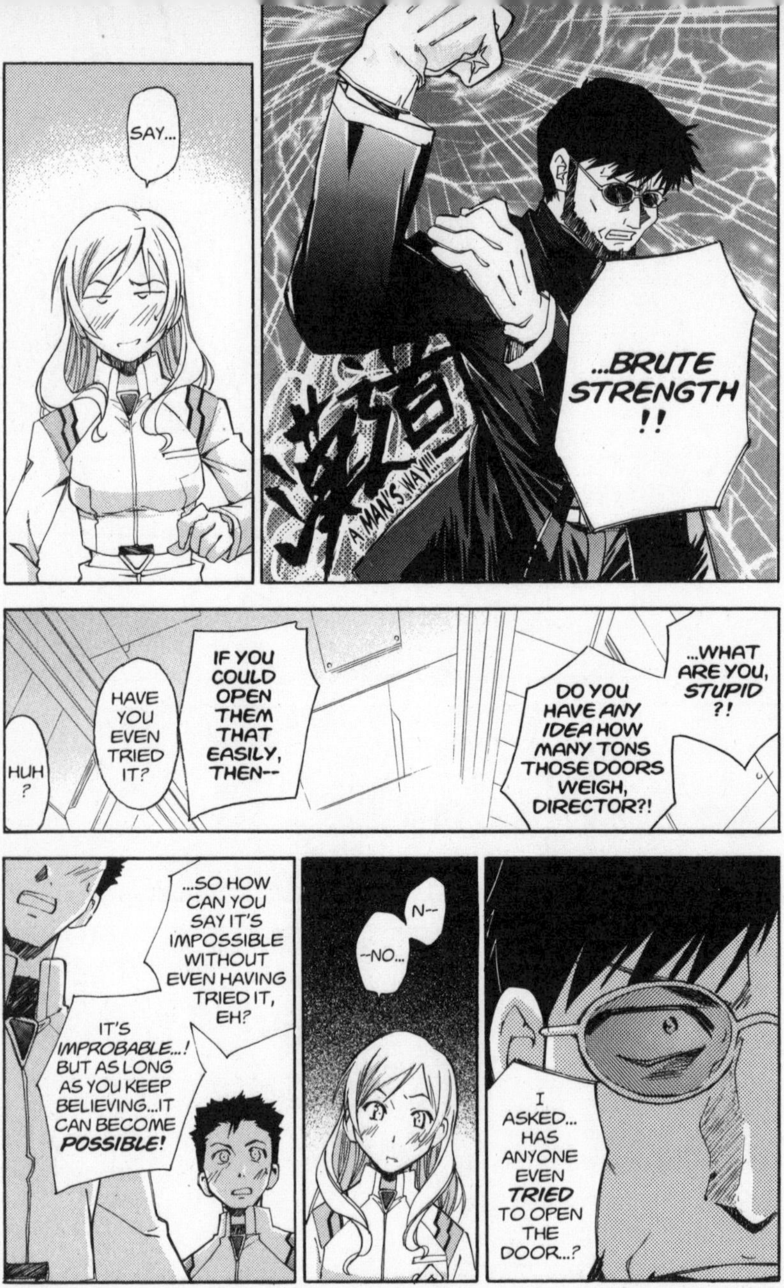
...BRUTE STRENGTH !!
A MAN'S WAY!!!!
SAY...
...WHAT ARE YOU, STUPID?!
DO YOU HAVE ANY IDEA HOW MANY TONS THOSE DOORS WEIGH, DIRECTOR?!
IF YOU COULD OPEN THEM THAT EASILY, THEN--
HAVE YOU EVEN TRIED IT?
HUH?
I ASKED... HAS ANYONE EVEN TRIED TO OPEN THE DOOR...?
N--
--NO...
...SO HOW CAN YOU SAY IT'S IMPOSSIBLE WITHOUT EVEN HAVING TRIED IT, EH?
IT'S IMPROBABLE...! BUT AS LONG AS YOU KEEP BELIEVING...IT CAN BECOME POSSIBLE!

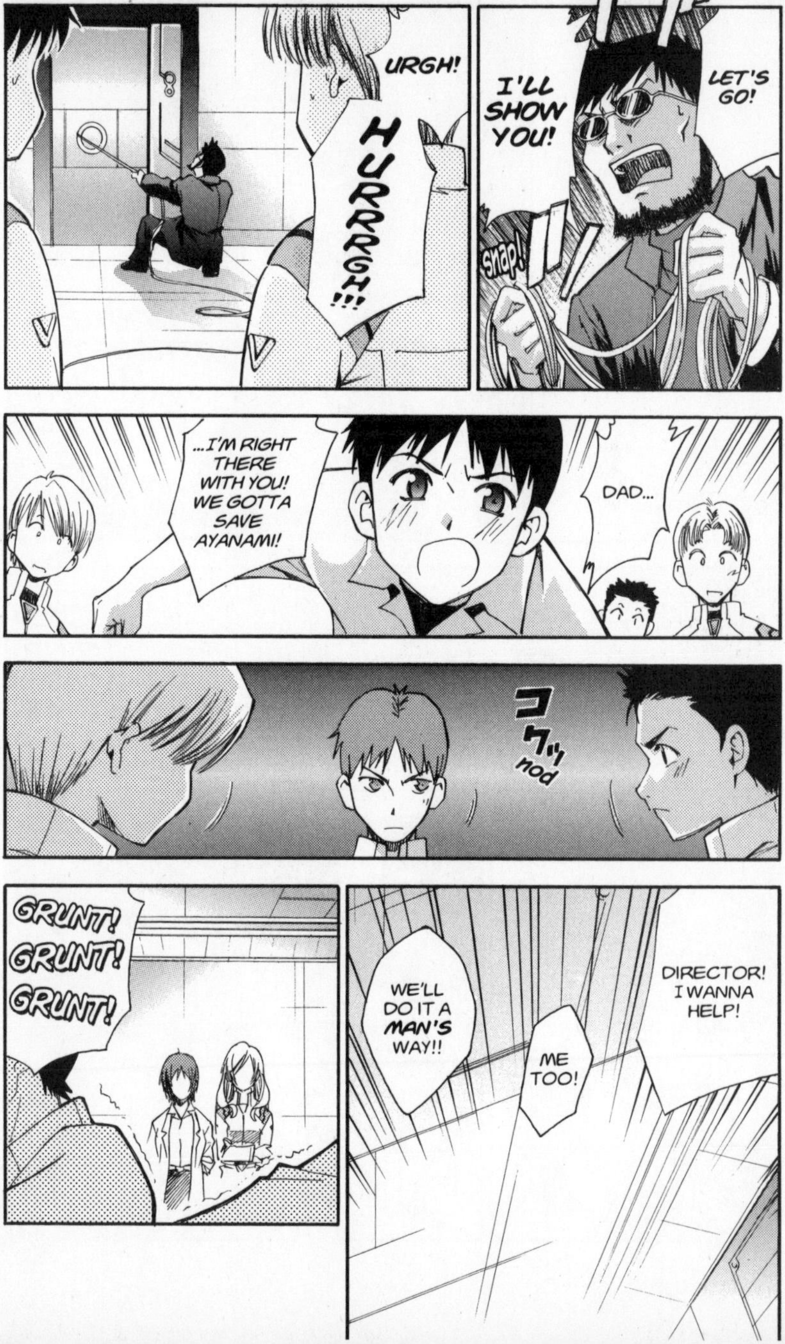
LET'S GO!
I'LL SHOW YOU!
snap!
URGH!
HURRRGH!!!
DAD...
...I'M RIGHT THERE WITH YOU! WE GOTTA SAVE AYANAMI!
コクッ
nod
DIRECTOR! I WANNA HELP!
ME TOO!
WE'LL DO IT A MAN'S WAY!!
GRUNT! GRUNT! GRUNT!

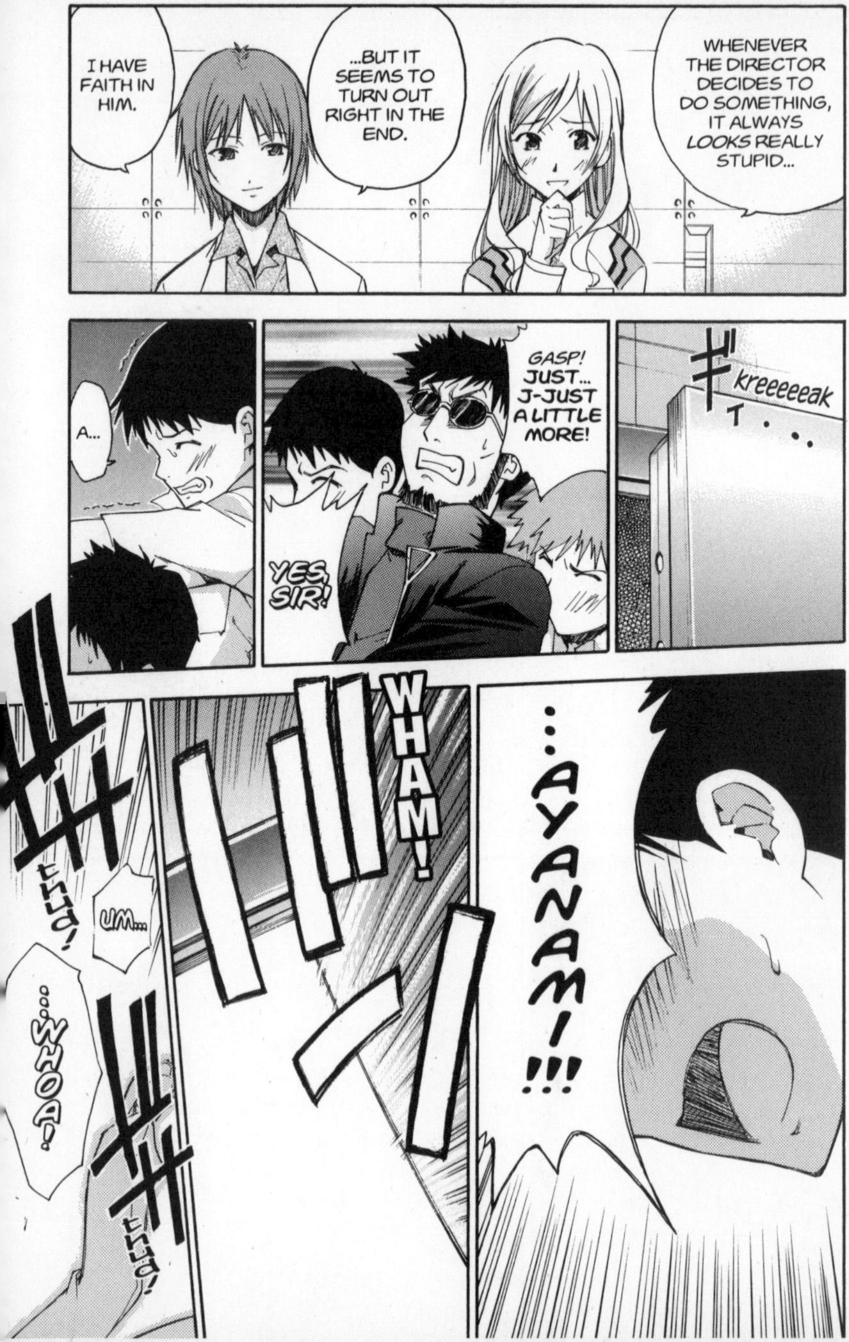

WHENEVER THE DIRECTOR DECIDES TO DO SOMETHING, IT ALWAYS LOOKS REALLY STUPID...
...BUT IT SEEMS TO TURN OUT RIGHT IN THE END.
I HAVE FAITH IN HIM.
kreeeeeak
GASP! JUST... J-JUST A LITTLE MORE!
YES, SIR!
A...
...AYANAMI!!!
WHAM!
UM...
thud!
...WHOA!
thud!

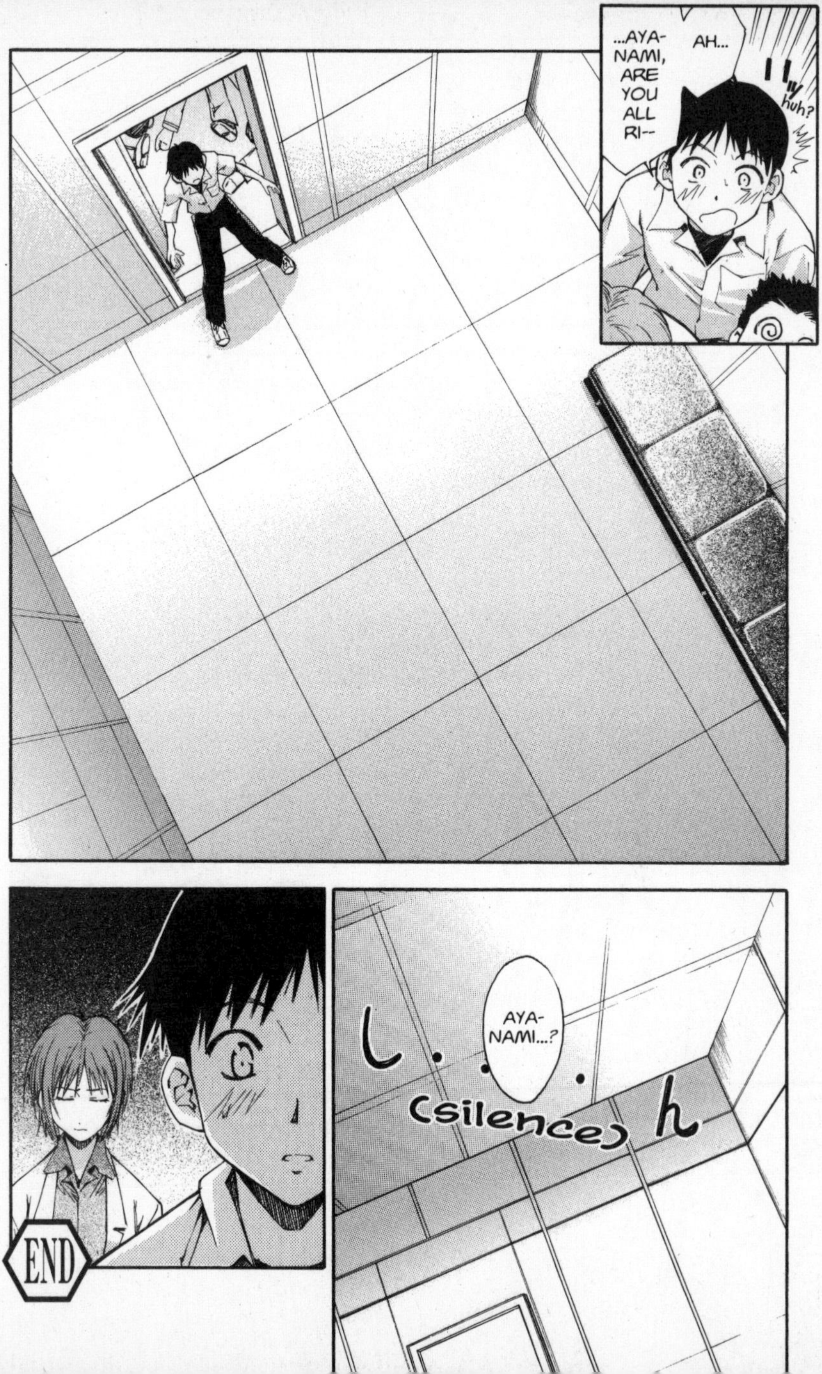
AH...
huh?
...AYA-NAMI, ARE YOU ALL RI--
AYA-NAMI...?
(silence)
END

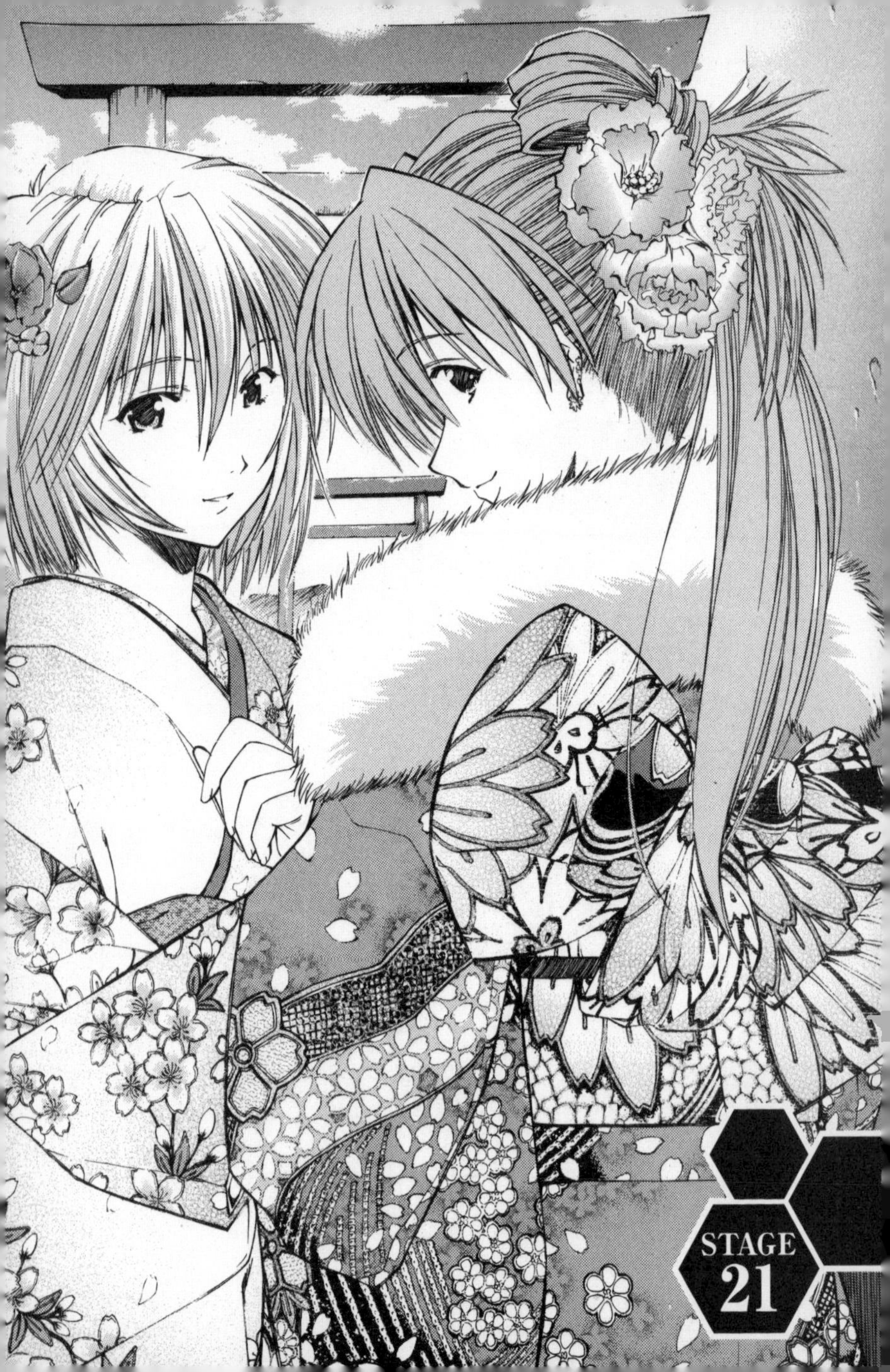
STAGE
21

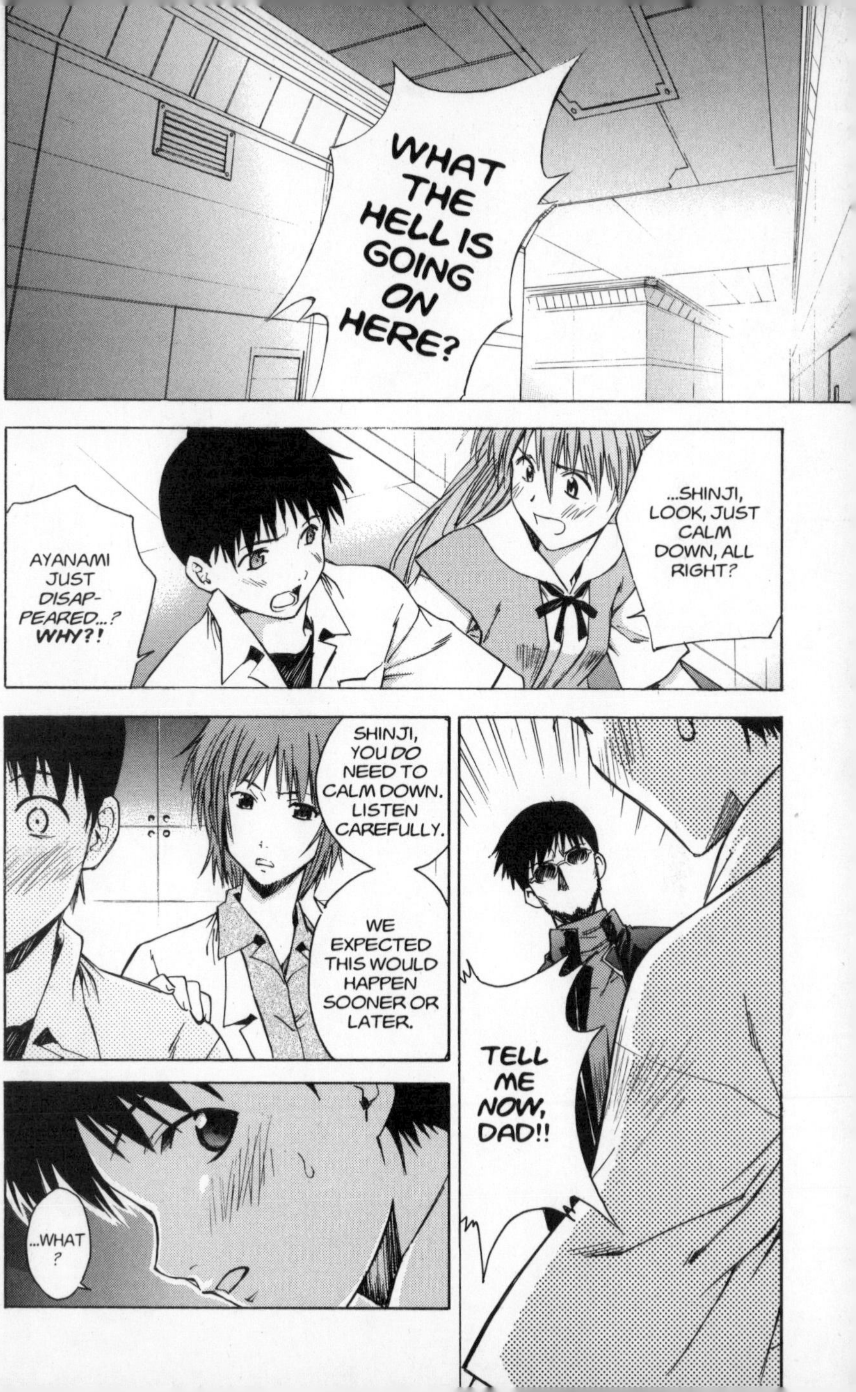
WHAT THE HELL IS GOING ON HERE?
...SHINJI, LOOK, JUST CALM DOWN, ALL RIGHT?
AYANAMI JUST DISAP-PEARED...? **WHY?!**
TELL ME NOW, DAD!!
SHINJI, YOU *DO* NEED TO CALM DOWN. LISTEN CAREFULLY.
WE EXPECTED THIS WOULD HAPPEN SOONER OR LATER.
...WHAT ?

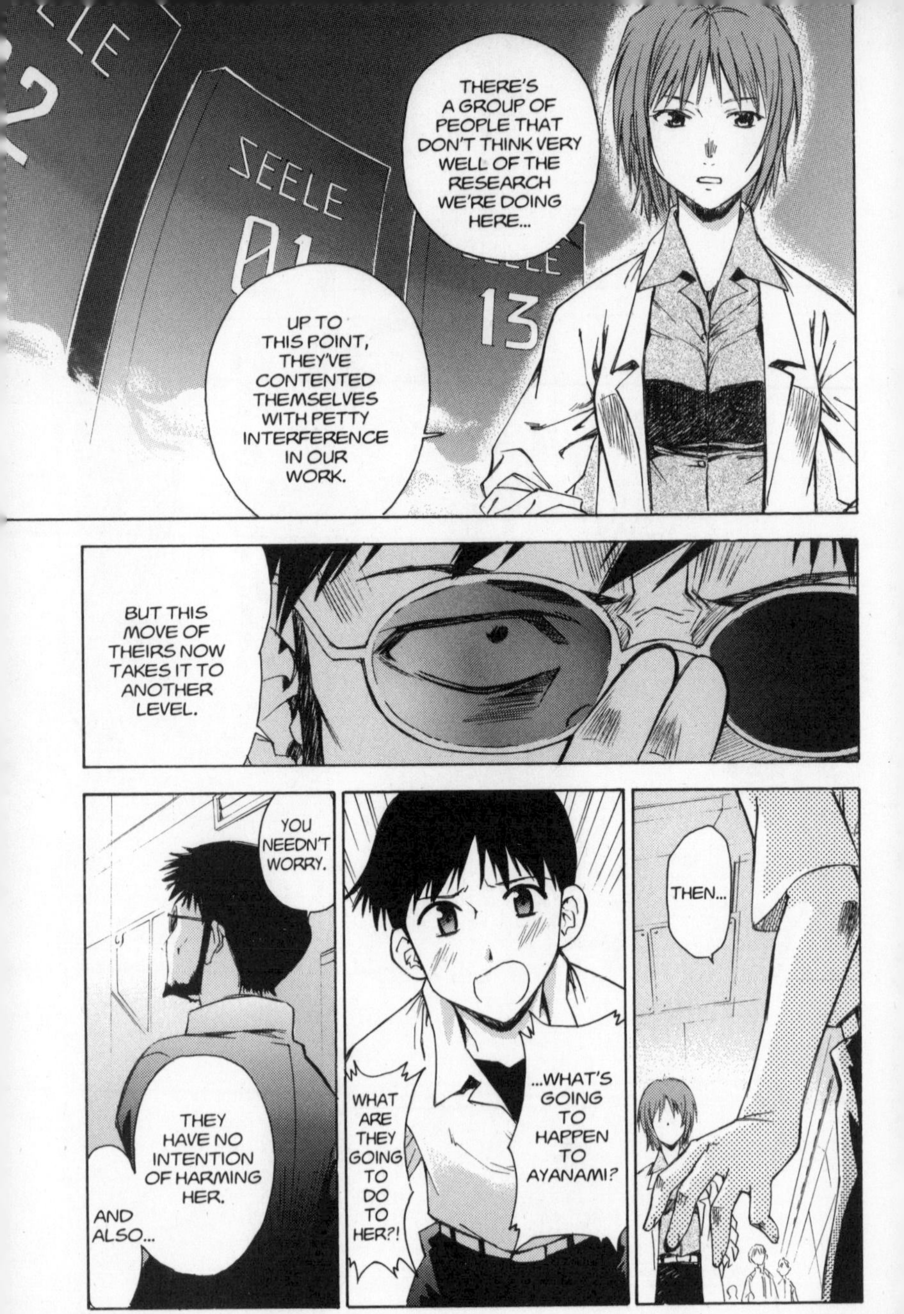
THERE'S A GROUP OF PEOPLE THAT DON'T THINK VERY WELL OF THE RESEARCH WE'RE DOING HERE...
UP TO THIS POINT, THEY'VE CONTENTED THEMSELVES WITH PETTY INTERFERENCE IN OUR WORK.
BUT THIS MOVE OF THEIRS NOW TAKES IT TO ANOTHER LEVEL.
THEN...
...WHAT'S GOING TO HAPPEN TO AYANAMI?
WHAT ARE THEY GOING TO DO TO HER?!
YOU NEEDN'T WORRY.
THEY HAVE NO INTENTION OF HARMING HER.
AND ALSO...

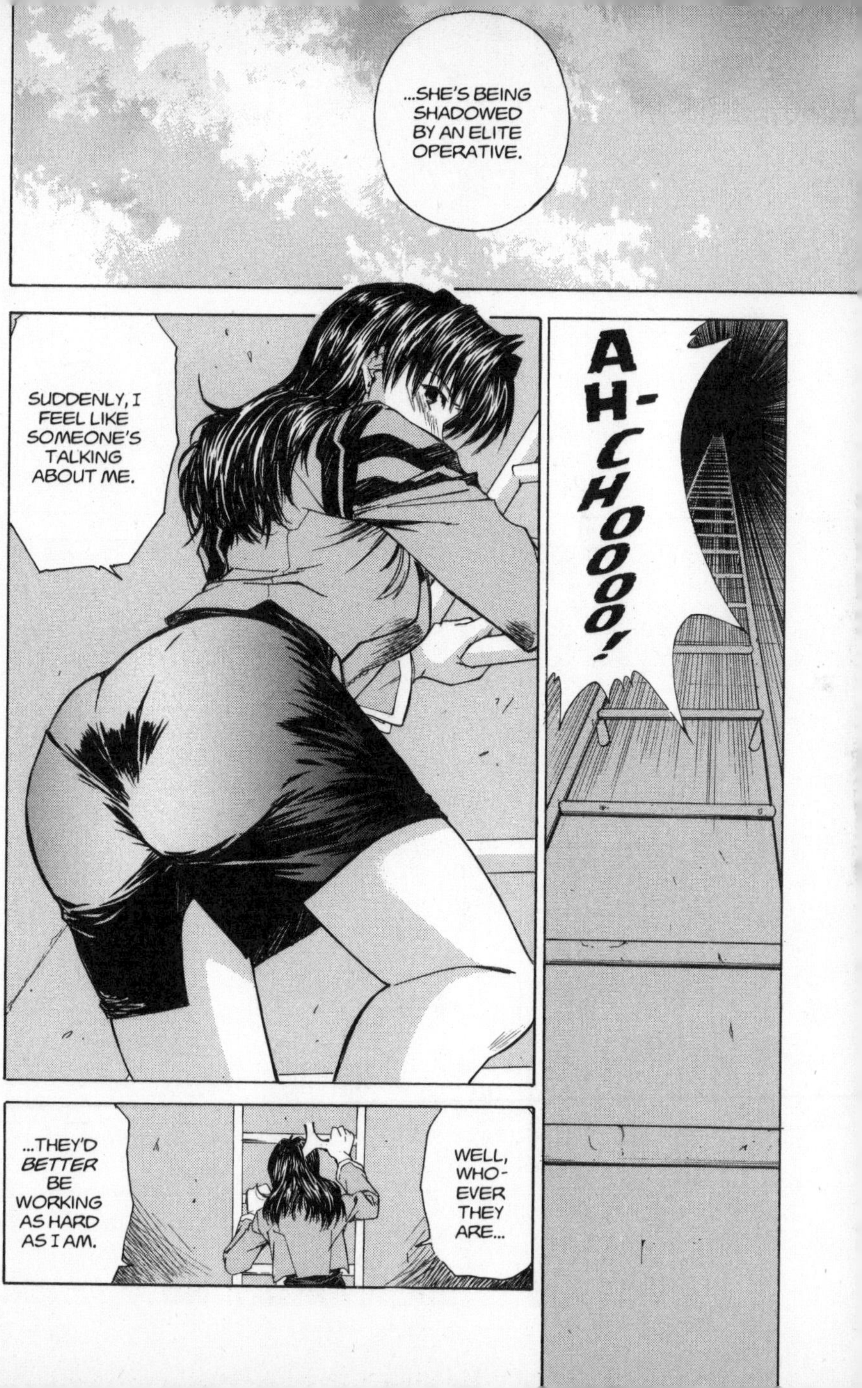
...SHE'S BEING SHADOWED BY AN ELITE OPERATIVE.
AH-CHOOOOO!
SUDDENLY, I FEEL LIKE SOMEONE'S TALKING ABOUT ME.
WELL, WHO-EVER THEY ARE...
...THEY'D *BETTER* BE WORKING AS HARD AS I AM.

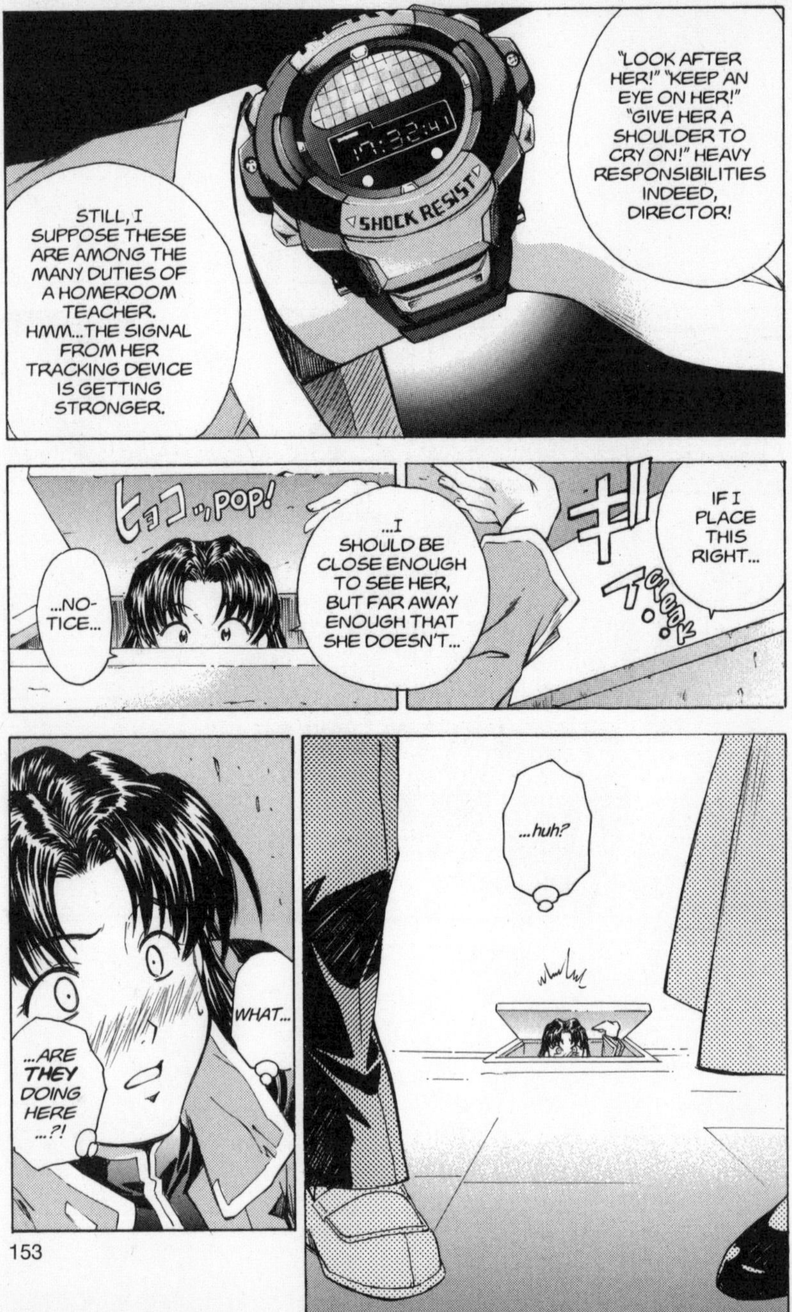
"LOOK AFTER HER!" "KEEP AN EYE ON HER!" "GIVE HER A SHOULDER TO CRY ON!" HEAVY RESPONSIBILITIES INDEED, DIRECTOR!
SHOCK RESIST
STILL, I SUPPOSE THESE ARE AMONG THE MANY DUTIES OF A HOMEROOM TEACHER. HMM...THE SIGNAL FROM HER TRACKING DEVICE IS GETTING STRONGER.
IF I PLACE THIS RIGHT...
...I SHOULD BE CLOSE ENOUGH TO SEE HER, BUT FAR AWAY ENOUGH THAT SHE DOESN'T...
POP!
...NO-TICE...
...huh?
WHAT...
...ARE **THEY** DOING HERE ...?!

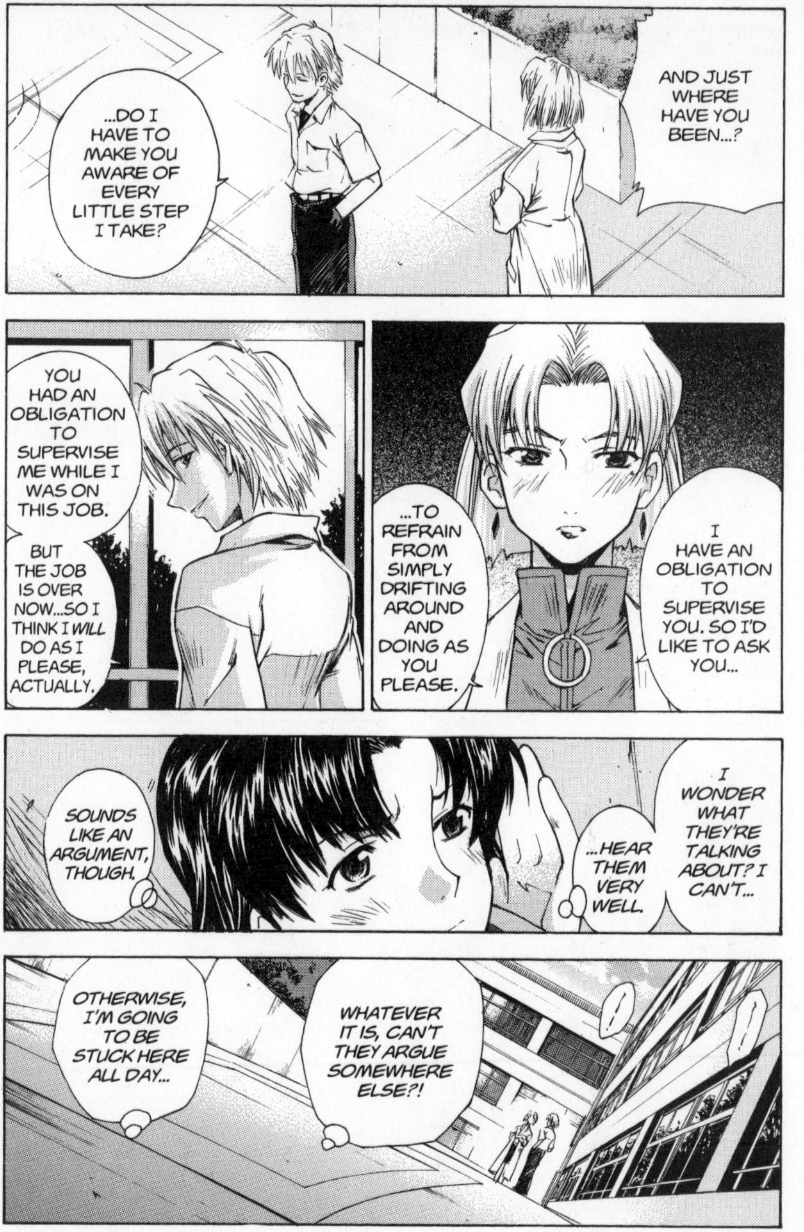
AND JUST WHERE HAVE YOU BEEN...?
...DO I HAVE TO MAKE YOU AWARE OF EVERY LITTLE STEP I TAKE?
I HAVE AN OBLIGATION TO SUPERVISE YOU. SO I'D LIKE TO ASK YOU...
...TO REFRAIN FROM SIMPLY DRIFTING AROUND AND DOING AS YOU PLEASE.
YOU HAD AN OBLIGATION TO SUPERVISE ME WHILE I WAS ON THIS JOB.
BUT THE JOB IS OVER NOW...SO I THINK I *WILL* DO AS I PLEASE, ACTUALLY.
I WONDER WHAT THEY'RE TALKING ABOUT? I CAN'T...
...HEAR THEM VERY WELL.
SOUNDS LIKE AN ARGUMENT, THOUGH.
WHATEVER IT IS, CAN'T THEY ARGUE SOMEWHERE ELSE?!
OTHERWISE, I'M GOING TO BE STUCK HERE ALL DAY...

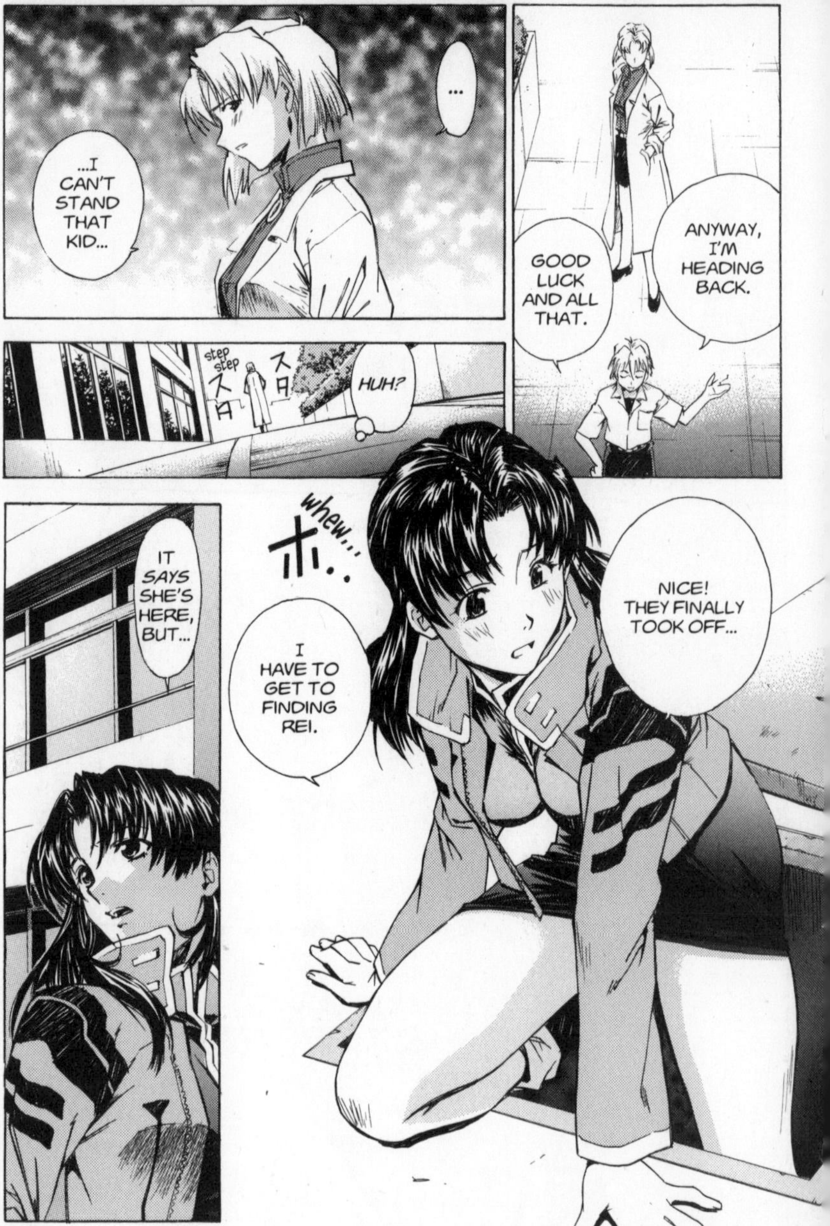

ANYWAY, I'M HEADING BACK.
GOOD LUCK AND ALL THAT.
...
...I CAN'T STAND THAT KID...
step step
スタ スタ
HUH?
whew...
ホ..
NICE! THEY FINALLY TOOK OFF...
I HAVE TO GET TO FINDING REI.
IT SAYS SHE'S HERE, BUT...

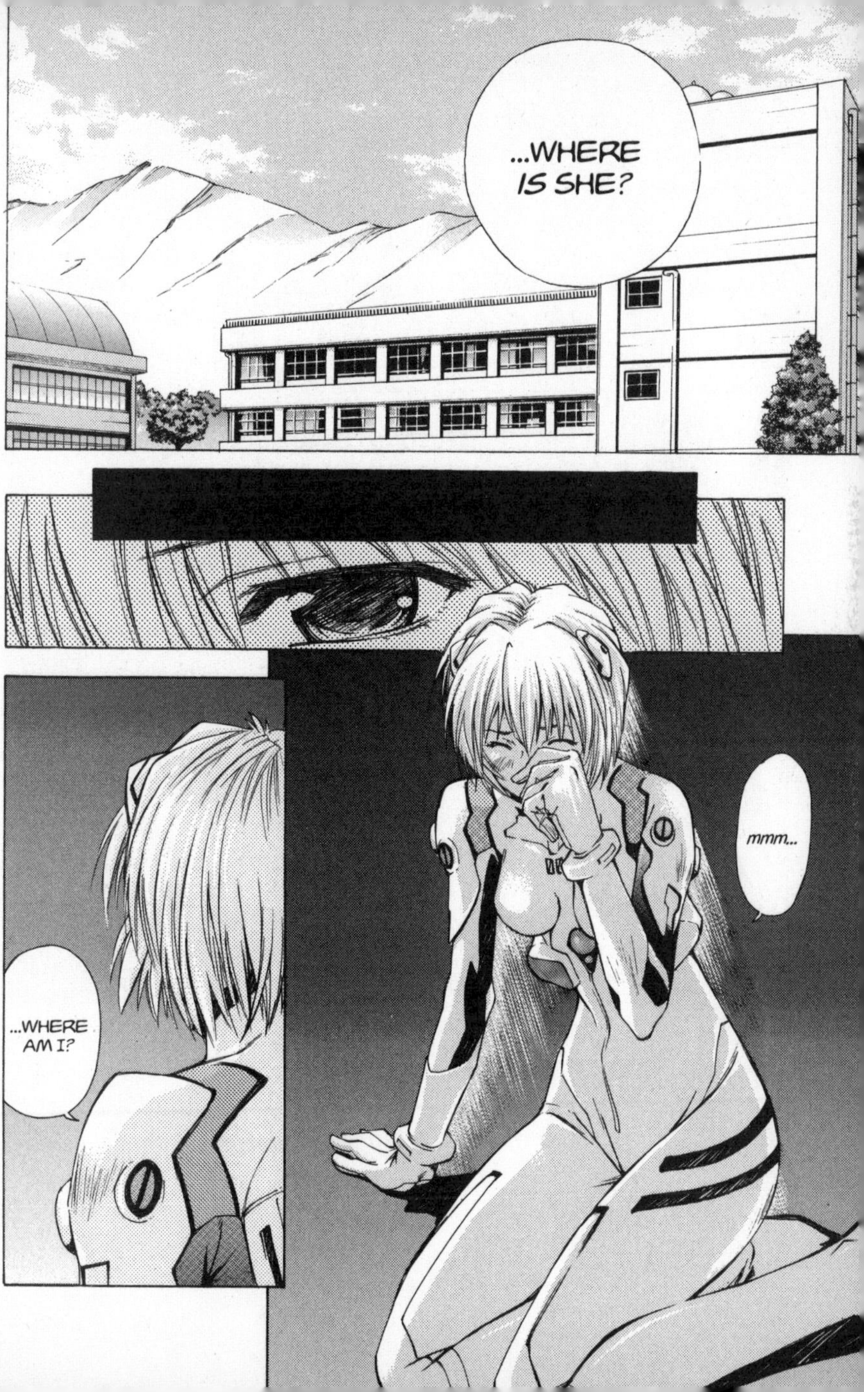
...WHERE IS SHE?
mmm...
...WHERE AM I?

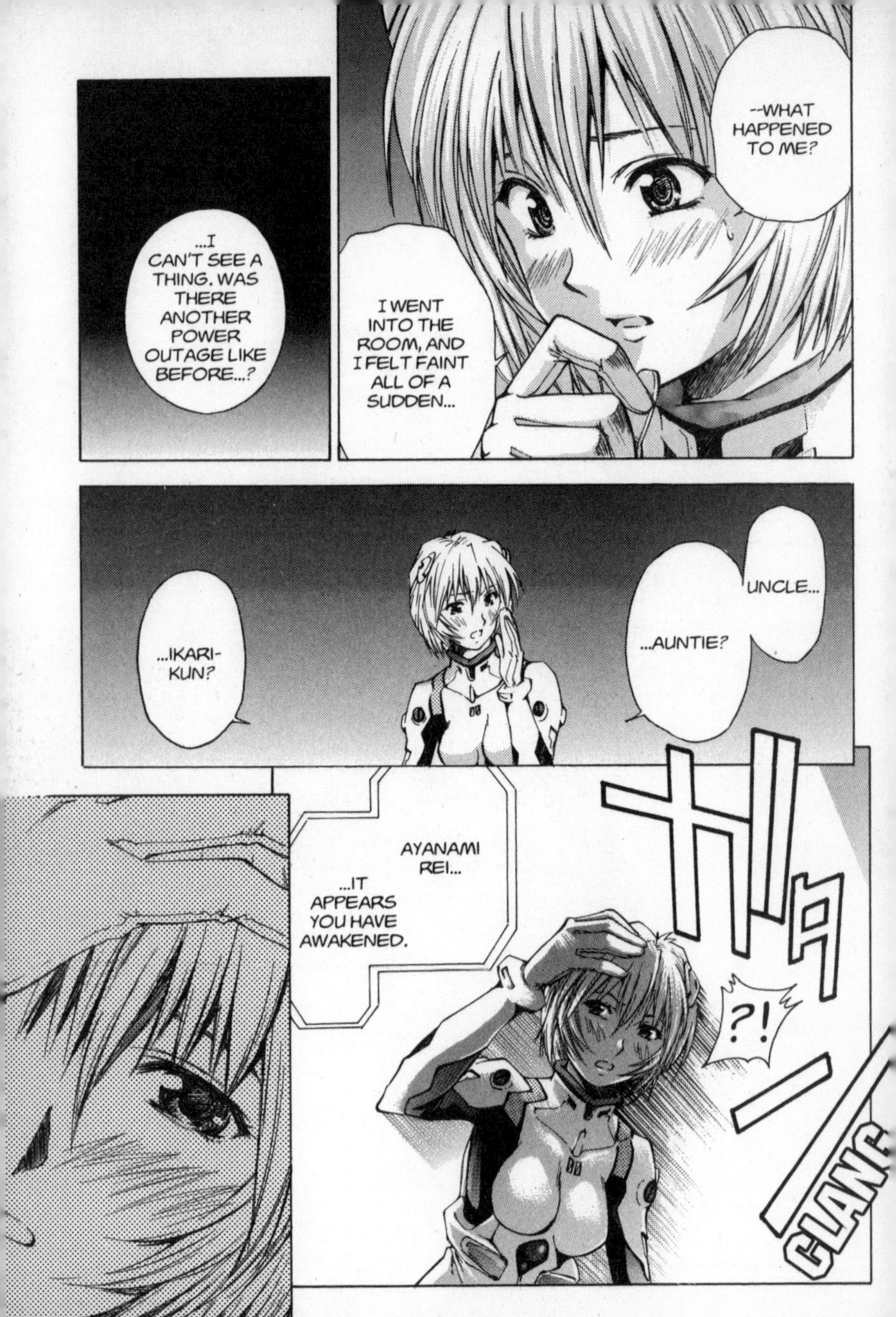
--WHAT HAPPENED TO ME?
I WENT INTO THE ROOM, AND I FELT FAINT ALL OF A SUDDEN...
...I CAN'T SEE A THING. WAS THERE ANOTHER POWER OUTAGE LIKE BEFORE...?
UNCLE...
...AUNTIE?
...IKARI-KUN?
?!
CLANG
AYANAMI REI...
...IT APPEARS YOU HAVE AWAKENED.

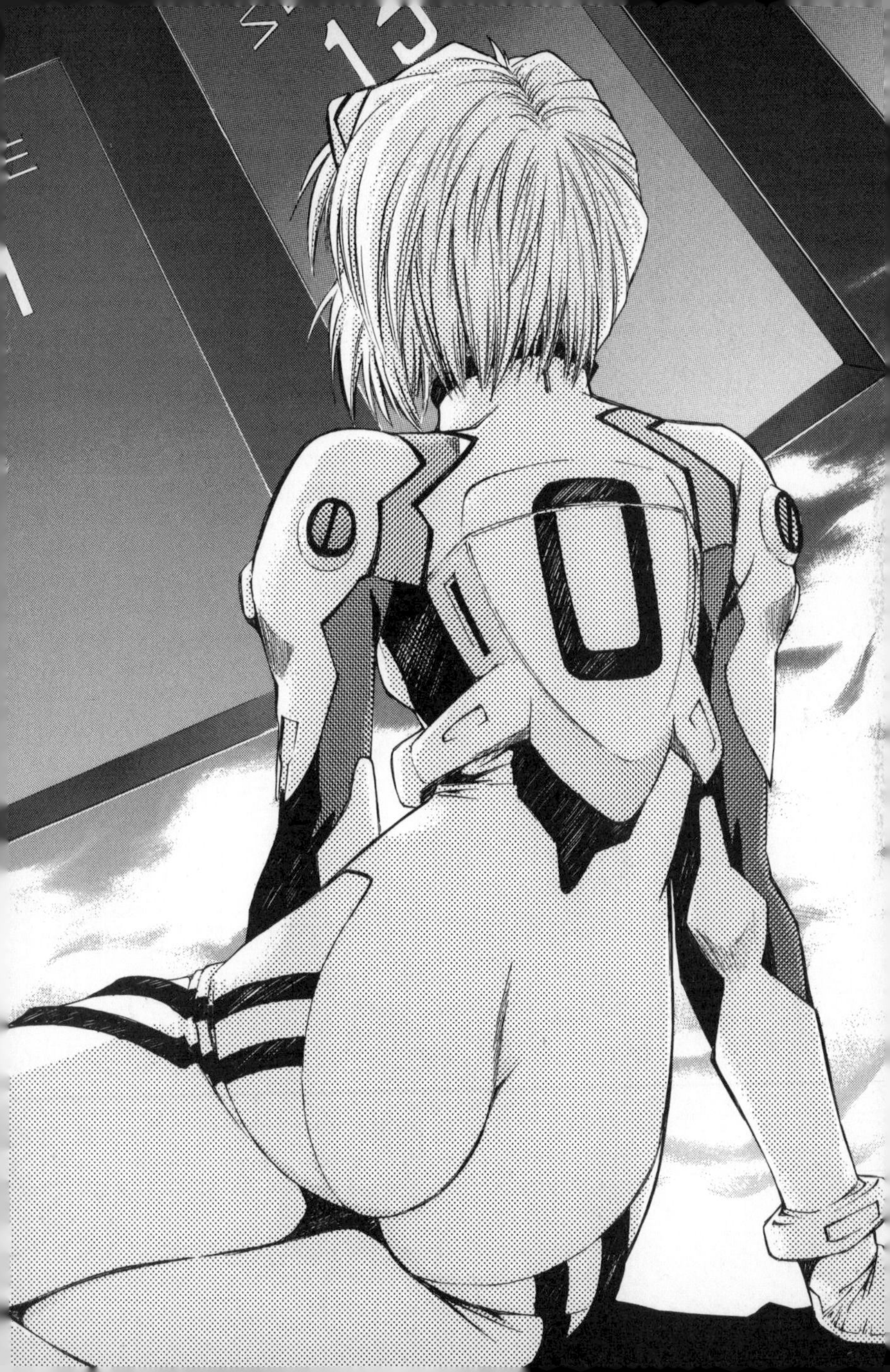

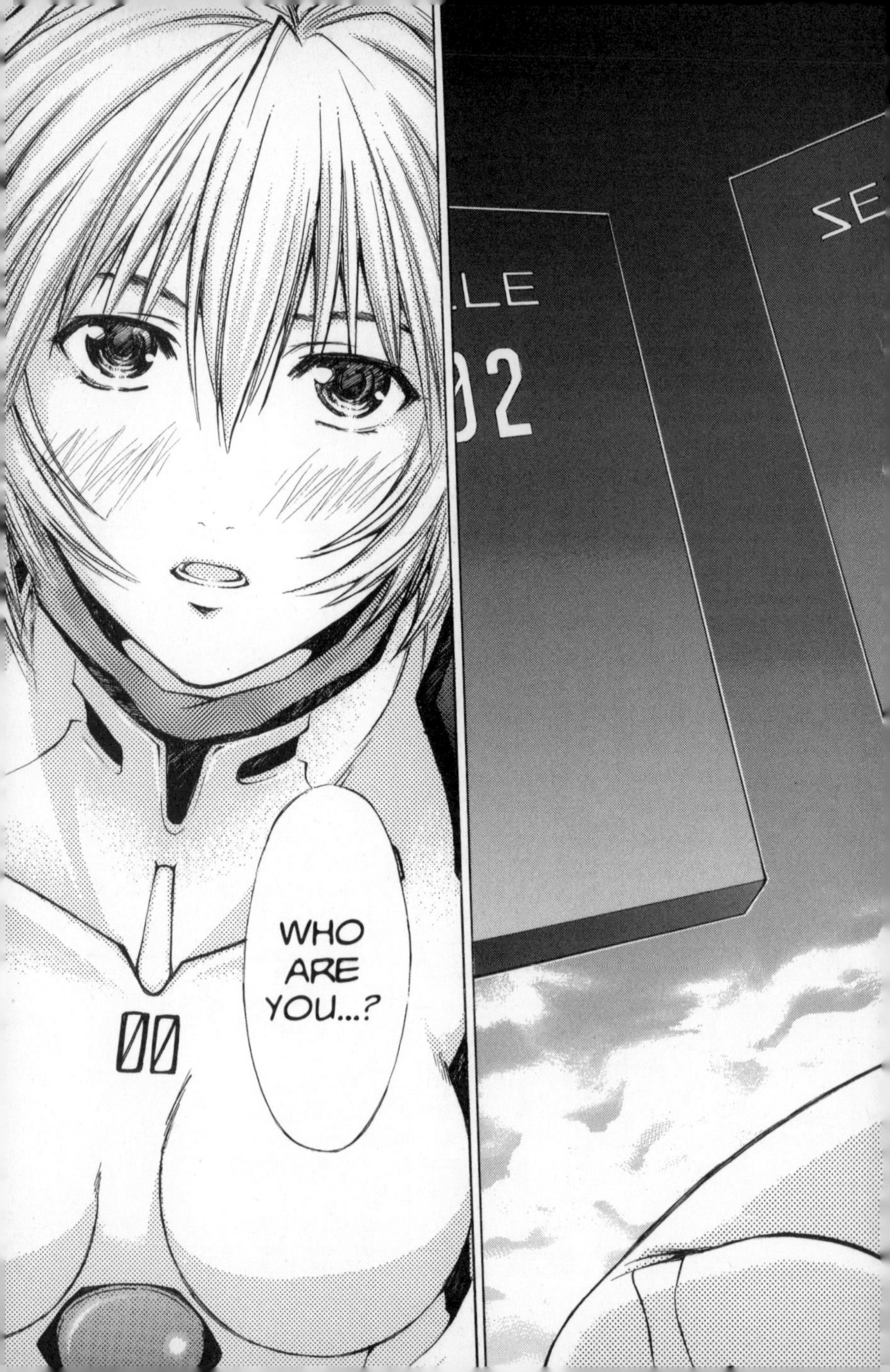
WHO ARE YOU...?

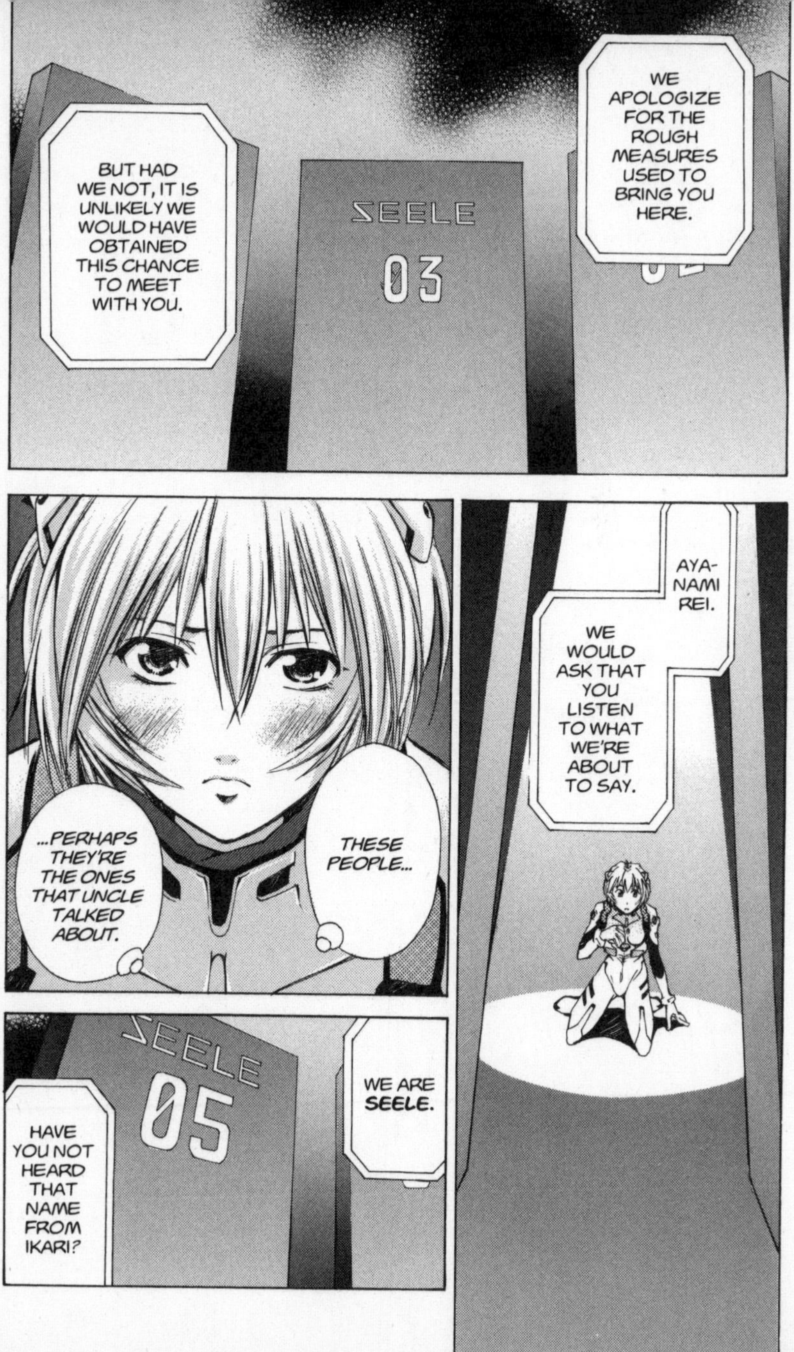
WE APOLOGIZE FOR THE ROUGH MEASURES USED TO BRING YOU HERE.
SEELE 03
BUT HAD WE NOT, IT IS UNLIKELY WE WOULD HAVE OBTAINED THIS CHANCE TO MEET WITH YOU.
AYA-NAMI REI.
WE WOULD ASK THAT YOU LISTEN TO WHAT WE'RE ABOUT TO SAY.
THESE PEOPLE...
...PERHAPS THEY'RE THE ONES THAT UNCLE TALKED ABOUT.
WE ARE SEELE.
SEELE 05
HAVE YOU NOT HEARD THAT NAME FROM IKARI?

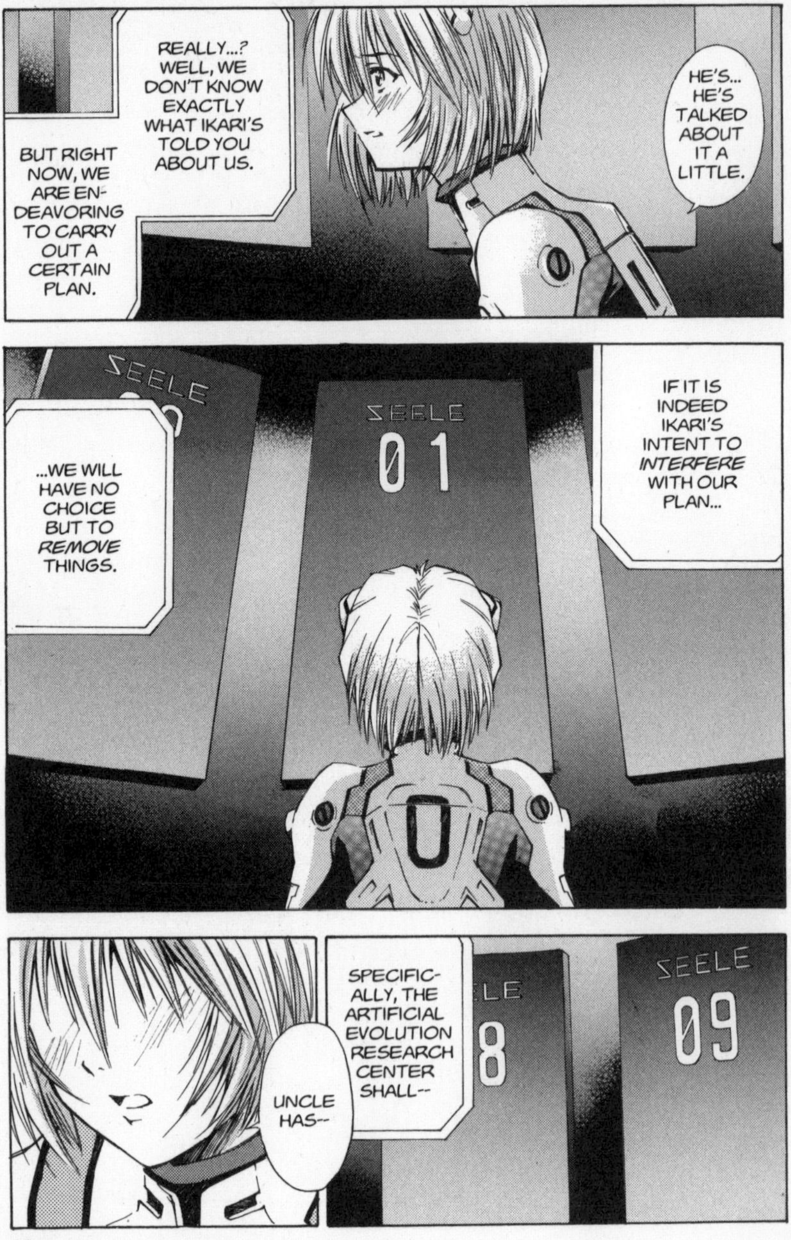
HE'S... HE'S TALKED ABOUT IT A LITTLE.
REALLY...? WELL, WE DON'T KNOW EXACTLY WHAT IKARI'S TOLD YOU ABOUT US.
BUT RIGHT NOW, WE ARE EN-DEAVORING TO CARRY OUT A CERTAIN PLAN.
IF IT IS INDEED IKARI'S INTENT TO *INTERFERE* WITH OUR PLAN...
SEELE
01
SEELE
...WE WILL HAVE NO CHOICE BUT TO *REMOVE* THINGS.
SEELE
09
SPECIFIC-ALLY, THE ARTIFICIAL EVOLUTION RESEARCH CENTER SHALL--
UNCLE HAS--

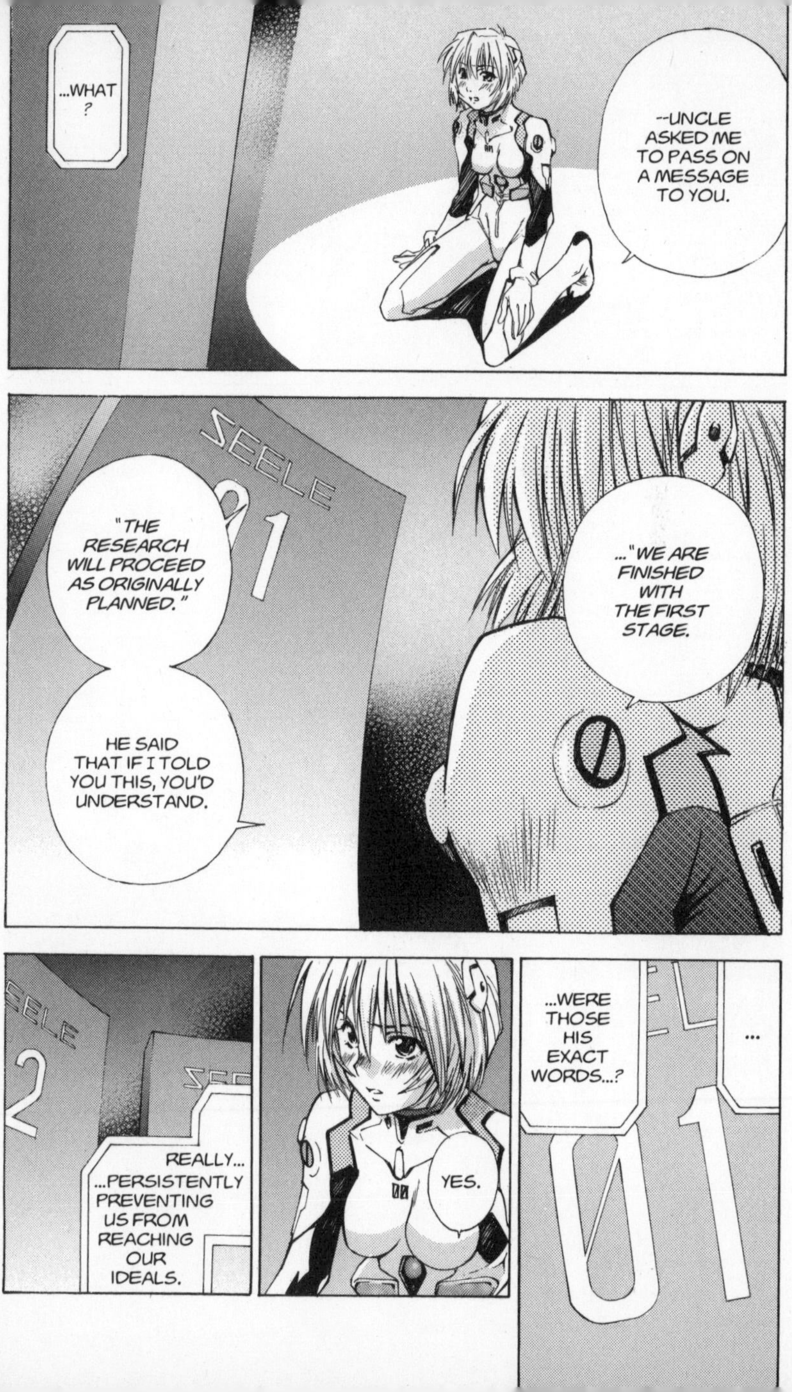

--UNCLE ASKED ME TO PASS ON A MESSAGE TO YOU.
...WHAT?
..."WE ARE FINISHED WITH THE FIRST STAGE.
"THE RESEARCH WILL PROCEED AS ORIGINALLY PLANNED."
HE SAID THAT IF I TOLD YOU THIS, YOU'D UNDERSTAND.
...
...WERE THOSE HIS EXACT WORDS...?
YES.
REALLY... ...PERSISTENTLY PREVENTING US FROM REACHING OUR IDEALS.

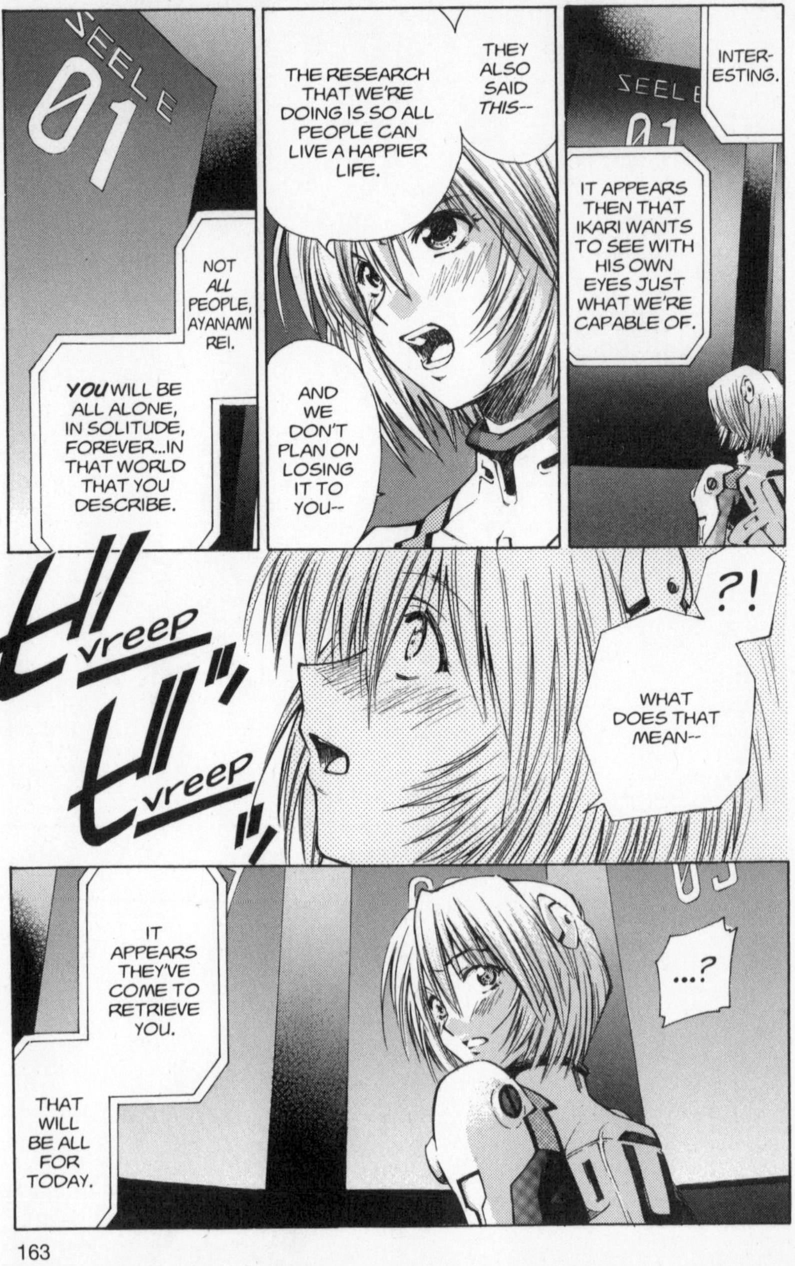

SEELE
01
INTER-ESTING.
IT APPEARS THEN THAT IKARI WANTS TO SEE WITH HIS OWN EYES JUST WHAT WE'RE CAPABLE OF.
THEY ALSO SAID THIS--
THE RESEARCH THAT WE'RE DOING IS SO ALL PEOPLE CAN LIVE A HAPPIER LIFE.
AND WE DON'T PLAN ON LOSING IT TO YOU--
SEELE
01
NOT *ALL* PEOPLE, AYANAMI REI.
YOU WILL BE ALL ALONE, IN SOLITUDE, FOREVER...IN THAT WORLD THAT YOU DESCRIBE.
?!
WHAT DOES THAT MEAN--
vreep
vreep
...?
IT APPEARS THEY'VE COME TO RETRIEVE YOU.
THAT WILL BE ALL FOR TODAY.

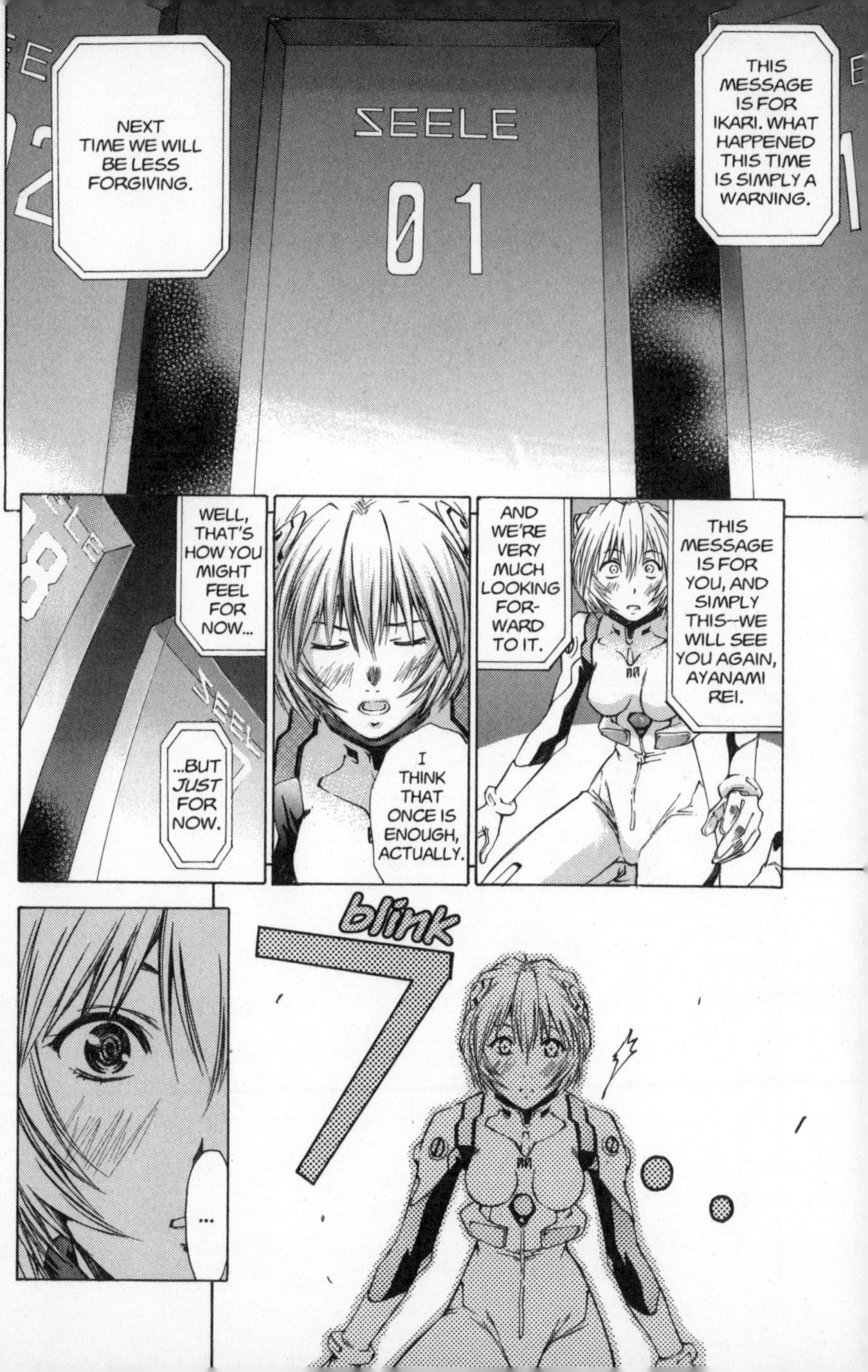
THIS MESSAGE IS FOR IKARI. WHAT HAPPENED THIS TIME IS SIMPLY A WARNING.
SEELE
01
NEXT TIME WE WILL BE LESS FORGIVING.
THIS MESSAGE IS FOR YOU, AND SIMPLY THIS--WE WILL SEE YOU AGAIN, AYANAMI REI.
AND WE'RE VERY MUCH LOOKING FOR-WARD TO IT.
I THINK THAT ONCE IS ENOUGH, ACTUALLY.
WELL, THAT'S HOW YOU MIGHT FEEL FOR NOW...
...BUT JUST FOR NOW.
blink
...

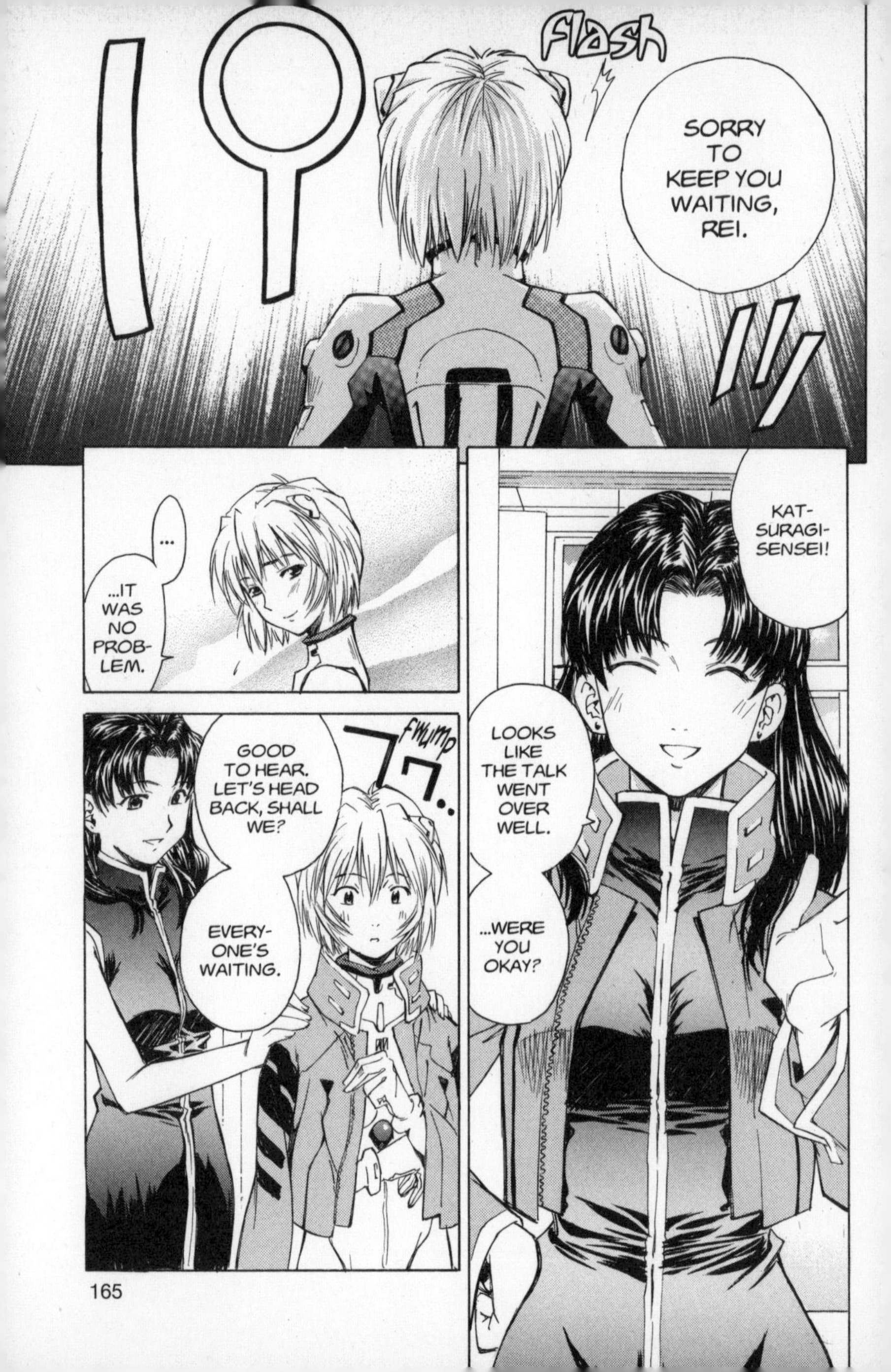
Flash
SORRY TO KEEP YOU WAITING, REI.
KAT-SURAGI-SENSEI!
LOOKS LIKE THE TALK WENT OVER WELL.
...WERE YOU OKAY?
...
...IT WAS NO PROB-LEM.
GOOD TO HEAR. LET'S HEAD BACK, SHALL WE?
fwump
EVERY-ONE'S WAITING.

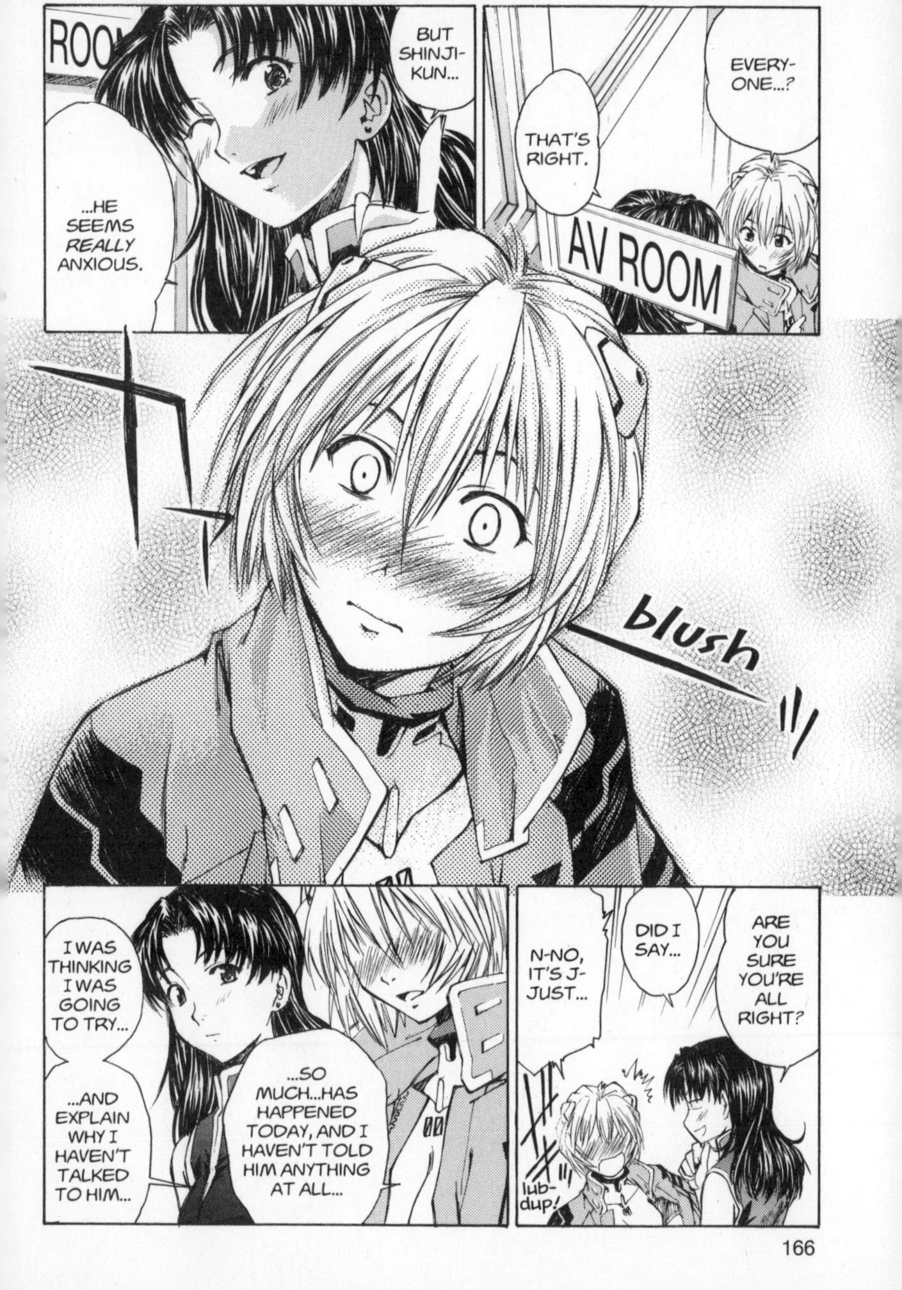
EVERY-ONE...?
THAT'S RIGHT.
AV ROOM
ROOM
BUT SHINJI-KUN...
...HE SEEMS *REALLY* ANXIOUS.
blush
ARE YOU SURE YOU'RE ALL RIGHT?
DID I SAY...
N-NO, IT'S J-JUST...
lub-dup!
I WAS THINKING I WAS GOING TO TRY...
...AND EXPLAIN WHY I HAVEN'T TALKED TO HIM...
...SO MUCH...HAS HAPPENED TODAY, AND I HAVEN'T TOLD HIM ANYTHING AT ALL...

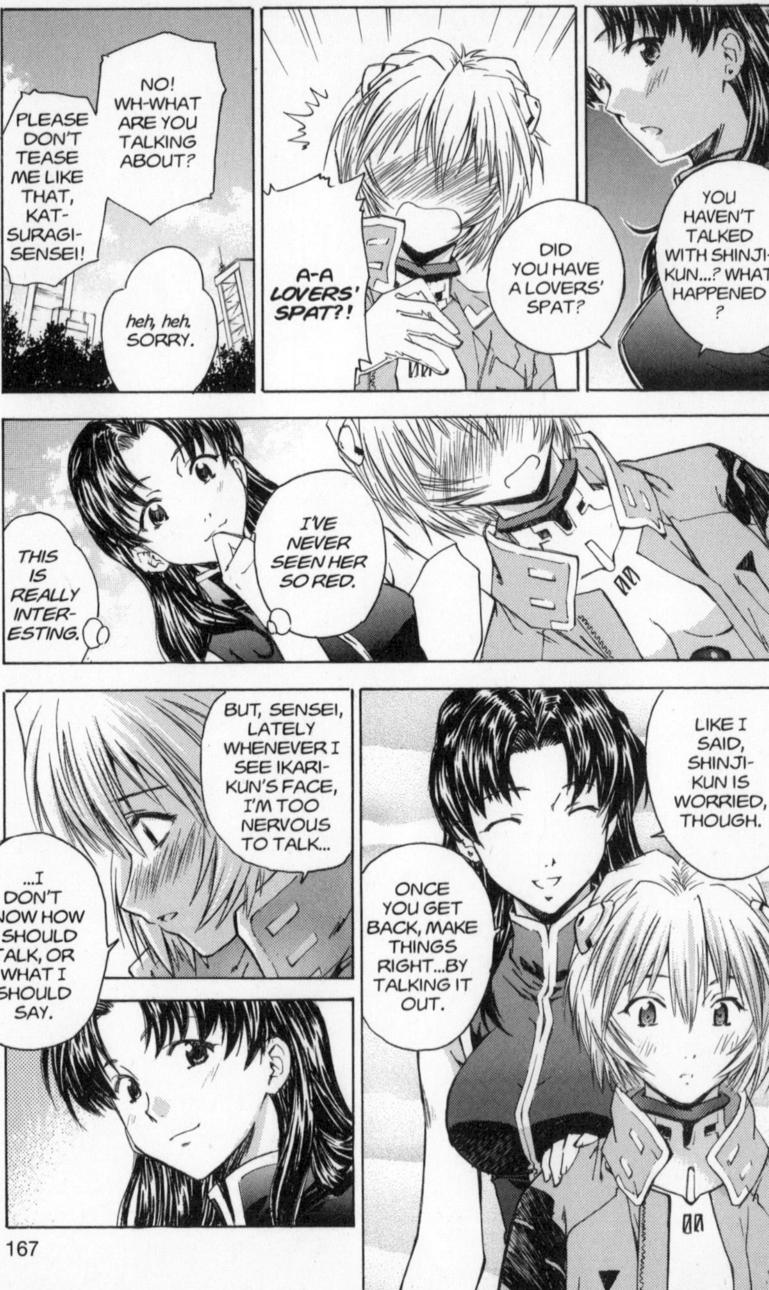
YOU HAVEN'T TALKED WITH SHINJI-KUN...? WHAT HAPPENED?
DID YOU HAVE A LOVERS' SPAT?
A-A LOVERS' SPAT?!
NO! WH-WHAT ARE YOU TALKING ABOUT?
PLEASE DON'T TEASE ME LIKE THAT, KAT-SURAGI-SENSEI!
heh, heh. SORRY.
I'VE NEVER SEEN HER SO RED.
THIS IS REALLY INTER-ESTING.
LIKE I SAID, SHINJI-KUN IS WORRIED, THOUGH.
ONCE YOU GET BACK, MAKE THINGS RIGHT...BY TALKING IT OUT.
BUT, SENSEI, LATELY WHENEVER I SEE IKARI-KUN'S FACE, I'M TOO NERVOUS TO TALK...
...I DON'T KNOW HOW I SHOULD TALK, OR WHAT I SHOULD SAY.

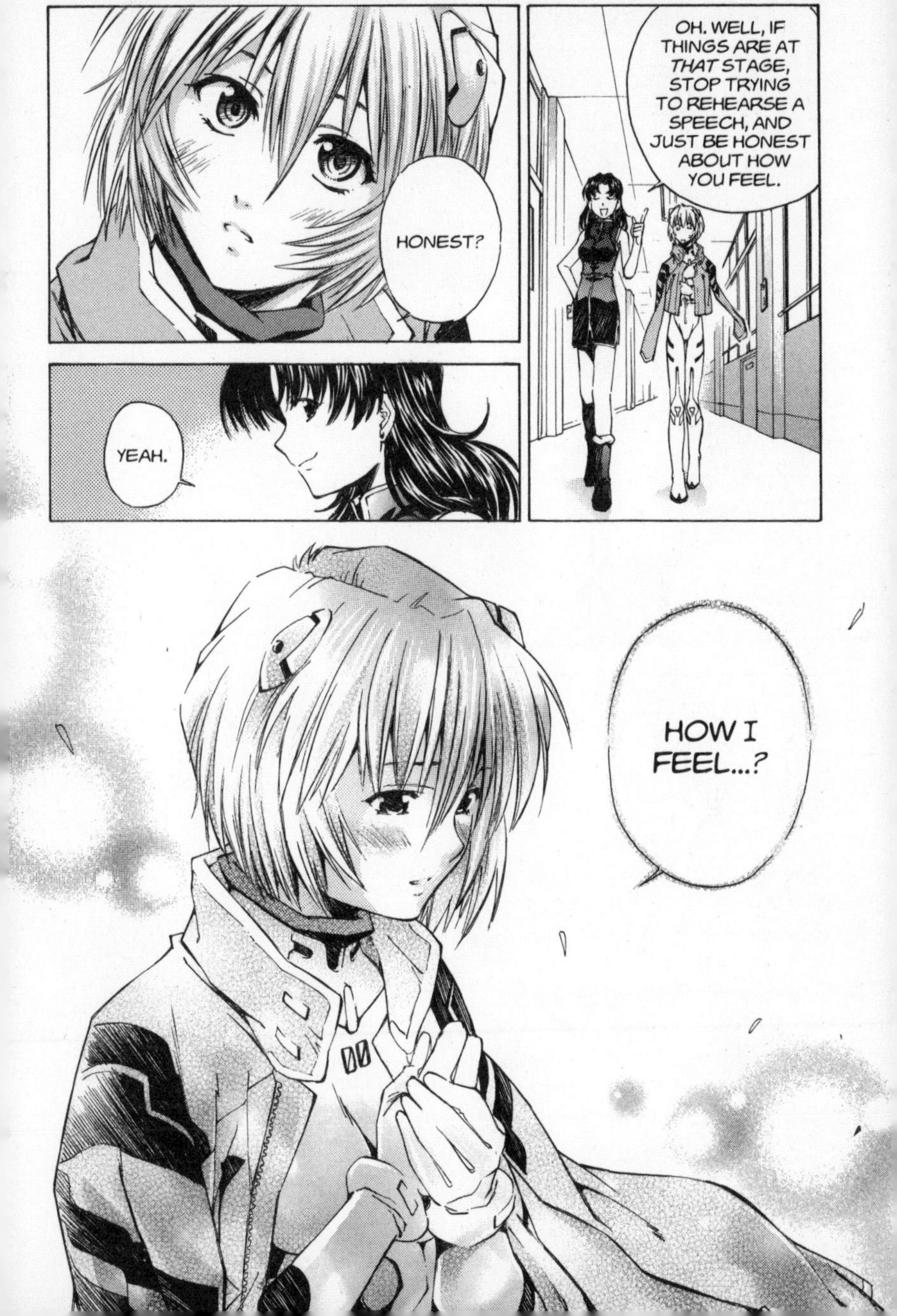
OH. WELL, IF THINGS ARE AT *THAT* STAGE, STOP TRYING TO REHEARSE A SPEECH, AND JUST BE HONEST ABOUT HOW YOU FEEL.
HONEST?
YEAH.
HOW I FEEL...?

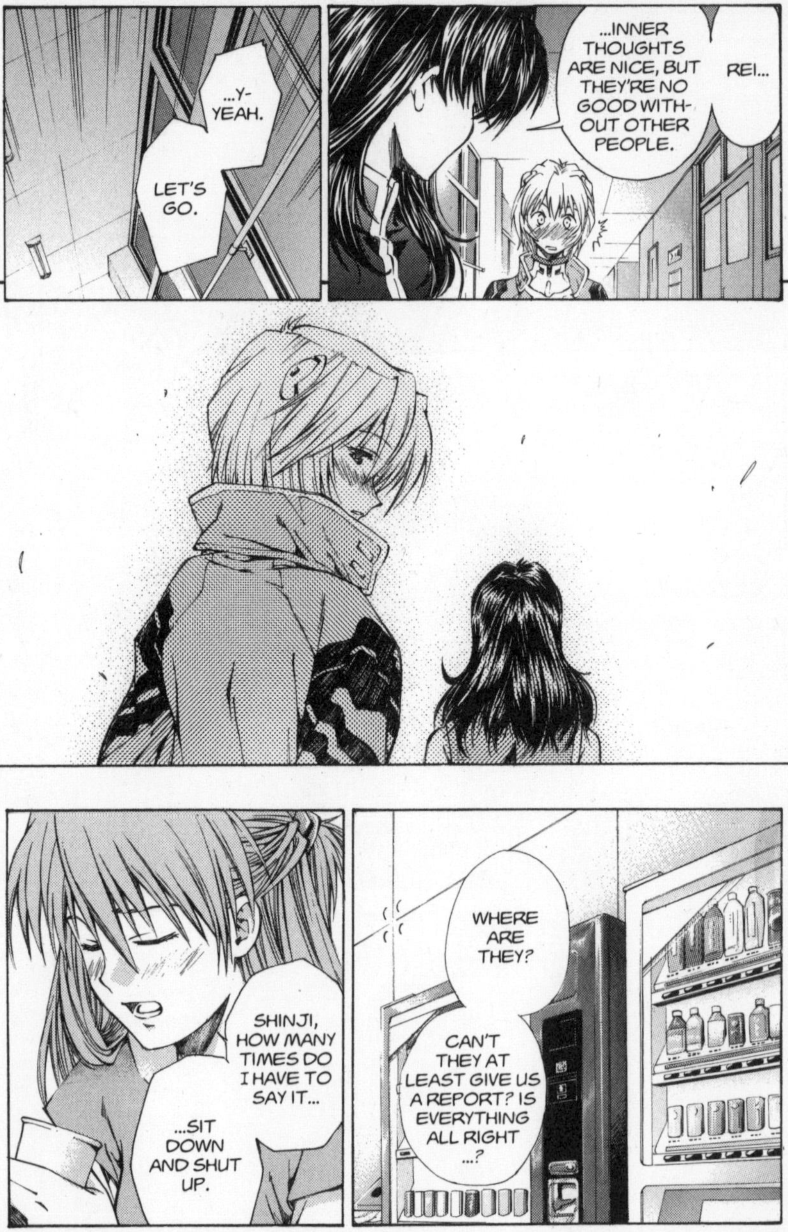
REI...
...INNER THOUGHTS ARE NICE, BUT THEY'RE NO GOOD WITH-OUT OTHER PEOPLE.
...Y-YEAH.
LET'S GO.
WHERE ARE THEY?
CAN'T THEY AT LEAST GIVE US A REPORT? IS EVERYTHING ALL RIGHT ...?
SHINJI, HOW MANY TIMES DO I HAVE TO SAY IT...
...SIT DOWN AND SHUT UP.

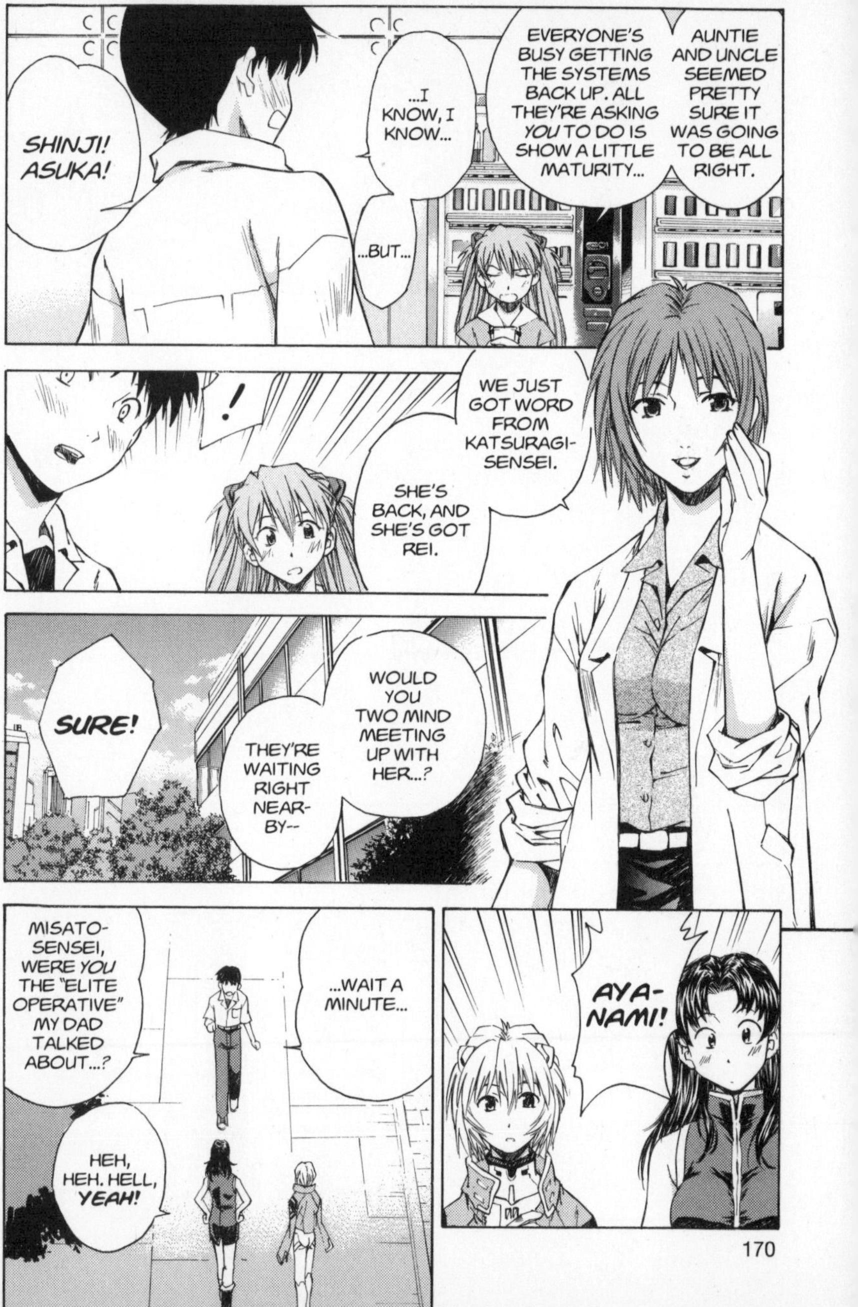
AUNTIE AND UNCLE SEEMED PRETTY SURE IT WAS GOING TO BE ALL RIGHT.
EVERYONE'S BUSY GETTING THE SYSTEMS BACK UP. ALL THEY'RE ASKING *YOU* TO DO IS SHOW A LITTLE MATURITY...
...I KNOW, I KNOW...
...BUT...
SHINJI! ASUKA!
WE JUST GOT WORD FROM KATSURAGI-SENSEI.
SHE'S BACK, AND SHE'S GOT REI.
!
WOULD YOU TWO MIND MEETING UP WITH HER...?
THEY'RE WAITING RIGHT NEAR-BY--
SURE!
AYA-NAMI!
...WAIT A MINUTE...
MISATO-SENSEI, WERE *YOU* THE "ELITE OPERATIVE" MY DAD TALKED ABOUT...?
HEH, HEH. HELL, **YEAH!**

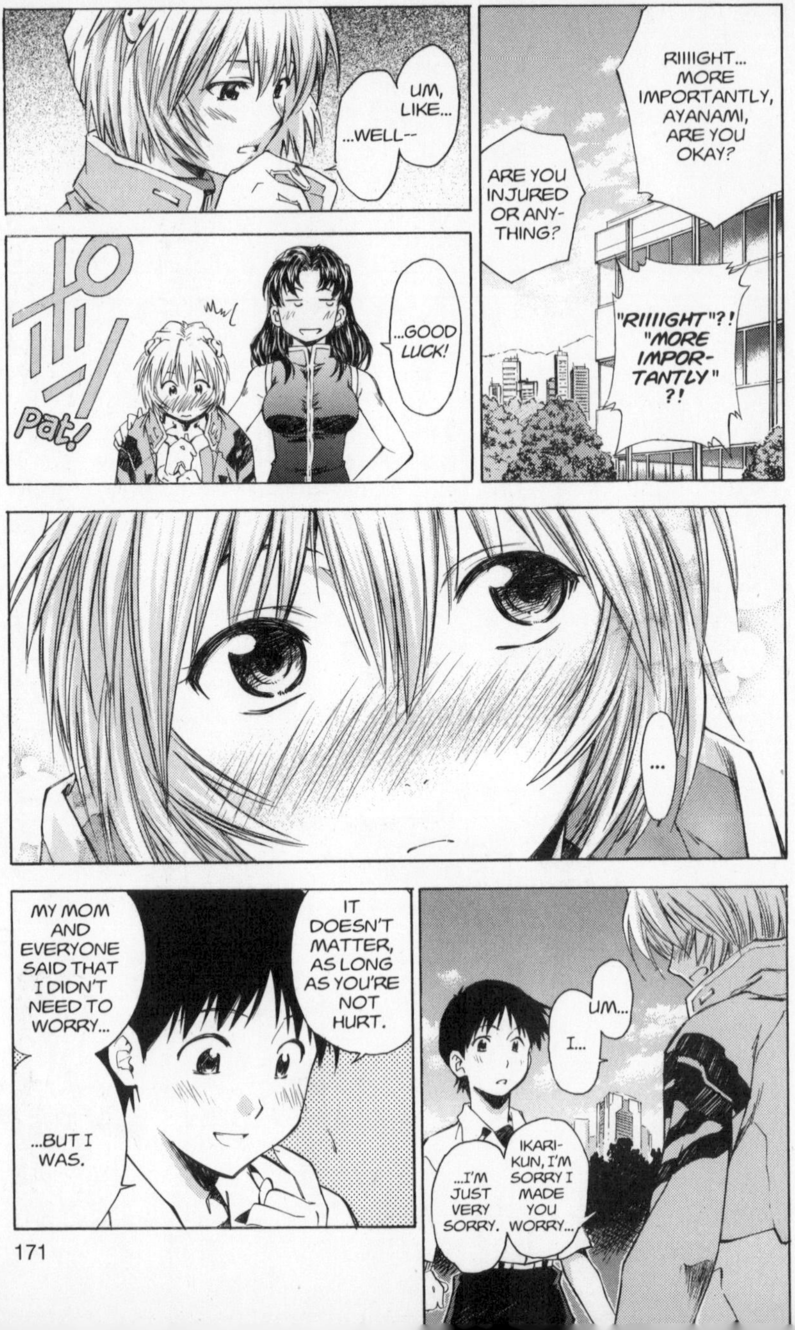
RIIIIGHT... MORE IMPORTANTLY, AYANAMI, ARE YOU OKAY?
ARE YOU INJURED OR ANY-THING?
"RIIIIGHT"?! "MORE IMPOR-TANTLY"?!
UM, LIKE... ...WELL--
...GOOD LUCK!
Pat!
...
UM... I...
IKARI-KUN, I'M SORRY I MADE YOU WORRY...
...I'M JUST VERY SORRY.
IT DOESN'T MATTER, AS LONG AS YOU'RE NOT HURT.
MY MOM AND EVERYONE SAID THAT I DIDN'T NEED TO WORRY...
...BUT I WAS.

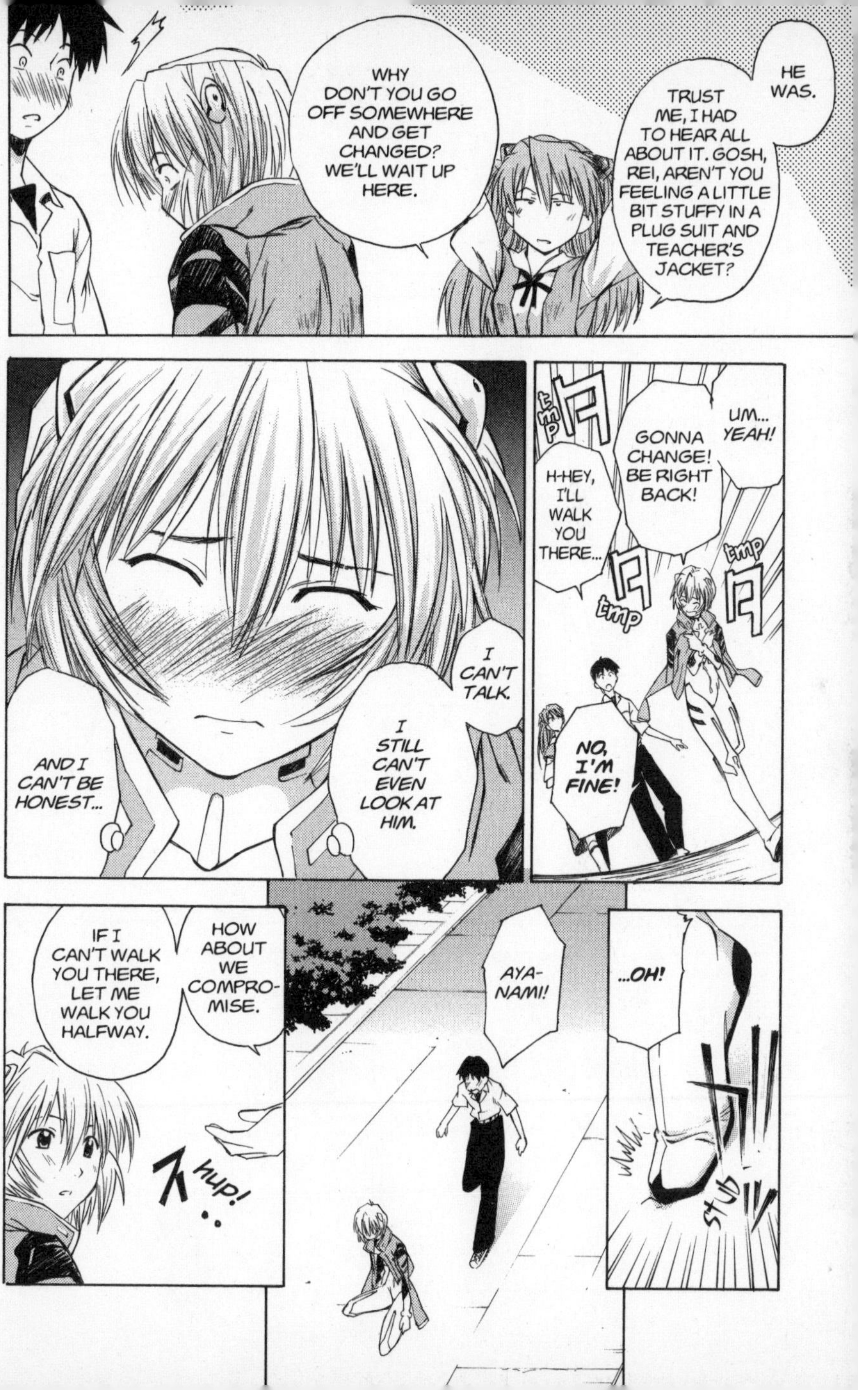
HE WAS.
TRUST ME, I HAD TO HEAR ALL ABOUT IT. GOSH, REI, AREN'T YOU FEELING A LITTLE BIT STUFFY IN A PLUG SUIT AND TEACHER'S JACKET?
WHY DON'T YOU GO OFF SOMEWHERE AND GET CHANGED? WE'LL WAIT UP HERE.
tmp
UM... YEAH!
GONNA CHANGE! BE RIGHT BACK!
H-HEY, I'LL WALK YOU THERE...
tmp
tmp
NO, I'M FINE!
I CAN'T TALK.
I STILL CAN'T EVEN LOOK AT HIM.
AND I CAN'T BE HONEST...
...OH!
stub
AYA-NAMI!
HOW ABOUT WE COMPROMISE.
IF I CAN'T WALK YOU THERE, LET ME WALK YOU HALFWAY.
hup!

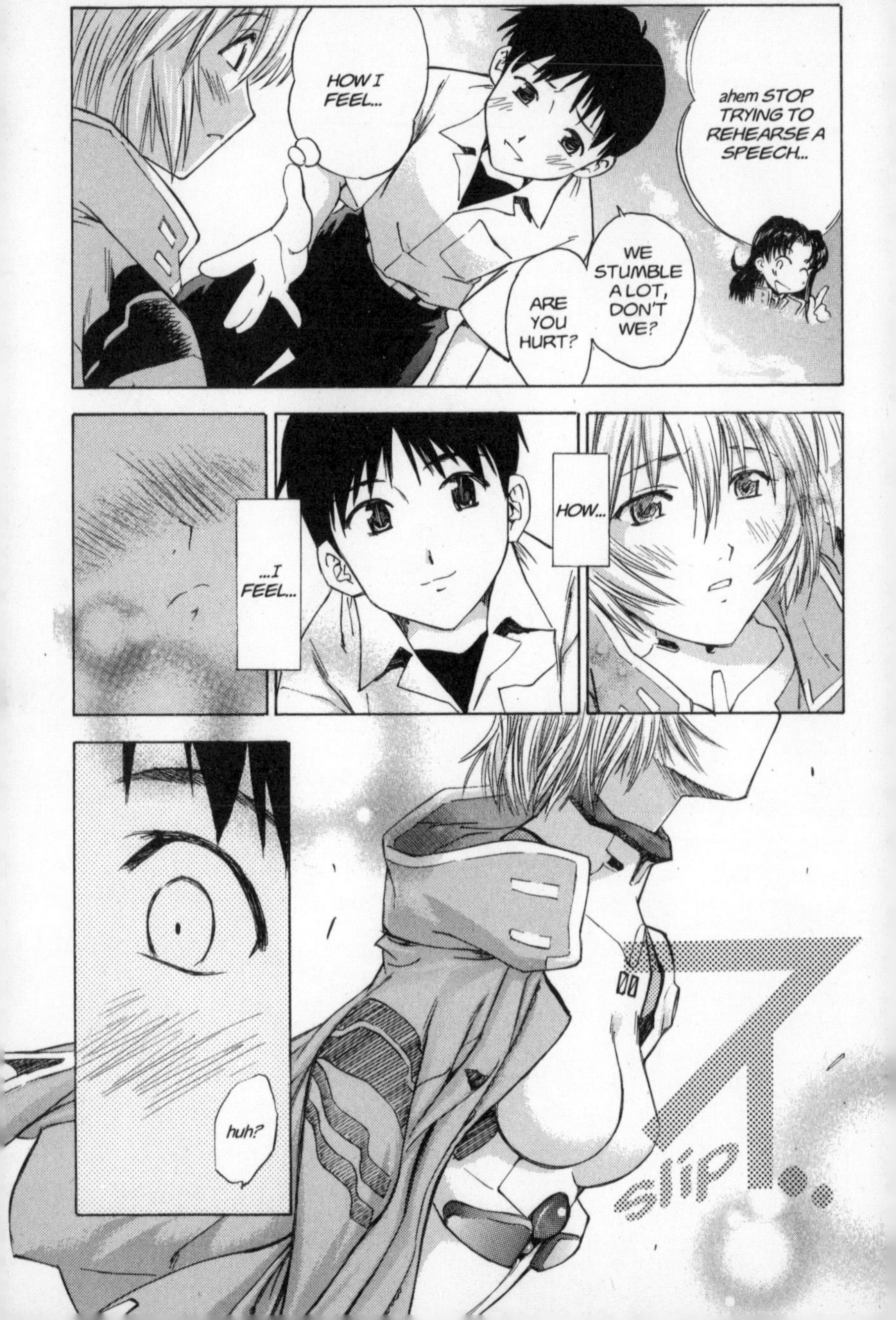
WE STUMBLE A LOT, DON'T WE?
ARE YOU HURT?
HOW I FEEL...
ahem STOP TRYING TO REHEARSE A SPEECH...
HOW...
...I FEEL...
slip
huh?

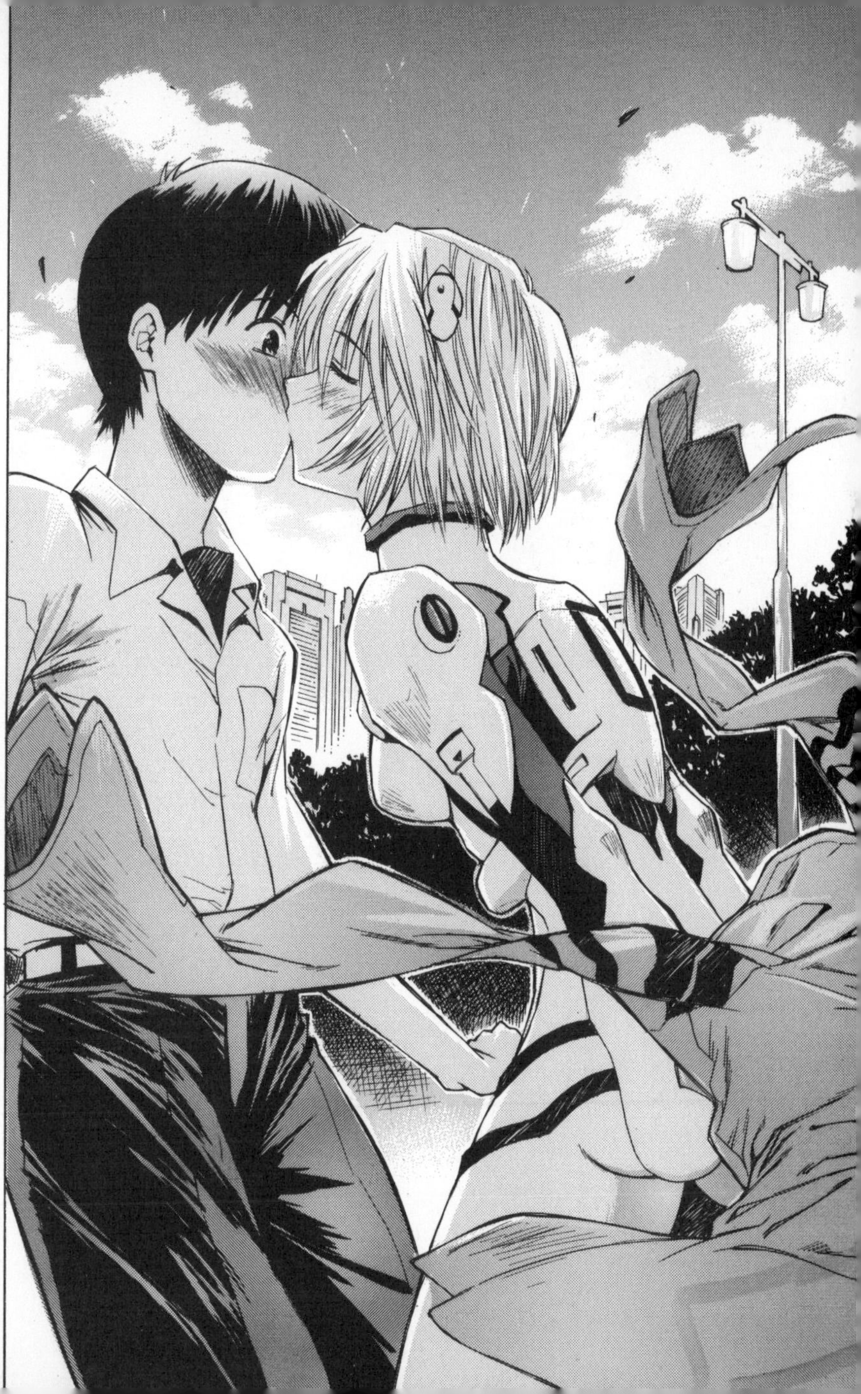

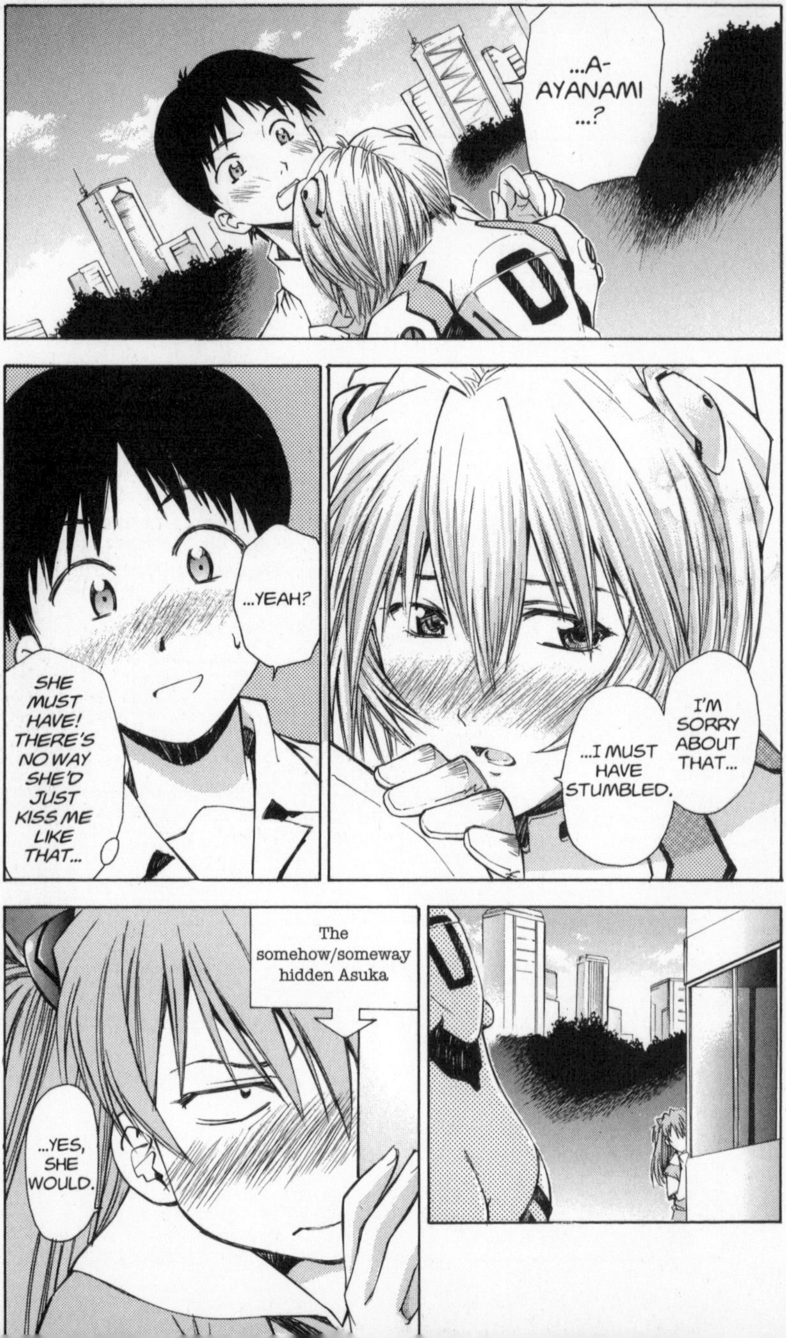
...A- AYANAMI ...?
I'M SORRY ABOUT THAT...
...I MUST HAVE STUMBLED.
...YEAH?
SHE MUST HAVE! THERE'S NO WAY SHE'D JUST KISS ME LIKE THAT...
The somehow/someway hidden Asuka
...YES, SHE WOULD.

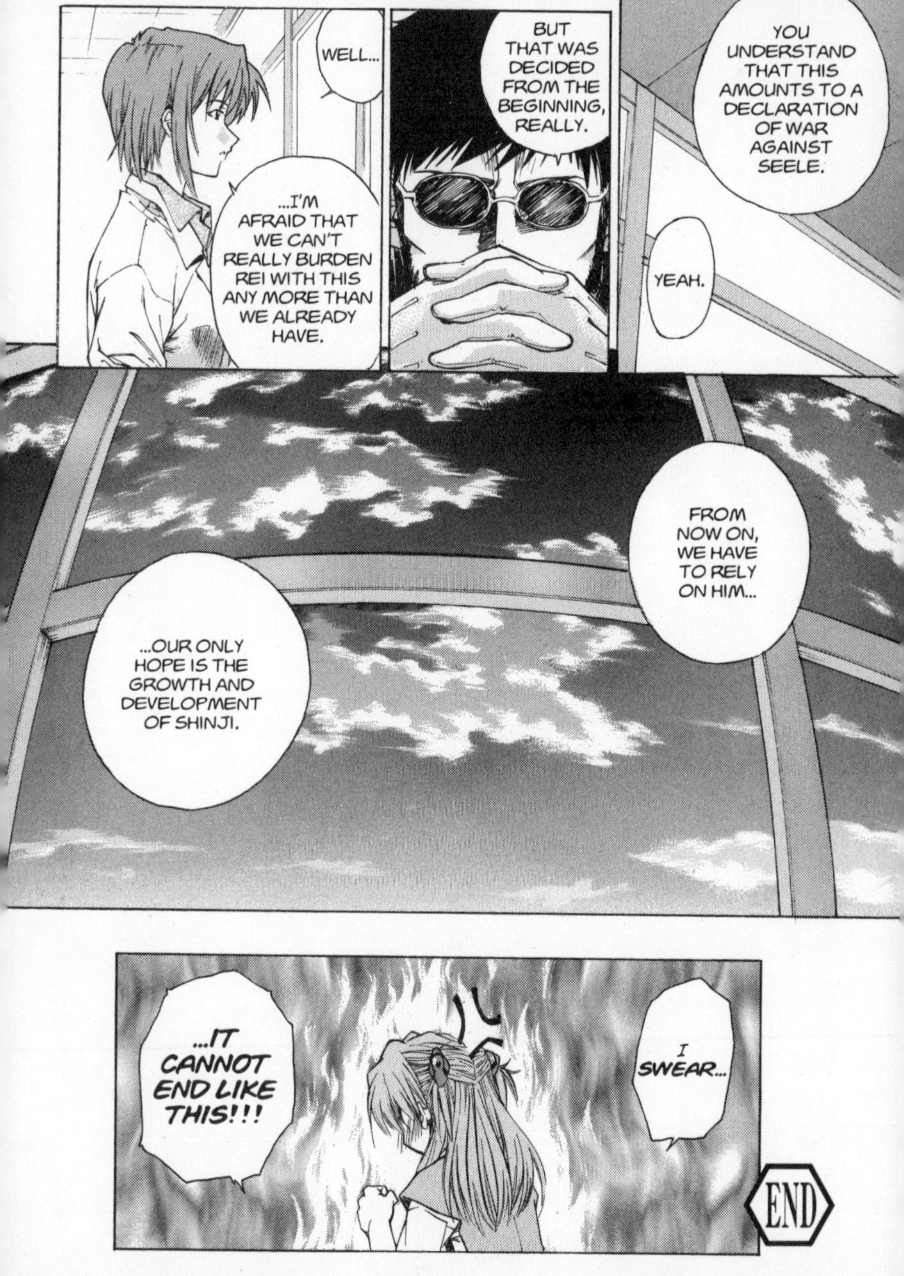
YOU UNDERSTAND THAT THIS AMOUNTS TO A DECLARATION OF WAR AGAINST SEELE.
YEAH.
BUT THAT WAS DECIDED FROM THE BEGINNING, REALLY.
WELL...
...I'M AFRAID THAT WE CAN'T REALLY BURDEN REI WITH THIS ANY MORE THAN WE ALREADY HAVE.
FROM NOW ON, WE HAVE TO RELY ON HIM...
...OUR ONLY HOPE IS THE GROWTH AND DEVELOPMENT OF SHINJI.
I SWEAR...
...IT CANNOT END LIKE THIS!!!
END

AFTERWORD

While working, there are many different things that some people can't be without, all particular to that individual. In my case, one of my things is listening to the radio.

There are times when I am listening quite intently, and other times when I swear that the sound never even reaches my ears. The great thing about the radio is that—unlike television—you can use it without having to stop working.

And with that, these last couple of years, I have lived a life virtually television free.

-Osamu Takahashi

~STAFF~

Kanna
Miki
Takuji
Masanori suzuki
Yuuta Nagano

COVER DESIGN
seki shindo

see you in vol. 4 . . .

EDITOR
CARL GUSTAV HORN

EDITORIAL ASSISTANT
ANNIE GULLION

DESIGNER
STEPHEN REICHERT

PUBLISHER
MIKE RICHARDSON

English-language version produced by Dark Horse Comics

Neon Genesis Evangelion: The Shinji Ikari Raising Project Vol. 3

First published in Japan as NEON GENESIS EVANGELION IKARI-SHINJI IKUSEI KEIKAKU Volume 3. © OSAMU TAKAHASHI 2007 © GAINAX • khara. First published in Japan in 2007 by KADOKAWA SHOTEN Publishing Co., Ltd., Tokyo. English translation rights arranged with KADOKAWA SHOTEN Publishing Co., Ltd., Tokyo, through TOHAN CORPORATION, Tokyo. This English-language edition © 2009 by Dark Horse Comics, Inc. All other material © 2009 by Dark Horse Comics, Inc. All rights reserved. No portion of this publication may be reproduced or transmitted, in any form or by any means, without the express written permission of the copyright holders. Names, characters, places, and incidents featured in this publication either are the product of the author's imagination or are used fictitiously. Any resemblance to actual persons (living or dead), events, institutions, or locales, without satiric intent, is coincidental. Dark Horse Manga™ is a trademark of Dark Horse Comics, Inc. All rights reserved.

Published by
Dark Horse Manga
A division of Dark Horse Comics, Inc.
10956 SE Main Street
Milwaukie, OR 97222

darkhorse.com

To find a comics shop in your area, call the Comic Shop Locator Service toll-free at 1-888-266-4226

First edition: December 2009
ISBN 978-1-59582-447-9

1 3 5 7 9 10 8 6 4 2
Printed in Canada

MISATO'S FAN SERVICE CENTER

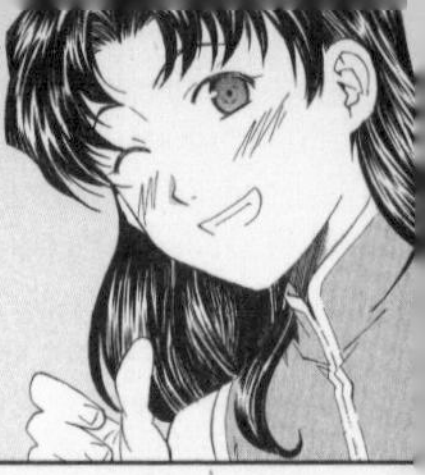

c/o Dark Horse Comics • 10956 SE Main Street • Milwaukie, OR 97222 • evangelion@darkhorse.com

In the immortal words of Cheech Marin (whom you may know as the killer priest from *Machete*), *"Well, all right, homes!"* The fans have come through, and that can mean only one thing—service, service! But before we reveal the three winners of the *Evangelion* folding fans shown back in vol. 1, allow us, in the best *The Price is Right* fashion, to sweep back the curtain and reveal what we'll be giving away to three readers in vol. 4!

Yes, she looks kind of small in this picture, but Mari Illustrious Makinami has been on the big screen recently in Japan, starring in the latest *Eva* movie this last summer, *Evangelion: 2.0 You Can (Not) Advance*. The first of the new *Evangelion* movies, *1.0 You Are (Not) Alone*, was based around the plot of the first six television episodes, but *2.0* goes much further in featuring scenes and events that were never shown (or occurred) in the original story; including, of course, this brand-new character.

Mari, like several other characters in *Evangelion* (as discussed in last volume's Misato's Fan Service Center), is presumably named after a naval vessel of the Second World War; perhaps two in her case. The Japanese destroyer *Makinami* (which means "rolling wave"), was sunk with the loss of two hundred crew, twenty eight surviving, by the U.S. Navy at the Battle of Cape St. George in the Solomon Islands, November 25, 1943. The British aircraft carrier HMS *Illustrious* survived the infamous Battle of Okinawa (whose brutality is said to have influenced the attack on NERV in *The End of Evangelion*), although it was severely damaged by kamikaze attacks and spent its final years of service after the war as a training ship.

Mari has already attracted a lot of attention, perhaps because she's the one thing the original *Evangelion* lacked, a *meganekko*—though I suppose Gendo might qualify. I'm not forgetting about Kensuke either, but with no girlfriend and no Eva, he always gets the short end of the stick, like Anthony Michael Hall in *The Breakfast Club* ("Could you describe the ruckus, Misato-sensei?"). Come to think of it, though, instant fame is not a new thing with *Neon Genesis Evangelion*—in the original TV show Kaworu only showed up for *thirteen minutes*!

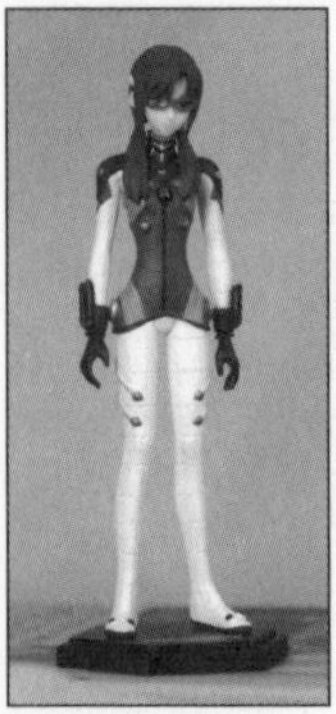

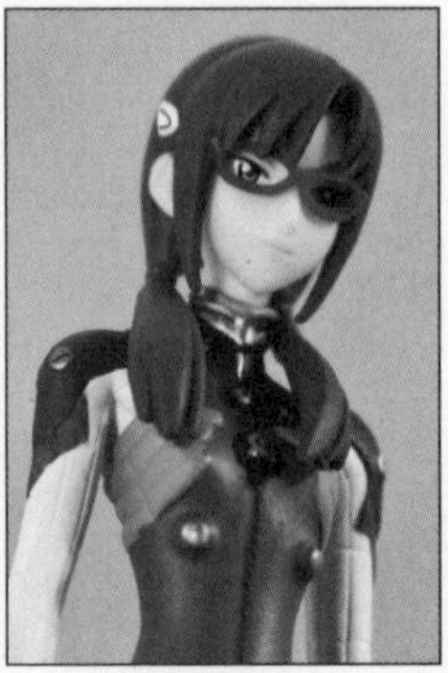

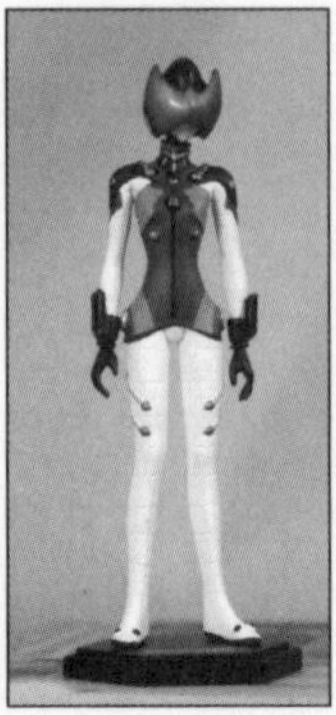

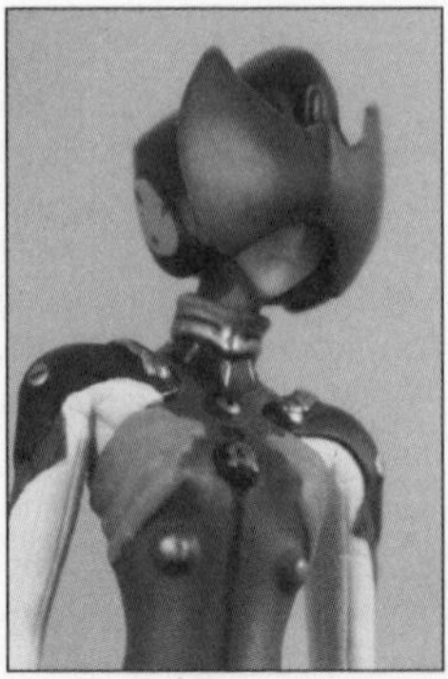

And, of course, introducing a new character to the actual anime itself is bound to attract notice, especially because the original cast and their dynamic have become so famous in the years since *Evangelion* first premiered (how many times have you looked at some other anime and thought, "Oh, that's the 'Shinji' character," or "that's the 'Misato' character"?). Of course, we're hoping that Funimation's North American release of *1.0* to theaters and home video will prove successful enough that an announcement of *2.0* will not be long in coming. At the recent Anime Weekend Atlanta, Funimation indicated they're hard at work on acquiring the rights to it.

We've been lucky enough to have our local showing of *Evangelion: 1.0 You Are (Not) Alone* at the Living Room Theater, across from Powell's Books—which claims to be, and may very well be, the largest bookstore in the world: it's four stories high and takes up the entire block. It says something very positive about Portland that the pride of the city is our bookstore, and you can bet they carry a lot of manga—not only a big English section, but a big used Japanese section! Powell's even accepts yen at the cash register as well as dollars (not to mention euros, pesos, and British pounds), since at any moment people from a dozen different nations might be shopping inside. It's pretty much the ultimate bookstore; the only thing it's missing is Yomiko Readman—although, since I've noted that before, perhaps I should just accept she's doing her best to avoid me.

Our local paper, the *Willamette Week,* had an interesting review of *Evangelion: 1.0 You Are (Not) Alone.* I say "interesting" because, owing to the fact very little anime comes to U.S. theaters, we don't often get the chance to see such reviews, and, when such reviews *do* happen, of course, they're as likely as not to be written by people who aren't familiar with anime. And thus the *Willamette Week*'s Aaron Mesh, in a "Highly Recommended" review, had this to say about *You Are (Not) Alone*: "This apocalyptic anime contains some vertiginous fantasy landscapes—check out the world's longest future escalator—and all the delicious angst of good boarding-school fiction. I'm granting that the thing is perfectly nice for whatever it is. Plus, it has a penguin that reads a newspaper." Did that bit about "boarding-school angst" mean that the *Harry Potter* movies have somehow helped the masses understand anime better . . . ?

Thanks to everybody, by the way, who came to the Dark Horse *Evangelion* panel at Anime Weekend Atlanta, too. We were proud to have an announcement of our own—that in August 2010 we're going to begin releasing a *second* manga based on *Evangelion,* entitled *Neon Genesis Evangelion: Campus Apocalypse.* The first thing that makes *NGE: Campus Apocalypse* so interesting is that it's done in a noticeably different style from *The Shinji Ikari Raising Project*—namely, it's a *shojo* style. I know that word gets thrown around a lot, but it's from an honest-to-goddess *shojo* magazine, the somehow fittingly named *Asuka,* published in Japan by Kadokawa (the *Shinji Ikari Raising Project* comes from another Kadokawa magazine, the contrastingly titled *Shonen Ace*).

As you may know, in Japan, almost all manga run in a magazine first before they get collected in graphic novels. It's a good way to get exposure for a story and to follow it chapter by chapter, but it's also an expensive way to publish, especially in America, which is why although we have the current manga magazines *Shonen Jump* and *Yen Plus,* we've also seen various others canceled over the years, including *Shojo Beat, PULP, Raijin Comics, Manga Vizion, MixxZine,* and Dark Horse's own *Super Manga Blast.*

Another way manga magazines are used in Japan, of course, is to provide a place to feature different styles of manga—hence there are *shojo* magazines like *Asuka* and *shonen* magazines like *Shonen Ace.* I think "style" may be a better word than "genre" to describe terms like *shojo* and *shonen,* because genre suggests a certain kind of story. The old stereotypes were that *shojo* stories involved relationships, and *shonen* stories involved action—but that hasn't been true for a long time now; just look at *The Shinji Ikari Raising Project,* which is from a *shonen* magazine but is mainly about relationships.

By contrast, our new *shojo Evangelion* manga, *Campus Apocalypse,* is full of action! As well

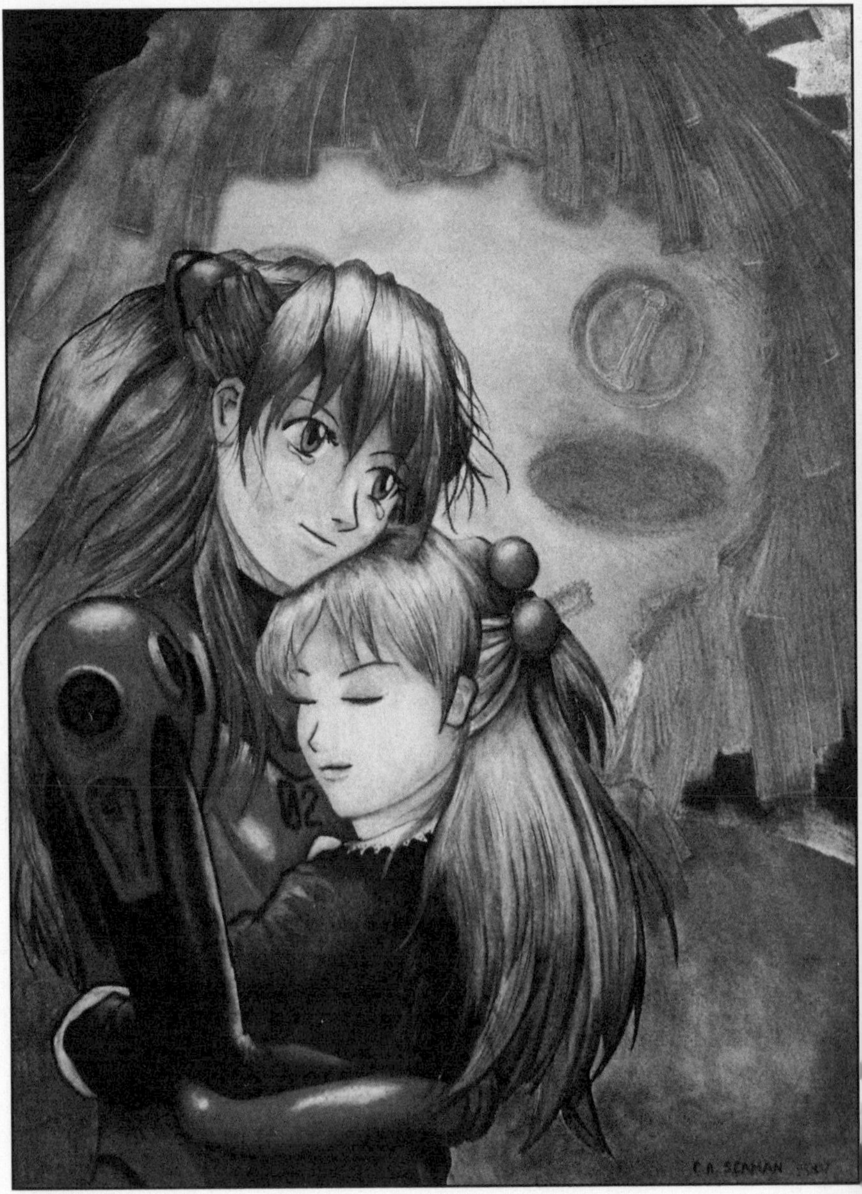

it might be, since the magazine it comes from, *Asuka*, is also the home of *Code Geass* and *Trinity Blood*! What's *Campus Apocalypse* about? Well, in this alternate version of the story, Shinji Ikari's parents are gone, and he lives with his legal guardian, Ryoji Kaji, while attending the private NERV Academy. But no one ever told Shinji about its secrets . . . or that he'd find his fellow students Kaworu, Rei, and Asuka out on the streets late at night—fighting with sword, spear, and whip against an enemy that looks very human, but who Kaworu insists are beings called the Angels . . .

On the previous page is the art that accompanied the first of the aforementioned winning three letters of vol. 3!

The artist, Christopher Seaman of the Toronto area, comments in his letter:

The original drawing was 11" x 14", done in coloured pencil and graphite; hence the shine on the rag doll portion of the work. Asuka and her younger self are represented in colour against the black and white representation of the doll to juxtapose the duality of her personality and the inner pain she has endured since she was a child. Asuka's inability to live with herself and the trauma she endured as a child was an intriguing theme developed in the series, and the doll always seemed to be part of the nightmare she repressed until the Angel attack that incapacitated her. I show her embracing her younger self in a gesture of healing—trying to extract some happiness out of a grim situation. If she could learn to love herself again, she would have to learn to love the person she was when her mother died—the child we see. Only then could she move on and grow once more to become a more complete person. Fluffy psychobabble, to be sure. However, I did this piece when one of my parents was undergoing cancer surgery, so I think this must have had some bearing on the content.

Well, if there's one thing the psychobabble is never in *Evangelion*, it's fluffy! Usually, it's of the rough and thorned variety. Our next folding fan goes to someone whose letter alone merited it.

Hi, my name is Komyar Moghadam, and I am an Evangelion fanatic.

Now before I begin, I would like to apologize for writing this so late. I had it slip my mind many times, and I felt as if I was betraying a promise I made to very good friends of mine. I was thankfully reminded by a Nicholas Walstrom, AKA Walrus-Guy, who posted a video on YouTube saying that the first volume of The Shinji Ikari Raising Project *is available at all major bookstores. First, my reaction was, "Awesome, I have been waiting for this to be available, now I'm only a five minute drive away!" Second, I thought to myself, "Oh crap! I was supposed to e-mail them about my story!" So that brings me here. I know Mr. Horn and Mr. McCoy were very surprised when they heard this account, and I want everyone else at Dark Horse to know of my beginnings as an anime fanatic. So, here it goes.*

It all started at a very impressionable age for me, around six or seven, if I remember correctly. I was a trouble making child who could never pay any attention to anyone. Most of the time I was either being indoctrinated into the values of the Bible at the private school I attended, or watching mind numbing amounts of television. The programs I viewed included Barney, Teletubbies, *and* Sesame Street, *among other kids', television programs. There were a fair share of cartoons I also enjoyed, but nothing I could really sit down and pay any mind to. Unless it was interesting, my short attention span would not allow me to think much of it.*

That was until a fateful weekend visit to my cousins' apartment in Sacramento. Me, my brother, and my father planned to stay over on a Saturday night. We enjoyed a delicious dinner, after which my brother and I played with some of our cousins' action figures he had collected, and watched him play some Warcraft. *Before we hunkered down, he decided to watch a DVD before we all went to bed. It was late, and I should have gone to sleep a while ago, but I was particularly hyper that day. So lo and behold, when he inserted that disk, what did I see? Why, none other than the first episode of one of the greatest anime ever conceived,* Neon Genesis Evangelion.

Let me ask you a question: what was the first anime you ever saw? At my age, one would say such series as Pokémon, Dragon Ball, Sailor Moon, *or even* Transformers. *These shows were marketed to children, and one would expect children to be drawn towards the characters and plots involving training creatures, fighting monkeys, pretty girls, or robots. But I was not exposed to any of this at first. I was completely in the dark about anime, so I had no idea what I was in for. So how did a young boy react to a violent, risqué, and intellectual work?*

Well, to tell you the truth, I didn't react at all. From the opening sequence to the ending credits, I was in another world within my own self, having no comprehension of what I had just witnessed. The scene of Shinji screaming in agony as his "arm" was torn off may have frightened me a bit, but other than that, I just viewed it as something of unknown importance to me. I did not get any of it. I believe it was a great shock to me, to go from Barney, *a show about a purple dinosaur, to* Neon Genesis Evangelion, *an anime about a boy who fights "angels" in a purple cyborg. After that immersion, I began to experience anime more and more. Unfortunately, I had forgotten about* Eva *as I grew up, and would not remember until almost ten years later.*

I finally remembered one day as I was browsing in the anime section of a Blockbuster, where I saw the complete series, as well as both movies, sitting on the shelves. Over the next week, I rented and watched every episode in Japanese with English subtitles, including Death and Rebirth *and* End of Evangelion. *No sooner was my mind blown after seeing the series in its entirety. I would forever set* Neon Genesis Evangelion *as a benchmark for any future anime I would view. It truly is, in my opinion, the greatest anime franchise on this earth. And with the new comic and movie coming out, I can't help but feel that the series is finally getting a long awaited revival into the twenty-first century.*

Thank you for taking your time to read this, and I hope you enjoyed this delving into my youth.

If you have any questions, please e-mail me back!

My generation might have said "greatest anime *franchise*" with a tinge of irony, but the youth of the twenty-first century are, as Frank Miller would say, a "purer breed." Komyar, as he mentions, was one of the people kind enough to attend the aptly named "Endless *Evangelion* Panel" at FanimeCon 2009, where Sean and I did some sort of *manzai* routine, only without the folded fans, and with two *boke*.

Well, I did have a follow-up question for Komyar. I thought he might have been the same guy who did an AMV that won an award in the action category at Fanime, but in searching his name, I also started getting high-school football scores. So Komyar explained:

Yes, I am the same guy who entered "That Girl Is So HONEY!" at Fanime. As a little backstory, being a fan of Evangelion *and Gainax, I wanted to see all works related to my all-time favorite anime. Re: Cutie Honey happened to come up, and even had direct relation to* Evangelion *in terms of characters and their development. I happened to be listening to Akon's "Dangerous" while watching the first episode, and found that they matched up pretty well (especially in the opening animation.) The rest is history, winning third in the action category (which I think it shouldn't have been in. I felt like it was a mix of most of the categories).*

I am also the same guy who plays on the MSJHS football and wrestling teams. I feel that it is the most distinct thing that separates me from other anime fanatics, as I feel that staying home watching anime all day is not the healthiest thing to do. You don't have to be a geek or untalented or whatever the stereotype is to be an anime fan, which surprises many people when I tell them I enjoy anime. In fact, I am the president of the school anime club. Besides watching anime, I argue with them on why Evangelion *is better than anything currently out, or most of the time ever. Of course, they don't take too kindly to that. ^_^*

Well, all I can say is that of the three biggest *Robotech* fans at my school back in 1986, one was on the water-polo team, one was on the football team, and the other one was me. ^_^ How big of fans were we? We called ourselves "The Triumvirate"—

which would be the *Evangelion* equivalent of, if there happened to be thirteen people in your anime club, holding all meetings standing in a circle while wearing boxes labeled "SOUND ONLY."

So I completely agree with you, Komyar. I think anime is far too interesting to belong to any one group or clique. I was so concerned about this when I started college (Pomona College, not UC Berkeley—but I had several friends at Cal, one of the reasons I ended up hanging out there a lot) that I decided not to start an anime club per se, but instead to just have regular showings of anime on campus, everyone invited (and lots of people came). Maybe I was overly worried, but I didn't want people to think you had to belong to any kind of group just to watch anime; I wanted people to treat it as normally as watching an American movie or TV show.

It is limiting to assume that only one kind of person can like anime. If only one type of person likes it, then new perspectives will not develop—and new perspectives are what anime needs to keep moving forward. As you know, one of the things that made *Evangelion* noteworthy in Japan was that it took risks and acquired an audience outside of traditional anime fans.

And I believe that wasn't because of *Evangelion*'s twists or trivia, but because people could sense this show was trying to be honest, was trying to reach out. As Hideaki Anno said when he visited the U.S. in 1996, "Look outwards first of all . . . Please have diverse interests, in things other than anime . . . Most anime makers are basically autistic. They have to try and reach out to others, communicate with others now." When asked what he thought the greatest thing was that anime had achieved, Anno said, "I guess the fact that we can hold a dialogue right here, in this time and place."

As for the first anime I ever saw, Komyar, it was, heh-heh, *Speed Racer*. Now, if anyone reading this happened to see the recent live-action film, and it wasn't to your taste, this was one time when it wasn't Hollywood's fault—screwing up the Japanese creators' vision—because the movie actually *was* a lot like the original anime. Very strange, you

know. *Speed Racer*, known in Japan as *Maha go go go* (*maha go* is a way of saying "mach 5" in Japan, whereas the hero's original name in Japanese was "Go Mifune," and it can also mean, well, *go go go*), was one of the first anime series ever broadcast in the U.S., hitting TV screens here in 1967.

The anime version of Osamu Tezuka's *Astro Boy*, which aired here in 1963 (manga available from Dark Horse Comics, I'm pleased to say), was the more popular series in Japan, but the reverse was true in America. I guess when it comes to a choice between a kid robot in shorts and a teen racer in a sports car, the racer is going to win every time. But *Speed Racer* is perhaps the anime best known to the largest number of Americans over the past four decades, something proved through what Robert Heinlein once called the sincerest form of flattery: money. Namely, *Speed Racer* has been used in commercials for NASCAR, Volkswagen, GEICO, and Pitney Bowes (Now *there's* an idea for future contributions to Misato's Fan Service Center. Suppose you could make a commercial for American TV using *Evangelion*. What would be the ideal product or service to advertise?).

But I actually didn't first see *Speed Racer* in America; I saw it in Tehran, where my family lived in the early 1970s, helping to expand the old international airport, Mehrabad. The fact the new one is named for the Ayatollah Khomeini shows how things have changed in the meantime, and I've wondered if *Speed Racer* is still on the air, and, if so, if they used CG to give Trixie a headscarf and Speed a faceful of beard stubble.

A lot of people don't realize anime has been just as popular in the Middle East and Central Asia as it is everywhere else in the world. I think one of the things that keeps this fact obscure is a kind of built-in limitation of Internet searches; that is, they not only depend on your search term itself, but also what writing system you use to type it. Most Western languages are written in the same Roman alphabet as English uses, so even if you just type the name of a show in English, you may still get hits from, say, Spanish and French fan pages. Many *gaijin* fans can also type a little Japanese, at least enough for web searches.

But if you don't know the Arabic alphabet (which is used not only to write Arabic itself, but also important unrelated languages like Persian/Farsi and Urdu—the same way Japanese uses Chinese kanji and vocabulary, yet spoken Japanese is not actually related to any Chinese dialect), you're much less likely to ever run across fan pages from that part of the world. Which, since it contains about half a billion people, includes quite a few anime fans as well.

At Kumoricon, for example, I was talking with a woman who grew up in Jordan watching ليدي أوسكار dubbed into Arabic on local TV. What, you don't know that show? ^_^ Well, it was one that we English-speaking fans never got to see, even though it was the anime version of perhaps the most famous *shojo* manga of all time—*The Rose of Versailles*, created by Riyoko Ikeda and directed by Osamu Dezaki, the guy who most recently did *Cobra the Animation* (don't worry; his work on *Rose of Versailles* was more feminine, although, as Anime World Order points out, *shojo* heroines in the '70s could kick the ass of most of today's *shonen* heroes most efficaciously. It was the spirit of Billie Jean King).

Yet *The Rose of Versailles* was only one of several Japanese classics Arabic-speaking anime fans got to see that were left out of our history in the English-speaking world. نينـجا مـغـامرات, which was the professional debut of director Mamoru Oshii (*The Sky Crawlers*). How about the show هايدي, directed by Isao Takahata (*Grave of the Fireflies*), or a TV series like ولـينا عدنان, directed by Hayao Miyazaki (*Ponyo*)? And . . . what about Hideaki Anno's biggest hit before *Neon Genesis Evangelion*? Yes, fans in the Arabic-speaking world got to watch الزرقاء الماسة on TV, but we didn't!

Oh, those shows in the last paragraph were *The Wonderful Adventure of Nils*; *Heidi, Girl of the Alps*; *Future Boy Conan* (one of Hideaki Anno's favorite TV shows, BTW); and *Nadia: The Secret of Blue Water*. Of course, what's acceptable in one country in a region may not be acceptable in another, more conservative one. And politicians and preachers in any country are not necessarily fans of anime. But I think it's not quite that simple, either. In last volume's "Misato's Fan Service Center," I talked about the legendary anime club at the University of California, Berkeley, Cal Animage Alpha. One of the things I remember about meetings there in the mid-'90s is that there was a Muslim girl who would always attend. She wore an *abaya* that covered everything but her face. Some students at Cal might do so for political reasons, but because she kept to herself and seemed shy, I guessed in her case she just came from a very conservative family. But here's the thing—whatever her cultural background or personal beliefs, she always showed up, for each and every anime showing. That included *The End of Evangelion*, and looking back, I wish I'd tried to discuss it with her, like I did with everyone else.

I was talking to a visiting Saudi fan after the *Evangelion* panel at Anime Central. Several countries in the Middle East, such as Iran, Egypt, Israel, Syria, Lebanon, and Palestine, have had differing levels of religious diversity, so people you meet who come (or whose families come) from those countries might likewise have differing backgrounds. But if you're talking to a Saudi citizen, it's a pretty safe bet they're Muslim. I'd heard panels before that discussed Jewish and Christian perspectives towards *Evangelion*, but hadn't had the chance to hear a view from a Muslim (I never noticed any specifically Islamic references in the series itself, although, in the Japanese tabletop RPG version of *Evangelion*, there are two "new" Angels, one of which is named Iblis—a name from the Koran; but Iblis was a jinn rather than an angel). Anyway, I asked him what they thought of *Evangelion* in Saudi Arabia, and he kind of scratched his head for a few seconds and looked as if he were trying to figure out just how to explain this to me, then finally he said, "Saudis are more into *Gurren Lagann*."

But what about the Irish? John Hanley from Celbridge, County Kildare, Eire, weighs in with the third of three winning letters for this volume. It was accompanied by the piece on the next page: Why, it's that Mari girl everyone's talking about, again (with a kind of Haruko Haruhara expression on her face, don't you think?). John writes:

I decided to go with Mari, Eva Unit-05, Kaworu, and Eva Unit-06 because I guessed you wouldn't get much of her, plus I think Unit-05 is really cool (need to get the model) and Kaworu finally getting his own Eva kicks ass. The Eva series doesn't count (dummy plugs, boo). Since all I had to go on for Unit-06 was the silhouette at the end of Evangelion: 1.0 You Are (Not) Alone (Hong Kong DVD—not a bootleg!) I used an altered Unit-01 body and what detail I could make out with help from the zoom button. I wonder how close to the real thing I was. For Unit-05 I had the trailers for Evangelion: 2.0 and some shots of the awesome model but I couldn't make out all the detail, especially for the . . . I guess you'd call them legs? So I ended up using some artistic licence and a lot of guesswork.

Now as for Evangelion: 1.0 You Are (Not) Alone— amazing movie, I really liked the reworked scenes, in particular the scene between Misato and Shinji after the fight with Shamshel (my least favourite angel, my favourite being Sahaquiel, who I assume was inspired while Anno and co. were sitting in front at a sumo match saying, "He's going to fall"). Misato definitely should have slapped him. I also

liked the climax to Shinji's attempt to run, where it goes all Wizard of Oz with Shinji's "there's no place like home" (or Misato's, apparently). It had a far larger impact on me than Shinji getting picked up at Kensuke's tent.

There are so many more scenes I could blab about: Misato and Shinji before Lilith for example, and of course, Operation Yashima is incredible, one of the most visually impressive battles I've seen anywhere. By the way, the Chinese voice actor for Shinji is terrible, far too masculine, and not a patch on Megumi Ogata and Spike Spencer. Thank God the DVD has Japanese audio and English subs. Speaking of voice actors, I wept like Shinji after hearing that Amanda Winn Lee isn't playing Rei for the English dub of Evangelion: 1.0, as her voice was beautiful—she's a fantastic Yui as well.

Wow, this e-mail went on far too long . . . Sorry, but it's Eva; I could talk forever—so, bye.

That's all right, John; talking forever is our specialty here at Misato's Fan Service Center. I can't name my favorite Angel offhand . . . That's a very serious issue

to consider. I want to say Zeruel, but is that more "best fight with an Angel"? What about appreciating an Angel for its charm? Is Iruel, the littlest Angel, therefore the most *moe*? Also, Iruel is inspired in part by the original 1971 *The Andromeda Strain*, which has to be one of the greatest "let's make this secret underground base look cool" films ever. I'm glad we mentioned Amanda Winn Lee, as she was the first person from the original ADV dub cast I ever had the chance to interview (this was in 1997, when I was an assistant editor at *Animerica*), and I remember being pleased at the thought and consideration she expressed towards Rei's character and what kind of person she was.

Anyway, I had to quiz John more on what it's like to be an anime fan in Celbridge (pop. 17,262). He said that although there may be other fans—"pockets of resistance" he calls them—scattered around Kildare, you can't even rent anime locally, the closest thing available being some J-horror films by Shinya Tsukamoto ("I adore *Vital*") or Takashi Shimizu ("*Marebito* is his best"—I must here mention that Dark Horse released the *Ju-on* manga).

For anime or manga in the Republic of Ireland, John says you really have to go into Dublin, "merely half an hour's journey by bus from Celbridge (lucky me)," advising that the local branch of Forbidden Planet (a famed comics-store chain whose home store is in London) is the best place to find manga, although "Sub City has some great anime deals—forty-five euros for a *Noein* box set that's ninety-nine everywhere else." John continues:

Actually, buying manga and anime is really easy. As well as the comic book stores, all the major bookstores carry manga, often titles not sold in the specialist shops, e.g. With the Light: Raising an Autistic Child by Keiko Tobe (one of my favourites). For anime it's the same thing, with all the high street stores [in Ireland and the UK, "high street" means the main downtown shopping district—ed.] *stocking it. Unfortunately recently they seem to not bother getting in new anime titles unless someone orders a copy. Only for manga can you seem able to get new stuff on shelves regularly, but later volumes tend not to be stocked, although you can still order a copy.*

Now as for your question about how I got The Shinji Ikari Raising Project *and why it's here in Ireland, there's one word to sum it all up: IMPORT. That word covers the anime and manga scene here; even if fans aren't aware of it, our manga shelves are lined with U.S. editions, often years before the UK edition comes out* [another example of this is Dark Horse's English edition of *Oh My Goddess!* which is produced for the North American market, but was later licensed by Titan Books for the UK and Ireland. The Titan edition is exactly the same as the Dark Horse edition—it can just be sold directly in that part of the world, and fans don't have to pay extra for the North American import. If you're wondering why all this is necessary, it's because licenses for books are granted for certain territories. It's a bit like how Ireland and the UK have a different DVD region code than North America, even though they share English as a common language—ed.]

Our biggest anime cons in Ireland are EirtaKon, which has been held for the last four years (I've been to them all) and had 600+ attendees at the most recent one [That may not sound very big to someone in the U.S., but bear in mind Ireland has only 4 percent our population, so that would be like having 45,000 people come to a con in America!—ed.], *and Q-Con in Belfast (I know, over the border— but we all go). There's also a load of tiny ones all over the place. They're all more or less the same, held on college grounds—no convention centers for us (you're so lucky)—always having a pub quiz (well, we are Irish), yaoi-crazed fangirls (of whom I know a few), and cosplayers. A lot of them are store-bought costumes, but on the whole, we Irish are always looking for a chance to dress up—you should see the Dublin City Women's Marathon, which features hundreds of dudes in drag. All in all, nothing special, but fun.*

By "over the border," John means of course that Q-Con is in Northern Ireland, which is under the jurisdiction of the United Kingdom, rather than the Republic of Ireland—it's a long story, but thankfully a more peaceful one of late. A pub quiz is, as you might guess, a trivia contest held at a bar, and is a popular way to draw people in for an evening's drinking and thinking. As you read in last

volume's MFSC, I'm actually rather fond of anime cons held on college campuses, but the grass is always greener, as they say (although wouldn't the grass be greenest in Ireland? ^_^). John tells us more about the scene in Eire:

Something that I hope isn't unique to Ireland (if it is, I feel special) is that our Japanese embassy is heavily involved in promoting anime and manga, and has been holding festivals since March 2008. The first one was in the Chester Beatty Library (currently showcasing ancient books, including The Tale of Genji*), whereas the second one was held in a Cine World theater the same weekend as EirtaKon. The latter caused me all sorts of trouble, as I had to pick between a* Soulcalibur IV *tournament and seeing* The Girl Who Leapt Through Time*. I picked the tournament, and got my ass handed to me by a teenage girl dressed as Sakura from* Naruto*. I did learn some life lessons from the experience. The third event was held last March, featuring talks by Helen McCarthy (she's awesome) and the Irish premiere of* Sword of the Stranger *(pretty cool).*

As for what we're into in Ireland, a big thing is Full-metal Alchemist *(I'm not a huge fan, though). The amount of people I know who reckon it's the best thing ever is only rivaled by the* Death Note *crowd and the* Naruto *contingent. We also seem to have a lot of people who are either allergic to or don't realise anime existed before 2000, except* Akira *and* Ghost in the Shell *(my first anime and manga). I don't know how many times I've been talking to someone about their favourite anime, and they'll say* "Fullmetal Alchemist," *and I'll go,* "Evangelion," *and then the answer nearly always is,* "Heard of it, but I haven't seen it; it's a bit old."

Ahem! Well, *Evangelion* first came out in 1995—like, literally, the previous millennium. ^_^ But I guess for people who don't like its original style, there is always the new movie version. We do have local Japanese consulates and the embassy get involved sometimes in anime and manga events in the U.S., but I get the impression the diplomats in Ireland have been leaders in this regard. Yes, Helen McCarthy is pretty cool; I was able to see her again at Anime Weekend Atlanta and, thanks

to Lloyd Carter, got an advance copy of her amazing new book *The Art of Osamu Tezuka: God of Manga*, a beautiful, oversize hardcover full of images and photos (it even comes with a DVD), that gives you the fullest appreciation of the man who basically founded both anime and manga (and, yes, whose influence can be seen even in *Evangelion*).

In last volume's MFSC, I talked about how I was fortunate to be involved, if only in a minor way, with *Animag*, a pioneering English-language anime magazine in the 1980s. Helen McCarthy was another person I was fortunate enough to be able to write for in the early and mid-'90s; she was the editor of two dynamic UK-based anime magazines: first *Anime UK*, and later *Anime FX*. Both shared *Animag*'s ambition of high production values and professional-looking original art. Not surprisingly, I wanted to write about Gainax ^_^ and I was particularly grateful to Helen for letting me write "Find, Find Your Place, Speak, Speak the Truth" in *Anime FX* #10.

I say grateful, because it was a somewhat experimental piece, almost a cross between an article and an AMV. Some readers will already get the title; the article was published in 1995, just before the premiere of *Evangelion*, but also approaching the end of the iconic era of bands such as Nirvana, Pearl Jam, Soundgarden, Alice in Chains, and Smashing Pumpkins (all referenced in the article), which had seemed to put new passion and meaning into music in the early '90s. At that same time, I was trying to think about what it meant to be an *otaku*, and I was getting my understanding of it through Gainax. Whereas a lot of the defining of *otaku* has been done by social scientists, trend spotters, or tabloid journalists, Gainax were the first to proclaim it as artists—which to me is the most worthwhile perspective. I was finding the same artistic passion in their anime that I heard in the bands I admired, and the article speculated on what their new series, *Evangelion*, might have to say about their struggles as a studio. It turned out, of course, to be a very dramatic struggle indeed . . .

I'd like to pass on some comments on this volume of *The Shinji Ikari Raising Project* from the

translator of the manga, Michael Gombos—also our director of Asian licensing, meaning that on this particular book, he not only translated it, but made it possible to publish it in the first place! About that *hanbagu* Asuka requests on page 17 . . . It sounds like "hamburger," and the word is related, but it's not the same dish. *Hanbagu* is like meatloaf, in that you make it by forming a patty out of ground beef, bread crumbs, onion, egg, milk, and spices, but it differs from meatloaf in preparation, in that you then fry the patty in a skillet, instead of baking it in an oven. Although it would be oddly charming to use the word "meatloaf" in *Evangelion* (this would also give Rei the chance to say, "I dislike meatloaf"), I decided to leave it at *hanbagu*, and explain it here.

On page 56, Yui talks about Shinji being *shookyoku-teki*, which Gombos notes can be translated as either "negative" or "passive," of which the latter seemed more appropriate here (It seems to me as editor that one of the running gags in *The Shinji Ikari Raising Project* is that Gendo understands what their son is actually like better than Yui does. Of course, there's an inevitable tension between *raising* a child as parents, and having him be part of a *project* as scientists . . .). Another contrasting term used here (which Gombos notes is used several times in vol. 3; for example, Gendo uses it on page 78, panel 2, and Misato on page 110, panel 5) is *sekkyoku-teki*, meaning positive, active, constructive. So Shinji's parents want to see less *shookyoku*, and more *sekkyoku*. I'm sure Shinji will take a note of that.

On page 60, panel 2, Rei said to Shinji in the original Japanese, *"otsukaresama."* Gombos notes that this is the typical phrase used by coworkers to mean "good job today." You may have heard it in anime when people have a toast after work; the better-known toast *"kampai!"* would be less likely in such a situation—*kampai* usually means celebrating something special, rather than the end of a regular day.

On page 68, panel 4, Gombos notes that the original Japanese version of this phrase is *ame futte, ii katamaru*, meaning "the ground gets stronger after it rains" (this doesn't seem to make any sense, but the implication is ". . . after it rains and dries up again"). He also remarks that on page 72, panel 1, "the exaggerated '*Ehhhhh?*' is one of the funniest things about the Japanese language." I agree, and soon Dark Horse will get to publish one of the greatest *"ehhhhhh?!"* scenes in the history of manga—the moment in *Cardcaptor Sakura* where Tomoyo informs Sakura that Li likes Yukito, too. Sakura's school-shaking ***EHHHHHH?!*** is accompanied by thirty-one separate drops of sweat.

As you may already know, Dark Horse is releasing a number of classic CLAMP titles in collected omnibus format, with newly remastered artwork (scanned from the original art) and many bonus color pages. *Clover* is already available as a one-book omnibus from Dark Horse, but look out for the premiere of *Chobits* in January 2010 (book 1 of 2), the aforementioned *Cardcaptor Sakura* in July 2010 (book 1 of 4), and *Magic Knight Rayearth* in fall 2010 (book 1 of 2). The number of books in the omnibus edition, of course, depends on how long the original series was; that's why *Clover* could be all collected in one volume, but *Cardcaptor Sakura* will take four.

Getting back to the manga of the moment, Gombos remarks that on page 75, panel 4, the original Japanese term is *sanshamendan*. That actually sounds pretty cool when you say it, but unfortunately, it means student-parent-teacher conference (it actually can refer to any three-party conference). These conferences tend to happen when a student has reached a senior stage of middle or high school, and a common purpose is to discuss where the student, given their grades, might consider applying for high school or college, respectively.

In stage 18, the underlying joke is that, while they do have days in Japanese schools where a parent will sit in on their child's class, everyone knows the day is going to happen well in advance, and the teacher and student practice for it so that everything goes perfectly and sounds brilliant. In other words, it's a bit staged. By just dropping in without warning, Gendo inadvertently experienced a more honest example of Shinji's class life. ^_^

On page 103, Ritsuko tells Shinji he has a fever, but actually, in the original Japanese, she said he had a *kaze*, a cold. Gombos notes that *kaze* is the all-purpose word for being sick in Japan, even if you're projectile vomiting. By the way, this scene makes me think that school nurses, like nuns, are a profession that is considerably more glamorous in manga than in real life, although I can't help but wonder how much of what's going on in pages 104–105 is Ritsuko, and how much of it is just Shinji paying close attention. I would certainly pay close attention to Akagi-sensei, even though in this manga she's been demoted from doctor to nurse. ^_^

In 137.3, the original term used is *imeeji eizoo*, which could be translated as "imaginary image"—this is often used on Japanese TV when events are reenacted, although it's also used for things that haven't actually happened yet, or things that only might happen. In 140.5, the term *terekakushi* is used, which means to cover one's embarrassment with a smile (it can also be used when a girl likes a boy, or vice versa, but one goes about ignoring the other because they like them). I think it takes a bit more skill to actually smile when you're embarrassed, instead of just keeping a stiff upper lip . . .

For next time! Don't forget, it's not a requirement that you send in actual fan art (although we love to see it) in order to have the chance to win the prizes. We're also looking for interesting *Eva*-related projects, letters, commentary, etc. It's obvious that this isn't the fastest way to exchange ideas on *Evangelion*, but that's not the point. The idea behind Misato's Fan Service Center is instead to bring *your* ideas, your expression, into an official *Evangelion* release, even in just a modest way such as this. **Looking forward to seeing you in vol. 4 . . .**

—CGH

P.S.! Before we go, you'll remember that in vol. 2's MFSC, there was some speculation that the next of the new *Evangelion* movies, that is, *3.0*, wouldn't come out until 2011, based on the fact it was two years between the Japanese releases of *1.0* (in 2007) and *2.0* (in 2009). We're now hearing, though, that we might not have to wait that long for the Japanese release of *3.0*—that it might come out in Japan next summer; i.e., in summer 2010. That would be great; it's true that we only had to wait a year between, say, the *Lord of the Rings* films, but, of course, they were all shot simultaneously, and on an anime film, you have to literally draw everything that you want to happen—you can't just switch the camera on and say, "Okay, Elijah, Sean . . . Start walking."

Kosuke Fujishima's **Oh My Goddess!**

Dark Horse is proud to re-present *Oh My Goddess!* in the much-requested, affordable, Japanese-reading, right-to-left format, complete with color sections, informative bonus notes, and your letters!

$10.95 each!

AVAILABLE AT YOUR LOCAL COMICS SHOP OR BOOKSTORE
*To find a comics shop in your area, call 1-888-266-4226

For more information or to order direct:
• On the web: darkhorse.com • E-mail: mailorder@darkhorse.com
• Phone: 1-800-862-0052 Mon.–Fri. 9 AM to 5 PM Pacific Time.

STOP!

止まれ

THIS IS THE BACK OF THE BOOK!

This manga collection is translated into English, but arranged in right-to-left reading format to maintain the artwork's visual orientation as originally drawn and published in Japan. If you've never read comics this way before, take a look at the diagram below to give yourself an idea of how to go about it. Basically, you'll be starting in the upper-right-hand corner, and will read each word balloon and panel moving right to left. It may take a little getting used to, but you should get the hang of it very quickly. Have fun! If this is the millionth manga you've read this way, never mind.

1
WELL, THERE IS A CUTE GIRL SITTING NEXT TO YOU...
2
...SO I SUPPOSE IT'S UNDERSTANDABLE YOU CAN'T CONCENTRATE--
3
--BUT IF I CATCH YOU SPACING OUT AGAIN, YOUR NOVEL WILL BECOME REQUIRED READING.
4
MISATO-SENSEI...!!
5
JUST KIDDING! ♡
THUD!!
6
A NOVEL.